GOD'S WAY OF
RECONCILIATION

God's Way Of Reconciliation

(Studies in Ephesians chapter 2)

D. MARTYN LLOYD-JONES

BAKER BOOK HOUSE
GRAND RAPIDS, MICHIGAN

© *D. M. Lloyd-Jones 1972*
First published 1972
ISBN: 0-8010-5519-9

Printed in Great Britain by
Billing & Sons Limited, Guildford and London.

CONTENTS

PREFACE

This volume consists of sermons preached on successive Sunday mornings at Westminster Chapel, London. In other words this is not a commentary as such but, as every sermon should be, it is exegesis plus homiletics and application. Its object is not merely to impart information and to lead to understanding but to bring out also something of the glory and the moving aspect of truth.

The title seemed quite inevitable. In an age of confusion, turmoil, violent divisions and wars, and at the same time a lingering belief in a false and superficial idealism which maintains that men and nations can be reconciled and peace and concord obtained by appealing to the best that is in man, the message of this second chapter of Paul's Epistle to the Ephesians is more needed than ever.

Here, we have expounded and laid before us clearly God's way of reconciliation—the only way. It deals with the profoundest and most elevating themes of the Bible. It shows us man's desperate need, it unfolds the glory of God's grace, the wonder of the cross of Christ, the breaking down of middle walls of partition, and the reconciliation of Jews and Gentiles, and all others who believe in the Lord Jesus Christ, in the kingdom of God.

I know of no chapter in the Bible which states so clearly and so perfectly at one and the same time the essential evangelistic message for the unbeliever and the status and the privileges of the believer.

Here lies the only hope for the individual and for the world, and as the apostle unfolds God's eternal plan one cannot but be thrilled by the glorious prospect that awaits all who have become 'fellow members with the saints and of the household of God'.

These sermons were originally printed in the Westminster Record month by month and have now been adapted to this book form by my wife. To her and to Dr Frank Crossley Morgan, who has been urging me to do what I have now done for the past ten years or so, I am deeply grateful.

January 1972   D. M. LLOYD-JONES

INTRODUCTION

And you hath he quickened, who were dead in trespasses and sins.

Ephesians 2: 1

As we begin to study the second chapter of this great Epistle, there are certain things of which we should remind ourselves if we are to do so in an intelligent and profitable manner. For instance, there arises at once the question of the relationship of this chapter to the previous chapter. Originally when this letter was written it was not divided into chapters, but for the convenience of Christian people, and to enable us to understand its message more clearly, these chapter divisions were adopted and introduced, and they are undoubtedly of very great value. And there can be no question but that here the division was made at the right point. We come to the end of a certain statement in the last verse of the first chapter, and here the apostle takes up a different aspect of the question. But clearly there is a connection between the two, because he starts off with the word 'and'—'And you hath he quickened. . . .' Obviously, therefore, the apostle is referring back to something he has already said, and to a subject which he is going to continue. In other words, if we are to understand this great chapter correctly we must remind ourselves of its setting and its background.

These New Testament Epistles are generally constructed around a central argument, and, roughly speaking, the first half of each Epistle is devoted to this. You can divide all the Epistles generally in that way; the first part is doctrinal, and the second part is more practical. In the doctrinal section there is always an argument which is worked out. It is sometimes a sustained argument. As we come to study the Scripture therefore it is very important that we should do two things. We should have a general grasp of the argument; and, having that, we can proceed to the particulars. Both these things are important, so important that they can be regarded as pitfalls that always confront any expositor or expounder of the Scripture. There are those who forget the generalities altogether, and are concerned only with the particulars, and who therefore tend to lose their way; and there are those who are simply concerned with the general and never really get down to the particular. Now the two things, I say, are of great importance. We must have a firm grasp in our minds of the general argument, but we must also follow the apostle as he works it out in all its details. Here we are driven therefore to remember what he has been telling us in the first chapter. We cannot possibly understand the argument of this second chapter if we are not clear about the argument of the first.

Let me then remind you of that very briefly. The great point which the apostle makes in this Epistle, its central theme in a sense, is the theme that he announces in the tenth verse of the first chapter: 'That in the dispensation of the fulness of times he might gather together in one all things in Christ, both which are in heaven and which are on earth; even in him'. Now that is beyond any question the theme of the Epistle. That is the ultimate matter which the apostle was anxious to make clear to these Ephesians and others. But of course he does not stop at this bare statement. He goes on to show us how God is doing it.

The first thing of which he keeps on reminding us is that *it is God's plan and that it is God's activity*. He starts by saying, 'Blessed be the God and Father of our Lord Jesus Christ, who hath blessed us. . . .' That is the starting point. We are concerned about something God has done. We are not interested here in human activity, we are looking at something that the Lord God Almighty has brought to pass. This is His plan, to bring and to reunite, to head up again once more in Christ all things. That at once throws us back to the doctrine of the fall—where the division came in, where things went wrong. God's plan and purpose is to bring them all together again in Christ. It is His plan and it is God who is active in it. It is something that God is bringing to pass. I do not pause at each point to emphasise the extreme relevance of all this to our present position, not only as Christians, but as citizens in this world. The thing that is being forgotten by the vast majority of people is that the really important fact in the world today is God's activity—what God is doing, not what men are doing. Of course men are doing things, and it is right that they should do them. I am not trying to detract from the importance of statesmanship and all such things; but according to the apostle the thing to understand above everything else is what God is doing. There is this unseen history which is at the back of the visible history, and which is much more important. There is this spiritual history which, as it were, underlies all secular history, and in the light of which secular history becomes relatively unimportant.

Well now, this is all a part of God's plan and it is the result of His activity. The apostle reminds us that it is something that

God has planned 'before the foundation of the world'. Here we have the very foundation of our faith. There is nothing contingent about God's plan. What God is doing is not dependent upon man, not even dependent upon the response of man; it is all ultimately of God. If God's plan were dependent upon us and our response, then I would be without any hope whatsoever. You have but to read the history of the Church to see that the Christian Church would have lasted probably not more than a century were it dependent upon man. But these things do not depend upon man, they depend upon God Himself. He has planned it all before the foundation of the world, and therefore it is absolutely certain.

The next thing he reminds us of is that *it is entirely due to God's grace and love and mercy and compassion*: entirely of grace. I remind you of these things because as we come to work through this second chapter we shall see that the apostle goes on repeating himself. Everything is 'to the praise of the glory of his grace'. He has said that in the first chapter in verse 6, then again in verse 12—'that we should be to the praise of his glory, who first trusted in Christ', and once more in verse 14—'which is the earnest of our inheritance until the redemption of the purchased possession, unto the praise of his glory'. It is all the result of the grace of God—the very fact that we sit together in a Christian church, that we commemorate the death of Christ, that we are going to consider this great salvation. It is all the result of God's exceeding, abundant grace, the riches of His grace. We must hold on to these themes and keep them in our minds.

That leads us to the next thing, which I have just mentioned: that *it is all in and through the Lord Jesus Christ*. There is no such thing as salvation without Christ at the centre. We must not listen to people who tell us how God is blessing them, unless Jesus Christ is central. They may think their prayers are being answered, that they are being guided and various other such things; but God, according to this argument, does not deal with us at all except in Jesus Christ. All blessings come in Him, through Him, from Him, by Him. I would remind you that the apostle in the first fourteen verses of the first chapter refers to the Lord Jesus Christ fifteen times. He knows how ready we are to forget Him, and how ready we are to think that we can have some direct dealings with God. Nothing is so tragic in the history of mankind as the fact that though God has placarded the cross before us we turn our backs upon it and seem to think that God can bless us without it. But He does not. 'In whom we have redemption through his blood, the forgiveness of sins.' His purpose is 'that in the dispensation of the fulness of times he might gather together in one all things in

Christ.' It must all centre upon Him; and if He is not absolutely central to us we have no right whatsoever to the name Christian. How vital it is that we should be clear about these things!

And then the apostle has told us in a memorable phrase in the third verse *what it is that God has done for us and offers to us* in and through our Lord and Saviour. Here it is: 'Who hath blessed us with all spiritual blessings in heavenly places in Christ.' Let us remind ourselves of these things. We have obtained pardon—'the forgiveness of sins'. That is the first thing we all need. Without that we are hopeless, but we have received it—pardon and forgiveness. Not only that—adoption, sonship, heirship, a wonderful inheritance, 'joint heirs with Christ'; yes, and God has sealed all this to us by the Holy Spirit. He wants us to be sure and certain of it all, and He wants us to know that we are in union with Christ, that He has made us one with Christ—that we are 'in Christ'. Such are the blessings. 'Who hath blessed us with all spiritual blessings in heavenly places in Christ'. We are here on this earth, yes, but we are in the heavenly places also—a truth we shall see him working out in this second chapter. But all the blessings that we are enjoying are spiritual blessings. The lot of the Christian in this world is sometimes a difficult one; he is surrounded by problems and trials and tribulations; but he is 'blessed with all spiritual blessings in the heavenly places'. And if he realises this and dwells there, and sets his affections on things above, not on things on earth, he will rejoice with a joy unspeakable and full of glory.

That is a summary of the great statement of the apostle in the first ten verses of that first chapter. But then toward the end of the chapter he moves on to something else. He emphasises *the importance of our understanding these things* and of our being clear about them. He says to these Ephesians, 'Wherefore I also, after I heard of your faith in the Lord Jesus, and love to all the saints'— he has heard this about them and he rejoices in it—'cease not to give thanks for you'. But he does not stop at thanking God for them; he makes mention of them in his prayers, and this is what he prays for them: that they may have 'the spirit of wisdom and revelation in the knowledge of him'. He prays that the eyes of their understanding may be enlightened, that they may come to know certain things. They have been brought into this realm, he tells them, but if they are really to enjoy the Christian life, if they are to live it fully, if they are to function as God's people here on earth, they must have this spiritual understanding of certain things. What things? The greatness of this salvation, and the glory of it: 'That ye may know what is the hope of his calling'. But then he goes on to say that he wants them to know also the certainty of it: 'the riches of the glory of his inheritance in the saints'. You see, the apostle is not merely writing a theological treatise. His aim all along is very practical, it is very pastoral. He wants to help these people, he wants them to rejoice in all this. Very well, he says, that is the way to do so. Do not start by looking at yourself, but look away to these great, glorious things: the hope of His calling; the riches of the glory of His inheritance in the saints; and then this other thing—'the exceeding greatness of his power to us-ward who believe'. We are conscious of feebleness, we are conscious of diffi-culties, we see the opposition against us, the world organised in sin, the malignity of men, the devil, hell, everything that is set against us. I know, says Paul, in effect; therefore the one thing you must know is this, 'the exceeding greatness of his power to us-ward who believe.' If only they knew that! They must have the eyes of their understanding enlightened to do that, so he prays that this may happen to them.

He not only prays for them in this way but he proceeds at once to give them a certain amount of instruction concerning it. He tells them that the power working in them is the same power 'that raised the Lord Jesus Christ from the dead and set him at the right hand of God in the heavenly places, far above all principality and power and might and dominion, and every name that is named, not only in this world but also in that which is to come'. That is the power that is working in us! We would not be believers were it not for that: 'what is the exceeding greatness of his power to us-ward who believe, according to . . .' We believe 'according to' the working of His mighty power, that is to say, in virtue of, as the result of, the working of His mighty power.

He then works it out in terms of the Church, and shows that we are members of the body of Christ, and that the power of the Head spreads through the whole body. We are not isolated indivi-duals, loosely attached to a church, vaguely related to Christ. No, we are members of His body, of His flesh and of His bones; it is an organic unity. So the power of Christ is in us; we belong to Him, we are in Him and He is in us. The apostle is anxious that they may know that nothing can frustrate this purpose of God, nothing can withstand Him. These things are absolutes, they are certain. What you and I have to realise is that it is that very power that is working in us, and that if we are Christians at all it is because that power has already begun working in us.

The apostle has already reminded these Ephesians that that had happened to them. He has two themes and he now works them out together at the same time: this great idea of *everything being reunited in Christ, and the power of God which brings that to pass*. He did the same thing in the first chapter in this way. He says in verse 11: 'in whom also we have obtained an inheritance'; then in verse 13, 'in whom also ye trusted'—you have also got an inheritance. He has already stated his theme there: this great purpose of God is already being put into action. There was nothing that ever surprised this man so much as the fact that he of all men should be 'the apostle to the Gentiles'. Here he is writing an epistle to Ephesians, who were Gentiles—he, who was a Hebrew of the Hebrews, of the tribe of Benjamin, a Pharisee, trained at the feet of Gamaliel, one of the most intense nationalists that the world has known—here he is, this intense Jew, actually writing to people who had been pagan Gentiles, and addressing them as equals, rejoicing with them that they are sharing the same experience. How had this come to pass? There is only one answer; it is the power of God. He has already stated his theme in that way in verses 11 to 14 in the first chapter. But now in chapter 2 he comes to work it all out in detail. The purpose of chapter 1 was to make a grand general statement. But he never stops at that. He now says, in effect: Let us go on and see in actual practice what God has done. You have become fellow heirs, 'in whom ye also trusted, after that ye heard the word of truth, the gospel of your salvation: in whom also after that ye believed ye were sealed with that holy Spirit of promise, which is the earnest of our inheritance (our inheritance together) until the redemption of the purchased possession.'

But this is so staggering that we must realise how it has come to pass. So in this second chapter the apostle tells us in detail how *the Jews and the Gentiles have been made one*, how God has succeeded in reuniting in Christ these utterly opposed elements. His way of doing it is to put it like this. What were the obstacles to this union in Christ? What were the things that separated the Jews and Gentiles? What was the task, if I may so phrase it, with which God was confronted in His desire to bring them together again? The apostle tells us that there were two main difficulties.

The first was the state and condition of these people by nature. That is what the apostle deals with in verses 1 to 10 in this chapter; the woeful condition, the sinful state of these Ephesians before their conversion. Before they could be made fellow heirs with the Jews, the Christian Jews, in the kingdom, this condition and state of sin had to be dealt with. 'You hath he quickened who were *dead* in trespasses and sins'. That has got to be dealt with.

But there was another matter also, and it was a very serious obstacle, and that was the relationship of the Gentiles to the law, to the law of God. The law of God had only been given to the Jews; it was never given to the Gentiles. It was something that God gave to His own people and to nobody else. And, of course, it raised up a great middle wall of partition at once. Here were the Jews under the law: there were the Gentiles, the dogs, outside the law, strangers to the commonwealth of Israel, without hope and without God in the world. Now this was a tremendous problem, and in the second half of the chapter, from verse 11 to the end, the apostle proceeds to show us how God has dealt with that second difficulty of overcoming the obstacle of the law. God, says Paul, has done this, has overcome both these obstacles. He has 'made of twain one new man', He has overcome every difficulty, all has been dealt with.

But you notice that at once he reminds us of *how it has been done*. And here he goes back again to his great themes and his great principles outlined in the first chapter. You notice he starts by saying 'And you hath *he* quickened'—God! It is God all the time from beginning to end; it is God who has overcome the obstacles, it is God who has brought us together. And again he reminds us at once—he does not delay for a second—that it is in Christ that God has done it; yes, and by the blood of His cross—it is all repeated. How these apostles repeat themselves, and go on saying the same thing! Why? Because it is so crucial, because there is no salvation without it, and because we are so constantly prone to forget these things. We will persist in trying to bring in our own righteousness and our own deserts, and we keep on asking, Well, is there nothing for me to do? We are so anxious to do something and to justify ourselves. No, says Paul, it is all in Christ, and all by the blood of His cross. The problem necessitated that; nothing else could do it. He would never have come on earth, He would never have died, if there had been another way. It is all in Christ. And again you will find that he keeps on emphasising that it is all of grace. You notice that it is in brackets—'even when we were dead in sins, hath quickened us together with Christ'—and then in brackets '(by grace ye are saved).' 'You shall not get away from this,' says Paul in effect. 'I will not allow you to get away with your constant assertion of yourself and your merit and your powers. Get rid of it all; you will never glory in this until you see that it is all of grace; "by grace ye are saved".' And he keeps on elaborating it and repeating it.

But the thing that he wants to emphasise above everything in the immediate context is this, that nothing less than the mighty power of God could have done it. That is where this chapter links up immediately with the end of the previous chapter where he has been telling us about this great power of God, manifested in Christ in raising Him from the dead and putting Him there at His own right hand in that place of supreme exaltation. Then, 'and you hath he quickened'—He has done it to you in Christ, because you belong to Him, you are in Him, you are members of His body, and nothing but the power of God could have done it.

So, as I understand him here, the apostle seems to ask a question. Are we clear about this? Are we quite happy about it? Do we understand that nothing but this almighty power of God that was manifested in the resurrection and exaltation of our Lord, nothing but that, nothing less than that, could make us Christian? Do we understand these matters to this extent, that we see not only that God has done something, but that God had to do something, that our condition was such that nothing less than this could suffice for us?

The apostle seems to be asking these questions. Do we know this? Do we realise this? Or, put in another form, we can put it like this: Do we realise what our salvation means? If we do not, says the apostle, consider these things. First, consider *what we were before God began to act in us*; consider the condition of man before God visits him graciously in salvation. If we are not clear about that we will never realise why the power of God was essential. And ultimately— there is no question about this—the whole trouble with people who are in difficulty about salvation is that they have never understood the biblical doctrine about sin. The greatest trouble always is an inadequate conception of sin. People say that if you only pull yourself together, if you only live a good life, and so on, you will satisfy God and He will be well pleased. The real trouble with such people is that they do not understand the meaning of the word *sin*. They think they can save themselves. They have never seen the necessity of this almighty power of God. That is entirely due to the fact that they have never seen themselves as they really are.

Well, the apostle starts with that—that is the theme of verses I to 3 of this second chapter: 'And you hath he quickened, who were dead in trespasses and sins; wherein in time past ye walked according to the course of this world, according to the prince of the power of the air, the spirit that now worketh in the children of disobedience: among whom also we all had our conversation in times past in the lusts of our flesh, fulfilling the desires of the flesh and of the mind; and were by nature the children of wrath, even as others'. That is man in sin, that is what we all would still be if God left us to ourselves. That is how all are who are not Christians. And the apostle's argument is this: if you want to know the greatness of God's power you have got to realise the depth of sin, you have got to realise the problem which confronted God, you have got to realise the problem that confronts you. The apostle wants to show us this power. He says that we must go down first, and that we can only realise the height to which we have been brought up if we realise the depths to which we had sunk. That is the first thing.

The second, of course, follows. He goes on to show us *what God has done for us*. That is the theme of verses 4 to 7: 'But God who is rich in mercy . . . even when we were dead in sins' —we were down in the depths of that grave as Christ was down in the grave—God, even when we were there, because of His rich mercy, for His great love wherewith He loved us, 'even when we were dead in sins, hath quickened us together with Christ . . . and hath raised us up together and made us sit together in heavenly places in Christ Jesus'. And it is only as we understand and realise something about that, that we shall realise the greatness of God's power. Many think of salvation, and of Christianity, in terms of a little bit of morality and of decency. What an insult to the Christian! as if the Christian were just a good and a nice and a harmless individual. Not at all! He is a man who has undergone this tremendous change. There has been this dynamic action. He has been raised, resurrected; he is in the heavenly places. This is the power of God! And if you think of your Christianity in those terms you will see that nothing but the power of God could do it. The apostle puts it before us in detail and we have to consider it.

Then he comes to the third thing, which he can never leave out. You say to yourself at this point, 'Is all this true? Was I really like that, dead in trespasses and sins, walking according to the course of this world, dominated by the prince of the power of the air, living for the lusts of the flesh and of the mind, a child of wrath and disobedient? Was I once in that position? Is it true that I am now in Christ, in the heavenly places? Is it true that God has done all this and has translated me from that to this? *Why has He done it?*' There is only one answer: it is all according to the riches of His grace, that in the ages to come he might show the exceeding riches of his 'grace in his kindness toward us through Jesus Christ. For by grace ye are saved through faith, and that not of yourselves, it is the gift of God; not of works lest any man should boast, for we are his workmanship. . . .' Now you see the apostle's argument. You see how this chapter follows on from the first chapter.

But before we go any further let us reflect on certain points. Is it not quite clear that it is only as we realise these things that *we shall praise God as we ought*? Think of Psalm 103: 'Bless the Lord, O my soul, and all that is within me, bless his holy name'. That is the norm for the Christian: every Christian should be like that, continually blessing God. Why are so many not doing so? There is only one answer to that question; it is because we do not realise what God has done for us; it is because we do not know what sin is, what sin is in us; because we do not realise what we were and what God has done for us, and how He has done it and why He has done it. If we realised these things we could not help praising God. It is because we do not realise these things that there is so little sense of wonder in our Christian life. There is to me nothing more appalling than the glibness with which many speak about these things, and the way we take them for granted. There is nothing so lacking in Christian life today as a sense of wonder. Read this man's epistles, read the epistles of the others, and notice how as they mention this great salvation they stop and begin to praise. They are filled with wonder, they are amazed, they are astounded. Are you surprised at yourself? Are you amazed at yourself? Is it to you an astounding thing that you are at this moment reading this kind of thing? That you are interested in these things—does it amaze you? If you realised the truth it would. It is failure to realise these things that accounts for our loss and our lack of the sense of wonder and of worship.

It is this that accounts for our lack of love to God. Are you worried about the coldness of your heart? I am sure you are, as we all ought to be. Is it not appalling that we can come and eat the bread and drink the wine at the communion table and be so unmoved, that our hearts are not overflowing with love to God? Why are they not overflowing with love? It is because we do not realise the greatness of His love. If you want to love God do not try to work up something inside yourself: realise His love, and pray that the eyes of your understanding may be enlightened, that you may realise the pit out of which you have been hauled up, the depths to which you had sunk, your former terrible, precarious, perilous position, and what God has done for you, by His grace, in Christ. That is the way to realise it. 'We love him because he first loved us', says John, and it is the same argument. The understanding of these things is essential to a sense of wonder, love and praise.

But come to something still more practical. It is because we do not realise these things as we ought that *we do not feel the burden of the souls of others* as we ought. Christian people are but a handful in the world today. The masses are outside Christ, outside the Church, in godlessness and irreligion, and in a terrible state of sin. Are we concerned about them? Does their condition burden us? Have we a missionary sense with regard to our fellowcitizens in this country? Does the condition of the benighted masses in other lands weigh upon us at all? Are we concerned about the missionary enterprise?

Do we think about these things, do they burden us, do we pray to God about them? Are we asking, 'What can I do, how can I help, what contribution can I make?' If we are not, there is only one explanation—we have never realised the truth about people who are in a state of sin. We are just irritated by them, we are just annoyed. But that is not enough; we must be concerned about souls, we must be concerned about sin. We must see them as they are, the children of wrath, hell-bound, in this degradation, in this pollution that the apostle here describes. If we only saw it, our hearts would go out to them; we would see them as our Lord saw them, and He had a great heart of compassion for them. The poorness of our missionary and evangelistic zeal is entirely due to this. We have not seen the position of those outside truly—what they are, what they might be, and what Christ has done.

The third thing that it brings home to us is that if we but saw these things truly *it would also control our evangelism*. The trouble with all false evangelism is that it does not start with doctrine, it does not start by realising man's condition. All fleshly, carnal, man-made evangelism is the result of inadequate understanding of what the apostle teaches us in the first ten verses of this second chapter of the Epistle to the Ephesians. If you and I but realised that every man who is yet a sinner is absolutely dominated by 'the prince of the power of the air, the spirit that now worketh in the children of disobedience,' if we only understood that he is really a child of wrath and dead in trespasses and sins, we would realise that only one power can deal with such an individual, and that is the power of God, the power of the Holy Ghost. And so we would put our confidence, not in man-made organisations, but in the power of God, in the prayer that holds on to God and asks for revival and a descent of the Spirit. We would realise that nothing else can do it. We can change men superficially, we can win men to our side and to our party, we can persuade them to join a church, but we can never raise the spiritually dead; God alone can do that. The realisation of these truths would of necessity determine and control all our evangelism.

You see then why it is that the apostle Paul is so concerned about these things, why he prays for these Ephesians that the eyes of their understanding may be enlightened. You see that the doctrine he brings to us affects the whole of our Christian life. It affects me individually, my prayer life, my praise, my worship, my love, my relationship to Him, my relationship to other people—all is controlled by this. The apostle has stated it all in principle in the first chapter. Yes, but he says that you must not only see it in principle; you must understand and grasp it in detail. So he takes us to the details, and he starts doing so in this second chapter. And you and I must do the same. We must contemplate men in sin until we are horrified, until we are alarmed, until we are desperate about them, until we pray for them, until having realized the marvel of our own deliverance from that terrible state, we are lost in a sense of wonder, love and praise.

That is the introduction to this second chapter of Paul's Epistle to the Ephesians. That is the essential prolegomenon. It is pointless to rush to the details without that background. And we must go on to consider the details, not simply that we may work through these great verses and enjoy ourselves as we do so, but because our whole Christian life is involved here, and we must understand these things. So let us commit ourselves to God and pray that the eyes of our understanding may be enlightened, that we may see and know these things, that we may see God's great plan and purpose being worked out; see that He alone can do it, but that He does it in Christ and that nothing less than that could do it. Let us therefore dedicate ourselves to a new consideration of these things, that we may truly be 'to the praise of the glory of his grace', and be of immediate practical help to our fellowmen and women who are 'the children of wrath', lost and doomed and condemned in sin.

2

MAN IN SIN

And you hath he quickened, who were dead in trespasses and sins; Wherein in time past ye walked according to the course of this world, according to the prince of the power of the air, the spirit that now worketh in the children of disobedience: Among whom also we all had our conversation in times past in the lusts of our flesh, fulfilling the desires of the flesh and of the mind; and were by nature the children of wrath, even as others.

Ephesians 2: 1–3

In these words the apostle is concerned to show the Ephesian Christians, and all the other Christians to whom he was writing, and therefore to us, the greatness and the glory of the Christian salvation. These Ephesians had already believed the gospel. He had already thanked God for their faith in the Lord Jesus and their love to all the saints. They had been sealed with the Holy Spirit and they had the earnest of the inheritance within them. And yet the apostle prays that the eyes of their understanding may be enlightened. They are merely at the beginning, they are merely as babes. He wants them to grasp something of the largeness and the greatness and the majesty of this wonderful salvation. And subject as they still are to temptation, and living in a gainsaying world and surrounded by paganism and opposition in various forms, the apostle is particularly anxious that they should be clear about the greatness of the power of God toward all that believe. And that is surely the one thing we need to know and to be certain of in the Christian life. Nothing is more vital than that we should be clear about the power of God that is manifested in this Christian salvation.

The apostle writes in order to help in that respect. He is not only praying for them, he is also instructing them. And the two things must always go together. He prays that the eyes of their understanding may be enlightened by the Holy Spirit. That is absolutely vital. Without the understanding that the Holy Spirit alone can give us, words such as these we are going to consider will obviously be quite meaningless to us. Moreover, we shall probably hate them and feel they are pessimistic and morbid. Man, by nature, says that he wants something to cheer him up, not a terrible analysis of human nature such as this, which is so depressing. In other words,

13

without a spiritual mind we cannot hope to understand them. So the apostle puts that first. His prayer comes first. Then, having prayed, he puts the knowledge and the instruction before them.

How can we have a true conception of the greatness of God's power in salvation? This is a constantly recurring theme in the letters of the apostle Paul. Take that magnificent statement in Romans 1: 16, 'I am not ashamed of the gospel of Christ'. Why? Because 'it is the power of God unto salvation to everyone that believeth'. The power! How do we measure it? The apostle gives us the precise measurements here.

The first measurement is the depth of sin out of which we have been raised. In other words, *in order* to *measure the greatness of this power* you have got to go down first, and then you have to go up. Man never starts on ground level, as it were. We do not start neutral, we do not start in a kind of indeterminate state, neither good nor bad. No, we start down in the depths of a pit. We are first raised up from that; and then we are raised right up into the very heavens themselves. So the apostle starts where we must start. Salvation comes to us where we are; not where we would like to be, not as we would like to think of ourselves idealistically. The gospel of Jesus Christ is thoroughly realistic, and it starts with us exactly where we are, and that is, at the bottom of a pit of corruption.

The apostle's case is that we shall never have *an adequate conception of the greatness of this salvation* unless we realise something at any rate of what we were before this mighty power took hold of us, unless we realise what we would still be if God had not intervened in our lives and had rescued us. In other words, we must realise the depth of sin, what sin really means, and what it has done to the human race. We must start with this because it is a fact; not because it is a theory but because it is a fact. The Bible is a book of facts; it is concerned about us as we are; it is historical. We must start with facts, whether we like them or not. If we want to be honest in our reasoning, we have got to face facts, and here is the first one.

Let me show you how absolutely vital it is that we should start here. No man will ever have *a true conception of the biblical teaching with regard to redemption* if he is not clear about the biblical doctrine of sin. And that is why so many people today are so loose and vague in their ideas of redemption. The common idea is that our Lord is a sort of friend to whom we can turn in difficulties, as if that were all. He is that—thank God for that! But that is not redemption in its entirety or even in its essence. You cannot begin to measure redemption until you realise something of what the Bible teaches us about man in sin and the whole effect of sin upon

man. Or let me put it in another way. You cannot possibly understand the doctrine of the incarnation unless you understand this
doctrine of sin. The Bible tells us that man was in such a condition
that it necessitated the coming of the Second Person in the blessed,
holy Trinity from heaven to earth. He had to come down and take
to Himself human nature and be born as a babe. That was absolutely
essential before man could be redeemed. Why? Because of sin,
because of the nature of sin. Therefore, you see, you cannot understand the incarnation unless you are clear about sin. In the same
way look at the cross on Calvary's hill. What is it? What does it
mean? What is it telling us? What is happening there? I say again
that you cannot possibly understand the death of our Lord and
what He did there on the cross unless you are clear about this doctrine
of sin. The utter vagueness of many people's ideas about the death
of our Lord is entirely due to this. They do not like the doctrine of
substitution; they do not like the doctrine of penal suffering. That
is because they have never understood the problem. It is because
they do not start with man in sin. These are the great cardinal
doctrines of the Christian faith, and they cannot be understood
except in the light of man's terrible plight in sin.

But let me be still more practical. There may be someone who
says: Ah well, you talk about your doctrines. I am not interested
in doctrines, I am not one of your theologians, I am a hard-headed
man of the world, a man of affairs, and I want to know something
about life and how to live. Very well, let me meet such a case.
I am asserting that you cannot *understand life as it is in this world* at
this moment unless you understand this biblical doctrine of sin. I
go further, I suggest that you cannot understand the whole of human
history apart from this, with all its wars and its quarrels and its
conquests, its calamities, and all that it records. I assert that there
is no adequate explanation save in the biblical doctrine of sin.
The history of the world can only be understood truly in the light
of this great biblical doctrine of man, fallen and in sin. Read your
books on the philosophy of history and you will find that they
fumble. They do not know how to interpret the facts, they cannot
give an adequate explanation; all their ideas are utterly falsified
by history. That is because they never realise that the starting point
is man's fallen sinful condition.

Those then are some of the reasons why we must consider this
matter. In the last analysis, there are only two proffered explanations as to why man is as he is and why the world is as it is today,
and why it always has been what it has been. There is the biblical
teaching: and there are all the other non-biblical teachings. Over

against the biblical teaching is the popular teaching of today that man is as he is, and things are as they are, because man has not had sufficient time yet, to advance to perfection. He was once an animal, so we are told, and that not so long ago. Millions of years are nothing, and just a few millions of years ago man was an animal. There he was in the forests, climbing trees, and so on. You cannot suddenly expect him to become perfect, they say. He is sloughing off these bestial relics and vestiges, but he has not done it all yet. He is doing it increasingly, of course, but you must give him time. The problem of humanity, in other words, is purely one of time. Such thinkers have not much comfort to give us who are alive now because they say that in many billions and millennia of years to come, man will probably have succeeded in arriving at perfection. It is all a question of time, a question of knowledge, a question of growth and instruction, and so on. Now, you either believe that, or some variation of that, or else you believe what the Bible says about man. Here we are told exactly what the biblical view is.

The differences between the biblical view and all those other views are these. This biblical view is *realistic*. All those other views do not face the facts, they gloss over a number of facts. They are so pleasant and so ingratiating; they want us to think well of ourselves and to think well of man, so they say: Give man a chance; he has never had a full chance yet or a right opportunity, but give him time, and so on. The Bible, on the other hand, with a stark realism, comes to us and tells us that man is a fool, that man has brought calamity upon himself, that it is because man is, as Paul puts it here, 'a child of disobedience' that he is what he is and his world is what it is. It asserts that there is no excuse for man, that he has got to admit it, and that he must face it, and that there is no hope for him until he does so. That is called repentance. It is realistic. And if I had no other reason for believing the Bible, and for believing that the Bible is the Word of God, that would be enough for me; it tells me what I know to be the stark truth about myself. And I know of nothing else that does so. Your novels do not—they praise me and tell me not to think too hardly of myself. They are trying to boost up my morale, they are treating me psychologically; but what they say is not true. This alone is realistic.

Not only so, it is also *radical*, it gets down to the depths. It does not merely face certain aspects of the problem of man, and the individual, it faces them all. Though the process is painful, it takes up its scalpel as it were and it dissects and dissects until the canker is exposed. It is radical. And that is why it is extremely difficult at times not to be impatient with what the world is so ready to believe. The world with its ideas and philosophies is but medicating symptoms, giving its pheno-barbitone in a spiritual sense, and its ano-dynes, its aspirins, and so on; and because our pain is a little eased for a time we think we are well. But the condition has never been diagnosed, it has never been exposed; it is not faced. The world does not like that which is unpleasant; it is afraid of it, so it does not face it. It is never radical. But the Bible is very radical as we shall see.

Then the last thing I would say about it in general is this: that this biblical view is, at one and the same time, *more pessimistic and more optimistic* than all the other views. Man has always been reaching after Utopia, he has been doing so throughout the centuries. But he never gets there. All that, therefore, is finally and utterly pessimistic. There is only one truly optimistic view of life, and that is the one which tells us that, though man is down in the depths of sin, the power of God can come and take hold of him and can raise him to the heights, and that it has done so in Jesus Christ our Lord.

There we have taken a general view of this position. But now let us come to the details, to the specific teaching. The apostle in these three verses summarises in a most amazing, and perhaps in the most perfect manner found anywhere in the whole of the Bible, the biblical doctrine, the scriptural view, of man in sin. He says four things about him. First of all he describes man's state in sin. Secondly he gives us an explanation of this state and why man is in this state. Thirdly he tells us what this state and condition leads to in practice. And fourthly he tells us how God views man in this state. That would be my analysis of these three verses: the condition; why man is in it; what results in practice because he is in it; and what God thinks of it. It is all in these three verses.

Let us begin our consideration of these matters by starting with *man's state in sin*. What is it? Here is the answer: 'And you hath he quickened who were *dead*'. Now certain words have been added here by the translators which are not in the original. The original reads like this, 'And you who were dead'. You notice in your Bibles that the words 'hath he quickened' are in italics, which means that the translators have added them (and rightly) in order to help us to read more smoothly. But Paul was full of his matter, and he says: 'And you who were dead'—not 'in' trespasses and sins but dead 'on account of' them, or 'because' of them, which is a yet better translation. But the vital word is the word 'dead'. 'You were dead,' says Paul. What does he mean? Well obviously he is dealing with a condition of spiritual death and not actual physical death, because he goes on immediately: 'wherein ye walked' and 'in which we all had our conversation in times past'. In other words the apostle's teaching is that *life for the non-Christian is a living death*. He is spiritually dead. I go on repeating the terms because they are so vital. You notice what a strong term it is. There is not a stronger term than 'death'. How categorical he is! You cannot say anything beyond saying that a man is dead. It is not 'almost dead', he is actually dead; it is not 'desperately ill', it is 'dead'. There is no life there. Now it is the apostle's word, not mine, the word that is used everywhere in Scripture; and it is the word that is used about man in a state of sin before the power of God unto salvation in the gospel comes and does something to him. He is dead!

What does this mean? The best way, I suppose, of defining death is to say that it is the exact opposite and antithesis of life. What then is life? Well, in the Bible life is always described and defined in terms of our relationship to God. Take the words of our Lord and Saviour Jesus Christ in John 17: 3: 'And this is life eternal, that they might know thee, the only true God, and Jesus Christ whom thou hast sent'. That is life! What is death? The opposite of that. God is the Author of life—'Who alone hath life and immortality'. He is the source of life, the sustainer of life. God is Life and gives life, and apart from God there is no life. So we can define life like this: life is to know God, to be in relationship to God, to enjoy God, to correspond with God, to be like God, to share the life of God, and to be blessed of God. According to the Bible that is life. Therefore as we come to define death we must define it as the opposite of all that. And as we do so you will see at a glance that what Paul says here about the man who is not a Christian is nothing but the simple truth. He is dead, says Paul: 'You were dead'; and those who are not Christian are still dead. What does he mean? He means that they are ignorant of God; they do not know God. The apostle puts that clearly later in this very chapter. He says here that these people before their conversion were in that very condition. He says in verse 12 'that at that time ye were without Christ, being aliens from the commonwealth of Israel, and strangers from the covenants of promise, having no hope and without God . . .' 'You were without God,' you did not know Him. You were estranged from the life of God, you were not in fellowship with God. Oh, you may have talked about God, but God was some sort of philosophic term for you, He was some imaginary Being somewhere, Someone to talk about only. You did not know Him, you were not in correspondence with Him; you were outside His life. Do you know God? I do not ask, Do you talk about God? But is God real to you? Do you know Him? 'This is life eternal, that they might know thee . . .' Can you say, 'My God'?

The second thing about this condition obviously is that *such a*

man is ignorant also of spiritual things and spiritual life. The apostle
puts it in writing to the Romans, in the eighth chapter, like this.
He says: 'They that are after the flesh do mind the things of the
flesh; but they that are after the Spirit do mind the things of the
Spirit'. Being interpreted it means that they that are after the
flesh are not Christian, they are interested in the things that correspond to the flesh, they are not interested in the things of the Spirit.
And this, of course, is sheer hard fact. The man who is not a Christian
knows nothing about these things, and he does not want to know
about them. He is not interested in them and thinks they are terribly
boring. The man who is not a Christian finds the Bible very boring,
and expositions of the Bible very boring. He does not find films
boring, he does not find the newspapers boring, he does not find the
novels boring; but he finds these things boring. He does not enjoy
conversations about the soul and about life and death and heaven
and God and the Lord Jesus Christ. He cannot help it, but he just
sees nothing in it and he is not interested. He is interested in men
and their appearance, and in what they have done and in what they
have said; the world and its affairs appeal to him tremendously.
The position is perfectly simple; these other things are spiritual,
they are God's things, and that kind of man sees nothing in them.
Why? Because he is 'dead', and has no spiritual life. The law
concerning affinities is true. Like appeals to like, like attracts like,
'birds of a feather flock together'. The child is born and it wants
milk; its nature demands it, but an inanimate object does not. That
is the second thing about man in sin.

But not only does he not like these things, let us go on and put it
as the Scriptures put it; he even hates them. He literally hates them,
not only because they are boring him but because he has a feeling
somehow that the fact that he does not like them condemns him.
And he does not like that feeling. Of course he is prepared to have
some sort of religion, but only as long as he can control it, control
what is said and for how long it is said, and such like things. Ah,
yes, there must be a time limit on God's things; but not on the
world's things. That is hatred of God. 'The carnal mind', says Paul,
'is enmity against God, for it is not subject to the law of God, neither
indeed can be' (Romans 8: 7).

We must go yet further: *this kind of person is obviously unlike God
and does not share the life of God.* In other words, to use a biblical
term, this kind of life is corrupt. It is corruption. God is holy, and
all who are like God are holy also. 'Be ye holy', He says, 'for I
am holy'. But these people are dead, they are outside His life,
they are corrupt. They are essentially evil. They delight in evil
things, they gloat over them, because their nature is an evil nature.

There is no righteousness in them, there is no truth in them. They believe lies, and are themselves liars, says the Bible, 'hateful and hating one another'. That is man in sin—dead, outside the life of God.

What follows, of course, is that *such a life is not blessed by God, and therefore it is miserable*. The life of man in sin is a miserable life. If you dispute that, there is only one thing to say to you and that is that you are not a Christian. If you do not agree that the godless life, the life of the world, is a miserable life and that the only happy life is the Christian life, you are just proclaiming that you are not a Christian. To hanker after that sort of life, that sort of existence, is just a proclamation that you have not a spiritual nature. The truth about that life is that it is wretched, it is unhappy. Look beneath the surface and you see it shouting at you. The way of the world, with all its changes, its constant changes, is a proclamation of the fact that those who follow it are profoundly miserable. That is why they have to go on changing. They get tired of everything, they must always be seeking after something new. They are always looking for thrills and they run after them. Why? Because it is intolerable to them to spend a few hours with themselves. They find their own company so miserable that they spend their lives in running away from themselves. That is the measure of the misery of a life of sin: no resources and no reserves, because they are outside the life of God. That is man in sin. He is dead.

The apostle indeed sums it all up perfectly in a statement in the sixth chapter of his Epistle to the Romans in the eleventh verse: he says, ' . . . reckon ye also yourselves, to be dead indeed unto sin, but alive unto God . . .' You were not alive to God before: you are now, as Christians, alive unto God. Do we realise that man in sin is dead in that way? Do you realise that that is what you were by nature? Do you not see that this is the way to measure salvation? That is what we all have been, says Paul. And those who are in sin are still there. Have you no heart of compassion for the unbelievers? Do you ever pray for them? Are you doing everything you can to bring this gospel to them, whether in this or in any other land? That is their condition. Oh, miserable wretches! Dead! Outside the life of God!

Let me hurry to a word on the second matter. The second thing he tells us about such people is that they are governed by this world, 'Wherein in time past ye walked *according to the course of this world.*' What a statement! 'The course of this world!' The actual word the apostle used was 'the *age* of this world'. What does he mean by that? I think he means that this kind of life is lived under the control of the outlook and the mentality of this present world—'this present evil world' as the Scriptures call it (Galatians 1 : 4). Now the trouble about man in sin is that he is carried along, he is controlled, he is absolutely governed by that kind of life and by that kind of outlook. This is something that is taught in the Bible from beginning to end. According to the Bible the world is always against God.

What is 'the world' in a biblical sense? It is the outlook and the mentality and the organisation of life apart from God. That is what is meant by 'the world'. It does not mean the physical universe, the mountains and the rivers and so on. The world is a mentality, an outlook, a view of life without God. God is shut right out; it is man himself viewing and organising life and controlling life. It is this mentality that is described as 'the world'. Paul has put it once and for ever in this very chapter we are considering. Look at verse twelve again: 'Wherefore', he says, 'remember, . . . that at that time ye were without Christ, being aliens from the commonwealth of Israel, and strangers from the covenants of promise, having no hope, and without God . . . in the world'. To be without God means that you are 'in the world'. And to be in the world means that you are governed by the outlook and the mentality of the world. The apostle says the same thing in Romans 12 : 2: 'and be not conformed to this world, but be ye transformed by the renewing of your mind. . . .' As a Christian, says the apostle, do not be conformed to this world with its mentality and its outlook; you are in another realm. 'Be transformed', 'have your mind renewed' to correspond to that new world. Or listen to the apostle John saying it very explicitly: 'Love not the world, neither the things that are in the world . . . the lust of the flesh and the lust of the eyes and the pride of life' (1 John 2: 15–17). That is the world. Do not love that, says John in effect, you do not belong to that, that is utterly opposed to God. Love not the world!

The apostle's statement here is *that the man who is not a Christian is a man who is simply governed and controlled by the world*, its mind, its outlook, its mentality. I know of nothing which is more sad about man in sin than just that. You see it all in your newspapers. Is it not sad to see the way people are governed entirely by what other people think and say and do? They are sorry for those of us who are Christian. They say, 'Fancy shutting themselves down to that one Book, those narrow miserable Christians!' So speaks the so-called broad-minded man of the world. How subtle the devil is to persuade people of that! For their little life is entirely controlled by the organization of the world. They think as the world thinks. They take their opinions ready-made from their favourite news-paper. Their very appearance is controlled by the world and its changing fashions. They all conform; it must be done; they dare not disobey; they are afraid of the consequences. That is tyranny, that is absolute control—clothing, hair style, everything, absolutely controlled. The mind of the world! There is no time to elaborate on the subtle, almost devilish influence that is displayed often in its fashions—sex rampant. This is a sex-ridden age. It comes out everywhere—photographs and pictures and placards suggesting it. Most lives are being controlled by it and governed by it, all their opinions, their language, the way they spend their money, what they desire, where they go, where they spend their holidays; it is all controlled, governed completely. Surely all this was never more evident in the world than it is today. When people talk so glibly about their emancipation they are giving a very clear proof of the fact that they are governed and dominated and controlled by this world, the mind of the world, the age of propaganda, the age of advertising, the mass mind, the mass man, the mass individual, without knowing it. Is it not tragic? But that is man in sin. He is spiritually dead because he is controlled by this mind of the world.

Not only that, but the apostle goes on to tell us that *that in turn is controlled by an evil principle that is in life.* Listen to him putting it like this: 'Wherein in time past ye walked according to the course of this world, according to the prince of the power of the air, the spirit that now worketh in the children of disobedience.' The 'spirit' here means the principle; there is an evil principle which, he says, is working in this world. And that word 'working' is a strong word. There is an energy, a force, a power about it. There is nothing more pathetic than to think of a life of sin as a passive life or a negative life. The fact is that there is a very powerful principle of evil at work in this world, and it is only the man who believes the Bible and has had his mind and his understanding enlightened by the Holy Spirit who can see that. Do you imagine that all that you see in life today just comes to pass anyhow, somehow? Cannot you see how organised it is, how uniform it is, how subtle it is, how it corresponds in every part? There is a principle of evil at work. In a very dark age let us thank God for every indication of improvement. I refer to the fact that there were certain philosophers who were honest enough to tell us that the last war actually convinced them of this. Think of a man like the late Dr. Joad. He was an atheist, an unbeliever, before the war. He then came to believe in the fact of God, and he tells us why. He said that the second war convinced him that the Bible was at any rate right as far as this, that there is a principle of evil at work. He said that he could not explain the war in any other way; he could see that it was not accident, not negative, but that there was a devilish evil power at work, 'the spirit that

now worketh in the children of disobedience.' It behoves us as
Christian people to recognise that these poor people who are without
God in the world are being dominated and controlled by this evil
principle.

But we must go yet one step further back. The apostle says that
that evil principle is governed by the devil and all his powers: 'Wherein
in time past ye walked according to the course of this world, according to the prince of the power of the air.' What a statement! But
surely, says some sophisticated person, you do not mean to say you
still believe in the devil! The simple answer is that I believe in the
devil because I have to. I have to, not merely because it is here—
this is enough for me—but I believe it because I cannot explain life
without it. And it is because the devil is ignored that the world is
as it is. The devil is so subtle that he dominates man and persuades
him at the same time that he is not being dominated. Man even
thinks he is emancipating himself by turning his back on the Bible.
The devil is also called 'the god of this world'. The Lord Jesus
Christ called him 'the prince of this world'. He is referred to as
'Beelzebub, the chief of the devils'. And it is he who is dominating
it all. He hates God. He was an angel created perfect by God, a
bright seraph. He stood up against God because he wanted to be
God; and he hates God, and his one object is to mar God's creation,
to ruin God's world. So he came into it and beguiled Eve and Adam,
and he has been doing it ever since. He dominates the life of man.
We are all under the dominion of Satan by nature. He has his
forces, his powers; he is 'the prince'. Of what? 'Of the powers of
the air.' You notice how Paul puts it in the sixth chapter of this
Epistle, verse twelve: 'We wrestle not against flesh and blood'. If
you think that the problem confronting the statesmen today is just
the problem of dealing with other men like themselves, then you
are tragically ignorant politically, let alone spiritually. If you think
that it is just a question of personalities, one man or another, like
Hitler or Stalin, you have not started to understand it. 'We wrestle
not against flesh and blood, but against principalities and powers,
against the rulers of the darkness of this world'—that is it, the
powers of the air, darkness—against 'spiritual wickedness in the
heavenlies'.

The Bible tells us that there are these unseen powers, and the devil
is 'the prince of the power of the air.' You can interpret that word
'air' in these two ways. You can say the prince of the powers of
darkness, or the prince of the unseen powers. They are not earthly
powers, they belong to another realm, they are ethereal as it were,
they are spiritual. They have no bodies, but they are there. And the
tragedy of man is that because he cannot see the spirits of evil he

does not believe in them. He cannot see the Holy Spirit so he does not believe in the Holy Spirit. He cannot see God so he does not believe in God. He does not realise he is in a spiritual realm. That is because he is dead. It is because he is without spiritual understanding. 'The prince of the powers!' Oh, the power of evil! The man who is not a Christian is absolutely dominated and controlled by, and is dead in the hands of, these powers.

We also, who are Christian people, are still confronted by them. That is what the apostle is saying in the sixth chapter of this Epistle. We as Christians have to wrestle against this power. 'Christian, seek not yet repose; cast thy dreams of ease away!' And it seems to me that many Christians are dreaming of ease, and are thinking and dreaming of some sort of a salvation in which there is no strife and struggle. Never in this world! There are these powers of evil, the powers of the air, with all their subtlety and malignity, with all their cleverness, and their chief transforms himself 'into an angel of light' in order that he may get us down. That is what is confronting us. The amazing thing is that any of us still stand in this Christian life at all. We are confronted by the one who did not hesitate to come to the Son of God and tempt Him and say with absolute confidence: 'If thou be the Son of God'. He is the one who repeatedly defeated all the patriarchs and all the saints of the Old Testament. Every one of them went down before him time and time again. And he is opposed to us with all his might and strength and power, with all the forces that he commands, with the evil principle that he has put into the whole outlook and mind of the world. It is organised in visible form, but it itself is unseen; it is everywhere.

How do we still stand? There is only one answer. It is by 'the exceeding greatness of his power to us-ward who believe'. The God who saves us is the God who keeps us, and without Him we could not stand for a second. The glory therefore must be entirely His. 'You hath *he* quickened, who were dead.' Oh, that our eyes may be enlightened that we may see the problem and appreciate its depths; and then know that this Power which holds us will never leave us nor forsake us!

3

ORIGINAL SIN

And you hath he quickened, who were dead in trespasses and sins; Wherein
in time past ye walked according to the course of this world, according to the
prince of the power of the air, the spirit that now worketh in the children of
disobedience: Among whom also we all had our conversation in times past
in the lusts of our flesh, fulfilling the desires of the flesh, and of the mind;
and were by nature the children of wrath, even as others.

Ephesians 2: 1-3

In our previous studies we have seen that the apostle's first principle
is that we cannot understand the greatness of the power of God's
salvation until we have realised that man by nature is spiritually
dead. Moreover we must grasp the fact that he is governed by
this world and the mind of this world, that he is governed by the
principle of evil that is operating in this world and which in turn is
governed by 'the prince of the power of the air', that great head,
the devil, Satan, the god of this world, the controller of all these
evil spiritual powers and forces that govern and rule men and
determine the kind of life that is lived by man in this world. That
is the state, the condition.

How vital it is that we should realise this! vital, not only from the
standpoint of understanding the gospel, but surely in a very practical
sense absolutely essential to an understanding of the times in which
we live, both internationally and in a national sense. There is
nothing so fatuous as the idea that Christian doctrine is remote
from life. There is nothing more practical, and the world is today
in its present condition of muddle because men simply will not recognise the truth of what the Bible tells us about man. Look at the
industrial, even the financial, situation. What is the trouble? Well,
we are told the main trouble is that production is not as high as it
should be. Why is production not as high as it should be? That is the
question. Why are we not producing more? And the answer is,
of course, that we are not producing more because man is in a state
of sin. You notice I say 'man', not 'the men'. I say man to include
all men. We are not producing as much as we should because
employers *and* employed are increasingly extending their notion as
to the length of the week-end. It applies to all. If one man has a
right to extend his week-end another has an equal right. And all,

because they are in sin and selfish, as I am going to show you, are doing that. Hence our major problem at this moment. 'Whence come wars amongst you?' James asks, and answers his own question. They come 'even of your own lusts that war in your members'. And the tragedy is that the world and its leaders and its statesmen, because they do not recognise the teaching of Scripture, think that they can explain it in some other terms. The various groups blame one another, and the various countries blame one another, not realising that they are all in sin together; and while they are in sin and are self-centred and selfish they will all consider themselves and nobody else, and the world will continue in its troubles. So you see this biblical doctrine of sin is the most practical thing in the world; and yet people dismiss it with disdain, including, alas, even Christian people also. How remote from the biblical teaching itself is the far too common idea that Christianity is simply a collection of a number of moral maxims, and that you go to church on Sunday just to have a little encouragement, to be told your duty and to be told you are good if you do it, and no more. That does not begin to consider the real problem. Before we can possibly realise the true nature of the problem we must understand exactly what man is in a state of sin. It is only then that we shall see clearly that nothing but spiritual renewal and the work of the Holy Ghost can possibly deal with the situation and deliver us in every respect. We are considering this teaching then, for these reasons.

Having looked at man, therefore, in his actual state and condition, we come to the second point, which is *the explanation of his condition*. Why is man in this condition? What has brought him into it, what accounts for it, what explains it? The apostle answers that question in a series of terms and words which he uses in these three verses. Let us look at them. The first term that is of importance is the expression 'the children of disobedience'. 'Wherein in time past', he says, 'ye walked according to the course of this world, according to the prince of the power of the air, the spirit that now worketh in the *children of disobedience*'. What a significant and important term this is! If you prefer it you can translate it 'sons of disobedience'— it is the same thing. What does it mean? It does not just mean disobedient children or disobedient sons. This is a characteristic biblical expression. You will find a similar kind of expression used in many places. You remember how our Lord turned to the Jews one day and said, 'Ye are of your father the devil, and the works of your father ye will do'. Then you remember how in the Old Testament you often find that certain wicked men are referred to as 'sons of Belial' or some such term. Therefore we must regard the term as saying that disobedience is the source of this distinctive character. We are children of disobedience in the sense that it is disobedience that leads to our being exactly what we are. Now that is the thing the apostle is stressing here.

That is always the essential point in the biblical explanation of why man is like this. The essential, primary trouble is disobedience. That is the thing that has led to all our troubles and all our disasters. In other words, it is man's relationship to God. And you notice that the emphasis is this, that sin is not merely something negative, not merely the absence of qualities, not merely the absence of something; it is positive, it is active, it is deliberate. It is dis-obedience, it is departure from obedience, it is a querying of the right of God to command us; in other words it is rebellion. And that is what the Bible tells us from beginning to end about man. He is not just a poor creature who has never had a chance, and to whom therefore you should be very sympathetic and very lenient. That is the modern idea, as you know. The biblical doctrine of sin really went out of men's thinking some sixty or seventy years ago, and psychology came in in its place. That is why discipline and punishment have gone. The idea now is that we are all, essentially, really very good, and the trouble is that we have never been given a chance. What we need, we are told, is encouragement. We do not believe in law and moral sanctions. That is regarded as very harsh and cruel. The result of it all is the breakdown of discipline in every department of life—in the home, in the schools, on the streets, in industry, in commerce, everywhere. You see how vital this doctrine is! The Bible teaches that our troubles are all due to this initial disobedience; that man is a rebel against God and deliberately rebels against God. And it all arises, of course, from his self-love. It is man's self-assertion, it is man setting himself up against God, his desire to be as a god himself.

This works itself out along three main lines. The first thing, obviously, is that *man denies his own creatureliness*. He objects to that. Man does not like the idea that he is a creature made and created by God. He feels that this idea of his creatureliness is insulting to him, that it somehow detracts from him and his essential greatness and glory. He does not like the idea that there is anybody, even God, who is above him. He likes to think that man is supreme, is above everything, and can look down upon everything. That is the very heart and nerve of the natural man's objection to God and his opposition to God. Man resents by nature the idea that there is anything or anybody whom he cannot comprehend with his mind; and when he is told that he is only a creature and that his attitude towards the Creator, the Lord God Almighty, should be one of humbling himself and falling down upon his face before Him, he objects to it. He feels that it is insulting, and he asserts that he is not a creature, and that there is nothing beyond him. So you have the modern man's atheism, his objection to God, and his godlessness. It all arises on account of the fact that he objects to this idea of his own creatureliness, that he is someone whom God has made and created and fashioned for Himself.

Another way in which it manifests itself—and it follows obviously from the first—is that *man always wants to assert his own self-sufficiency*. He believes that he is sufficient in and of himself. The Bible, of course, says the exact opposite—that man was not only made by God and for God, but that he is dependent upon God, and that he can only be happy when he is in correspondence with God and when he obeys God. The whole biblical conception of man is that man is thus in a state of complete dependence upon God, and that his well-being depends upon his realisation of that and his practice of that. But this, of course, cuts right across what man has always felt about himself. He has always had the feeling that he is self-sufficient, that he has the necessary powers and that he has but to exercise them to make a perfect world and to make a perfect life for himself. He feels competent to order his affairs in the right way, and that he needs no aid and no assistance.

That is why there is nothing that so offends the natural man as the gospel which tells him that he is saved by the grace of God alone which he as a pauper has to accept as a free gift. He says: I have not sunk as low as that, I am not perfect, perhaps, but I am not a pauper, there is still something that I can do, and I am capable of doing it. It is the doctrine of the grace of God that man hates most of all. That is 'the offence of the cross'; and it exists because man believes in his own self-sufficiency, his own capacity, his own inherent power. That is an expression of his disobedience. He will not accept grace, he will not believe it, he rebels against it, and fights against it.

Or perhaps we can explain it in this way: it is man's assertion of his autonomy, his independence of God. Autonomous man is the notion of man as one who can in every way manage his own affairs and who needs no help and no assistance from anywhere, not even from God Himself! Autonomous man, self-sufficient man, self-determinative man, independent man, man as a god, man as the lord of the universe, man on the throne and on a pedestal!

All must surely recognise that that is nothing but a description of man as he is at the present time outside the Christian faith. He is utterly disobedient, and proud of it, and arrogant in it. He is asserting himself and his self-sufficiency. It is essential that the matter be pressed to that point. Disobedience is, as I have said, active, and it is active to the point of enmity. If we fail to realise that, we have not really understood this doctrine. So let me interpret what the apostle says here by what he says in the Epistle to the Romans in the eighth chapter and the seventh verse: 'The natural mind', he says, 'is enmity against God; is not subject to the law of God, neither indeed can be'. What a statement, and what an important addition! Man disobeys because he is at enmity against God; he hates God. Ah but, you say, I know many people who are not Christians but who say that they believe in God. No, they do not! They believe in a figment of their own imagination; they do not believe in God. If they believed in God they would believe in His Christ, as our Lord Himself argues in John 8: 30–45. But they do not. They believe simply in what they think and imagine God is, the god that they have manufactured themselves. That is not God! 'The natural mind is enmity against God; is not subject to the law of God, neither indeed can be.'

This is important in this way, that it shows that man as the result of sin, as the result of being dominated by the devil and the principle of evil which he has introduced, and by the mind of this world, is in such a state and condition that *he cannot obey God*. That is what the great Martin Luther called 'the bondage of the will'. But what a hateful doctrine to man in sin and to the modern man! 'The bondage of the will!' My will is free! says man. Man likes to think that he is absolutely free to choose anything he likes, that he can choose to serve God if he so desires; that he can choose to be a Christian if he wants to do so. Assertion of man's will, free will, is the order of the day. But the Bible speaks of 'children of disobedience'; and 'Ye are of your father the devil, and the works of your father ye will do'. Our Lord says that you cannot help it. The natural man 'is not subject to the law of God, neither indeed *can* be'—he is incapable of it. There has been no such thing as free will as regards obeying God since Adam fell. Adam had free will; no one else has ever had it. Freedom of the will was lost in the Fall; man there became a slave of sin and under the dominion of the devil. His will is bound. 'If our gospel be hid', says the apostle Paul to the Corinthians (2 Corinthians 4: 3 and 4) 'it is hid to them that are lost; in whom the god of this world hath blinded the minds of them which believe not' lest they believe the glorious gospel of Christ. The devil will not allow them to believe. 'The strong man armed keepeth his goods in peace.' That is the condition of man under the dominion of the devil; he is not free. He is not free not to sin. 'Children of disobedience!' 'Neither indeed can be!' He is incapable of it. Such is the depth to which man has sunk in sin. And yet this is where the paradox, as it were, comes in. In spite of that, everything man does he does deliberately. He wills to sin, he enjoys sinning, he glories in sinning. He does exert his will negatively in sin; what he cannot do is to will positive good, to will spiritual good. He is incapable of that and that is why he needs to be 'born again' and to have a new nature. But he can will evil and he delights to do so. What he does not realise is that he is rendered incapable of willing good and willing anything in the direction of salvation. He is not free to do that. Children of disobedience, the spawn of disobedience, the progeny of disobedience! There is in the universe an evil mind and we are the offspring of it. That is the biblical teaching. Is it not extraordinary that anybody who has understanding in these matters can dispute that for a moment? The world today is just demonstrating and proving its truth. Men and women are the slaves of the devil, the bondslaves of the devil; they are under the power and dominion of Satan.

So much for the first term, but let us look at the second term. The second term is found at the end of the third verse: 'and were *by nature* the children of wrath, even as others'. I pick out the words 'by nature'. This is obviously a most important term. This is the thing which explains why we are children of disobedience and why we have this particular attitude with respect to God. The apostle uses it primarily here in explication of his teaching that we are 'under the wrath of God'. We are under the wrath of God, he says, 'by nature'. I hope to deal with that later. Now I want to show that it means something in addition to that. We are what we are in every respect 'by nature'. If you prefer another translation you could substitute the words 'by birth', 'and we were by birth the children of wrath, even as others'.

In other words the teaching here is the teaching of the whole Bible with regard to man in sin, and it is that *we are born into this world with a disobedient nature*. We are not born neutral into this world. We are not born evenly balanced with the possibility of going either that way or this way. We are born heavily biased to one side. David puts it memorably in Psalm fifty-one in the fifth verse: 'Behold, I was shapen in iniquity, and in sin did my mother conceive me'. What a profound bit of self-analysis and of psychology! If you want psychology, go to the Scriptures. Here is a man, David, examining himself. He has been reminded of what he has done, the adultery and the murder following it. He is awakened and he examines himself, and seems to be saying to himself, How could I do it? How could a man ever do such a thing? What renders a man capable of that? What is it? And, he says, There is only one answer, it is as deep as this: I was shapen in iniquity—'shapen' in iniquity—and 'in sin did my mother conceive me'.

This doctrine is not popular today. Man in sin has never liked it. What he likes to say, of course, is that we are all born neutral. Look at that little child, how wonderful, how perfect! Well, why does he sin when he grows up? Ah well, they say, you see that is the trouble; it is the sinful world into which he comes: he sees bad things, he sees bad habits, and he is gradually influenced by them. They say that the child is all right but that the environment is not. If only that child could be put into a perfect world he would remain perfect; but he comes into an imperfect world and he sees and he picks up habits, he listens to talk, and he sees the things that people do, and he gradually picks them up and he practises them. It is nothing but bad environment, bad example, bad influence. No, says the Bible, it is not. That little child was shapen in iniquity and born and conceived in sin. Our very natures when we come into this world are already polluted. We inherit a sinful nature from our forefathers and parents; we start with it. The tendencies and the desires are all there, and all the world does is to give us an outlet. There is rebellion within us, a desire for the prohibited. It comes out at once. It is one of the first things we manifest, all of us. Why? Well, 'by nature'.

In other words, the central fallacy arises at this point in this way. We tend to think of sin in terms of separate acts of the will; and therefore we tend to lose sight of the fact that we are ourselves sinful apart from our actions, that sin is in us and is a part of our very nature. We must get rid of the notion that we ourselves are all right until temptation comes and we fall. That is true of *a* sin, a sinful action. I have exerted my will and I did what I should not have done! But that is not the whole explanation. The real question is this: What was it that ever led to that act? The answer is, that 'something' within me. Take the words of our Lord Himself, who put it once and for ever: 'Not that which goeth into the mouth defileth a man; but that which cometh out of the mouth, this defileth a man. . . . For out of the heart proceed evil thoughts, murders, adulteries, fornications. . . .' and all the rest. The trouble is in the heart of man. It is this fallen, sinful nature. It is what Paul calls, in the seventh of Romans, 'the law in my members'; 'in me, that is to say, in my flesh, dwelleth no good thing'. It is corrupt, it is evil, by nature. 'We are, by nature, the children of wrath even as others.'

This is of the most vital importance. If the other theory is right and man is born more or less neutral, and if his troubles are due to the fact that bad things or evil environment lead him astray, then all you have to do is to deal with the environment. And that has been the controlling philosophy for the last sixty to seventy years. The problem has been regarded as one of education, housing, and economic improvement almost exclusively. We had only to give man the right conditions, and give him the right environment and adequate knowledge, and he would be all right. But by now, surely, we must all be beginning to realise that that is not true, that it does not work. You can give man the most ideal conditions and he will go wrong in them. It was in Paradise that man fell! And if man in his original righteous condition could fall into sin, how much more so man who has already fallen. This is a principle that shows itself in all human relationships everywhere. The problem and the tragedy of man, alas, lie at a very deep level. The Bible is not alone in teaching this. Shakespeare has stated it memorably: 'The fault, dear Brutus, is not in our stars but in ourselves, that we are underlings.' 'By nature!' We start with it, with a bias towards evil, with a will that is in bondage, under the dominion of Satan, with lusts and evil desires, as we shall see, already there and waiting for an opportunity to demonstrate and to manifest themselves.

We come next to the most important word 'all'. 'Wherein in time past ye walked according to the course of this world, according to the prince of the power of the air, the spirit that now worketh in the children of disobedience; among whom also we *all* had our conversation in times past, in the lusts of our flesh, fulfilling the desires of the flesh and of the mind, and were by nature the children of wrath'—and again he says it—'even as others'. Or, if you prefer another translation—'like the rest of mankind'. 'All,' *it is universal*. Now this is a startling thing. This point was very germane to the apostle's particular argument just here. His theme is, you remember, how God in Christ in the fulness of the times is going to reunite all things in Christ, 'both which are in heaven and which are on earth, even in him'. And he says that He has already started to do this. In chapter one, verse eleven, he states that some who are Jews have believed the gospel and are in the kingdom. He goes on to say that some who were Gentiles have also obtained an inheritance. Here he comes back to that again—'you hath he quickened'. He has done it to you Gentiles. But he is most anxious that no one should think that he is only saying these things about the Gentiles. No, we 'all' had our conversation, we 'all' were the children of wrath, even as others. What he says here about man in sin is as true about the Jew as it is of the Gentile.

How difficult it was for the Jew to believe that! For centuries he had believed that he was quite apart: the Jew! Outside were the dogs, the Gentiles, the strangers. They were 'outside the common-wealth of Israel'. He, a Jew, was a child of God, he was safe because he was a Jew. He was altogether right and better than all others who were sinners, dogs of the Gentiles, outside. How difficult for him to accept a doctrine which says that he was as much a sinner as was the Gentile! That was the stumbling block to the Jew, he did not like it. And this classification of mankind is still to be found in different forms and guises. But here the apostle says, 'not only Gentiles' but 'also Jews'. And you notice that he even puts himself in. Having started with 'you', he now says 'we'. This is true of Paul, the apostle! The thing is unthinkable, is it not? But that was the whole tragedy of his life before his conversion. As Saul of Tarsus he was satisfied with his life; 'as touching the righteousness which is of the law, blameless'. And he tells us (in Romans 7) how it was that he came to see his error. It was when he understood the law to say 'Thou shalt not covet'. Then 'sin revived and I died'. When the law began to say 'you must not desire', 'you must not covet', he saw the real meaning of the law and he saw that he was a terrible sinner. In writing to Timothy he says, 'This is a faithful saying and worthy of all acceptation, that Christ Jesus came into the world to save sinners, of whom I am chief'. He is the chief of sinners. 'We all had our conversation in times past. . . .'

This is true of 'all'. But people are still very slow to see that. They say, Take this description of sin which you have in those three verses. Of course, says the man, I can see quite well that that applies to certain people. I walk along the streets and I see that poor drunkard, and that fallen woman. I see sin in its rags and in its vices. You are quite right in what you say as regards such people and when you talk about an evil nature and the lusts of the flesh, the lusts of the mind, and so on. I quite agree with you. But we are not all like that. Are there not good people, and moral, and decent people, and upright people, and religious people? Are you saying that about them? The answer of the apostle Paul is 'all', 'even as others'; the whole of mankind; not a single exception. We are 'all shapen in iniquity', conceived in sin. We 'all' have this sinful nature.

The fatal mistake is to think of sin always in terms of acts and of actions rather than in terms of nature, and of disposition. The mistake is to think of it in terms of particular things instead of thinking of it, as we should, in terms of our relationship to God. Do you want to know what sin is? I will tell you. Sin is the exact opposite of the attitude and the life which conform to, 'Thou shalt love the Lord thy God with all thy heart, and with all thy soul, and with all thy mind, and with all thy strength'. If you are not doing that you are a sinner. It does not matter how respectable you are; if you are not living entirely to the glory of God you are a sinner. And the more you imagine that you are perfect in and of yourself and apart from your relationship to God, the greater is your sin. That is why anyone who reads the New Testament objectively can see clearly that the Pharisees of our Lord's time were greater sinners (if you can use such terms) than were the publicans and open sinners. Why? Because they were self-satisfied, because they were self-sufficient. The height of sin is not to feel any need of the grace of God. There is no greater sin than that. Infinitely worse than committing some sin of the flesh is to feel that you are independent of God, or that Christ need never have died on the cross of Calvary. There is no greater sin than that. That final self-sufficiency, and self-satisfaction, and self-righteousness, is the sin of sins; it is sin at its height, because it is spiritual sin. So when you realise that, you realise that the apostle is not exaggerating when he says 'we all', 'even as others'.

That is man in sin, and it is true universally. There is only one adequate explanation of this. It is what is given at the beginning of the book of Genesis. It is the biblical doctrine of the Fall and of original sin. You cannot understand the modern world apart from the doctrine of original sin. It has all come about in this way: one man, Adam, the representative of humanity, sinned, rebelled, and fell. And the consequences have devolved upon all his progeny. I defy you to explain the universality of sin in any other terms. It simply cannot be done. Every other theory breaks down. That is why we must believe the early chapters of Genesis if we are to believe the New Testament. You cannot have a true doctrine of salvation apart from this. The two things go together as Paul proves in the fifth chapter of the Epistle to the Romans and again in exactly the same way in the fifteenth chapter of the First Epistle to the Corinthians. That is the problem of man; that is why man is as he is. Adam fell, Adam sinned; and the result is that all the seed of Adam are born in corruption, with a polluted nature. It is universal, everywhere. It is this that 'makes the whole world kin'; it is this that makes nonsense of all your various 'curtains' and all your colour bars and all your philosophies. The whole world is one here. We are all in sin, children of disobedience, inheritors of a fallen nature that expresses and manifests itself in the way which we shall go on to consider—'in the lusts of the flesh, fulfilling the desires of the flesh and of the mind', and therefore under the wrath of God and utterly helpless.

I leave it there, because I am preaching on the assumption that I am addressing Christian people. But if I were preaching this to a mixed gathering I would not stop there, I would not dare stop there. I would go on to say, '*But*, even when we were like that, in His infinite grace and love and mercy, God has quickened us'. Nothing less could do it. What else could deal with man in such a condition? Nothing less than the almighty power of God—the power, as Paul has said at the end of the first chapter, that brought the Lord Jesus again from the dead and raised Him and 'set him in the heavenly places, far above all principality and power and might and dominion and every name that can be named'. Nothing less than the power of God can rescue and redeem and save man. But He has done so in Christ. And we who are Christians have been raised out of that terrible plight, in which we once were, solely because of His wondrous grace.

4

LIFE WITHOUT GOD

And you hath he quickened, who were dead in trespasses and sins; Wherein in time past ye walked according to the course of this world, according to the prince of the power of the air, the spirit that now worketh in the children of disobedience: Among whom also we all had our conversation in times past in the lusts of our flesh, fulfilling the desires of the flesh and of the mind; and were by nature the children of wrath, even as others. Ephesians 2: 1-3

As we come back to a consideration of this tremendous and most vital statement, we remind ourselves that the apostle introduces it in order to bring out the great idea which he had started expounding in the previous chapter, namely, that we as God's people should realise 'the greatness of his power to us-ward that believe'. He says that what we need to do is to measure this great power. The way to do so, he says, is to realise first of all the depth out of which God has had to raise us, and then consider the height to which he has taken us. As we understand the depth and height we shall have some conception of the exceeding greatness of God's power.

So the apostle first describes our state and condition in sin, what we were like before this power took hold of us. The second thing he does is to give us an explanation of how we ever got into that state. There he introduces us to the great doctrine of original sin.

Now he comes to the third point which is, *the actual way in which all this shows and manifests itself in practice,* in our ordinary life and living. As he deals with this he incidentally introduces us to the third great power against which we have to struggle in this our earthly life. He has already dealt with the world and the devil; now he comes to deal with the flesh. We have a conflict against the world and the flesh and the devil—and we are now going to look at this conflict against the flesh. Man in sin, according to the apostle, is living a life controlled by 'the lusts of the flesh'. This is so because he is born with a polluted nature as the result of original sin, which in turn resulted from that original transgression and rebellion of man against God which produced the Fall. In other words we find ourselves here in these three verses in the very centre of the greatest profundities of Christian doctrine; and Paul

36

reminds us of them in order to enable us to see the greatness, not only of the power of God, but of His love and of His grace and of His mercy. The astounding thing is that He has ever looked upon such people or ever troubled about us at all.

Let us then look at these things. Man's life, in a state of sin and outside grace, is, according to the apostle, *a life of trespasses and sins*—'you hath he quickened, who were dead in trespasses and sins'. That sums it all up. You can sum up the life of the whole world today in those two words—'trespasses' and 'sins'. What do they mean? The apostle is obviously concerned about shades of meaning here; otherwise he would not have used the two words. He has done so quite deliberately.

What is a trespass? A trespass is an outward transgression. The actual root meaning of the word is that it is a falling away from the true and from the upright. Man was meant to be upright and true and righteous and holy; he has fallen away from that, he is deflected from it, he is no longer upright. It is like something leaning or falling to the ground, it has gone out of its true position, out of the perpendicular.

What does he mean by the word 'sins'? This is a very large and comprehensive term. It is a term which includes all the manifestations of sin considered as an inward principle. That is what he means by the term 'sins'. Sins are the outward manifestations of this inward principle called sin which we have been considering. There is in every one of us this polluted principle, and it manifests itself in what we call sins. Here then, we have a very comprehensive definition of man's life apart from grace—a falling away from the true and the right and the upright and the righteous, and all the outward manifestations of this evil principle that is within us. That is what is meant by trespasses and sins. And according to the apostle that is the life of man apart from the grace of God; that is how he 'walks', he says. You notice how he puts it, 'wherein in time past ye walked'. And then he has another phrase, 'among whom also we all had our conversation in times past'. What he means by 'conversation', as is generally the case in the Authorised Version, is not 'speech' but 'tenor of life'. You remember the apostle says at the end of the third chapter of the Epistle to the Philippians: 'Our conversation is in heaven'. That does not mean speech or talk. This is a term which was used in the sixteenth and seventeenth centuries to express a general mode or manner of life.

That is the description of our actions. But actions after all are expressive of something else. There is a saying to the effect that

'as a man thinketh, so he is'. Examine a man's conduct and behaviour and you will discover his philosophy, if you examine it
truly. We all express our ideas of life in the way in which we live.
That is exactly true of man in sin, says the apostle. What you
see are the trespasses and sins. Yes, but what is it that leads to the
trespasses and sins? He has his answer for us. It is all due to this
polluted nature, which he explains in the words, 'among whom we
all had our conversation in times past, in the lusts of the flesh, fulfilling the desires of the flesh and of the mind'.

That is the statement which we are considering now. That is
man's life without the grace of God in Jesus Christ. It is polluted. It
is *a life lived in the lusts of the flesh*. And the thing that the apostle
emphasises, and which I am anxious to emphasise therefore, is:
that this is true of all men, without exception. This is universally
true of the whole of mankind; not only of certain bad people but of
all people; 'we all had our conversation in times past . . . and were
the children of wrath, even as others'. We must hold on to this
idea of the universality of the condition. All men by nature are
living a life in the lusts of the flesh.

Let us examine this great statement. You notice the extraordin-
arily logical development of the apostle's statement. The trespasses
and sins are the result of this 'lust of the flesh'. But that is a general
expression so the apostle subdivides it. The lusts of the flesh manifest themselves along two main lines—'the desires of the flesh'
and 'the desires of the mind'. The fundamental trouble is that
we are living in 'the lusts of the flesh'; and that manifests itself in
our obeying 'the desires of the mind' and 'the desires of the
flesh'.

What is the meaning of this term *flesh*? It is a very important
term in the New Testament, and it is very important that we should
understand clearly what it means. There are systems of theology
which err mainly because they have never understood this scriptural term 'flesh' aright. You notice that this term is used twice in
this third verse: 'among whom also we all had our conversation
in times past, in the lusts of our flesh, fulfilling the desires of the
flesh and of the mind'. It is obvious at once that the word 'flesh'
is used there by the apostle in two different senses, otherwise
he is just repeating himself. He uses 'flesh' first in a general sense,
and then he uses it in a particular sense. So it is very important that
we should know the precise connotation each time he uses his
term.

This word 'flesh' is used in the Scripture in four main ways,
Two of them are general and two are particular. What I mean is
this: the word 'flesh' is sometimes used in Scripture to represent the

whole of mankind. Take a phrase like this, 'All flesh is grass, and all the goodliness thereof is as the flower of the field'. Flesh is used there to cover the term mankind, 'all flesh'. That is one, very general way. But it is also sometimes used to describe the covering of our bones. What does a man's body consist of? Well, there is the skeleton, the frame which consists of bones and so on. But you do not see the bones because they are covered with that we call flesh—muscles, fat, ligaments, etc. Now the term 'flesh' is sometimes used like that. Job says, 'I shall yet see him in my flesh', and he means there really 'in the body'. Those are the two general meanings.

But there are two other meanings which are more particular, and more spiritual, in their connotation. And these are the important ones for our purpose now. The first is again fairly general or has a fairly wide meaning. 'Flesh' is used by the apostle to denote that which is the complete antithesis to the Spirit, the Holy Spirit. There is a perfect example of this in Galatians 5 :17: 'for the flesh lusteth against the Spirit (with a capital S), and the Spirit against the flesh: and these are contrary the one to the other'. There he is using the term 'flesh' in a wide spiritual sense; it represents everything in man that is opposed to the working and the power and the influence of the Holy Spirit. Now this is tremendously important, so let me give you further definitions of it. Flesh in this sense means human nature in a state of sin, man in sin. Or take a yet more comprehensive definition of it. It is the entire nature of man apart from the renewing grace of Christ; so it embraces the soul, and the moral and the intellectual faculties, as well as the body. Flesh in this wide, general, spiritual sense is the entire man in sin apart from the grace of Christ. It includes, therefore, my body and its workings, my mind, my affections, my everything; the total man, the whole of man in a state of sin.

But finally the apostle uses this term 'flesh' in a more restricted spiritual sense, referring only to what you may call the sensuous part of our nature, to the body, to the animal part of nature and the manifestations of that animal portion. It is important that we should have these four definitions clearly in our minds, and especially the second two, those that have the spiritual reference—the whole man in sin, and secondly the animal part of man in sin, the bodily part of man, the sensuous, sensual part of man in sin.

It is important that we should be clear about this because we have this word 'flesh' twice over in this third verse, with the apostle using it in two different senses. Well, someone may say, is not this very muddling and confusing? How am I ever to know which he is using at any given point? The answer is quite simple. If you take the context into consideration you can never go wrong. Keep your eye on the context, and the context will always put you right. Take, for instance, this example here: 'among whom also we all had our conversation in times past, in the lusts of our flesh' —there is the whole thing, the whole man; particularly, he says 'fulfilling the desires of the flesh and of the mind'. Now in this second instance 'flesh' is the opposite of 'mind', so it is no longer the whole man. What is it then? Well it is the bodily part of man only, the animal part of man's nature only. You see, the context gives the answer. The first time, flesh is general: the second time it is particular, the opposite to the mind, the intellect, the higher part. So that flesh in general covers the desires of the body and the desires of the mind. We must always be careful to observe these distinctions as we read these Epistles.

What the apostle is saying is that man lives his life of trespasses and sins because he is governed and controlled by the lusts of the flesh—flesh in the general sense. But what is meant by lusts? Again we have a very important term. A lust is a strong desire. And actually the term 'lust' means no more than that. The strong desire may be good or it may be bad. For instance, there is a well-known statement made by our Lord in which He said as He ate the Last Supper with His disciples, 'With desire I have desired to eat this passover with you' (Luke 22 :15). What He actually said was: 'With lust I have lusted to eat this passover with you"—it is exactly the same term as is used here. In general, therefore, a lust means a strong desire. But again, obviously, if you pay attention to the context you will find whether the meaning is a good one or a bad one. Generally speaking the term 'lusts' in Scripture has reference to a strong, urgent craving for something which is prohibited or forbidden.

Now, then, having understood our basic definitions, we can look at man in sin, we can look at all who are not Christians, we can see what we ourselves were, before God in His infinite grace took hold of us and dealt with us and gave us new life. That is the picture of the natural man, controlled by strong and urgent cravings after that which is opposed to God and His holy laws. The apostle, however, is so anxious that we should get this clearly that he does not leave it as a general statement. He wants us to see how complete this pollution is; he wants us to see and to realise how it affects the whole man and every part of man. When Adam fell, the whole man fell; it was not merely his body that fell, everything in Adam fell, his mind, his affections, his will; the whole man fell. And it is because so many in their theological systems do not realise that, that they go astray; they make the term refer only to the sensuous part of man's nature, and therefore their whole outlook must be wrong. They think that they can choose salvation, almost that they can save themselves and decide to be sanctified, and so on. They have never realised the totality of man's fall in sin. The whole man is involved.

The apostle shows us that by dividing it up here into these two main sub-divisions. You see how important it is to grasp that. We all refer at times to certain people as being sinners. And when we say that, we think of a certain class of person—drunkard, murderer, adulterer, and so on. On the other hand there are nice people, and good people, who have never been guilty of such things, and we would never dream of saying that such people live according to the lusts of the flesh! 'Lusts of the flesh!' we say, 'of course we read about them in the newspaper. There they are, the people who are crowding through the divorce courts.' Lusts of the flesh! But the apostle's teaching is that we all by nature live in the lusts of the flesh, without a single exception. There has not been a single exception since Adam fell. The whole of mankind lives in the lusts of the flesh. Let us see how the apostle demonstrates this.

First of all he refers to the *'desires of the flesh'*. What does he mean by a desire? He uses a different word to express desire as distinct from lust. A desire is a command. A desire is a strong behest. I will go further, a desire is an imperious will, urging us to action, driving us to action. I remember once hearing an expression used by a mother concerning her children, her daughters. This poor woman was not over-blest with the goods of this world, and yet we saw her daughters very well dressed on a certain occasion, like everybody else. We knew that she could not really afford to do it. Certain people made remarks to her about this and wondered how it was done. Her reply was, 'They must have it'. Must have it!— there was no arguing. She could not really afford it, but the children must have it! That is a desire, this imperious demand that comes and will not be resisted. The lusts of the flesh manifest themselves in the desires of the flesh. Here flesh means the body, the animal part of our nature.

Of what is the apostle thinking? He is thinking of hunger, thirst, the desire for sleep, the desire for pleasure, the desire for happiness, the desire for contentment, sex, the desire to attract and be attractive. Now all those things are an essential part of our bodily, animal nature and make-up. There is that side of man, and it has been made by God. Therefore in and of itself it is essentially good— hunger, the desire for food, the desire for drink, the desire for rest and sleep and repose, for joy and happiness and pleasure, sex, the desire to be attractive. You see it in the whole of animal creation, in the animals and birds. It is equally true of man. And there is nothing wrong in it. Man was made thus by God and endowed with these various qualities and powers and propensities and instincts. And they are all good. When God had made man in addition to the rest of creation, he looked upon it all, man included, and 'saw that it was good'. Well, what is the apostle talking about? He is describing man in sin. How does sin show itself? It shows itself like this. These things which, in and of themselves, are right and good, suddenly take control, become imperious in their demands, begin to assert themselves and to drive us. I am using a technical term here; the psychologists talk about 'drives' manifesting themselves in the sick person's whole life and living, and it is a good term. It is a drive, a power, a force. You see that golfer 'driving', and the power, and the force he uses; well, these things begin to drive us. There is a very good scriptural term which is even better; it talks about 'inordinate affections'. There is nothing wrong in your being hungry, but if you live to eat it is all wrong. If the desire for food is controlling you, you are suffering from the desires of the flesh, and it is a manifestation of the lusts of the flesh. Eating! Drinking! People today like to talk about it and to write about it. A man is a 'connoisseur', he can give you the exact age of the bottle, he knows all about the vintage! He is meticulous about what to drink with each course! That is a desire of the flesh. You see, the man is not merely drinking to quench thirst, or even to have enjoyment; no, it has gone beyond that, it has become a desire of the flesh. And it applies to sleep. We are all meant to sleep, but there is such a thing as being a glutton for sleep, and at that point it has become a desire of the flesh and can ruin a man. Likewise with pleasure: pleasure is all right, there is nothing wrong with pleasure. But when pleasure begins to dominate and becomes so important that you are prepared to quarrel with people about it, then it is a desire of the flesh. Need I say anything about sex? God ordained sex—but God never ordained sexuality and the modern sex-mania. God never ordained the kind of thing that is staring at us and glaring at us in the newspapers every day. That is not the thing God made; that is man extracting sex out of its setting, isolating it, painting it up, placarding it, with the result that it is dominating life. Desires of the flesh! It is exactly the same with the desire to attract, which in and of itself may be quite innocent. There is nothing wrong in everybody desiring to look nice and attractive; but when you begin to have your whole mind centred upon it, and when you live for it and think about it and talk about it, and spend too much money on it, it has become a desire of the flesh.

We could go on illustrating this endlessly. Work these things out for yourselves. There you have the desires of the flesh. These things are in us, they are there, they are put there by God; but they are meant to be subordinate, they are meant to be kept in order. We are meant to be in control. What has happened to man is that these things have gained control; they have entered into a position of authority and they are driving us and urging us. We all know all about it—the urges, the desires that can even make a man tremble! The power of it all! 'The desires of the flesh!'

But wait, we have not finished. That is only one subdivision of the lusts of the flesh. Everybody will be prepared to agree with what I have been saying so far. 'Yes, of course,' they say, 'look at them, we see it, how terrible it is.' But my dear friend, I am now going to show you that however respectable you may have been all your life you are equally guilty of 'living in the lusts of the flesh'; for the lusts of the flesh not only manifest themselves through the desires of the body but also, you notice, through '*the desires of the mind*'. It is at that point a man like Charles G. Finney goes wrong in his theology. He does not recognise that. He confines it all to what I have been saying, and does not realise that this is as true of the mind, the intellect and understanding, as it is of the other.

Let us begin by defining the word 'mind'. It stands for the whole process of thinking; and it includes the emotional, the affective part, as well as the purely intellectual; the whole process of thinking—because thinking is not purely intellectual. We all think emotionally up to a point. Even the scientist does; that is why he has his prejudices. We all think with the whole man, intellect and affections. The desires of the mind then are as much an expression of the lusts of the flesh as are the desires of the body. How does this show itself? I can give you a general definition by putting it like this. Anything which tends to control and to absorb and govern your attention and your activity is a desire of the mind. Anything for which you live apart from God is a desire of the mind, a kind of lust of the mind. Does anyone need to be convinced about this matter? Is there anyone who does not realise that he has as much trouble with his mind as he does with his body? We know all about the lusts of the body, but have we realised the truth about the lusts of the mind, and how the mind can run away with us—all this power and force that exercises itself there?

Let us consider some illustrations. I find it very difficult to suggest a classification. Let us take the lusts of the mind at their very lowest level. Jealousy, envy, malice, pride, hatred, wrath, bitterness; what are they? They are nothing but manifestations of the desires of the mind—every single one of them. And you see the lust element coming in. Have you not seen people literally shaking in a rage, trembling in a passion, in anger and wrath? Have you seen malice and envy? It will stop at nothing—'Killing Kruger with your mouth', as the poet puts it. All these things are manifestations of the desires of the mind. People who have never got drunk or have never been guilty of adultery, have often been guilty of these! They are manifestations of the lusts of the flesh. And another way in which it is seen so commonly and prominently today is in what the Scriptures call 'foolish talking and jesting'—the desire to be clever and to say something clever, and to produce a laugh. How common that has become in life! People who would never dream of doing those other things, live for this kind of thing, the smartness, the glibness, the cleverness. It is a 'desire of the mind', it is a lust of the mind; it is as much a lust as is the other. There it is at its lowest level.

Let us now look at it on a somewhat higher level. Take ambition. What a driving force ambition is. It is as great a power as is a lust of the body in the animal part of our nature. The lust for wealth; the desire for position; the desire for a given social status; the desire for importance in life; the desire for power; the desire for success! Keep your eyes open, keep your ears open, read the biographies and autobiographies, and you will see that the lives of some of the most respectable men the world has ever seen have been full of this kind of lust. Ambition, governing and driving; men spend fortunes on it, they stop at nothing in order to have a name or reputation. It is a 'desire of the mind', it is a true expression of lust. Or take another example, the craving for something new. You remember that illuminating phrase about the Athenians in that seventeenth chapter of Acts: we are told that 'all the Athenians and strangers that which there did nothing else but to tell or to hear some new thing'. Desire of the mind! The restlessness of the modern man!—always out for a new thrill and excitement—and manifesting itself particularly, perhaps, in gossip. 'Have you heard?'—and at once the power enters; the one who says it is already being driven by the desire; he knows something the other one does not. 'Have you heard?' It is nothing but a lust, and the whole world is living on it; it is rampant, even in Christian circles. Gossiping and talk governed by the desire to be important; we know something somebody else does not, and we gloat over that fact. It is a lust. Hence the denunciation of gossiping and such talk so constantly in the New Testament. And in exactly the same way we see it in clever talk, and argument and disputation! I do not know what you feel as I go through this sorry and terrible list, but as I was preparing this sermon it filled me with a loathing and a hatred of myself. I look back and I think of the hours I have wasted in mere talk and argumentation. And it was all with one end only, simply to gain my point and to show how clever I was. The other disputants and myself would claim, I suppose, that we were interested in truth, but so often we were not; it was the mere enjoyment of argument and disputation and scoring, and being clever. It is a lust, it is a desire of the mind. Then think of it in terms of reading—reading books I mean, and journals, and so on. So often it becomes a lust, and instead of thinking and of meditating and of praying, we read. One of the tragedies of the modern world is that reading has become a substitute for thinking in the case of the vast majority of people. At that point it is a desire, a lust; it has become a disease.

Have you not known it? I could tell you a great deal about this. This is one of the ways in which it shows itself. Reading is an excellent thing; we can never know too much and we should read to have greater understanding and to improve our minds. But, you know, it becomes a lust like this: you have started reading one book, then you suddenly hear about another book and you get that also. You have not finished the first yet, but you start reading the second. Then a third comes, and you are reading three books! Well, it is a lust at that point. You are no longer in control, the thing has mastered you, it has run away with you, it has captured you. And it can happen at all levels. I have seen people read novels exactly in the same way as others take drugs. I remember the case of a poor woman who could be seen walking round her house with a novel in her hand. Even while she was cooking she was still reading her novel. It may sound laughable, but I am not sure that it is not something to weep at. I see no difference in principle (and leaving out the social consequences) between that and taking drugs and taking alcohol, or giving way to a lust of the body. I see no difference whatsoever; it is equally a lust, but it is a desire of the mind and not of the flesh. It manifests itself like that. Then you can think of it in terms of people with their hobbies and their games and their interests. These things are quite innocent. A hobby is all right, a game is all right; but if you live for it, it is not all right; it has become a desire of the mind.

Let us go to the highest level of all: the lust for knowledge, the lust for learning! Literature, art, music, drama, philosophy, they all come in. These things are good, but not if you live for them, not if they master you, not if they have become a drive in your life which you cannot control. And is not that true of some of the most respectable people in the land? I mean the people who say, 'Well, of course, that gospel of salvation and conversion and regeneration is all right in the east end of London, but not in the west; it is all right for people who have lived in gutters and have been adulterers and so on, but I have never done . . .' There they are, and they may be in high academic positions in the universities. They say: 'Surely I do not need to have this rebirth you are speaking of!' The answer is, 'You do, because you are as much a creature of lust as is the other'. And it does not matter whether the lust is in the mind, the intellect, or whether it is in the animal part, it is the same thing exactly, and it is equally opposed to God. And there is this lust, this quest, for more knowledge as knowledge, and understanding; it is pervasive, it runs right through the whole of life. There is not a living person who is not guilty of this lust of the flesh. Such is man in sin. Sin is as deep and as profound and as pervasive as that.

You see the importance of all this. I can imagine a kind of person saying to himself, 'Well of course that is very interesting if you are interested in that kind of thing, but after all this country is passing through a time of crisis at the moment; and the whole world and its future is in a most precarious position. Why do you not say something about that?' Will it surprise you if I say that I have been preaching about that the whole time? 'How do you make that out?' says someone. My answer is, that it is as you understand this doctrine of sin that you see the ultimate futility and fatuity of trusting only to political action. The politicians think that this kind of situation is to be met by calling upon men and women to discipline themselves voluntarily. We must eat less, we must smoke less, we must import less and, disciplining ourselves, we must work harder. They have already made the appeal but we do not seem to have responded; so they put on a purchase tax. They say that that will do it. But it is not doing it. Why not? Because they have never realised the meaning of the word *lust*. Men simply cannot respond, because they are driven, they are captives. Lust is a force, it is a power. You put up the price but they will still have it; they may moderate their smoking for a week or two after a Budget, but after a few weeks, the statisticians tell us that it goes back to the former level. And it will go on. Why? Because man is driven by desires, by lusts. He cannot discipline himself.

I can prove that. If we are in the midst of a terrible war and we are actually fighting for our lives, then you will find men will smoke less and drink less and discipline themselves in various ways up to a point. But you see what is happening; a bigger instinct has driven out the lesser instincts. The instinct of, and desire for, self-preservation has driven out the other lusts—but it is still a lust. So that the moment the crisis passes men drop back exactly to where they were before. The whole fallacy of mere political thinking is based upon a failure to realise the biblical doctrine of sin. It is not enough to tell men what is right and what is wrong; they cannot help themselves because they are slaves and victims of the lusts, the passions, the desires that control them.

There is only one thing that can deal with a situation like this. It is that which I mentioned at the beginning. It is 'the exceeding greatness of his power toward us that believe'. It is what Thomas Chalmers called 'the expulsive power of a new affection'. So if you are thinking simply of this country, and a particular crisis, the direct route to the answer is to be found in this Scripture. But over and above this, if you are thinking, as you ought to be thinking, about the end of your life in this world and about the end of the whole world, and God, and judgment, and eternity, well then you must still think about this; because in that state of lust you cannot stand before God and you cannot enjoy Him. You must be delivered from this control of the lust of the flesh, manifesting itself in the desires of the body and the desires of the mind. And it is only the power of God in the Lord Jesus Christ through the Holy Spirit that can deliver us. But blessed be the name of God it can, it does, it will. Sin!—oh, the depths, the foulness, the ugliness, the power of it all! There is only one place of safety, and that is ever to be looking unto Him, receiving of His fulness, relying on the power of His might. For there we are safe.

5

THE WRATH OF GOD

Among whom also we all had our conversation in times past in the lusts of our flesh, fulfilling the desires of the flesh and of the mind; and were by nature the children of wrath, even as others.　　　　Ephesians 2 : 3

We now come to look at the apostle's final statement about man in sin; and that is, that he is under the wrath of God. In other words Paul deals with sin, as sin affects man's standing before God. He shows what God says and thinks and does about man in that condition which we have already considered: There can be no question at all but that this is the most important aspect of the subject. The others were vitally important, but there is nothing which is as important as this. It is because we so constantly forget this that the world is as it is today—and indeed that the Church is as she is. We are so self-centred and concerned about ourselves that we fail to remember that the most important thing above all else is the way in which God looks down upon it all. That is the subject with which we now have to deal.

The apostle puts it like this. He says that '*we were all by nature the children of wrath, even as others*'. Here we have a twofold statement. And there is no doubt at all but that these two matters that we are compelled to look at together are two of the most difficult and perplexing subjects in the whole realm and range of biblical doctrine. That is why they have often led to great misunderstanding, and are subjects which people often in their ignorance not only fail to understand but bitterly resent. There is no subject, perhaps, which has more frequently led people to speak—albeit unconsciously—in a blasphemous manner, than this very matter which we are now going to consider. The apostle says two things: that we are all under the wrath of God; and secondly that we are all under the wrath of God by nature.

Why should we examine these things? Someone may well ask that question. Why spend our time on a subject like this, a difficult subject? There are so many other things that are interesting at the present time and attracting attention. Why not deal with them?

And in any case, amid all the problems that confront the world, why turn to something like this?

Well, lest there be someone who is harbouring some such idea, and is provoked to put such a question, let me suggest certain reasons why it behoves us to consider this matter. The first is that *it is part of Scripture*. It is here in the Bible and, as we shall see, it is everywhere in the Bible. And if we regard the Bible as the Word of God, and our authority in all matters of faith and conduct, we cannot pick and choose; we must take it as it is and consider its every part and portion.

Secondly, we must do so because what we are told here is, after all, *a question of fact*. It is not theory, it is a statement of fact. If the biblical doctrine of the wrath of God is true, then it is the most important fact confronting every one of us at this moment; infinitely more important than any international conference that may be held, infinitely more important than whether there is to be a third world war or not. If this doctrine is true, then we are all involved in it, and our eternal destiny depends upon it. And the Bible states everywhere that it is a fact.

Another reason for considering it is this: that the apostle's whole argument is that *we can never understand the love of God until we understand this doctrine*. It is the way in which we measure the love of God. There is a great deal of talk today about the love of God, and yet were we truly to love God, we would express it, we would show it. To love God is not merely to talk about it; to love God, as He Himself points out constantly in His Word, is to keep His commandments and to live for His glory. The argument here is that we really cannot understand the love of God unless we see it in the light of this other doctrine which we are now considering. So it is essential from that standpoint.

Let me put it in this way. I suggest that we can never truly understand why it is that the Lord Jesus Christ, the eternal Son of God, had to come into this world unless we understand this doctrine of the wrath of God and the judgment of God. As Christians we believe that the Son of God came into this world, that He laid aside the insignia of His eternal glory, was born as a babe in Bethlehem, and endured all that He endured, because that was essential for our salvation. But the question is, Why was it essential to our salvation? Why did all that have to take place before we could be saved? I defy anyone to answer that question adequately without bringing in this doctrine of the judgment of God and of the wrath of God. This is still more true when you look at the great doctrine of the cross and the death of our blessed Lord and Saviour. Why did Christ die? Why had He to die? If we say that we are saved by

His blood, why are we saved by His blood? Why was it essential that He should die on that cross and be buried and rise again before we could be saved? There is only one adequate answer to these questions, and that is this doctrine of the wrath of God. The death of our Lord upon the cross is not absolutely necessary unless this doctrine is true. So, you see, it is a vital matter for us to consider.

Lastly, I would put it in a very practical form. *This doctrine is essential from the standpoint of a true evangelism.* Why is it that people do not believe in the Lord Jesus Christ? Why is it that people are not Christians and not members of the Christian Church? Why does the Lord Jesus Christ not come into their calculations at all? In the last analysis there is only one answer to that question: they do not believe in Him because they have never seen any need of Him. And they have never seen any need of Him because they have never realised that they are sinners. And they have never realised that they are sinners because they have never realised the truth about the holiness of God and the justice and the righteousness of God; they have never known anything about God as the Judge eternal and about the wrath of God against the sin of man. So you see this doctrine is essential in evangelism. If we really believe in salvation and in our absolute need of the Lord Jesus Christ, we must start with this doctrine. There, then, are the reasons for considering it. The apostle supplies them; I am simply repeating them.

Now let us look at the two statements themselves. The first thing the apostle says is that *all who are born into this world are under the wrath of God.* He says we 'were all the children of wrath, even as others'; we were all the children of wrath, as the rest of mankind —that is what 'even as others' means. Here we come face to face with this tremendous doctrine which I know full well is not only unpopular at the present time but is even hated and detested. People can scarcely control themselves as they speak about it. The whole modern idea has been for a number of years, that God is a God of love and that we must think of God only in terms of love. To talk about the wrath of God, we are told, is utterly incompatible with any idea of God as a God of love. The way in which it is put is this. They say: Of course that idea of the wrath of God stems from the ancient idea of God as a sort of tribal God. The trouble is that there are still certain Christians who believe in that God of the Old Testament, who was nothing but a tribal God. The gods of mythology were all of that type and of that kind; they displayed their anger and their wrath; but, of course, we know now from the New Testament and from Jesus that this is quite wrong and quite false. We no longer believe in the God of the Old Testament, we believe in the God of the New Testament, in the God and Father of our Lord and Saviour Jesus Christ. You are familiar with the argument. Indeed, some go even further, and say that it is only during the past century that we really have become sufficiently enlightened to understand these matters, and that, until the beginning of this present century, people still believed in the wrath of God, and, therefore, had a completely false conception of God. I remember reading a very learned book in which the author stated that this idea of the wrath of God was nothing but a kind of projection into the character of God of the notion of the typical Victorian father, the stern repressive father who kept his children down and disciplined them severely and punished them. His suggestion was that people just carried that idea over and projected it right into God Himself. But that, he held, was nothing but a false bit of psychology from which we have by now delivered ourselves, and we now know that the idea of wrath in a God of love is something that is self-contradictory.

Is there any answer to such contentions? Let me dispose of one preliminary misunderstanding. There are some people who completely misinterpret the very term *wrath*. They think of wrath instinctively as some uncontrolled manifestation of anger. They cannot think of it apart from the idea of somebody trembling in a rage and pale with passion, who has lost self-control and is speaking in a violent manner and doing violent things. Now that is quite a false and wrong idea of the meaning of wrath. Sinful man, it is true, does sometimes manifest his wrath in this way, but all that does not enter at all into the term as used of God in the Bible. Wrath is nothing but a manifestation of indignation based upon justice. Indeed, we can go further and assert that the wrath of God, according to the scriptural teaching, is nothing but the other side of the love of God. It is the inevitable corollary of the rejection of the love of God. God is a God of love, but God is also and equally a God of justice and of righteousness; and if God's love is spurned and rejected there remains nothing but the justice and the righteousness and the wrath of God.

Now let us demonstrate the contention that this is something which is taught everywhere in the Scripture. In the Old Testament it is to be found at the very beginning. When man fell in the garden of Eden, God visited and spoke to him and pronounced judgment upon him. He drove him out of the garden, and there at the eastern gate of the garden He placed the cherubim and the flaming sword. What is the meaning of the flaming sword? It means just this very thing; it is the sword of God's justice, it is God's sword of wrath and of punishment, punishing man for his sin and making it impossible for him to come back and eat of the tree of life and live for ever. There, at the very beginning, is a manifestation of God's righteous judgment and His wrath upon sin. It is to be found running right through the Old Testament: in the story of the flood, the story of Sodom and Gomorrah, and in the various punishments of the children of Israel, whether as a nation or as individuals. The Old Testament is full of this. God has given His law and He has pronounced that if men break it He will punish them—that is His wrath. And when they have done so He has punished them. He has punished individuals, He has punished the nation, even His own chosen people. He punished them, He poured His wrath upon them by raising up the Chaldean army which came and sacked Jerusalem and carried away the people as captives into Babylon. That was a manifestation of the wrath and the righteous judgment of God. It is everywhere in the Old Testament; you really cannot believe the Old Testament unless you accept this doctrine of the wrath of God.

When you come to the New Testament, in spite of all that modern critics would have us believe, the doctrine is again present everywhere. The first preacher in the New Testament is John the Baptist. What did he say? He said, 'Flee from the wrath to come'; 'Repent and be baptised every one of you, flee from the wrath to come'. The Pharisees came to be baptised of John, and he looked at them and said, 'Who hath warned you to flee from the wrath to come?' It was his great message. Indeed it was the message of the Lord Jesus Christ Himself. But, and most surprising of all, we find it in the verse that is generally quoted as the supreme statement of God as a God of love—John 3: 16, 'God so loved the world that he gave his only begotten Son'. Why did He do so? The answer is 'that whosoever believeth in him should not perish, but have everlasting life'. The alternative to everlasting life is perishing. And it is John 3: 16 that teaches it. But the thirty-sixth verse of that third chapter of John is still more plain, 'He that believeth on the Son hath everlasting life, and he that believeth not the Son shall not see life; but the wrath of God abideth on him'. In other words, all men are under the wrath of God, and unless we believe on the Son of God the wrath of God abides upon us. What can be more plain or explicit? There it is in the Gospel of John the apostle of love.

The apostle Paul teaches the same truth equally clearly. Preaching in Athens he says that, 'God hath appointed a day in which he will judge the whole world in righteousness by this man whom he hath appointed'. Judgment! The wrath of God! In Romans 1: 18, we read: 'For the wrath of God is manifested [is already revealed] from heaven, against all ungodliness and unrighteousness of men'.

Paul has no gospel apart from this; it is because of the wrath of God that he is preaching the gospel. In this Epistle to the Ephesians which we are considering, in the fifth chapter and the sixth verse, you get exactly the same thing, 'Let no man deceive you with vain words', says Paul 'for because of these things cometh the wrath of God upon the children of disobedience'. Again, in summarising his gospel to the Thessalonians in the First Epistle and in the first chapter and the last verse, Paul says that the Thessalonians have turned to Christ and await Him from heaven—what for?—well, he says, because He 'delivered us from the wrath to come'. The same idea is to be found in the Epistle to the Hebrews in several places. And if you go right on to the Book of Revelation you will find it there in a most remarkable phrase. It is a phrase about the 'wrath of the Lamb'. It seems quite contradictory, quite paradoxical. You think of a lamb in terms of innocence, harmlessness. And yet there is this pregnant phrase, 'the wrath of the Lamb'. It is the Lamb of God that takes away the sins of the whole world who is to judge the world in righteousness. So it is quite clear that the idea that love and wrath are incompatible is a complete denial of the plain teaching of the Scriptures. Indeed I would go so far as to say that unless we start with this idea of the wrath of God against sin we cannot possibly understand the compassion of God, we cannot understand the love of God. It is only as I realise God's wrath against sin that I realise the full significance of His providing a way of salvation from it. If I do not understand this I do not understand that, and my talk about the love of God is mere loose sentimentality which is indeed a denial of the great biblical doctrine of the love of God.

The apostle's teaching, then, is that until we believe on the Lord Jesus Christ we are under the wrath of God. And the wrath of God is an expression of God's hatred of sin, an expression of God's punishment of sin. It is a clear statement to this effect, that if we die in our sins we go on to eternal punishment. That is the teaching of Scripture. The wrath of God against sin manifests itself finally in hell, where men and women remain outside the life of God in misery and wretchedness, slaves to their own lusts and desires, selfish and self-centred. The apostle's teaching is that that is the position of all who are not Christians. They are under the wrath of God in this life, they will remain under the wrath of God in the next life. That is the position of the sinner, according to Scripture. If you object to the idea you are objecting to the Scriptures, you are setting up some philosophic idea of your own contrary to their plain teaching. You are not arguing with me, you are arguing with the Scriptures. You are arguing with these holy apostles, you are arguing with the Son of God Himself. If you believe that the Bible is divinely inspired, then you must not say, 'But I don't understand'. You are not asked to understand. I do not understand it, I do not pretend to understand it. But I start from this basis, that my mind is not only finite but is, furthermore, sinful, and that I cannot possibly understand fully the nature of God and the justice and the holiness of God. If we are going to base everything on our understanding, then we might as well give up at this point. For the Bible tell us that 'the natural man' and 'the natural mind' cannot understand the things of the Spirit of God (see 1 Corinthians 2). It was the desire to understand that led to the Fall. Intellectual pride and arrogance is the first and the last sin. The business of preaching is not to ask people to understand; the commission of the preacher is to proclaim the message. And the message is that all are under the wrath of God until they believe in the Lord Jesus Christ. But indeed we must go even one step further.

That brings us to the second matter. The apostle says that *we are all in that condition by nature*—'we were all by nature the children of wrath, even as others'. What does this *by nature* mean? We have already shown in a previous study in this series that this has one meaning only, and that is, 'by birth'. We were all by our very birth the children of wrath even as others. You notice that the apostle does not say that we 'become' the children of wrath because of our nature; he says we 'were'. In other words the apostle, in line with the whole of the Bible, does not teach that we are born into this world in a state of innocence or in a state of neutrality, and that then, because we sin, we become sinners and thereby come under the wrath of God. That is not what he says: he says the exact opposite. He says that we are born into this world under the wrath of God; from the moment of our birth we are already under the wrath of God. It is not only something that is going to happen to us, neither is it something that results only from our actions. There are people who teach that, but that is a blank denial not only of the teaching here but, as we shall see, of the teaching elsewhere in Scripture. He does not say that we are under the wrath of God only because of our nature or because of the manifestation of our nature. He says that we are in that position 'by birth'.

What, then, does this mean? The answer is to be found in the fifth chapter of the Epistle to the Romans where it is argued out in detail and thoroughly from verse twelve to the end of the chapter. What is the argument? Let me summarise it. In that chapter the one great truth the apostle is concerned to prove is *that our relationship, as believers to the Lord Jesus Christ is exactly analogous to our relationship formerly to Adam.* He keeps on repeating the comparison and goes back and forth. He talks about what was true of us in Adam and then shows what is true of us now in the Lord Jesus Christ. He starts in verse twelve saying, 'Wherefore, as by one man sin entered into the world and death by sin; and so death passed upon all men, for that all sinned', and so continues. Any careful and unbiased reading of that argument, which is basic to Paul's doctrine of assurance, will compel us to see that all along he says that our relationship to Adam was identical with our present relationship to Christ. If, therefore, we believe that we are what we are in Christ because of what God has imputed to us in Christ, we must also believe exactly the same on the other side about what was imputed to us in Adam. That is the argument. But the apostle is not content merely to state it generally, he states it in particular also. Let me pick out the important verses. Take verse twelve: 'Wherefore, as by one man sin entered into the world and death by sin, and so death passed upon all men, for that all sinned . . .'. The punishment of sin is death. Adam sinned and death came upon him, yes, but not only upon Adam—upon all men. As a result of Adam's one sin, death passed upon all men. Why? The last part of the verse explains —'all sinned' in Adam. That is the statement which we will expound later.

Then take verses thirteen and fourteen of that chapter. Paul introduces a statement in a parenthesis, beginning at verse thirteen, 'For until the law sin was in the world, but sin is not imputed where there is no law. Nevertheless, death reigned from Adam to Moses, even over them that had not sinned after the similitude of Adam's transgression'. Are you tempted to say, What does all this mean? I cannot follow it, I want some simple gospel of comfort. That is how we tend to speak, we who think that because we live in the twentieth century we are greatly superior to all generations that have ever lived before us. We pride ourselves on our being so learned and intellectual and able to understand great things, whereas previous generations were primitive. But we do not realise that the apostle Paul wrote these words to people who lived nearly two thousand years ago, and that he meant them to understand them. He was not writing to great philosophers; he was writing to simple Christian believers, many of whom were but slaves, and others soldiers in Caesar's household; and he meant those people to understand these things. Shame on us modern Christians who must be spoon-fed, and who just want something nice and easy and simple. If you do not accept this doctrine, then it is God's Word you are rejecting.

I again ask, What does it mean? Paul says that until the law sin was in the world. The law was given through Moses, you remember; but there was that long interval between Adam and Moses, at the least it was probably a period of some two thousand five hundred years. Now during that whole long period sin was in the world, but sin, he says, is not imputed when there is no law. In other words, if there is not a law to define sin, the sin is not brought home to a man. The business of law is to bring the sin home to man's mind and heart and conscience. If there were no laws, for instance, about parking and about motoring, you and I might still do wrong things, but if there were not a law about these matters we could not be punished. That is what he is saying, 'sin is not imputed when there is no law'. 'Nevertheless', he says, 'death reigned from Adam to Moses'. Here is the problem: though the law was not given until Moses, nevertheless, from Adam to Moses people died. All the people born into the world died. Why did they die? What is it that produced death in those people though there was no law imputing sin at that period? The apostle's answer is that there is only one explanation; they all died because they were involved in the sin of Adam. There is no other explanation. The only reason why death reigned from Adam to Moses is that that one sin of Adam brought death upon the whole of his posterity. In other words, we are born 'by nature the children of wrath'.

Notice then the next thing, which is still more extraordinary. He says that death reigned from Adam to Moses, 'even over them that had not sinned after the similitude of Adam's transgression'. What can that mean? It means that death reigned even over those persons who had not actually committed an act of sin as Adam did when he fell. Who are they? And there is only one possible answer; they were infants who died in infancy. All other men sinned. Everybody who has lived since Adam has committed deliberate acts of sin. The only people who have not sinned after the similitude of Adam's transgression, who have not deliberately sinned, are infants who are too young to exercise their will because they are not conscious. Death reigned, says Paul, from Adam to Moses, even over infants also. Why do infants die? There is only one answer. Infants die because Adam's transgression involves them. 'Death passed upon all men, even upon them that had not sinned after the similitude of Adam's transgression'.

But going on to verse fifteen we read, 'But not as the offence, so also is the free gift; for if through the offence of one many be dead'. There it is again. Then he turns to the other side about Jesus Christ. In verse sixteen, we have, 'And not as it was by one that sinned so is the gift'—and then, 'for the judgment was by one to

condemnation, but the free gift is of many offences unto justification'. The judgment, the condemnation, was by one to condemnation: the one sin of Adam brought this upon the whole of mankind.
But conversely, he says, many sins are forgiven in the righteousness
of One, even Jesus Christ. Then once more in verse eighteen:
'Therefore, as by the offence of one judgment came upon all men
to condemnation'. Is not that as explicit as anything could be?
'As by the offence of one judgment came upon *all* men'—no
exception—'to condemnation'. We are 'born the children of wrath'.
And finally, in verse nineteen, 'For as by one man's disobedience
many were made sinners'. You and I and all mankind were made
or, as a more accurate translation puts it, 'constituted' sinners by
that one sin of Adam. That is the teaching. We are 'all by nature
the children of wrath even as others'.

Ah, you say, I do not understand that, I cannot grasp that, it
seems to me almost immoral. Of course you do not understand it.
Who can understand such things? It is not a question of understanding, it is a question of whether you believe the Scriptures or
not. For the apostle says exactly the same thing in 1 Corinthians 15,
that great and wonderful chapter which is read at funeral services,
'As in Adam all die, so in Christ shall all be made alive', and so
on. It is precisely the same argument. It is the basis of the Christian
faith. Whether we understand it or not, it is the truth. You have to
explain the universality of sin; you have to explain the universality
of death, and especially the death of infants. And this is the biblical
answer. Adam was the whole of humanity and he represented the
whole of humanity. He was our federal head. As the Lord Jesus
Christ is the Representative of all who are saved, as His righteousness is imputed to us, so Adam was our representative and his sin
is imputed to us. We fell in him, we are damned in him and because
of his action. In exactly the same way those who believe in Christ
are redeemed by Him and saved in Him and righteous in Him
because of His action on our behalf. That is the argument. If you
believe the one side about Christ, you must believe the other about
Adam. If you deny this, you are virtually denying that.

Let us be careful therefore. There is nothing more tragic than the
way in which Christian people bring the relics of their philosophies
and their own understanding into the Christian faith. Many who
claim to believe the Bible, and who regard it as authoritative,
reject it at this point because they do not like the doctrine, or
because they cannot reconcile certain matters. But the reconciliation
is here before us. Though we were dead in trespasses and sins, hateful
and hating one another, polluted by sin, sinful in practice, living

in trespasses and sins and under the wrath of God, and absolutely helpless and hopeless, the very God against whom we have sinned, the very God whom we have offended, has Himself provided the way of deliverance for us. He does so in the Person of His own dearly beloved Son, whom He did not spare even from the suffering and the agony and the shame of Calvary and that cruel death. He has offered us, and provides for us, the way of complete deliverance and reconciliation to Himself in spite of the fact that our sin in Adam and our own sins, and our own sinful state deserve nothing but His eternal wrath. That is the love of God! That is the 'love so amazing, so divine'! God has done that for us, who deserve nothing but eternal wrath, which we could never have done for ourselves.

May God in His grace enable us to receive these things so that we may go on to consider the next verse with its glorious 'but'. Though all we have been considering was true of us, 'God who is rich in mercy, for his great love wherewith he loved us, even when we were dead in sins, hath quickened us together with Christ'. Blessed be the name of God!

6

THE CHRISTIAN MESSAGE
TO THE WORLD

But God . . .   Ephesians 2: 4

We now come to look at two wonderful words—'But God'. These words obviously suggest a connection with something that has gone before. The word 'but' is a conjunction, and yet it suggests always a contrast; and here we have the connection and the contrast. Look at them in their context, 'And you hath he quickened, who were dead in trespasses and sins; wherein in time past ye walked according to the course of this world, according to the prince of the power of the air, the spirit that now worketh in the children of disobedience: among whom also we all had our conversation in times past, in the lusts of our flesh, fulfilling the desires of the flesh and of the mind; and were by nature the children of wrath, even as others. But God . . .'

With these two words we come to the introduction to the Christian message, the peculiar, specific message which the Christian faith has to offer to us. These two words, in and of themselves, in a sense contain the whole of the gospel. The gospel tells of what God has done, God's intervention; it is something that comes entirely from outside us and displays to us that wondrous and amazing and astonishing work of God which the apostle goes on to describe and to define in the following verses.

We shall take these words now in a general manner only. I do so for several reasons. One is that the text itself compels one to do so, but there are also certain special reasons for doing so. A charge frequently brought against the Christian message, and especially the evangelical form of that message, is that it is remote from life, that it is irrelevant to the immediate circumstances in which men and women find themselves. In other words, there is an objection on the part of some to the expository method of preaching the gospel; it is that it never seems to come to grips with the realities of the situation in which men and women find themselves from day to day, and that it is irrelevant to the whole world situation in which we find ourselves. I desire to show, therefore, that that charge is entirely unfounded; and further, that the idea that the business of Christian preaching is just to make topical references to contemporary events is, indeed, in a sense, to depart from the Christian message altogether. I would go so far as to say that there is nothing which really does deal with the contemporary situation save the Scripture, when its doctrines are understood, believed and applied.

That is what I propose to do now. I want to show the relevance of the gospel on a day such as Remembrance Sunday when instinctively almost, and certainly as the result of what is happening in the world in which we live, our minds are compelled to face, and to think of, the general situation in addition to our own particular situations. And, claiming as I do that the gospel deals with the whole of man and with the whole of his life in this world, it is important that we should see what it has to say about, and to do with, the position in which we find ourselves. You notice that the thing I am emphasising is the all-importance of method. The many who do not think in a Christian and biblical manner believe that the business of the Christian Church on a day such as this is to announce, for instance, a subject such as 'The Geneva Conference—Possibilities', and then go on to say what we think the statesmen should do. That, it seems to me, is entirely false and contrary to the biblical method. The biblical method, rather, is to display God's truth, and then to show the relevance of that to any given situation. You do not start with the situation, you end with the situation. The Bible invites us at the outset to stop looking on the horizontal level, as it were, to stop merely looking at the world and at men; it invites us at the very beginning to lift up our eyes and to look at God. In other words, the whole case presented in the Bible from beginning to end is that life and man and the world simply cannot be understood until we see everything in the light of the truth about God, and in that context. Therefore we must start with the truth of God and only then go on to the immediate situation.

Let us proceed to show how that is done, and how it is done in the very passage which we are considering. We have considered in detail these first three verses in this chapter, and we have been doing so in order that we might see what we ourselves are like by nature and what the world is like by nature. You cannot begin to solve the problems of mankind until you know the truth about man. How futile it is to attempt to do so apart from that. You must start with the character, the nature, the being of man. Instead of starting with international conferences and talk about contemporary events, we need to go much further back and ask, Well now, what sort of a creature is man? Obviously all our conclusions and all our proposals are going to be governed by the answer to that question. If man is really an essentially good creature who only needs a little more instruction and knowledge and information, obviously the treatment is going to be comparatively simple. But if what the apostle Paul says here about man as he is by nature, and without Christ, is true, then equally obviously, treatment along such lines is going to be entirely hopeless, and to attempt it is sheer waste of time.

We must start with this doctrine. *What is true of man in sin?* What characterises man as he is in sin without the grace of God? We have already looked into this matter. Man is dead spiritually; he is governed by the devil, who operates through the mighty spiritual forces under his command, which in turn produce and control the mind and the outlook of the world. That is the position of man. And the result is that man, dominated by that evil power, lives a life of trespasses and sins; indeed he has been born in such a way, as the result of his descent from Adam, that his very nature is fallen. He starts with a polluted nature. And finally he is under the wrath of God. That is the apostle's statement in the first three verses.

What then is the relevance of all that to the present situation; what has it to say to us as we face the whole world situation at this present time? It is clear that a number of things can be very easily deduced from this teaching.

The first is that here we are given *the only real and adequate explanation of why there are such occurrences as wars.* Why do we have them? Why is man guilty of this final madness? Why is it that men kill one another and have even gloried in war? Why? What is the explanation of it all? There is only one answer; it is because man is as the apostle describes him. It is not only the teaching of the apostle Paul. You remember how James puts it in the fourth chapter of his Epistle, 'Whence come wars among you?'—and answers the question—'even of the lusts that war in your members'. That is the cause of war. It is man in his fallen condition. Now the realisation of this truth and fact is absolutely vital for us as a starting point. This is true of nations, it is true of classes, it is true of individuals. There is surely nothing which is quite so illuminating and contradictory as the way in which people think along one line when they are thinking of nations and along a quite different line when they are thinking of individuals. There is little point in talking eloquently about the sanctity of international contracts while you are dealing with people who break their own marriage contracts and other personal contracts, for nations consist of individuals. The nation is not something abstract, and we are not entitled to expect conduct from a nation which we do not find in the individual. All these things have to be taken together.

This is a principle that operates throughout society from top to bottom, from the individual to the nation, to the continent, to the whole world itself. The explanation of the state of the world according to the Bible is that man is governed by these desires of the flesh and of the mind. He is not so much interested in whether a thing is right or not, he is interested in the fact that he wants it, that he likes it, that he must have it. Of course we stand back aghast when a nation behaves like that. When Hitler walks in and annexes Austria we are horrified. Yes, people are horrified who do the very same thing in their personal lives. They do it in the matter of other men's wives; they do it in the matter of another man's post or position or business. It is the same thing exactly. There then is the principle. It is this lust that governs mankind. 'Walking according to the course of this world' says the apostle, 'we all had our conversation in times past in the lusts of the flesh, fulfilling the desires of the flesh and of the mind'. The first deduction, therefore, is that here and here alone do we have an adequate explanation and understanding of why things are as they are.

The second deduction follows quite logically. It is that *while man continues to be thus governed, the world will continue to be as it is.* This is surely obvious. If it is the state of man in sin that has been responsible for the history of the past, obviously, while man remains unchanged, the history of the future is going to be unchanged. Here we confront and come into collision with the optimism of the natural man who is always so sure and confident that somehow or another we in our generation can put things right. He feels that whereas all other generations who have gone before us have failed, we are in a different position, in a superior position. We are educated, and cultured; we know whereas they did not know; we have advanced so much, we must succeed; we are going to succeed. But if you believe this biblical doctrine of man in sin you must see at once that that is a fatal fallacy. If our troubles are due to the lusts that are in mankind in sin, and which control men, while they remain, there will be wars. We have specific teaching to that effect from our blessed Lord Himself, who said, ' There will be wars and rumours of wars'. He said, also, 'As it was in the days of Noah, so shall it be also in the days of the Son of man'; 'Likewise also as it was in the days of Lot'—in Sodom—'even thus shall it be' (Luke 17: 26–30). That is our Lord's view of history.

If we grasp this teaching we shall be delivered at once from all the false enthusiasm and the false hopes of men who really believe that by bringing in some new organisation you can outlaw war and banish it for ever. The answer of the Bible is that you cannot do so while man remains unregenerate. Is this depressing? My reply is that, whether it is depressing or not is not our concern; we should be concerned to know the truth. The modern man claims to be a realist. He has objected to Christianity because, according to him, it does not face the facts. It is not realistic, he says; it is always 'pie in the sky', and you go into your chapels and you shut yourselves off and do not face the facts of life. Yet when we give him the facts he objects on the grounds that they are depressing. It is the political and philosophical optimists who are not realists; it is the people who have never faced the facts about man in sin who are shutting their eyes and turning their backs upon reality. The Bible faces it all; it has a realistic view of life in this world, and it alone has it.

Now let us look at *the specific, direct teaching of the gospel*. What has the Christian message to say about this state and this condition, the explanation of which we have just been considering? The answer is that it says, 'But God'. That is its message. What does that mean? The most convenient way of analysing this matter is to put it first of all negatively and then positively. I regret that I have to start with a negative again. I must do so, because so many forget these negatives, and thus deliver messages which cannot possibly be regarded as Christian at all. And yet they will be delivered in the name of Christianity and of the Christian Church. I am profoundly convinced that what is keeping large numbers of people from Christ and from salvation, and from the Christian Church is this terrible confusion of which the Church herself has been, and is, so guilty. There are many outside the Church today because in the first world war the Christian Church so frequently became a kind of recruiting office. Men were offended—and in a sense they were right to be offended. There are certain things which should never be confused. Let us note some of them.

What is this Christian message? We start by saying that *it is not a great appeal for patriotism*: That is not the Christian message. The Christian message does not denounce patriotism, or say that there is anything wrong in it. The man is to be pitied who does not love his country and his nation. There is nothing in the Scriptures against that. It is God who has divided up the nations and defined their bounds and their habitations. It is God's will that there should be nations. But it is not God's will that there should be nationalism, an aggressive nationalism. There is nothing wrong in a man honouring his own country and delighting in it: but it is utterly un-Christian to say 'My country right or wrong'. That is always wrong, that is fatally wrong; that is a complete denial of the teaching of Scripture. Take this great apostle who wrote this very Epistle to the Ephesians. Here is a man who was a Jew, and if ever a man was proud of the fact of his nationality it was the apostle Paul—'A Hebrew of the Hebrews, of the tribe of Benjamin. . . .' He was once a narrow nationalist who despised others. The Gentiles were dogs, outside the pale. But the thing in which he glories in this Epistle, you remember, is this, 'in whom ye also trusted'. The Gentiles have come in, have been made 'fellow heirs' with the Jews, the middle wall of partition has been broken down. 'There is no longer Jew nor Gentile, barbarian, Scythian, bond nor free, male nor female; all are one in Christ.' That is the Christian position. 'But God. . . .' Here is the way to break down that nationalistic spirit that leads to war. To believe that we are always right and everybody else wrong is as wrong in nations as it is in individuals. It is always wrong. The Christian message is not just an appeal to patriotism. And if Christianity is portrayed in that form it is a denial, a travesty of the message, and it is misleading in the eyes and the ears of those who listen to it.

But, secondly, *the Christian message is not just an appeal to courage, or heroism*, or to the manifestation of a great spirit of self-sacrifice. Let us be clear about this also. Christianity does not condemn courage, it does not condemn self-sacrifice, or heroism. These qualities, these virtues are not specifically Christian. They are pagan virtues, which were taught and inculcated, admired and praised, before the Lord Jesus Christ ever came into this world. Courage was the supreme virtue according to the Greek pagan philosophers; it was the very essence of Stoicism. And that was why they regarded meekness, the meekness taught by the Christian faith, as weakness. There was no word for meekness in Greek pagan philosophy. Courage, and strength, and power—those were the things they believed in. That is why, you remember, Paul tells us that the preaching of the cross was 'to the Greeks foolishness'. That someone who was crucified in weakness should be the Saviour, and that that should be the way of salvation, to them was nonsense and rubbish. They placed no value on meekness and on humility; courage and power and heroism were the great virtues. So it is very important that we should realise that it is no part of the Christian message to exhort people to courage and heroism and to self-sacrifice. There is nothing specifically Christian in such ideas. Christianity does not condemn them, but that is not the Christian message. And the point I am emphasising is this, that when that has been presented as the Christian message it has confused people, and has led to the very division which the gospel itself was meant to heal.

But let us go on to a third matter. There are many people who seem to think that the Christian message is that we should just appeal to the world to put into practice the Christian principles. *Now this is the pacifist position, so-called.* They say, Now, you Christian people, you are always preaching about personal salvation and about doctrines and so on; why do you not do something about wars? Well then, we say, what do you want us to do? They reply, What you have to do is to tell the people to practise the Sermon on the Mount. Why do you not tell them to turn the other cheek and to love one another, and so on, then there would be an end of war? You have the solution; just get people to put into operation the principles of the teaching of Christ. What is the answer to that? The answer is the teaching of the first three verses in this second chapter of Paul's Epistle to the Ephesians. You can preach the Sermon on the Mount to people who are 'dead in trespasses and sins' until you have exhausted yourself and you will be none the wiser, neither will they. They cannot practise it. They do not want to. They are 'enemies and aliens in their minds'. They are governed by 'lusts'. They 'fulfil the desires of the flesh and of the mind'. They are governed and ruled by this. How can they practise the Sermon on the Mount?

There is only one hope for man in sin, says Paul—'but God'. Men need to be regenerated; they must be given a new nature before they can even understand the Sermon on the Mount leave alone begin to put it into practice. So it is but a travesty of the Christian message to speak of it as if it were but an appeal to men to rise up and to follow Christ in their own strength, and to put into operation Christian principles of teaching. It is as much a travesty of the gospel as is the preaching of patriotism and imperialism. It is equally non-Christian. It is indeed dangerous heresy, the ancient Pelagian heresy, because it fails to realise that man, being what he is in sin, cannot possibly implement such teaching. To expect Christian conduct from people who are not yet Christians is dangerous heresy. You see how important our teaching is, and how essential it is that we should be clear about the true application of the Christian message to the modern world. That is why we do not spend our time in talking about international conferences and about politics and international relationships, or industrial disputes, or in preaching always on the question of pacifism and against physical warfare. To do so is simply to waste time—though it would probably attract publicity. What is needed is that we should start with this fundamental principle, the doctrine of man in sin, in his deadness, in his hopelessness, in his complete helplessness.

To sum up at this point, the negative principle is that the Christian faith, the Christian gospel, has no direct message for the world except to say that the world as it is, is under the wrath of God, that it is under condemnation, and that all who die in that state will go to perdition. The only message of the Christian faith to an unbelieving world, in the first instance, is simply about judgment, a call to repentance, and an assurance that if they do repent and turn to Christ they shall be delivered. The Church, therefore, the Christian faith, has no message to the world apart from that.

But the Bible also teaches very plainly and clearly that while that is the message of God to the unbelieving world, God, nevertheless, has done something about that unbelieving world. What He has done in the first instance is this. *He has put a control upon the power of sin and of evil.* He has done so in this way. As I have already reminded you He has divided up the peoples of the world into nations. Not only so, He has ordained that there should be states and governments. He has ordained 'the powers that be'. 'The powers that be', says Paul, in Romans 13, 'are ordained of God'; whether it be a king or an emperor or a president of a republic, 'the powers that be are ordained of God'. It is God who has ordained magistrates and given them the sword of power. Why? Simply to keep the manifestations of evil within bounds and under control. For if God had not done this, if the lusts that operate in us all by nature and by inheritance from Adam were allowed unlimited and uncontrolled manifestation, the world would be hell, and it would have hurtled itself to perdition long ago and would have destroyed itself. God has put a limit upon it. He has put a bound even upon evil, He has held it in, He has restricted it. Indeed the apostle Paul in a most extraordinary statement in the Epistle to the Romans (chapter 1, verses 18 ff.) proves the matter by saying that sometimes, for His own end and purposes, God withdraws that restraint partially. He says that God 'had given them over to a reprobate mind'. There are times and seasons when God seems to relax the restraint that He has put upon sin and evil in order that we may see it in all its horror. It may well be that we are living at such a time. But that is what the Bible tells us about what God does directly about man in sin; He controls the manifestations of his foul and evil and fallen nature. That is the *general* message.

But what is the *particular* message? This is the thing that the apostle is concerned to emphasise most of all in this immediate paragraph. *The message to individuals is that we can be delivered out of this present evil world,* that we can escape the condemnation that is coming for certain upon this world. That is the message the apostle preached. It is a message to individuals. It does not say that the world can be put right if we only implement Christian teaching; it is not an appeal to people to reform themselves and to do this or that. No, it is a message which says that as the result of what God has done in Christ Jesus, His Son, our Lord and Saviour, we who were in the very warp and woof of that sinful, condemned world can be delivered out of it—'Who gave himself for our sins', he says to the Galatians, 'that he might deliver us from this present evil world'. *1:4* The world is doomed, the world is going to be destroyed and punished, the devil and all his forces are going to perdition, and all who belong to that realm will suffer the same punishment. But the message of the gospel to men and women individually is that they need not be participators in that. You can be taken out of it—'out of the kingdom of darkness' brought out from the power of Satan, unto God. That is its message to individual men and women. The world will remain as it is, but you can be delivered out of it, you can be taken out of it.

Not only that; we can also be introduced into and become citizens of a kingdom which is not of this world. As we go through this chapter we shall find Paul elaborating his own words. The marvellous thing, he says, is that you Gentiles are in Christ, and because of His blood, have become fellowcitizens with the saints; you have become citizens in the kingdom of God, the kingdom of Christ, the kingdom of light, the kingdom of heaven—a kingdom that is not of this world, a kingdom which cannot be shaken, a kingdom which cannot be moved. That is the kingdom into which we enter.

This is the most thrilling news a man can ever hear. Now we are all citizens of this country, our native land, and we are all involved in what happens to this country. If this country goes to war we shall be involved. We did not escape the bombs in the last war any more than anybody else simply because we were Christians. We are all involved in it, we are citizens of this world and we share in the fate of this world. But thank God, here is something different. While remaining citizens of this world we become citizens of another kingdom, this other kingdom that has been opened to us by Christ— a spiritual kingdom, a kingdom that is not of this world, eternal in the heavens with God. That is the teaching of this message. 'But God. . . .'

The doctrine works itself out in practice like this. If I believe this message, from now on *I am not going to pin my hopes, nor rest my affections finally, on anything in this world.* The natural man does so, of course; he pins his hopes on this world and its mind, its outlook, its statesmen, its mentality, its pleasures, its joys. He lives for it, and all his hopes are centred here, his affections are here. Not so the Christian. The Christian, having been given to see that this world is doomed, that it is under the wrath of God, has fled from 'the wrath to come'. He has believed the gospel, he has entered this other kingdom, and his hopes and affections are set there now, not here.

The Christian is a man, who, to use a scriptural phrase, knows that he is but 'a stranger and a pilgrim' in this world. He is a mere sojourner, he does not any longer live for this world: he has seen through it, he sees beyond it. He is but a journeyman, a traveller, and, as James puts it (chapter 4) he is a man who has realised that his life is 'but a vapour', a breath. So he does not regard this world as permanent; he does not lay down his plans and say, I am going to do this or that. Not at all! But rather, 'If the Lord will . . .'; it is all under God, and he realises how contingent it is. He does not any longer pin his faith or set his affections on this world.

But still more marvellous! *He is never taken by surprise over anything that happens in this world.* That is why I said earlier, that there is nothing that I know of that is so relevant to worldly circumstances as this gospel. The Christian is a man who is never surprised by what happens in the world. He is prepared for everything, prepared for anything. He is not at all surprised when a war breaks out. The non-Christian, and especially the idealist, of course, is greatly surprised. He really did believe at the end of the first world war that the League of Nations was going to abolish war for ever. There were many who believed that the Locarno Pact of 1925 was finally going to do it, and they were very happy. They were confident that there would never be another war like that of 1914-18. And when it came in 1939 they did not know how to explain it. But the true Christian, knowing that man is a creature who is governed by lusts, and that lust always produces war, knew perfectly well that no Locarno Pact or anything else could outlaw or abolish war. He knew that war might come at any time, and when it came he was not surprised. As Psalm 112 puts it in the seventh verse: 'He shall not be afraid of evil tidings; his heart is fixed, trusting in the Lord'. Believing as we do this biblical doctrine of man in sin, we should never be surprised at what happens in the world. Are you surprised at all the murders, the thefts, the violence, the robbery, all the lying and the hatred, all the carnality, the sexuality? Does it surprise you as you look at your newspapers? It should not do so if you are a Christian. You should expect it. Man in sin of necessity behaves like that; he cannot help himself, he lives, he walks in trespasses and sins. He does it individually, he does it in groups; therefore there will be industrial strifes and misunderstandings and there will be wars. Oh, what pessimism! says someone. I say, No, what realism! Face it, be prepared for it, do not expect anything better from a world like this; it is a fallen, sinful, godless, evil world; and while man remains in sin, it will be like that. And it is as much like that today as it was in the days of Sodom and Gomorrha and in the time of the flood!

But, thank God, I have not finished. I go on to say that the

Christian is a man who, realising that he is living in such a world, and who, having no illusions at all about it, yet knows that he is linked to a Power that enables him not only to bear whatever may come to him in such a world, but indeed *to be 'more than conqueror' over it all.* He does not just passively bear it, he does not merely put up with it, he does not just 'stick it' and exercise courage. No, that is stoicism, that is paganism. The Christian, being in Christ, the Christian knowing something of what the apostle calls 'the exceeding greatness of God's power to us—ward that believe', is strengthened, is enabled to endure; his heart does not quail, he is not defeated, indeed he can rejoice in tribulations. Let the world do its worst to him, let hell be let loose, he is sustained. 'This is the victory that overcometh the world, even our faith.' So that if things really do become impossible, the Christian has resources, he still has comforts and consolations, he still has a strength of which all others are ignorant.

Finally, the Christian is absolutely certain and assured that whatever the world and men may do *he is safe in the hands of God.* 'We can confidently say', say the Scriptures, 'the Lord is my helper, and I will not fear what man shall do unto me.' Indeed he knows this, that man in his malignity may insult him, may persecute him, may ravage him, may even destroy his body; but he also knows that nothing shall ever be able to 'separate him from the love of God which is in Christ Jesus our Lord'. He knows that whatever may happen in this world of time, he is a son of God, an heir of glory. Indeed he knows this, that a day is coming when even this present sinful world shall be entirely redeemed, and there 'shall be new heavens and a new earth wherein dwelleth righteousness'. The Christian can look forward to this, that he, some glorious day in the future, when his very body shall be renewed and glorified, when it shall no longer be weak, when it shall be no longer subject to sickness and old age and disease, when it will be a glorified body like that of the risen Christ—he knows that he in this glorified body shall even walk the face of this very earth, out of which evil and sin and vileness shall have been burned by the fire of God. He will dwell in a perfect world, of which the Lamb, the Son of God, is the Light and the Sun, the Brightness and the Glory, and he shall enjoy it for ever and ever. That is what the Christian message, the Christian faith has to say to this wretched, distracted, unhappy, confused, frustrated, modern world. It is all the outcome of these essential doctrines which can be learned only in this Book which is God's Word. There is the world!—'But God . . .'

7

IN CHRIST JESUS

But God, who is rich in mercy, for his great love wherewith he loved us,
Even when we were dead in sins, hath quickened us together with Christ,
(by grace ye are saved;) And hath raised us up together, and made us sit
together in heavenly places in Christ Jesus: That in the ages to come he
might shew the exceeding riches of his grace in his kindness toward us
through Christ Jesus.   Ephesians 2: 4–7

We have already looked at this majestic and most moving statement
in a more or less general manner. We have observed the way in
which the apostle introduces it, and especially that word *But* which
introduces the transition point from the hopelessness and the despair
of man in sin to the hope and comfort of the gospel. It is the only
hope; apart from it there is none whatsoever. As we see ourselves
in an entirely lost and parlous condition, suddenly there comes this
message to us, unexpectedly, surprisingly, from a different realm,
causing us to lift up our faces. Furthermore, its great emphasis is
that it is God who has done this. It is when we were dead and could
do nothing that God did that which He alone could do. It is the
power of God. It is here, also, we see the contrast between God and
ourselves most clearly: He is rich in mercy, He has great love
toward us, He has grace which is exceeding rich, and He is kindly
and benignly disposed toward us.

But the apostle is not content merely to introduce the gospel,
and merely to paint these striking and wonderful contrasts. He is also
anxious that we should be quite clear in our minds as to the great
thing God has done for us. What can be more wonderful than the
way in which, when we see ourselves as we are in sin, we meet this
blessed 'But'. Yet we must not simply stand amazed and astonished;
we must learn and realise exactly what God has done for us. So
the apostle puts it before us in detail. There is a sense in which we
can say quite rightly and truly that we have here one of the profoundest statements with respect to the condition and the position
of the Christian that can be found anywhere in Scripture. What has
happened is, that 'when we were dead in sins, God hath quickened
us together with Christ, and hath raised us up together and made
us sit together in heavenly places in Christ Jesus'.

Now there are obviously a number of preliminary remarks that one must make about a statement like this. The first that I feel constrained to make is that *this is true Christianity*; that it is the very essence of Christianity, and nothing less than that. What is described in these words is the very nerve of this whole matter. It is what God has done to us and for us, and not primarily anything that we have done. Christianity, in other words, does not just mean that you and I have taken a decision. Of course it includes that, but that is not the essence of Christianity. People can decide to stop doing certain things and to start doing other things; that is not Christianity. People can believe that God forgives them their sins; but that is not Christianity in and of itself. The essence of Christianity is the truth we have here—and this is the real thing, and nothing less than this is the real thing.

I would emphasise, also, that *this is true of every Christian*. We shall see later that here we come face to face with the wonderful teaching and doctrine about the union of the Christian with the Lord Jesus Christ. Now there are certain schools of Christian thought which have done very great harm at this point by giving the impression that this is something that only certain Christians arrive at, that if you really give yourself to the cultivation of the Christian life, you may hope, ultimately, to achieve this union with Christ. They obviously think that there are many Christians who are not yet in that position and who need to be exhorted and urged and stimulated to strive until they get to that condition. Now that is entirely wrong, entirely false. You cannot be a Christian at all apart from the truth we are now examining; this is what makes us Christians; and apart from this we are not in the Christian position at all.

It is important therefore that we should understand at once that we are really dealing here with something that is basic and fundamental and primary. At the same time, of course, the doctrine is so glorious and great that it includes the whole of the Christian life. The Christian life is a whole, and you, as it were, have the whole at once and then proceed to appropriate it in its various parts, and to understand it increasingly. This is Christianity, that 'when we were dead in sins God hath quickened us together with Christ, and hath raised us up together and made us sit together in heavenly places in Christ Jesus'. What happens, I wonder, when we examine ourselves in the light of such a declaration? Can we say that we always think of ourselves as Christians in these terms? Is this my way of thinking of myself as a Christian? Or do I still tend to think of myself as a Christian in terms of what I am attempting and striving to do, and what I am trying to make myself or to make of myself? Now this is obviously quite basic, because the apostle's whole emphasis here is that the primary thing, the first thing, is this which God does to us, not primarily what you and I do ourselves.

There are two ways of looking at this great statement. There are some people who take a *purely objective view* of it. They think of it exclusively in terms of our position, or our standing, in the presence of God. What I mean is, that they think of it as being something which, in a sense, is already true of us in Christ, but is not true of us in practice. They regard this as a statement of the fact that beyond death we shall be resurrected and shall share the life of glory which is awaiting all who are in Christ Jesus. They hold that the truth is that the Lord Jesus Christ has already been raised from the dead; He was quickened when He was dead in the grave, He was raised, He appeared to certain witnesses, He ascended into heaven, He is in the glory in the heavenly places. Now, they say, that has happened to Him, and if we believe in Him it will happen to us. They say that it is true of us by faith now, but actually only by faith. It is not real in us now, it is entirely in Him, but it will be made real in us in the future. Now that is what I call the purely objective view of this statement. And of course as a statement it is perfectly true, except that it does not go far enough. All that is true of us. There is a time coming when all of us who are Christians shall be resurrected, unless our Lord returns before we die. Our bodies will be changed and will be glorified; and we shall live, and we shall reign with Him, and enter into and share His glory with Him. That is perfectly true.

But it seems to me that to interpret this statement solely in that way is very seriously to misinterpret it. And that I can prove. There are two arguments which make it quite inadequate as an interpretation. The first is that *the whole context here is experimental.* The apostle is not so much concerned to remind these Ephesians of something that is going to happen to them; his great concern here is to remind them of what has already happened to them, and of their present position. It is important that we should always carry the context with us. What the apostle is concerned about in this whole statement is that we may know 'the exceeding greatness of his power to us-ward who believe, according to the working of his mighty power which he wrought in Christ when he raised him from the dead'. He is praying, in other words, that these Ephesians may have the eyes of their understanding so enlightened that they may know what God is doing for them now, at that very time, not something that He is going to do in the future. It is important that we should be clear about death, that we should lose the fear of death, that we should be so certain of the resurrection and our glorification that we can smile in the face of death; that is right, but that is not what the apostle is teaching here. He is concerned that they should appreciate now in the midst of all their difficulties what is actually true of them.

But there is still stronger proof, it seems to me, in the fifth verse. The apostle says, 'even when we were dead in sins, hath quickened us together with Christ', and then in a parenthesis '(by grace ye are saved)'. In other words, he says, What I am talking about is your salvation at this moment. 'By grace ye are saved' means 'by grace *you have been saved*'. That is the tense, 'you have been saved'. Clearly that is something which is experimental. This is something subjective, not something purely objective. The tragedy is that people so often put these things up as opposites, whereas in reality the Scripture shows always that the two things must go together. There is an objective side to my salvation, but thank God there is a subjective side also. It is wrong to teach, as the modern Barthian movement tends to teach, that it is all objective, that it is all in Christ and that there is nothing in me at all. That seems to me to be a grievous error, because the Scripture, fortunately for us, always emphasises the experimental, the experiential, the subjective, what I enjoy in the here and now. My salvation is not altogether and exclusively in Christ; because I am in Christ it is also in me.

That is the thing the apostle is so anxious for us to understand. In other words this must be interpreted *spiritually and subjectively*, it must be understood experimentally. What God has done to us spiritually, says the apostle, is comparable to that which He did to the Lord Jesus Christ in a physical sense when He raised Him from the dead and took Him to Himself to be seated in the heavenly places. We must go back to the end of the first chapter. The power which is working toward us and in us who believe is the same power which God 'wrought in Christ when he raised him from the dead and set him at his own right hand in the heavenly places, far above all principality and power, and might, and dominion, and every name that is named, not only in this world but also in that which is to come; and hath put all things under his feet, and gave him to be the head over all things to the church, which is his body, the fulness of him that filleth all in all'. Now, says Paul, I want you to know that the self-same power that did that, is working in you spiritually. That, then, enables us to say, that all that has happened to us, if we are Christians, has happened by this self-same power of God. All the tenses the apostle uses here in these very words that we are studying are all in the past; he does not say that God is going to raise us, is going to quicken us, is going to put us to be seated in the heavenly places; he says that He has done so already, that when we were dead He quickened us. It is the aorist tense, it is the past, it is completed, and once and for all, it has already been done. So that we must say of ourselves as Christian people, that we have been quickened, we have been raised, we are seated in the heavenly places.

Or, perhaps, we can put it best like this—and surely this is the thing that the apostle had in his mind—the position of the Christian is the exact opposite of the man who is not a Christian. The man who is not a Christian is a man who is dead in trespasses and sins, he is being led about according to the course of this world, according to the prince of the power of the air, the spirit that now works in the children of disobedience; his conversation is in the lusts of the flesh, fulfilling the desires of the flesh and of the mind; he is under the wrath of God by nature. That is the non-Christian. What is the Christian? He is the exact opposite of that—quickened; alive; raised; seated in the heavenlies; entirely different, the complete contrast. The 'but' brings out everywhere this aspect of contrast. And obviously we cannot truly understand our position as Christians unless we realise that it is a complete contrast to what we once were. You see how important it is in interpreting the Scripture to take everything in its context. We must be clear about our state in sin, because if we are not, we shall never be clear about our state in grace and in salvation.

If that is the truth about us as Christians now, there are two main matters that must occupy our attention. The first is: *How has all this happened to us?* How has this come to be true of me as a Christian? The apostle answers the question. It is 'together with Christ'. Do you notice his constantly repeated emphasis?—'when we were dead in sins, hath quickened us *together with Christ*, and hath raised us up *together*, and made us sit *together* in heavenly places *in Christ Jesus*'. Here we are undoubtedly face to face with one of the greatest and most marvellous of all the Christian doctrines, one of the most glorious beyond any question at all. It is the whole teaching of the Scripture with regard to *our union with Christ*. It is a teaching which you find in many places. I would refer you to the fifth chapter of the Epistle to the Romans, which is in many ways the most extended statement of the doctrine to be found anywhere. But it is to be found in exactly the same way in the sixth chapter of the Epistle to the Romans. It is likewise found in 1 Corinthians 15, the great chapter which is read so often at funeral services; but it is seen equally clearly in 2 Corinthians, chapter 5. Similarly it is the teaching found in those beautiful words at the end of the second chapter of the Epistle to the Galatians—'I have been crucified with Christ; nevertheless, I live: yet not I, but Christ liveth in me; and the life which I now live in the flesh I live by the faith of the Son of God who loved me and gave himself for me'. This is the most wonderful and the most amazing thing of all, and to me it is always a matter of great surprise that this blessed doctrine should receive so little attention. For some reason or other Christian people seem to be afraid of it. I have no doubt that it is mainly for the reason I have already adduced, that Catholic teaching (whether Roman or Anglican or any other type) always has tended to give the impression that this is some final achievement of the mystic, the ultimate goal of the greatest saint, but that it has nothing to do with the rest of us ordinary Christians. Our reply is, that according to this teaching in Ephesians 2 and elsewhere, you are not Christians at all unless you are joined to Christ and 'in Him'. This doctrine of our union with Christ should not come at the end of Christian doctrine, it should come at the beginning where the apostle himself puts it.

What is meant by our being joined to Christ? It is used in two senses. The first is in what may be called *a federal sense*, or, in other words, a covenant sense. That is the teaching of the fifth chapter of Romans, verses 12–21. Adam was constituted and regarded by God as the head and the representative of the human race; he was the federal head, the federal representative, the covenant head. God made a covenant with Adam, made an agreement with him, made certain statements to him as to what He would do, and so on. Now that is the first sense in which this doctrine of union is taught. And what is said, therefore, about the Lord Jesus Christ is that He is our Federal Head, He is our Representative. Adam, our representative, rebelled against God; he sinned, and he was punished, and certain consequences followed. But because Adam was our representative and our head, what happened to Adam also therefore happened to all his posterity and to us.

Now that is one aspect of the matter, and a very important one. We know something about this in ordinary life and living. The ambassador of this country in a foreign court represents the whole country, and he engages in actions in which we are all involved whether we want to be or not. As citizens of this country we all suffer the consequences of actions that were taken before we were ever born. You cannot contract out of your nation, you are federally involved in the activities of your nation, and what the leader or the official representative of a nation does is binding upon all the citizens of that nation. Now that was true of Adam. It is also true of the Lord Jesus Christ. Adam was the first man; Jesus Christ is the

Second Man. You have the first Adam; you have the Last Adam. Now Jesus Christ, according to this teaching, is the Representative of this new humanity; and, therefore, what He did and what He suffered is something that applies to the whole of this new race that has come into being in Him. So that the union of the believer with Christ must be thought of in that federal sense.

But it does not stop at that. There is another aspect of the union which we may call *mystical or vital*. This is something which was taught by our Lord Himself, in the famous words in the fifteenth chapter of the Gospel according to John, where He says, 'I am the vine, ye are the branches'. The union between the branches and the vine is not mechanical, it is vital and organic. They are bound together; the same sap, the same life is in the stock as in the branches. But that is not the only illustration used. At the end of the first chapter of this Epistle Paul says that the union between a Christian and the Lord Jesus Christ is comparable to the union of the various parts of the body with the whole body, and especially with the head. Now, any one of my fingers is a vital part of my body. It is not simply tied on; there is a living, organic, vital union. The blood that flows through my head flows through my fingers. That indicates a kind of internal, essential unity and not merely a federal, legal or covenant union. Indeed there is yet another comparison which is used in this Epistle to the Ephesians in the fifth chapter, where we are told that the union between the Church and Christ, and therefore between every member of the Church and Christ, is comparable to the union between a husband and a wife—'they two shall be one flesh'. That is mystical union. Such is the union between Christ and the Church.

All these blessings that we enjoy become ours because we are joined to Christ in this double manner; in the forensic, federal, covenant manner, but also in this vital and living manner. We can therefore claim that what has happened to Christ has happened to us. This is the marvel and mystery of our salvation, and it is the most glorious thing we can ever contemplate. The Son of God, the Second Person in the eternal Godhead, came down from heaven to earth; He took unto Him human nature, He joined human nature unto Himself, He shared human nature; and as the result of His work we human beings share His life and are in Him, and are participators in all the benefits that come from Him. Now I reminded you at the beginning, and I must repeat it, that that, and nothing less than that is Christianity. And if we do not realise this, I wonder what our Christianity is? This is not something you arrive at, this is something with which you begin. You get no benefit from Christ except in terms of your union with Him—'of his fulness have all we received', says John, 'and grace for grace' (John 1: 16).

Now the apostle at this point is concerned primarily to emphasise the positive aspect of all this, and not the negative. He will deal with the negative a little later in this chapter. But of necessity the negative also has to be borne in mind. But what the apostle is primarily concerned to emphasise is, that *whereas we were dead, we are now alive*. The question arises at once, How can this happen? Something must happen before we who are dead and under the wrath of God can ever be made alive. I can derive no benefit whatsoever until something has been done to satisfy the wrath of God, for I am not only dead and a creature of lusts and controlled by the god of this world, I am under the wrath of God—'we were by nature the children of wrath, even as others'. And, thank God, that something has happened. Christ has taken upon Him our nature, He has taken upon Him our sins, He has gone to the place of punishment; the wrath of God has been poured out upon Him. That is the whole meaning of His death upon the cross, it is sin being punished, it is God's wrath against sin manifesting itself. And if we do not see that in the cross of Calvary, we are looking at that cross without New Testament eyes. There is that terrible aspect to the cross, and we must never forget it. We must never forget the cry of dereliction, 'My God, my God, why hast thou forsaken me?' That was because He was experiencing the wrath of God against sin, nothing less. But the apostle, here, is much more concerned to emphasise the positive aspect. Christ not only died and was buried; He rose again. God 'raised him from the dead and set him at his own right hand in the heavenly places, far above all principality and power and might and dominion and every name that is named'. All that involved a quickening, a raising, and an exaltation. And the same thing, says the apostle, is true of us, because we are in Christ—'hath quickened us together with him'. This has happened to everybody who is a Christian. It is God's action. Surely this does not need any demonstration? That man who is dead in sins and under the wrath of God, what can he do? He can do nothing; God does it to him, He quickens him. As He quickened the dead body of His Son in the grave, He quickens us spiritually.

What does 'to quicken' mean? It means 'to make alive', it means 'to impart life'. The first thing then that is true of the Christian is that he has *come to the end of his death*—we were dead in trespasses and sins, we were not born spiritually. There is no divine spark in anybody born into this world; all born into this world, because they are children of Adam, are born dead, born dead spiritually.

This whole idea of a divine spark remaining in man is a contradiction not only of this Scripture, but of the whole of Scripture. The position of every person born into this world is that he is dead. The comparison used to illustrate this is the dead body of the Lord Jesus Christ buried in a grave with a stone rolled over the mouth. This then is the first positive truth. I have come to an end of my death. I am no longer dead in trespasses and sins, I am no longer dead spiritually. Why? Because I have died with Christ; I have died with Christ to the law of God and to the wrath of God.

Now a Christian is a man who must assert this truth. The beginning of Christianity is to say 'There is therefore now no condemnation to them who are in Christ Jesus'. The Christian is not a man who is hoping to be forgiven; the Christian is not a man who hopes that ultimately he will be able to satisfy the demands of the law and to stand before God. If he is a Christian who understands Christianity he says, I am already there, I have ceased to be dead, I am alive, I have been quickened, I have been made alive. And the first important aspect of that statement is the negative one, which says that I am no longer dead. I have finished dying; I am dead to sin, I am dead to the law, I am dead to the wrath of God. 'There is therefore now no condemnation.' Can you say that? It is the statement that every Christian should be able to make. And if you have not got that assurance it is simply because you do not understand the Scriptures. The Scriptures make this definite assertion: I am not a Christian, I cannot be a Christian at all, without being in Christ. It follows that if I am in Christ, what is true of Him is also true of me. He has died unto sin once, and I have died unto sin once, in Him. When the Lord Jesus Christ died on that cross on Calvary's hill I was dying with Him as definitely and as certainly (and more so) as I am responsible for the actions of Great Britain, for instance, in China, in the last century when they so shamefully introduced the opium trade there. Though I did not do it personally, though it was done before I was born, I am responsible for it because I am a Britisher, and I feel my responsibility and I am conscious of shame. In exactly the same way, when Christ died on that cross and endured the wrath of God against sin, I was participating in it; I was in Him, I was dying with Him. I am dead to the law, I am dead to the wrath of God, I can say with Augustus Toplady:

> The terrors of law and of God
> With me can have nothing to do;
> My Saviour's obedience and blood
> Hide all my transgressions from view.

But, more, He has *quickened us*, He has *made us alive*; and if you are alive you are no longer dead. It must be one or the other—you cannot hope to become alive, you are either alive or else you are dead. Are you dead spiritually or are you alive spiritually?

But look at the case more positively. It means that God has put a new spirit of life into me. 'The law of the Spirit of life in Christ Jesus hath made me free from the law of sin and death.' 'The law of the Spirit of life in Christ' is in the Christian. This is the opposite of death and deadness. Before this new spirit of life in Christ Jesus came into us we were dead in trespasses and sins and subject to a very different spirit—'the prince of the power of the air, the spirit that now worketh in the children of disobedience'. But that is no longer true. There is a new spirit of life.

What is 'quickening'? Quickening is *regeneration*, and nothing else. When the apostle says here, 'You hath he quickened', he means, You He has regenerated; He has given you new life, you have been born again, you have been created anew, you have become partakers of the divine nature. What is regeneration? I cannot think of a better definition than this: regeneration is an act of God by which a principle of new life is implanted in man, and the governing disposition of the soul is made holy. That is regeneration. It means that God by His mighty action puts a new disposition into my soul. Notice I say 'disposition', not faculties. What man in sin needs is not new faculties; what he needs is a new disposition. What is the difference, you ask between faculties and disposition? It is something like this: the disposition is that which determines the bent and the use of the faculties. The disposition is that which governs and organises the use of the faculties, which makes one man a musician and another a poet and another something else. So the difference between the sinner and the Christian, the unbeliever and the believer, is not that the believer, the Christian, has certain faculties which the other man lacks. No, what happens is that this new disposition given to the Christian directs his faculties in an entirely different way. He is not given a new brain, he is not given a new intelligence, or anything else. He has always had these; they are his servants, his instruments, his 'members' as Paul calls them in the sixth of Romans; what is new is a new bent, a new disposition. He has turned in a different direction, there is a new power working in him and guiding his faculties.

That is the thing that makes a man a Christian. There is this principle of life in him, there is this *new disposition*. And it affects the whole man; it affects his mind, it affects his heart, it affects his will. It is something that happens to a man instantaneously, not gradually. Birth is sudden, birth is instantaneous, it is not a gradual

process. There was the man, at one moment dead, the next moment
he is alive. He has been quickened; this disposition, this principle of
life has come into him. And obviously it is something that happens
in our sub-conscious. Our Lord makes that quite plain (does He
not?) to Nicodemus in that famous statement, 'The wind bloweth
where it listeth; thou hearest the sound thereof but canst not tell
whence it cometh and whither it goeth; *so* is everyone that is born
of the Spirit'. It is secret, it is elusive, one does not understand it,
one cannot explain it fully; all one knows is that it has happened.
'Once I was blind, now I see.' I do not understand, I cannot explain
it physiologically, anatomically, or in any other way; all I know is,
I was blind, I could not see, but I am now able to see. I was dead,
I am now alive. It is secret, it is mysterious, it is miraculous, it is
marvellous, it is incomprehensible; but I know the effects, I appreciate the results, I am aware of the fact that it has taken place.
What is it then? It is a creative act of God. That is why you often
find this apostle and others referring to it as a new creation—'If
any man be in Christ he is a new creature (a new creation); old
things are passed away, behold all things are become new'. Yes, he
has the same eyes and he looks at the same things that he looked
at before, but he does not see them as he used to see them. The
poor drunkard had eyes and he could look at a public house, and
he saw certain things; he still has eyes, he still sees the same public
house, and yet it is not the same, it is entirely different. He is looking
at the same thing but he sees something absolutely different. Why?
—it is not the public house that has changed. He has changed, or
rather has been changed. A new man, a new disposition, a new
governing principle, new life!

Are you alive? Has God put this principle of life into you? Just
as you are at this moment, do you know that this has happened
to you, that there is this essential difference between you and the
man of the world? I shall have to go into the matter in detail later.
But this is the beginning of it all. Look at that little child that has
just been born. It cannot reason, it cannot think, it cannot give an
account of itself, its likes and its dislikes; but it is manifesting life;
it is alive, and as much alive as it will ever be. Its understanding and
all else will increase, but it is alive and it is proving it. Quickened!
We were dead, lifeless, could not move ourselves spiritually, had
no appetite spiritually, no apprehension or understanding spiritually.
But if we are Christians that is no longer true; we have been
quickened together with Christ, the life principle has come in, we
have been regenerated. There is no Christianity apart from that.
Merely to believe you are forgiven is not enough. This is Christianity,

to believe and know that, because we are joined to Christ, something of His life is in us as the result of this vital indissoluble union, this intimate, mystical connection. The life of the Head goes through the members—'ye are the body of Christ and members in particular'. Are you aware of Him? Do you know that He is in you and you in Him? Can you say, 'I live, yet not I, but Christ liveth in me'? Have you life? Have you been quickened? It is the beginning of Christianity. There is no Christianity apart from this. It is not that you and I should not be striving. Of course we have to strive, to study, to fast, to sweat and pray. We have to do all these things; but that is something which follows. The first thing is this knowledge of life. Are you aware of a principle that is working within you, as it were, in spite of yourself, influencing you, moulding you, guiding you, convicting you, leading you on? Are you aware of being possessed?—if I may so put it, at the risk of being misunderstood. The Christian is a possessed man; this principle of life has come in, this new disposition possesses him. And he is aware of a working within him. 'Quickened together with Christ!' What a tremendous thing! This is objective; but thank God it is also subjective. It is not something altogether in Him and which leaves me where I was. Not at all! God has begun a good work in me, and I know it. He has put this new life in me—in *me*! I am born again and in union with Christ.

May God by His Spirit enlighten the eyes of our understanding so that we may begin to comprehend this mighty working of God's power in us.

8

RISEN WITH CHRIST

But God, who is rich in mercy, for his great love wherewith he loved us,
Even when we were dead in sins, hath quickened us together with Christ, (by
grace ye are saved;) And hath raised us up together, and made us sit together
in heavenly places in Christ Jesus: That in the ages to come he might shew
the exceeding riches of his grace in his kindness toward us through Christ
Jesus.   Ephesians 2: 4–7

We continue our study of this statement of what God has done to
us in our helplessness and hopelessness as described in the first three
verses of this chapter. Surely there is no more wonderful, no more
striking statement of the truth concerning the Christian than that
which is to be found in these verses! We must therefore all admit as
we read the first seven verses of this chapter that most of our troubles
are due to the fact that we are guilty of a double failure; we fail on
the one hand to realise the depth of sin, and on the other hand we
fail to realise the greatness and the height and the glory of our
salvation. Oftentimes we are content to think of our salvation merely
in terms of the forgiveness of sins. Not that one wants to depreciate
that, for there is nothing more wonderful or more glorious. My point
is that to stop at that is surely tragic. And I verily believe that the
whole condition and state of the Church today is largely due to the
fact that we fail at both points. It is because we never realise the
depth of the pit out of which we have been brought by the grace of
God that we do not thank God as we ought. And then there is our
failure to realise the great heights to which He has raised us. That
is what the apostle is dealing with now. He is telling us about the
deliverance, the salvation. Here, of course, the apostle is not so much
concerned about the way in which we are saved. At this point, he is
not interested in evangelism; that is something that has already
happened; he is writing to people who are already Christians, and
he wants them to realise and to understand what is really true of
them as Christian people. He wants them to know 'the exceeding
greatness of God's power to us-ward who believe', and so he
expounds it.

We have already seen that what makes us Christians is our *union with Christ*. This doctrine of our union with Christ is absolutely vital. The first thing to which it leads is regeneration, as we have already seen.

We must now go on to the second step, because the Epistle not only tells us that we have been quickened together with Christ, but also that He '*hath raised us up together*'. We must bear in mind constantly as we deal with this teaching that the apostle is working out a comparison here. His case is that what is true of us spiritually is similar to what happened to our Lord physically when He was raised from the dead. He bore our sins in His own body on the tree, He died, His lifeless body was taken down, it was buried in a grave, the stone was rolled over the grave—there is no question about that; that is fact. He was dead, he literally died for our sins. But the morning of the third day He arose, He was raised from the dead. And the apostle works all this out in terms of our experience. So let us bear in mind what happened to our Lord. There He was for that period dead and in the grave, in the realm of the dead. But He came out from the state and place of death. The grave-clothes were left in the grave, but He was not there. You remember how graphically the evangelists describe that to us, and the surprise of the women and others who went to the grave. They went to see the body in the grave but there was no body, only the grave-clothes. He had arisen, He had been taken out, He was no longer dead, He was no longer in the grave, He was now in another realm, He was alive from the dead. And He appeared, you remember, to chosen people for forty days; at various times and in various ways He manifested Himself unto these chosen witnesses; and then He ascended into heaven.

Those are the facts that we must bear in mind. Our salvation, according to the apostle, is comparable to that, nothing less than that. There was this complete change in the realm in which our Lord was existing: dead, in the grave; alive, manifesting Himself, and in a new way. Now that is the truth, says the apostle, about all who are truly Christian. Nothing less than that. We have been raised together with Christ. Because of our union with Him, what happened to Him happened to us—not, as he points out here, in the physical sense but in the spiritual. It will happen in the physical sense also; that is to come, but what he wants them to understand now is that, spiritually, this selfsame power (as he has argued at the end of the first chapter) which raised the Lord Jesus Christ is working in us who believe, and is doing this wonderful work in us.

What then does this tell us about the Christian? What does this tell us as truth about ourselves? We can consider the matter in the way we considered the statement about our Lord Himself. We can look at this 'raising up together' *first of all in a negative manner*. Once our Lord was raised from the dead there were certain things that were no longer true of Him. And the same thing exactly can be said about the Christian. There are certain negatives which are of tremendous importance. And perhaps the best way for us to work all this out is to do so in terms of the sixth chapter of the Epistle to the Romans, because there you really have an extended commentary on this phrase which we are considering. In all these Epistles you have the same essential doctrine. Some of them work out one point in great detail, others work out another point in great detail, but the essential doctrine is the same in every one of them. And that is why the best commentary always on any Epistle of the apostle Paul is to read all the various other Epistles by the apostle Paul—and if you fail to do that you will sooner or later go astray. And another point which we make is this: if you really study any one of these Epistles carefully, exhaustively, and take time to do so, you will have covered the entire range of Christian doctrine; whereas if you skim lightly over the surface of all of them, you will not have any true conception of the apostle's teaching. Let us now see how he works all this out in the sixth chapter of the Epistle to the Romans.

What can be said about the Christian, clearly, is this. The Christian, by definition, *is no longer dead spiritually*. He is no longer in a spiritual grave. He was!—we were all dead in trespasses and sins. We were dead, we were in a grave, in a spiritual grave. But as Christians we have come out of it. As Christ came out of the grave we are out of the grave. We have left behind the grave-clothes, there is nothing else left. We are no longer in that realm, we no longer belong to that sphere, our condition is an entirely new one. Now that is just another way of saying that this whole matter of regeneration and salvation is the profoundest change possible; and to become a Christian is the most profound experience, the most profound fact, in the whole universe. It is nothing less than the difference between death and life, between being in a grave and walking at liberty and in freedom in the world.

But what does this mean in actual practice? The apostle says that there are certain things which we as Christians must hold on to most tenaciously. Here are some of the negatives. The fact that we are no longer dead and no longer in the grave is proof positive that we are *no longer under the wrath of God* and we are no longer under condemnation. The apostle puts this in a very interesting manner in the last verse in the fourth chapter of the Epistle to the Romans. Referring to our Lord, he says, 'Who was delivered for our offences and was raised again for our justification'. He means that our Lord's death was on account of our offences. He died because He bore our offences; He bore our sins and our transgressions, and as the punishment was death, He died. But how do we know that God was satisfied with that offering? The answer is the resurrection! 'Delivered for our offences, raised again for our justification!' The emergence of Christ from the realm of death and the grave, His appearing again, is an absolute proof that God is satisfied that sin has been truly punished. This obviously, therefore, applies with equal force to us. And the apostle goes on to make the point at once in the next verse, the first verse of the fifth chapter. 'Therefore'—you see the logic! 'Therefore, being justified by faith we have peace with God through our Lord Jesus Christ.' We are raised from the dead with Him and therefore we are justified, and therefore we are no longer under the wrath of God. He puts it still more strongly in the first verse of the eighth chapter: 'There is, therefore, now no condemnation to them that are in Christ Jesus'. No condemnation! Condemnation leads to death; but we are no longer dead, we are risen, therefore there is no condemnation. You remember the contrast. What were we? We were not only 'dead in trespasses and sins' but we were also 'by nature the children of wrath, even as others'. All of us born into this world are born under the wrath of God, under condemnation. But we are no longer there; we are risen from the dead, we have come out of the grave, we have finished with death; 'there is, therefore, now no condemnation to them that are in Christ Jesus'.

Every Christian should know that truth, and every Christian should enjoy that assurance. And why? Because you are in Christ, not because of anything in you. Because of your union with Him, because you have been raised together with Him. The first basis of assurance is that we believe this; we accept this by faith, we recognise that this is true. I have been put into Christ, I have been joined to Christ; and, therefore, as He rose and left that realm, so too I have left it. 'Delivered for our offences, raised again for our justification!' Do you realise that you are no longer under the wrath of God? Do you realise that there is, therefore, no longer any condemnation for you? Do you realise that the punishment has been borne, and that you no longer need fear that punishment that is to come? That is Paul's first deduction.

He then proceeds to another. He says that, because we are no longer dead but alive, we are also *dead to the law*. We are 'not under law but we are under grace', he says. And in the seventh chapter of the Epistle to the Romans he works it out with a comparison. He says that a woman, as long as her husband is alive, is bound by that husband and to that husband, and that she cannot marry another without being an adulteress. But when the husband dies she is free and is able to marry again; she is no longer bound to that husband and by that husband. He says that that is exactly our relationship as Christians to the law. We all of us are born 'under the law'. There is the law of God facing us, challenging us, and condemning us because of our failure; and God deals with us by law. But if we are in Christ we are no longer under law, we are under grace. That does not mean, of course, that we no longer have to keep the moral law, but it does mean that our relationship to God is no longer a legal relationship; it is a personal relationship, the relationship of father and child. Of course the father, if he is a good father, will see to it that the child is disciplined and that he has to obey certain laws, but the relationship has changed. Man in sin is an alien from God, and God deals with him in a purely legal manner. But those of us who are 'in Christ' have been brought right out of that realm. The law executed its full punishment in full measure upon the Lord Jesus Christ, and if we are in Him the law has no further demands upon us in that sense. I am no longer under law, I am under grace. That is the second deduction. And what a tremendous thing that is for us to realise, that we are in an entirely new relationship to God. That works out, as we shall see later, in certain practical respects.

But there is a still more striking statement. The apostle says that because we have risen with Christ we are now '*dead to sin*'. In the second verse of the sixth chapter of Romans, the apostle answers the question he had put in the first verse—'What shall we say then? Shall we continue in sin that grace may abound?'—by saying 'God forbid. How shall we that are dead to sin live any longer therein?' Because we have risen with Christ we are dead to sin. He says it again in verse six: 'Knowing this, that our old man is crucified with him, that the body of sin might be destroyed, that henceforth we should not serve sin'. Now this is obviously a very important and vital statement. What does it mean? It clearly does not mean that we are all perfect, and that we are without sin, and that we shall never sin again. We know that that is not true. 'If we say that we are without sin we deceive ourselves and the truth is not in us', says the apostle John, in his first Epistle, chapter one. What then does it mean? In what sense is it true to say of a Christian that he is dead to sin? It is true in this sense. Before we become Christians we are 'dead in trespasses and sins'; but as Christians that is no longer true of us. Before, we belonged to the realm of sin, to the dominion of sin, and we were under the power of sin. We were controlled by the lusts of the flesh, showing themselves as desires of the flesh and of the mind. Our life was a sinful life, we were controlled by sin, dominated by sin, governed in various ways by these lusts and

passions in mind and body. But that is no longer true of us. We are
dead to that realm of sin, we are no longer there, we have been taken
out of it. 'Sin shall not have dominion over you', he says in Romans 6.
We no longer walk in trespasses and sins as we used to do. Once
we were dead in trespasses and sins, even as others; 'we all had
our conversation in time past', in that way. But that is not true of
the Christian. He does not spend his time there, he does not walk
there, he does not exist there; he does not belong to that realm any
longer, he has been taken right out of that realm. I repeat that it
does not mean he is perfect; but he is no longer in that realm. It is
like a man moving from one country to another, it is like a man
taking out naturalisation papers; there is a complete change in his
status, in his relationship to the state. And that is the thing that is
true of the Christian. He no longer serves sin. Or, to use the apostle's
illustration again, he is no longer the servant of sin. He was a complete slave before. Whether we like it or not, the fact about every
unregenerate person is that he is the slave of sin, governed by an
evil principle. But that is no longer the case with the Christian.
We are no longer the slaves of sin, we have been taken right out of
that. It is true that we may still in our folly listen to the devil, we
may still yield to temptation, we may still respond to a sinful
impulse, but that does not mean that we are slaves to sin. We
no longer are controlled by it. That is the principle, and it is in
that sense that we are dead to sin. 'He that is dead is freed from
sin.'

   We have died with Christ, we have risen with Him and we no
longer belong to that particular realm of sin, law and death. If you
examine your experiences as Christians you will find that this is true.
It is a very remarkable and wonderful thing. There are many of
God's people who do not realise this because they cannot draw the
distinction between a temptation and a sin. Because there are evil
thoughts insinuated into their minds they think they are still in the
realm of sin. They are not. Those thoughts come from without. Of
course there are still sinful tendencies left in the body, and yet one
realises that one's whole attitude is entirely different. May I put it
like this in an illustration. You have heard of the conquest of Canada
in 1759 and the famous battle of Quebec, with General Wolfe
against the French General Montcalm. There was one battle and
one great victory, the battle of Quebec. And as the result of that one
battle Canada became a British possession. But if you go on reading
the history you will find that the British had to continue fighting in
Canada for a number of years. There were pockets of resistance left,
but Canada was no longer French, it was British. But the fact that
it had ceased to be French and had become British did not mean

that there was no longer any struggle or fight. There was; but that
one decisive battle changed the whole situation and the right of
possession. Now the position of the Christian is something like that.
He is no longer under sin; he is dead to sin, in the matter of position
and dominion and control. He has been brought out, he is in this
new life with his Lord and Saviour.

Perhaps we can put it still better in this way. The apostle says,
in the sixth verse of the sixth chapter of Romans, 'Knowing this,
that our old man is crucified with Christ'. A better translation is:
'Knowing that our old man was crucified with Christ'. We know
that, says Paul. As Christians, that is true of us. What does it mean?
What is the old man? The answer is found in the fifth chapter. The
old man is the Adamic man, the man who was in Adam. You
remember the comparison. We were all in Adam, we are lineal
descendants from Adam, and we were all in him. Again, he was our
federal head and representative; but not only that, we are bound
to him by ties of flesh and of blood and of descent; there is the same
double union, federal and vital—we were all in Adam. And every
one of us born into this world is born a child of Adam. We have an
Adamic nature, our standing before God is that of Adam. Adam
fell, and we all fell with him. Consequently, we were under the
wrath of God, subject to lusts, and under the control and the
dominion of sin and of Satan exactly as Adam was. That is the old
man, the Adamic man. But we have died with Christ, and when
we died with Christ the old man died also. As a Christian I am no
longer in Adam, I am in Christ. I am a member of a new humanity.
Christ is 'the firstborn among many brethren'. I am in Him. What
does this mean? It means this—and it is such a glorious truth!—that
God no longer looks at me as one who is in Adam. He looks at me as
one who is in Christ. I am a new man. Of course I am the same
personality, and yet I know that I am a new, a different man. My
whole position, my whole status and standing is absolutely different.
I do not belong to that old humanity any longer. I am still in the flesh,
but I am a member of a new humanity. That is what Paul means by
saying that our old man has been crucified with Christ. As I have
said, I am no longer under the wrath of God, I am no longer under
the law of God; I am no longer under the dominion of sin, I am no
longer under the dominion of Satan. That is because I am no longer
an Adamic man. The Christian must not be content with saying
anything less than that. That is the simple, primary, truth about the
Christian: he is 'in Christ' and not 'in Adam'. The old man that I
once was has gone and gone for ever. Now you notice that I am
saying 'the old man'. I am not saying that the sin that is in the body
and in the flesh has gone; I am simply saying that as the entity

that was in Adam, I am no longer there; I am an entity in Christ now. That is the negative side of the truth and of the fact that we have been 'raised together with Christ'.

Let us now look at *the positive*. This is the most amazing thing of all. What a contrast this is! We are sharing the life of Christ and we therefore become like Christ. As Christians we are basically different from what we were before. I use my terms advisedly. We are fundamentally and essentially different. In what respects? Observe how Paul puts it in Romans 6: 11: 'Likewise, reckon ye yourselves also to be dead indeed unto sin, but alive unto God through Jesus Christ'. Here is the positive aspect. Having risen with Christ I am *now alive unto God*. Before, I was not; before, I was dead in trespasses and sins, and you remember that we saw that the definition of that term *dead* was that I was dead to God. That is the terrible tragedy of every natural man who has not become a Christian; he is dead to God. He is living a life as if there were no God; he is not conscious of God, he has no living relationship to God. He lives in this world as if there were not a God. He is absolutely dead to God. But, being risen with Christ, we are 'alive unto God'. And that is the biggest thing you will ever know about yourself, that you are alive unto God, in tune with the Eternal, and have been awakened to something infinite and absolute.

Have you seen that flower? There it is at night, closed and shut; the sun comes out and suddenly it begins to open and to take in its life from that glorious sun. That is what happens to the Christian. He is 'alive unto God'. What does it mean? It means that we have an entirely new attitude towards God. We are no longer at enmity with God. The apostle goes on in the eighth chapter of the Epistle to the Romans to say that the natural mind, the natural man, is enmity against God. Indeed, in this very Epistle to the Ephesians which we are studying, we shall see that Paul says later that we were 'aliens and enemies in our minds through wicked works'. And how true it is! But it is no longer true of the Christian. The Christian is no longer at enmity against God. He desires God. He no longer has the feeling that God is some terrible monster set against us, waiting to crush us and to damn us and to destroy us. No, he has come to know God, and to know that God is love and that God is mercy and kindness and compassion. He no longer runs away from God and tries to hide behind the trees, as Adam once did, avoiding God at all costs. That is what the natural man still does; the natural man does everything he can to avoid God. That is why he hates the thought of death. Death is to him the most terrible enemy. Why? Because it means that he has to stand before God. He does not always put it in words, but he has that feeling in his bones. He knows it is true, and hates it for that very reason. It means standing before God, and that, he wants to avoid. He wants to get away from God. That is why he does not attend a place of worship, that is why he does not read the Bible, that is why he does not like funerals—God! It brings him near to Him and he hates it; he is terrified and so he avoids God.

But not so the Christian. 'As the hart panteth after the water brooks, so panteth my soul after thee, O God. My soul thirsteth for God, for the living God: when shall I come and appear before God?' (Psalm 42: 1-2). What a change! It is a change from death to life. It is an absolute change. It is an essential change. Is there a bigger change than this, that one now desires the Being that one feared before with a craven and trembling fear? God becomes our Father. And the greatest desire of the true Christian is to draw nearer to God. Can you say, honestly, that the greatest thing you desire at this moment is to know God better, and to realise His presence? If you can you are a Christian. If you cannot, you had better examine the foundations again; for when a man is in Christ he has a new nature, and this new nature cries out for God. Our Lord used to rise up long before the dawning of the day to pray to His Father; He would stay up all night. His Father! He wanted Him, He enjoyed the communion. And that is the characteristic of the Christian, he is 'alive unto God'. Think of the obvious illustrations. It is like an electric instrument: it is not switched on, and it is dead. But switch on and it becomes alive. The microphone receives my voice. Why?—because it is alive to me. But if you switch it off it is dead. That is how man once was, he was not alive to God; but now he is alive to God, sensitive to God, desiring God, loving God, seeking God. 'O that I knew where I might find Him!', is his cry. He cannot find God as he would like to, he does not know Him well enough. He is 'alive unto God'.

But not only is he alive to God, he is *walking in newness of life*. What a wonderful phrase! It is the complete contrast, you see, to death. The apostle says it again in the fourth chapter of this Epistle to the Ephesians, in this way: he talks about the 'new man, who after Christ is created in righteousness and true holiness'. What then is the truth about the Christian? It is that he is no longer walking in trespasses and sins, he is living this entirely new life, no longer governed by the flesh and its desires, but governed by this new outlook. How does it show itself? Let me summarise it. It shows itself in his mind, it shows itself in his heart, it shows itself in his will. That is the way to tell whether you are a Christian, or not. The Christian is one who, because he is risen with Christ, is walking in newness of life. And a man lives with his mind and his heart and his will.

The Christian has *a new mind*. What is it? Paul says in the twelfth chapter of the Epistle to the Romans, 'Be not conformed to this world, but be ye transformed by the renewing of your mind'. And the Christian has a new mind, which shows itself in these ways. He looks at everything in a different manner. He no longer thinks only in terms of time, he begins now to think in terms of eternity. The life of the man who is not a Christian is entirely bounded by time, he never goes beyond it, he does not want to, he is afraid. Thoughts of that 'unknown country from whose bourne no traveller returns', trouble him. No, he is not interested in eternity. But the Christian is interested. The Christian sees that this is a temporary life, a life in time. Eternity!—his mind begins to play upon that. And now he not only thinks in terms of the body and of the rational soul, he also begins to think in terms of the spirit. How does a man who is not a Christian think? Well, his 'thought world' is bounded by this world and its knowledge and its culture and its art and its business and its pleasures and all such things. Put anything you like into it— I do not want to keep anything out—put everything you have into it, but still I say that it is a life and an outlook that are bounded entirely by the body and by the rational soul, and by nothing beyond. But the Christian does not stop at that. He realises that there is that within him which is called spirit, there is that which makes him conscious of the fact that he belongs to another realm and to another sphere, and he begins to live more and more in that, and less and less in this other. It is not only time, it is not only the material; it is eternity, it is the spiritual, it is the everlasting. He is lifted up into an entirely new 'thought realm'. And he judges everything now in the light of it. He has a new standard of values, he assesses things in an entirely different way. What he wants to know about anything now is, not what sort of a 'kick' he will get out of it, not what sort of pleasure will it bring him; but rather what is its value to his soul? And how does it affect his relationship to eternity? How does it impinge upon his relationship to God and to Jesus Christ? He looks at everything in a different way and has an entirely new standard of values, because he has this renewed mind in Christ. He is walking in newness of life.

Another thing that is obvious is that he is interested in the Bible in a way in which he was not before. He put every other book before the Bible then; he puts the Bible before every other book now. He realises that this is the only book that brings him to God and to an increasing participation in the life of God. His mind begins to play upon this Book; it speaks to him, he revels in it, he glories in it, he is moved by it.

He finds also that he increasingly spends his time in meditation. What a lost art meditation has become! But the Christian meditates. He stops to think, he puts down his newspapers, he switches off his wireless and his television, he is not constantly rushing out to some form of entertainment; he settles down and he thinks about himself and God, and glory, and eternity. He has a new mind. You see what a complete opposite he is to the natural man? The one thing the natural man never does is to meditate. He does everything he can to avoid it, and the world caters for him; it knows his likes, and it helps him to run away from himself and from all these wonderful things.

Then consider the *manifestations of the new heart*. This man has entirely new desires. This is what our Lord says about him: 'Blessed are they that do hunger and thirst after righteousness, for they shall be filled.' His greatest desire now is not for more pleasure and momentary satisfaction; it is for righteousness, for true holiness. He says with David, 'Create within me a clean heart, O God, and renew a right spirit within me'. That is his greatest desire. The greatest desire of the true Christian is to be clean within, to be pure, to be holy, to be righteous, to have a heart that is free from sin. And he is grieved on account of sin. He does not now regard the pain that follows sin as an annoyance and a nuisance. He does not regard it as that inevitable concomitant of pleasure and the illicit. No, he realises now that sin is not merely an offence against law, but an offence against the God who so loved him as to send His only begotten Son to die for him. How do you regard your sins and your failures? What is the first thing that comes into your mind when you sin? Is it fear of punishment? If it is, you are still under the law in your thinking. If it is rather a feeling that you have grieved the One who loves you, then it is Christian thinking. The desires are absolutely new; they are no longer the desires of the flesh and of that sinful mind; they are desires, the desires of Christ Himself, to be well-pleasing in His Father's sight.

The new man also has a desire for prayer. I do not want to depress anybody, but if you have new life in you, you will want to pray in a way you never did before. You will long to be so intimate with God that you would sooner spend time speaking to God than anyone else. Do you know the very beginnings of that experience? It is essentially true of the Christian. Prayer! Then, too, he desires fellowship with the saints. 'We know that we have passed from death to life', says John, 'because we love the brethren'. The brethren, the children of Christ, the family of God, these people who are interested in these things, they are the people we love and long for. And the other thing, of course, is a concern about the souls of those who are outside these things. You cannot be a Christian without having that concern. They are dead in trespasses and sins; they are creatures of lust—they do not know it, but we know it; and there they are under the wrath of God. Our Lord felt a great compassion for the people; He saw them 'as sheep without a shepherd'; and the Christian of necessity must knows omething of that feeling. There is the changed heart.

And then a word about the will. The Christian *excercises his will in a new direction*. It is to please Christ and to please God. His question now is not, What do I like, what do I want? but, What is becoming in one who belongs to Him? What is His will for me? These are the things he now desires. The will, negatively and positively, is entirely renewed.

We have been 'raised together with him'. And because of this, we are different in mind, in heart, and in will.

We can summarise it all by asking a few simple questions. Have you been raised? Have you been raised together with Christ? Are you alive to God? Have you an awareness of God? Do you know God? Do you desire Him? These are the vital questions. 'Reckon yourself, therefore, to be dead indeed unto sin, but alive unto God through Jesus Christ.' And if you are, this is the apostle's exhortation: 'Yield yourselves, therefore, unto God, as those that are alive from the dead; and your members (your faculties) as instruments of righteousness unto God'. The Christian is one who is risen with Christ from the realm of sin and death to a new life in which he is 'alive unto God'.

9

IN THE HEAVENLY PLACES

But God, who is rich in mercy, for his great love wherewith he loved us, Even when we were dead in sins, hath quickened us together with Christ, (by grace ye are saved;)·And hath raised us up together, and made us sit together in heavenly places in Christ Jesus: That in the ages to come he might shew the exceeding riches of his grace in his kindness toward us through Christ Jesus.
                                                                Ephesians 2: 4–7

In working out what this great statement tells us about ourselves as Christians we have seen that we have been quickened into new life and then raised with the Lord Jesus to new life.

But the story does not end there. It goes even beyond that. God has not only quickened us and raised us with Christ, He has *'made us to sit together in heavenly places in Christ Jesus'*. For our Lord, after He had risen from the dead, did not remain indefinitely upon earth. He ascended into heaven, and He is seated at the right hand of God in the glory. So the apostle goes on to say that this also has happened to the believer. And, of course, it must happen to the believer. I say it must happen to the believer for this reason, that the doctrine of our union with Christ insists upon it. As we have been quickened with Him and raised with Him, so it must follow that everything else that has happened to Him must happen to us spiritually. Therefore, of necessity, we have been made to sit with Him in the heavenly places.

Another thing which we must bear in mind is that all these statements which are made by the apostle are in the past tense. He is not saying here that these things are going to happen to us; they have happened. You notice he puts that quite clearly—'by grace ye *are* saved', you 'have been' saved. In the same way you 'have been' quickened, you 'have been' raised, you 'are' seated. It is something that has taken place. It is not a prophecy, it is not a prediction, it is not holding out a hope before us of something that is going to happen. The real point the apostle is concerned about is that these Ephesians should realise that this is true of them. He says, I want the eyes of your understanding to be enlightened that you may know that this change has already taken place, it is already something that

is actually a fact. It must be, I repeat, because of our union with
our Lord.

The next point common to the three statements is this. We have
seen that the quickening and the raising together have got to be
considered objectively and subjectively. They have to be considered
as happening in Christ as our Head and Representative; and they
have to be considered also in terms of our mystical union with Him.
In the light of that let us now face this mighty statement. There is
no more wonderful statement about the Christian believer anywhere
than that which we have in the phrase we are examining at this
moment. This is the supreme truth of all, this is the highest glory,
this is the most priceless thing that is true of us as God's people.
We are 'seated together with Christ in the heavenly places' now;
at this moment we *are* in that position.

What does it mean? Perhaps the best plan is to start by considering
the term which is translated in the Authorised Version as *'the
heavenly places'*. The same expression is found in the first chapter in
verse three: 'Blessed be the God and Father of our Lord Jesus
Christ, who hath blessed us with all spiritual blessings in heavenly
places in Christ'; A better translation is 'the heavenlies'. 'Places'
is really a word that has been added by the translators, and it is
rather an unfortunate addition because it does not convey the full
idea that was in the mind of the apostle. It localises it too much.
The heavenlies! What is meant by 'the heavenlies'? It is the same
thing as the apostle has in his mind when, in that striking bit of
autobiography which we have in the Second Epistle to the Corinthians, in the twelfth chapter, he tells us, in the second verse, that
he knew a man fourteen years ago, who was 'caught up into the
third heaven'. That was the way in which people thought in those
days. The first heaven was the atmosphere, the clouds and so on
that we see; the second heaven was the realm in which you have
the stars and the moon and the sun; and the third heaven was the
place where God especially manifests His presence and His glory,
the place in which the Lord Jesus Christ in His glorified body now
dwells. That is the third heaven. Whenever you get this term
'heavenly places' or 'heavenlies' it generally carries that meaning
and connotation. So that is the realm into which we have been
introduced as the result of our regeneration. As the result of our
regeneration we belong to the third heaven, the heavenlies, this
place in which the glory and the presence of God are manifested
in this marvellous and wonderful manner. What does that actually
mean in practice for us? To answer that question we must expound
our passage.

As we do so we must bear in mind that in these verses, four, five, six and seven, we have the contrast to what we had in verses one, two and three. That is where we were—but God! He has raised us to an entirely new and different position. That is the contrast, and it works itself out, as we have seen, quite simply and naturally. Being dead, we were given life. The opposite to being spiritually dead is to be regenerated. The opposite to living a life of sin and being under condemnation is to be justified by faith, to be under condemnation no longer, to be living this new life unto God. It is exactly the same with this third step, described as 'seated in the heavenly places in Christ Jesus'.

Once again, to discover the meaning of the apostle's words we must start with our *negatives*, because they are not only important and interesting, but they are really essential. We read that the Christian is 'seated with Christ in the heavenlies'. The first thing that these words signify is this: *the Christian no longer belongs to this world*. What a statement! Previously he belonged entirely to this world. 'You hath he quickened who were dead in trespasses and sins, wherein in time past ye walked'. How? 'According to the course of this world'. He was bound by this world in every respect—in his mind and outlook and understanding, in his enjoyments, in his hopes, in his desires. The man who is not a Christian is entirely confined to this world. That does not merely apply to people who are guilty of the gross manifestations of sin, it does not apply merely to people who live for pleasure and nothing else, and who are purely the creatures of their physical, fleshly lusts; it is equally true of those who are governed by the lusts of the mind, it is equally true of the greatest philosophers. They cannot go beyond this world, they know nothing beyond it, they are entirely circumscribed by this world. And so the apostle says that the natural man, the unregenerate man, is a man of the world, he belongs to this world entirely and utterly and absolutely. It is our duty as Christians to restore the use of this term, which, regrettably, seems to have dropped out of use, and is not heard as often as it once was. People used to be described as either 'Christians' or 'men of the world'. Now that is the exact description of the man who is not a Christian—he is a man 'of' the world, he is entirely confined to it. But the Christian is no longer like that. He is no longer walking according to the course of this world, he does not belong to that realm any longer. The Christian cannot be a man of the world, because you cannot be at one and the same time in the world and out of it. It must be one or the other. And the truth about the Christian is that he has been taken out of 'the world'.

The apostle makes much of this idea. In writing to the Galatians, in the first chapter and the fourth verse, he says, referring to our salvation: that Christ 'gave himself for us that he might deliver us from this present evil world'. His point is that He does that now. It is not a reference to death and going out of this world. The Christian is a man who is delivered from this present evil world now. He is still in it, but he is no longer of it; he is no longer bound by it, his whole outlook is no longer determined by it. The apostle John is equally definite about this and equally rejoices in it, as we all should—'This is the victory that overcometh the world . . .' (1 John 5: 4). One difference between the non-Christian and the Christian is that the non-Christian is overcome by the world, he is absolutely controlled by it. There is no need to demonstrate this; the way in which people live is an absolute proof of it. It is all depicted in the newspapers. Non-Christians are entirely controlled by 'the thing to do', and by 'what everybody is doing'. Controlled by the world! The Christian, on the other hand, is a man who has a victory over the world. What a contrast! He is taken out of that realm.

This emphasis is found everywhere in the Scriptures. Have you noticed what we are told about those children of faith, those men of faith in Hebrews, chapter eleven? It is always true of them. This is what we read: 'They confessed that they were strangers and pilgrims on the earth'. That was their position though they were still in the world. You remember we are told that the patriarchs, Abraham and Isaac and Jacob, dwelt in tents, in tabernacles. Why?—well, their idea was to impress upon themselves and upon all others that they were but sojourners (that is the term that is used), strangers and pilgrims, travellers, just passing through this world. This was not their permanent dwelling place, they were marching, they were on the move. 'Here', they said, 'have we no continuing city, but we seek one to come'; 'strangers and pilgrims in the earth'. And you will remember how the apostle Peter, in pleading with the people to whom he was writing to live a life worthy of their high calling in Christ, puts it like this: 'Dearly beloved', he says, 'I beseech you as strangers and pilgrims, abstain from fleshly lusts which war against the soul; having your conversation honest among the Gentiles: that whereas they speak against you as evildoers, they may by your good works, which they shall behold, glorify God in the day of visitation' (1 Peter 2: 11, 12). Notice the terms of the appeal: 'Dearly beloved, I beseech you as strangers and pilgrims'; that is, You do not belong to this world. Realise that! Indeed this idea is one of the clear major themes of the entire Scripture. Once a man becomes a Christian one of the first things he is conscious of is that he has been separated from the world. He once belonged to it, he was of its very essence: he is aware now of separation, he is taken out of that, he no longer belongs to the world. He is estranged from it in his mind, his outlook, his tastes, his everything. Of course it may still tempt him, but he is conscious that he is outside it. He was in it, he is now outside it. And if he is foolish enough to look back at it and to be enticed by it, well, he is just contradicting what has happened to him. Because we are in the heavenlies with Christ we no longer belong to this world. 'Love not the world,' says John, 'neither the things that are in the world.' That is the first negative.

The second negative is this: because we are in the heavenlies with Christ, *we are no longer under the dominion of Satan and we are no longer in the kingdom of Satan.* We were once there—'wherein in time past ye walked according to the course of this world, according to the prince of the power of the air, the spirit that now worketh in the children of disobedience; among whom we all had our conversation in time past'. That is where we were, the victims and the serfs of Satan; not only controlled by the mind of the world, but controlled by the one who controls the mind of the world. We were in the kingdom of Satan, under the power of Satan, under the dominion of Satan. That is the position of the unbeliever. The world laughs at this and ridicules it. It is amazed that anybody still believes in the devil, thereby proving that it is under the dominion of the devil. It is so completely fooled and blinded that it is not even aware of it. 'If our gospel be hid', says Paul, 'it is hid to them that are lost, in whom the god of this world hath blinded the minds of them that believe not. . . . ' Such people think they are not Christians because they are so learned and so clever. What is really true of them, of course, is that they have been bludgeoned by the devil and so blinded by him that they cannot see. They are entirely under his dominion. But when a man becomes a Christian and is translated into the heavenlies, that is no longer true of him. That is the very point the apostle made in addressing Agrippa and Festus and the company when he appeared before them as a prisoner (Acts 26:18). He said that when Christ appeared to him on the road to Damascus and gave him His great commission, He said: I am going to send you to the people and to the Gentiles, 'to open their eyes and to turn them from darkness to light, and from the power of Satan unto God. . . .' That is the business of preaching, says the risen Lord to Paul, that is My commission to you; these people are under the power of Satan, I am sending you to preach the gospel to them in order that they may be brought from under the power of Satan to God. What a transference—right out of his dominion! John says the same thing in his First Epistle: 'We know that we are of God, and the whole world lieth in the wicked one'. The whole world is lying in the bosom and the embrace of the wicked one, but we are not there; we are of God, entirely removed. The same apostle says that that wicked one 'toucheth us not'. He not only touched us before, he controlled us; but we are now so removed out of his realm and dominion and power that he cannot touch us; he can shout at us and entice us, he cannot touch us. Or again take it as the apostle Paul puts it in writing to the Colossians. He says that the Christian is one who, among other things, has been translated from the kingdom of darkness into the kingdom of God's dear Son. I am convinced that if we who are Christians realised that we are no longer under the dominion of Satan, that he has no authority over us whatsoever, that we need not even fear him if we realise who and what we are, it would revolutionise our lives. That is the truth concerning us. We are in the heavenlies, not in the realm of Satan. And in this heavenly realm we are out of the dominion and kingdom of Satan and of evil.

The third negative is this: because we are in the heavenlies *we are no longer under the wrath of God* that is coming upon the whole world. You remember the final thing the apostle said about the unbeliever. 'We were by nature the children of wrath'—as it were, belonging to the realm of wrath—'even as others', as all others. But now God has acted upon us and has raised us up together with Christ, and we no longer belong to that realm, we belong to the realm of the heavenlies. This is the most tremendous and staggering thing of all. This world in which we find ourselves is a doomed world, it is a world under judgment. There is nothing which is stated more plainly in the Scripture from beginning to end than that. There is going to be a judgment of this world, and this world and all that is evil in it, in its very constitution, in addition to the people who belong to it, is going to be judged, and the wrath of God will be poured upon it. There will be an awful judgment and a terrifying destruction. It is adumbrated by the flood, by the destruction of Sodom and Gomorrha, by the various captivities of the Children of Israel, by the destruction of Jerusalem in A.D. 70. And all this is but a pale suggestion of the doom and the disaster that is going to overwhelm the world and all who are opposed to God, under the wrath of God. The Christian is taken right out of that; he has already passed from judgment to life. It will not touch him, it will not affect him, it will not harm him at all, he need not fear it in any sense; he is already out of that realm because he is in the heavenlies with Christ. There, then, are the negatives. Let us now look at the positives, which are glorious.

The first thing that is true of us on the *positive* side is that *we belong to the kingdom of God.* We now belong to a heavenly sphere. This is actual, this is fact. It is not that I am going to belong to it, I am already there. Look at some of the Scriptures as they describe this to us. Do you remember how the apostle Paul puts it in writing to the Philippians? He is talking about people who do not obey the truth, people whose god is their belly, who delight in their shame, and such like things, 'whose end', he says, 'is destruction'. 'But', he says, 'our conversation is in heaven'; which means that our citizenship is in heaven. It is not here, we are no longer citizens of the worldly realm, our citizenship is in heaven; or, as somebody has translated it, we are 'a colony of heaven'. That is the homeland, this is just a colony. We do not belong to that which is doomed to destruction. The kingdoms of this world and all that belong to it are passing away, but we who belong to God shall abide for ever. And therefore it is right to say of us that heaven is really now our home. I know that it has been the custom in this century to poke fun at the hymns which say 'I'm but a stranger here, heaven is my home'. But that is true of us who are Christians; our citizenship is in heaven. And I know of no better way of testing ourselves and our profession than to question ourselves on this point. Are you aware, have you a consciousness within you, that you are a stranger in this world? Do you feel estranged from it? Are you aware of a difference in yourself? Have you a feeling that you belong to another realm, that you are merely passing through this world? Our citizenship, the thing we are proud of, the thing we boast of, is that citizenship. Our citizenship, our conversation is in heaven. Look again at the words found in Colossians: The Father 'who hath delivered us from the power of darkness and hath translated us into the kingdom of his dear Son' (1: 13). But I suppose there is no more glorious statement of this truth than that found in the Epistle to the Colossians again, the third chapter and the third verse. Listen to this astounding statement about the Christian—'For ye are dead, and your life is hid with Christ in God'. That is true of you. If you are a Christian it must we true of you, you cannot evade it, because you are in Christ. You are dead. The Adamic man, the man you used to be, is literally dead, he is no longer in existence, he really is not there; you are dead, and your life is hid with Christ in God. You belong to a different sphere and to a different realm altogether. Christian people, do you know that? Are you aware of it? That is the vital question, this sense of belonging elsewhere, strangers and pilgrims on the earth—we are away from home, we are just away from home for a time, for God's own purpose; but our home, our homeland, our citizenship, abides there in heaven. That is the polity to which we belong.

The second thing follows of necessity. *We are under the control of the Holy Spirit*; no longer under the control of that evil spirit, but under the control of the Holy Spirit. '. . . work out your own salvation with fear and trembling', says Paul, 'for it is God which worketh in you both to will and to do. . . .' He is doing it by His Holy Spirit. What is a Christian? Paul's answer in writing to the Romans is, 'For as many as are led by the Spirit of God, they are the sons of God'. Led by the Spirit; no longer led by the mind of the world, no longer led by the evil spirit that now works in the children of disobedience; no longer led, and your whole life governed, by what you see other people doing, and the advertisements in the papers, and the flashy things to do. No, that is evil. Led by the Spirit of God—they are the sons of God. I do not see how a man has any right to call himself a Christian unless he is aware of heavenly influences in his life. 'In heavenly love abiding, no change my heart shall fear'—do you know that? Do you know the influence of the heavenly love drawing you and wooing you, and speaking to you? Heavenly-mindedness! It is a sad thing, but I have even heard evangelical people joking about this, saying of people, 'They have become so heavenly-minded that they are no earthly use'. And that is thought to be a clever statement. Oh, the tragedy! You can never be too heavenly-minded. The trouble with all of us is that we are not sufficiently heavenly-minded, we do not know enough about it, we do not dwell enough there. We have not realised what is true of us, the eyes of our understanding have not been enlightened. The Christian is of necessity a heavenly-minded man, the life of God has come into him, and his mind is changed, as we have seen. He used to be governed by the desires, the lusts of the mind and of the flesh. No longer is he governed by those—they tempt him, they try him; but he is not controlled by them because there is this other influence. He is aware of it, he knows it. The Spirit of God is dealing with him, and working in him, and moving him and drawing him and wooing him from that to this.

But that leads to a third matter, which is still more wonderful. The chief characteristic of the heavenlies is this: the heavenlies is the sphere in which God peculiarly and especially manifests Himself, His presence, and His glory. That is what makes heaven heaven. If you want proof of that, read the Book of Revelation, chapters four and five in particular. John, you remember, saw a door opened in heaven and he had his vision. The first thing he saw was the glory of God. That is the characteristic of the heavenlies. What the statement we are looking at therefore means, is this. We are in the heavenlies, and that means *we are in a realm where we are near to God*. Before, we were dead in trespasses and sins, in the grave of this world, away from God, estranged from Him, aliens and enemies in our minds, not knowing Him; now in the heavenlies we are near to God. Therefore, the apostle James can write: 'Draw nigh unto God, and he will draw nigh unto you'. Ah, says someone, but is it possible for me to draw nigh unto God? Can I get near to God? Of course you can; and, says the author of the Epistle to the Hebrews, for this reason, 'Seeing then that we have a great high priest, that is passed into the heavens, Jesus, the Son of God, let us hold fast our profession'. But not only that, 'Let us therefore', he says, 'come boldly unto the throne of grace, that we may obtain mercy, and find grace to help in time of need'. It is possible.

But let me put it still more plainly, as that same Epistle to the Hebrews puts it still more plainly in the tenth chapter and in verses nineteen and twenty. This is a proof that we are in the heavenlies and that we are near to God: 'Having therefore, brethren,' he says, 'boldness to enter into the holiest'—'the holiest of all,' we can enter in there—'by the blood of Jesus, by a new and living way, which he hath consecrated for us, through the veil, that is to say his flesh; and having an high priest over the house of God, let us draw near with a true heart, in full assurance of faith. . . .' Can you find a more explicit statement than that? The Christian is enabled to come into the holiest of all, that is into God's own presence, where the Shekinah glory is. Or listen to this other majestic statement of it in the twelfth chapter of the Epistle to the Hebrews. Where are we when we meet together in church as Christians? Where are we? Are we at Mount Sinai? Have we come to a place of morality and of law and of condemnation? Have we come to a place where we just commiserate with one another and bemoan our sins and failures and hang down our heads and feel that all is hopeless? If you have come like that you are not a Christian. No! We 'are come unto Mount Sion and unto the city of the living God, the heavenly Jerusalem, and to an innumerable company of angels, to the general assembly and church of the firstborn, which are written in heaven; and to God the Judge of all, and to the spirits of just men made perfect, and to Jesus, the mediator of the new covenant, and to the blood of sprinkling, that speaketh better things than that of Abel.' We have come there; not going to come there, we are there now. As a Christian you have arrived there. That is where we are—the heavenly Jerusalem. We are in the heavenlies with this innumerable company of angels; we cannot see them, but they are there, we are in that realm, we are seated there with Christ. That is where you have come; realise it, and live accordingly. Coming to God, we enter into the 'holiest of all,' and we have fellowship with God. Do you? Do you know God? I ask again. Are you enjoying fellowship

with Him? Are you able to find Him, can you draw near to Him
and know that He is there? You should if you are in the heavenlies.
Realise your position, and live accordingly.

But there is one further thing. Because we are in the heavenlies
we already know something of the life of heaven even in this world. And
this again is something essential and vital. Because we are Christians,
because we are with Christ in the heavenlies, we are already enjoying
something of the life of heaven even now. The apostle talks elsewhere about partaking of the first-fruits; he talks about having a
foretaste; the great harvest has not yet come, but the first-fruits are
available, we have got them in our hands, we are partaking of
them. There was a feast of the first-fruits, you remember, in Israel,
just to remind them and us of this. The foretaste! And glimpses of
glory! It is not given to many of us to be lifted up into the third
heaven as was the case with the apostle Paul. I have not had that
experience; but even so, we should know something about the
glory, we should have had an occasional glimpse. We should
occasionally have heard something of the music; we should have
some sensation of the life that is lived there. Isaac Watts was quite
certain of this; this is how he puts it in his verse:

> *The men of grace have found*
> *Glory begun below;*
> *Celestial fruits on earthly ground*
> *From faith and hope may grow.*

It begins here. 'The men of grace have found glory begun below'.
Do you know it? Have you experienced it? Have you felt at times
that what you are experiencing is not earth, but heaven, and a
foretaste of glory? It must be true of those who sit with Christ in
the glory.

A final word. This word *'seated'* is a fascinating word, and
obviously an important one. It is used about our Lord Himself in
connection with His resurrection and ascension. Let me give you
the quotation from Hebrews 1 : 3: 'Who, being the brightness of
his glory and the express image of his person, and upholding all
things by the word of his power, when he had by himself purged
our sins, sat down on the right hand of the Majesty on high'.
Again we read in the thirteenth verse: 'But to which of the angels
said he at any time, Sit on my right hand, until I make thine
enemies thy footstool?' And again in the tenth chapter of that
Epistle, verses twelve and thirteen: 'But this man (Christ), after
he had offered one sacrifice for sins for ever, sat down on the right
hand of God, from henceforth expecting till his enemies be made

his footstool'. That is what has happened to Him. Having done all this He sat down, waiting, expecting, until His enemies shall be made His footstool. And, in Him, we are seated with Him in the heavenly places. It means that He completed the work, and so He sat down. Sitting down is a sign of completion. When a man has finished his task he sits down. And Christ has sat down. What else does it mean? No longer labour, but rest. But still more important, victory!—'henceforth expecting until his enemies shall be made his footstool'. A sign of victory! He sits down victorious. And you and I are in Christ, and we are seated with Him in the heavenly places. The work of your redemption is already complete, you need nothing further, it has all been done—whom He has called, them has He also justified, and whom He has justified them He has also glorified.

If you are in Christ you are eternally safe, complete. *But are you enjoying the rest?* Do you realise that these things are true? Are you rejoicing in these things? Are you still trying to make yourself a Christian? If you are, you are misunderstanding your whole position, you are denying what has happened to you. Rest in the finished work of Christ—the rest of faith! 'There remaineth therefore a rest to the people of God'. Let us aim to enter into that rest, says the Word, just realising that He has done it all. But oh, that we might especially realise the victory! for we are still in the flesh and there are still the world, the flesh and the devil to contend with. We are timorous mortals, we faint and we shiver, and we are alarmed, and the devil can terrify us. We must learn to believe this truth.

Oh that God would enlighten the eyes of our understanding by His Spirit, that we may know 'the exceeding greatness of His power to us-ward who believe', that we may realise all that is true of us! 'Ye are of God, little children', says John, 'and have overcome them, because greater is he that is in you than he that is in the world.' If we only realised this truth about ourselves we would understand what James means when he says, 'Resist the devil and he will flee from you'. The devil! the one who did not hesitate to stand up against God in eternity and who dragged down a number of other angels with him; the one who was so powerful that when he approached Adam and Eve in their perfection and innocence he dragged them down! And yet it is said to you and to me: 'Resist the devil and he will flee from you'—not because he is afraid of you, but because he is afraid of the One in whom you live and who is with you, the One who has vanquished him and routed him and finally defeated him. The Apostle Peter puts it like this: 'Your adversary the devil, as a roaring lion, walketh about, seeking whom he may devour'. What do we do? Do we run and hide ourselves? Not at all!—you see this rushing beast coming at you, this devil, this Satan, this hellish power, and what do you do? 'Whom resist, steadfast in the faith.' And if you do so, he will not be able to touch you. 'They overcame him by the blood of the Lamb and by the word of their testimony.' Christian people, because we are seated with Christ in the heavenly places, the apostle Paul can say this about us in Romans 6: 14: 'Sin shall not have dominion over you, for ye are not under the law, but under grace'.

Do you know that you are in the heavenlies? Are you aware of the separation? Are you aware of the Presence? Can you draw near to God and know that He is with you and you are with Him, and all your fears are taken away? Do you see and hear something sometimes of the celestial glory and its music and its joy? Do you ever see 'the eternal glories gleaming afar to nerve your faint endeavour'? Can you say, looking at life at its very worst, 'Our light affliction, which is but for a moment, worketh for us a far more exceeding and eternal weight of glory; while we look not at the things which are seen, but at the things which are not seen: for the things which are seen are temporal; but the things which are not seen are eternal'? 'Set your affection on things above, not on things on the earth.'

10

THE EXCEEDING RICHES OF
HIS GRACE

That in the ages to come he might shew the exceeding riches of his grace in his kindness toward us through Christ Jesus.　　　Ephesians 2 : 7

These are the last words of the great statement which begins at verse 4—'But God, who is rich in mercy, for his great love wherewith he loved us, even when we were dead in sins, hath quickened us together with Christ (by grace ye are saved;) and hath raised us up together, and made us sit together in heavenly places in Christ Jesus: that in the ages to come he might show the exceeding riches of his grace in his kindness toward us through Christ Jesus'.

The apostle, you remember, has been reminding us of what God has done for us in and through our Lord and Saviour Jesus Christ. When we were in that hopeless state of sin God intervened, God acted, and quickened us together with Christ, He raised us up together with Him in newness of life, and He made us sit together with Him in the heavenly places. But now the question arises, why has God done all this? What was the motive? What was it that led God to do all this for creatures such as we are? The answer is given in this seventh verse, and is introduced by the word *that* which comes at the very beginning. He has done all this 'that', 'in order that', 'to the intent that', 'with the object, or with the objective in view, that'. . . . This word *that*, therefore, is a tremendously important word, and it is vital that we should consider together what the apostle tells us here concerning this great purpose.

How important it is for us to study the Scriptures carefully and to observe exactly what they say; because we can so easily misunderstand, as indeed we often do. Here, I think, as we consider this verse, we shall all probably feel, at least in some measure, that our view of Christianity, our view of the Church, our view of ourselves as Christian people, is defective and inadequate, that indeed our whole conception of salvation tends to be inadequate. We have already seen this as we have considered those three great steps in our salvation, and as we have seen what is already true of us as Christians because we are in Christ. We must have felt that we had never truly realised as we ought the meaning of regeneration; we had not fully grasped the completeness of justification and our standing and status in the presence of God. Still more, perhaps, as we considered that statement about our being seated in the heavenly places in Christ Jesus, we saw how we fail—and most regrettably fail—to realise that that is the truth about us even at this present moment. In other words, it seems to me, increasingly, that most of our troubles in the Christian life arise from the fact that we always start with ourselves and live so much in the realm of feeling and the subjective.

Let us be clear about this. I have been making that point constantly from the beginning of the chapter, and again it is of the very essence of what I shall have to say in expounding this seventh verse. Thank God there is a subjective element to salvation; thank God for every feeling, for every experience, for everything that we are aware of within ourselves. If we are not aware of this subjective element, then our whole position, it seems to me, is a very uncertain one. On the other hand *there is nothing which is quite so fatal to our welfare as to think only in that subjective manner and to fail to grasp with our minds and understanding this objective presentation of the truth which we have in this section* and in most of these New Testament Epistles. What I mean is, that if we only had this true scriptural conception of ourselves as we are as Christians and members of the body of Christ at this moment, most of the things which worry us would immediately fall off from us altogether. They would appear to be so trivial, so small, so unimportant.

This is something one can illustrate in this way. The best way to get rid of small things is to look at big things. Take for instance the interesting statistics which were provided, I think, by the medical authorities in Barcelona in Spain during the Spanish Civil War shortly before the second world war. They were very interesting. A given number of people had been receiving various forms of psychotherapeutic and psychological treatments; but the moment the Civil War came and affected Barcelona acutely, the number dwindled almost to nothing. What was it due to? It was the larger concern that had driven out the lesser concerns. And the same thing happened, of course, in this country during the last war. When suddenly the crisis came and husbands and sons had to go off to battle, many people forgot their aches and pains. These things which had been so prominent in their lives and which had meant so much to them were suddenly forgotten, for a greater fear had driven out the lesser fears; the bigger crisis had made other things so trivial as really to be quite irrelevant. We are all familiar with such facts.

Now all that is equally true in the Christian life. As we live our lives we are troubled by this and that, and we tend to grumble and to complain; we wonder why God is dealing with us like this and why certain things are allowed to happen to us. The antidote to all this is to see ourselves objectively as we really are in the purpose of God. And if we could but do so, all these difficulties would disappear. Or let me put it like this. If we had but some small conception of the glory which awaits us, and to which we are going, it would transform our view of our life in this world and of the things that happen to us in this world. That is the sort of treatment the apostle is going to apply in this seventh verse. This is the cure for the self-centredness and self-concern which lead eventually to introspection and morbidity and various other forms of trouble. The thing to do—and that is why the apostle writes this letter and why every New Testament letter was ever written—is to get such people to lift up their heads and to see themselves objectively in the grand purpose and plan of God.

Let us then look at this verse in this way. *Why has God done all this?* Why has He intervened? Why has he quickened us and raised us and set us to sit with Christ in the heavenly places? The answer, says the apostle, is that this is a part of His great and His grand purpose—'that', 'in order that . . .' Let us look at it in the form of a number of propositions.

The first is this: *The chief end, intent, and object of salvation is the glory of God.* That is why He has done it—'that in the ages to come he (God Himself) might show the exceeding riches of his grace in his kindness toward us through Christ Jesus'. God has done all this, says Paul, in order that He may present a spectacle to all future ages, not only in this world but also in that which is to come. God is going to give a great demonstration, He is going to manifest His own glory. You notice that that is the thing which the apostle puts first. That is the chief reason why God has done all this, he says. Now immediately, the question arises, Do we normally think of these things like that? Is it not the truth to say, of most of us probably, that we do the exact opposite? We start with ourselves; and we think of salvation as something for us, something we need, something we want, something we are concerned about. We are always subjective, we always start with ourselves. But the thing we have to learn is this, that the first objective and the first intent in salvation has in a sense—do not misunderstand me—nothing to do with us at all, but with the glory of God. That is the teaching of the whole Scripture from beginning to end. In other words we must not even start, as we habitually do, with our own sins, but with sin. We must learn to view all these things more historically. It is extremely difficult, is it not? It is extremely difficult for any generation to take the historical view, because we are in the world at a particular moment and there are various problems—we hear the news on the wireless, we see the headlines in the papers—and we are so immersed in them that we tend to see nothing else. It is extremely difficult, is it not, to realise that there were people in this world a hundred years ago, and that they had problems and difficulties? It is still more difficult to realise that there were people in this world a thousand years ago who never thought of us at all. We feel that we are so important and that our time in this world, just our little sector, is the whole of history. But those who were here before us felt the same; and we can be equally certain that in a hundred years', and, if our Lord does not return before then, a thousand years' time the generations then on earth will never give us a thought at all. But how difficult it is for us to realise that! And yet that is the very thing we have to do. We have got to learn to view ourselves and the whole problem of man, the whole crisis of history, and especially the whole subject of salvation, in this objective, historical manner.

What I mean is this. Instead of starting with myself and my own sins and my own problems, I must learn to think in terms of sin, and the whole problem of man, and the whole problem of evil in this world. Now it is only as I do this that I sha'l begin to see what the apostle means when he says that the first intent and object of salvation is the glory of God. It is very difficult for us to realise what sin and the Fall meant to God. Sin is that which is utterly opposed to God, and, therefore, what has happened as the result of sin and the Fall, and all its consequences in the world and amongst men, is (if I may put it reverently) a tremendous matter in the sight of God. But we will persist in thinking of this whole problem in terms of particular sins, this particular thing that gets me down, and the sins we put up in a list—you know them, drunkenness, gambling and so forth. That to us is the whole problem; we turn the problem of sin more or less into a social problem. It is either a social problem or the problem of our own personal happiness. We dislike the feeling of remorse and repentance, because it is painful. So we reduce the whole great problem of sin to such proportions and to such dimensions. But the Bible does not! The Bible views all sin as an attack upon God. The devil came forward and asserted himself against God, he raised himself up against the majesty and the sovereignty and the glory of God. He disputed this, he wanted to set himself up at the very least as a rival god. And when he saw God creating the world and creating man, and God looking at it and saying that it was all 'very good' and that He was pleased with it, the devil determined to ruin it. So he entered in. What was his object? Do you think that the object of the devil was merely to persuade Eve and Adam to do just one particular thing? Of course it was not! The devil had but one idea in his mind and that was to detract from the glory and the majesty and the greatness of God. He was little concerned in what should happen to Adam and Eve. The devil takes very little interest in you and me as persons. We are not persons to him, we are pawns, we are simply things that he can use in the great game. And yet we think of it all in terms of ourselves! The devil regards us with contempt, as he did Adam and Eve. He fawned upon them, he flattered them, because he knew that that was the way to make pawns of them. He had no interest in them at all as such. His one object was to detract from the glory and the majesty and the greatness of God. He was out to spoil God's work and God's world; he was out to ridicule it. He desired to stand up and to address all the holy angels and say: God makes claims for Himself, He says He has made a perfect world, but look at it, look at His perfect world!

That is the way to look at the problem of sin. The Fall is a terrible thing in God's sight. It is not primarily a social problem, it is a much more crucial problem in the sight of God. Of course there is a social problem. Sin raises many social problems, but they are the by-product, not the real thing that makes sin sin. If I may so put it, God would never have sent His Son from heaven to earth and to the cross of Calvary to solve a social problem. The problem to God was His own glory, His own majesty, His own everlasting greatness. This had been queried and questioned by the devil and all who belong to him. And what is salvation? Salvation, the whole purpose and object of salvation in the first instance, is to vindicate God, is for God again to manifest the truth concerning Himself. The devil is described in the Scripture as 'a liar and the father of lies'; and the apostle John tells us in the third chapter of his first Epistle that God sent His Son into this world in order to destroy the works of the devil. That is the first object, that the whole character of God should be vindicated. Of course, the devil in an ultimate sense did not, and cannot and could not, affect the being and the nature and the character of God, but in the sight of created beings he could, and he most certainly did. He succeeded in the case of all the fallen angels; he succeeded in the case of Adam and Eve and the whole of their posterity. And the whole problem in the world today is the attitude of man towards God. So God has initiated this great movement of redemption and of salvation primarily in order to declare and to manifest and to vindicate again His own glory, His own greatness and the truth about Himself. Why has He done it? He has done it 'that in the ages to come he might *show* (display) the exceeding riches of his grace in his kindness toward us through Christ Jesus'.

Have you thought of salvation like that? One question to ask is: Why did God ever send His Son? God forbid that we should give some sentimental, subjective answers only, and fail to see that God sent Him in order to vindicate Himself. It is the grandest theodicy of the ages; God is vindicating and declaring and showing the truth concerning Himself.

Let us now turn to a second proposition. *Salvation vindicates the greatness and the character of God in a special way and in a manner which nothing else does.* There is no question about this. We learn certain things about God in this whole movement of salvation and redemption which we would never have known otherwise. That may sound a daring statement, but I venture to make it. People have often asked the question—nobody can answer it, but it is a question that many have asked, indeed we all have asked it—Why did the almighty God ever allow the Fall? Why did He ever allow man to fall into sin? The ultimate answer is that we do not know, and we should not enquire because it is beyond us. But at any rate we can say this and we know this: If God had not allowed the possibility, man would not have been entirely free, and therefore he would not have been entirely perfect. Man, as God made him, really did have free will. He lost it by falling into sin, but he had it originally; and it was a part of man's perfection. But whatever the explanation, it is clear that God has overruled it in such a way that through redemption He has displayed certain attributes of His holy being and nature and character which otherwise could never be known, but which now most certainly are known.

The apostle has already mentioned some of them. Listen to him: 'God, who is rich in *mercy*'. Would it be possible to have the same conception of God's richness in mercy if man had not fallen into sin as he has done? It is through this that God manifests the endlessness of His mercy. 'Rich in mercy!' Then, 'For his great *love* wherewith he loved us'. Man certainly knew something about the love of God before he fell; Adam knew the love of God. I wonder, however, whether the love of God would ever have been known as it is now known were it not for the Fall and the movement of redemption? God is showing it, He is displaying it, He is manifesting it, there is an unfolding of it in a manner that surely is not conceivable apart from this. Then the apostle goes on to this next great term: 'Even when we were dead in sins hath quickened us together with Christ; (by grace . . .'—there it comes in—'by grace ye are saved); and hath raised us up together and made us sit together in the heavenly places in Christ Jesus, that in the ages to come he might show the exceeding riches of his *grace*'. There is nothing that enables us to have such an understanding of the extent of the grace of God as this does. It is the ultimate measure of it; and nothing can show it as this shows it. Then the last term is 'kindness'—'in his kindness', in His look of benignity. Adam knew something about the kindness of God, but I agree with Isaac Watts when he claims in his hymn—'In Him (in Christ) the tribes of Adam boast more blessings than their father lost'. I say it reverently, weighing my words, that we in Christ know something of God which Adam in his state of innocence did not know, and which, in a sense, Adam could not know. It may be speculation, but it seems to me to be the teaching of Scripture that God has shown these things here in a unique manner and in a way that He has never shown anywhere else.

But what is, perhaps, most important for us, is the third pro-position. *All this display and vindication of the character and the being and the greatness and the glory of God comes to pass through the Church.* God does this tremendous thing by means of us and through us, in the first instance. Look at it again: He has done all this 'that in the ages to come he might show the exceeding riches of his grace in his kindness toward us, through Christ Jesus'. This is to me the most overwhelming thought that we can ever lay hold of, that the almighty, everlasting, eternal God is vindicating Himself and His holy nature and being, by something that He does in us and with us and through us. This is Christianity, this is the meaning of church membership, this is what it is to be a Christian; nothing less than this! Here, we are taken right out of our little subjective states and moods and feelings and passing conditions, and we see ourselves suddenly in this great plan of eternity which God brought into being and into operation as the result of the Fall of man into sin.

Let us examine this glorious conception. The apostle teaches it very plainly in this verse. He states it still more clearly and explicitly in the tenth verse of the third chapter of this Epistle. The apostle is describing this great mystery which had been hidden but which now has been revealed. What is it for? It is 'to make all men see what is the fellowship of the mystery which from the beginning of the world hath been hid in God, who created all things by Jesus Christ' (v. 9). And then in verse ten: 'to the intent that'—the same idea; this is the object, this is the intent, this is the purpose—'to the intent that now unto the principalities and powers in the heavenly places might be known *by the church* the manifold wisdom of God'. That is the idea. God is using the Church, and is going to use the Church, in the future ages, in order to give a demonstration and an exhibition to the principalities and the powers in the heavenly places of His own eternal and amazing wisdom.

That is the way to think of ourselves as Christians and as members of the Christian Church. God is vindicating Himself and His character by you and by me, by people such as ourselves, by the whole of the Church gathered in Christ out of the world. He is going to put us on display, as it were; there is going to be a glorious exhibition. He is already doing it, but it is going to continue in the ages to come, and at the consummation God is going to open His last great exhibition and all these heavenly powers and principalities will be invited to attend. The curtain will draw back and God will say, Look at them! 'To the intent that now unto the principalities and powers in the heavenly places might be known *by the church* the manifold wisdom of God!' You and I are being prepared for that. You read of artists preparing their paintings and their drawings for exhibition, and of how they add the final finishing touches—the frame must be right, it must be put in the right position, the light must come from the correct angle, and so on. We all know about it; we have seen people preparing animals for horse shows; or fruit and vegetables for a horticultural show—the picking out, the preparing. Well, that is what is happening to you and to me. That is the meaning of a service of public worship and preaching—it is just a part of it. The exhibition, the show, the display is coming! And the astounding and amazing thing is that it is through people like ourselves, and as the result of what He is doing to us and has done to us and will do to us, that God is going to vindicate His own eternal wisdom and His majesty and His glory and all the attributes of His holy Person to the principalities and the heavenly powers.

It seems to me that this is expressed perfectly in the seventh chapter of the book of Revelation. John has his vision—'I beheld, and lo, a great multitude which no man could number, of all nations and kindreds and people and tongues, stood before the throne and before the Lamb, clothed with white robes, and palms in their hands, and cried with a loud voice saying, Salvation to our God which sitteth upon the throne, and unto the Lamb'. John saw these people clad in white robes and with palms in their hands, singing the praise of God and saying, 'Salvation to our God that sitteth upon the throne'. But what I particularly like is the question put by the elder who stood by to John, saying, 'Who are these?'—'What are these that are arrayed in white robes and whence came they?' These who are standing here with palms in their hands and singing the praises of God, who are they? That will be the question asked by the principalities and powers in the heavenly places. The curtain will be withdrawn and there we shall be in our white robes and with the palms in our hands, and the principalities and powers will ask—Who are these? what are they? what is this phenomenon? what are these people? where have they come from? And the answer will be that they are Christian people, the Christians of all centuries, of all nations and tribes and countries and colours, gathered out by the power of Christ's redemption through the ages, all finally gathered together there in the glory. 'Who are these?', where have they come from, what are they? And the answer is, These are the people redeemed by the wisdom and the power and the glory and the love and the grace of God. 'By the church!' You and I! Miserable creatures that we are, with our aches and pains and 'mumps and measles of soul', and our questions and queryings, and our, 'Why does God do this and that?' I beseech you, look into heaven, cast your mind into the glory. Shame on us, Christian people, for our wretched subjectivity, and our failure to realise who we are and what we are, and what is happening to us, and what God is doing in us and through us! This is the intent of salvation, that all this might be done to the vindication of the character and the glory of God.

The next proposition *helps us to see how God does this through the Church*. We need not stay with it as we have already considered it in part. There we are, of the Church, in the white robes, with the palms, in the glory, in the presence of God. How have we got there? how has it happened? The first wonder is that He has ever looked upon us at all, such as we were, 'dead in trespasses and sins, walking according to the course of this world, the spirit that now worketh in the children of disobedience; amongst whom we all had our conversation in times past, in the lusts of our flesh, fulfilling the desires of the flesh and of the mind, and were by nature the children of wrath even as others'. How could He ever have looked upon us? We deserved nothing but retribution and punishment and hell. If you feel that you deserve anything better, you do not know what you are as a sinner, and you know nothing, I am afraid, about the grace of God. Miserable, vile, foul, wretches and rebels—that He ever even looked upon us! What a display of His being and of His holy nature! We are a demonstration of that. If He had not looked upon us we would still be in our sins and going to perdition. But there we are, in glory, because He looked upon us and had mercy and pity upon us.

Not only that, He devised and planned a way of delivering us. He made the way of salvation Himself. Man did not ask for it, man did not want it, man did not know what he needed, man was not consulted, he has not put in a single suggestion. Salvation is entirely of God from beginning to end. That is the apostle's whole point: 'By grace you have been saved', and nothing less. What a display of the being and the character of God!

And then the wonder that He should have done to us what He has done, that He should have made of us what He has made, that we are already quickened, that He has put a principle of spiritual life into us who were utterly, absolutely, hopelessly dead! He has put new life into us, His own life; He has raised us up together with Christ, we are alive to Him, we have the new interests and the new outlook, we are seated in the heavenly places. He has done all this to us already, but when we are there in the glory with the white robe and the palm we shall be absolutely perfect, without spot or even a wrinkle, or any such thing. There will not be a suspicion of a blemish; the most powerful magnifying glass will find nothing wrong about us; we shall be absolutely whole and entire, purified from all traces of sin. It is not surprising that the elder asked, 'Who are these?' and 'How have they become like this? What is this spotless whiteness, this glory?' It is but the manifestation of God's character and being. Through the Church He does it in that particular way.

That brings me to the last proposition, which is simply a very practical question. *How should we think of ourselves in the light of all this?* Surely it is obvious. If you think at all of your own goodness, it just means that you have never seen this at all. If you think that you are a Christian and a good church member because you have lived a good life and never done anybody any harm, and because you are giving a good deal of your time to these things, you are just telling me that you have never understood it. If you can find anything in yourself at this moment to be pleased about, you have never seen this truth, that God has done it all to the intent that now unto the principalities and powers in the heavenly places might be known His own manifold wisdom, that He might display the exceeding riches of His grace. If you feel that you have got any plea to offer at the throne of grace and of mercy save the name of Jesus Christ, you have just never seen it, you are just blind. Our one thought should be this: 'A debtor to mercy alone, of covenant mercy I sing'; 'I am what I am by the grace of God'—nothing in me; 'Nothing in my hands I bring'; I find no good in myself; 'In me, that is, in my flesh, dwelleth no good thing' at all; I have nothing to recommend me, I have nothing to boast of at all. I am nothing; He is everything, GOD!—His grace in Christ Jesus! If you see this, then inevitably you will think in this way.

And it follows from that, that *we should also conduct ourselves in a given way*. 'Every man that hath this hope in him purifieth himself, even as he is pure' (1 John 3: 3). A man who has seen himself as a member of the Church and of the body of Christ in the way we are considering will no longer want to keep as near as he can to the world, and will not regard Christianity as narrow because it condemns certain things. Not for a moment! If we could but see those whom we know, who have now gone beyond the veil, we would say farewell to most of the things of this world. Any man who sees this, any man who has this hope in him, purifies himself, even as He is pure. If you know you are going to be absolutely pure and spotless, well, get on with it, wash your hands,' clear ;e your hearts, ye double-minded.' These are the New Testament appeals. Get as far away from the world as you can. 'Haste thee on from grace to glory.'

The other thing I find here is *the absolute certainty of it all* and the assurance of it all. If my confidence of my final salvation and of my ultimate perfection rested in myself, my own energy, my own zeal, my own purposes and desires, I know that I should never get there. My assurance is based on this, that God, the infinite, eternal God, is vindicating His own eternal character through me. And if He started saving me and then left the work undone or unfinished, and I duly arrived in hell, the devil would have the greatest joy of eternity. He would say, There is a being that God began to save, but it all ended up in failure. It is impossible, it cannot happen; there is no more monstrous idea than the idea that you can fall away from grace, that you can ever be born again and then be damned. The character of God is involved! It is impossible. His object is not merely to save me, it is to vindicate His own being and nature, and I am being used to that end. The end is absolutely certain because God's character is involved in it. 'He that hath begun a good work in you will perform it until the day of Jesus Christ.'

The last word is an obvious one. *The privilege of it all!* The privilege of being used of God in this way to vindicate His own eternal, glorious character! Why am I in this? Why did He ever look upon me? As the elder asks, 'Who are these?' I ask, 'Who am I?' You remember David asking the question when God gave him a glimpse of where he came in this great plan, 'Who am I or what is my house that this great honour should come to me?' And do we not all feel like saying that? Who am I, and what am I, that God should ever have looked upon me and chosen me to be a part of His plan and His purpose, to vindicate Himself, His greatness, His glory, His wisdom, His love, His mercy, His kindness, His compassion, before the principalities and the powers in the heavenly places?

Christian people, think of yourselves like that, and go on to glory.

11

THROUGH CHRIST JESUS*

That in the ages to come he might shew the exceeding riches of his grace in his kindness toward us through Christ Jesus. Ephesians 2:7

We must look once more at this magnificent statement which begins at the fourth verse. We can never do so too frequently. 'But God, who is rich in mercy, for his great love wherewith he loved us, even when we were dead in sins, hath quickened us together with Christ (by grace ye are saved); and hath raised us up together, and made us sit together in heavenly places in Christ Jesus: that in the ages to come he might show the exceeding riches of his grace in his kindness toward us through Christ Jesus'.

I want particularly now to consider those last three words: 'through Christ Jesus'. For there you have the whole gospel and particularly the whole essence of the Christmas message.

The apostle has been explaining that in doing all that He has done to us as Christians, God has been displaying the glory of His being and His ways. But in verse seven he goes on to tell us that God is displaying His glory, and the wonders of His grace, not only by what He has done and will do in us and through us and upon us, but still more by the way in which He has done it—'in His kindness toward us *through Christ Jesus*'.

Paul can never leave that out. I fear that many of us can and do leave it out, but Paul never forgets it. This name!—you find it everywhere, in all his Epistles. Watch them, read them and see how he keeps on repeating it—the name of Jesus Christ. If ever a man could use and appropriate the words of the well-known hymn: 'How sweet the name of Jesus sounds in a believer's ear', it is the apostle Paul. Notice how he keeps on repeating it here all along: 'in him'; 'together with Christ'; in heavenly places 'in Christ Jesus'. And having used it so often, you would have thought he might have ended by saying 'that in the ages to come he might show the exceeding riches of his grace in his kindness toward us'. But he must say it again—'in his kindness toward us through Christ Jesus'. Here we come to the point at which, of all points, we can

* This sermon was preached on the Sunday before Christmas.

really begin to measure these exceeding riches of God's grace. Some people would translate the words in this way: 'that He might show the immeasurable riches . . .'; or in the words that the apostle uses in the next chapter in the eighth verse: 'the unsearchable riches'.

But before we come to look at these expressions let me emphasise one point. *It is through Christ Jesus that we derive every benefit.* Is it not astonishing that it is still necessary to say this, and to emphasise it? What vast numbers of men and women still think of the blessings that come from God, apart from Christ Jesus! There are thousands of people in the world today who are worshippers of God, as they think, and are anxious to be blessed by God, and believe that they are being blessed by God, but they seem to be able to speak about all that without mentioning Christ Jesus. They talk about praying to God, they talk about being blessed by God, of being healed by God, being led by God, and so on, but they do not mention the name of Jesus Christ. The apostle was aware of that danger, that is why he never misses an opportunity of saying, 'through Christ Jesus'. The whole essence of Christianity is to say that God deals with man and blesses man *only* in and through Christ Jesus. Everything comes from God to us through Him.

It would be a very simple matter to prove this by endless quotations, but take just our Lord's own words: 'I am the way, the truth, and the life; no man cometh to the Father but by me' (John 14: 6). Surely that ought to be enough in and of itself. We cannot pray without Him; we pray in His name, we pray for His name's sake. We have nothing to plead but Him. How can we approach God without Him? How could anything come to us apart from Him? John, you remember, in the prologue to his Gospel puts it in exactly the same way. Referring to the Lord Jesus Christ he says, 'and of his fulness have all we received, and grace for grace'. It is all in and through our Lord and Saviour Jesus Christ. 'God was in Christ (through Christ) reconciling the world unto himself.' That is how He does reconcile the world; and all blessings from God come to us and flow into us through Him. He is 'the head of the church which is his body, the fulness of him that filleth all in all'. The Church is His body. We derive all our life, every blessing, every power and our very sustenance from the fact that we are members of Him. He is the Head, we are members in particular in the body. Everything comes from the Head, and we enjoy, therefore, every blessing that we possess, through Christ Jesus. Can I assume, therefore, that we are all clear about this, that (as Paul puts it elsewhere) we are entirely 'shut up unto Christ'? The very law itself was the schoolmaster, the pedagogue, to bring us to Christ, to shut us up to Christ, to make us see that we cannot know God or derive any blessing from God except in and through Christ Jesus. He is the only channel, the one and only Mediator between God and man. It is everywhere—'*through Christ Jesus*'.

The thing to which I want to advert particularly now, and to emphasise, is the way in which God has done all this through Christ Jesus. And it is here we most especially see something of the unsearchable character, *the immeasurable character of the riches of God's grace*. Here we are looking at the matter from the God-ward side. We have already been looking at it from our side, but now, I repeat, we are looking at it from the God-ward side. The way in which we do a thing is often much more significant than the thing itself which we do. And that is true about the way in which God blesses mankind through the Lord Jesus Christ. It is a wonderful thing, an amazing thing, and indicative of exceeding riches in God's grace that He should bless us at all. Let us imagine that God had blessed us, as it were, directly from the heavens, that He had looked upon us and that He had done certain things for us, as He indeed does in the regular working of providence. That in itself is wonderful for we deserve nothing. We have seen our character in the first three verses. There is nothing too bad that can be said about man in sin, nothing. He is as vile a creature as is imaginable; but in spite of that, God looks upon us and blesses us. 'He maketh his sun to rise on the evil and on the good, and sendeth rain on the just and on the unjust' (Matthew 5: 45).

The very fact that He even looks upon us is indicative of unsearchable riches of grace. But we have something here that goes beyond that. For it is possible for us sometimes to do a kindness to other persons without sacrificing anything ourselves at all. A multi-millionaire sees some poor pauper. He does not know him, he has no interest in him, and he may even find him to be an offensive person to look at. It would be a very fine and a very generous and a very noble thing for this multi-millionaire to make that man a gift, especially if the man has offended him in some way. Suppose he give him a thousand pounds! It is very generous, but it really has not cost that multi-millionaire anything; he is hardly aware of the fact that he has given anything at all. In and of itself, it is great generosity; it is very great kindness, especially if that poor fellow has done something unworthy or wrong with respect to the wealthy man. The act, in and of itself, is wonderful. But what would greatly add to the value of that act would be that the millionaire should actually make a personal sacrifice to help the man. In other words, the ultimate measure of our actions is what they cost us. I do not want to detract for a moment from the intrinsic value of generosity; it is fine in its place, but when it involves personal suffering or personal loss in order to help another, then it becomes immeasurably greater.

Now, it is something like that that we are considering here. I speak carefully and with reverence but I do suggest that it is as we look at it from this aspect that we really begin to have some kind of a measure of the immeasurable riches of God's grace. Such a statement is paradoxical, and yet it conveys true meaning. We never shall be able to measure it; it is beyond that; it is so wonderful that man's measures are totally inadequate; and yet the Scriptures exhort us to make the effort. Let us go on, let us go as far as we can go. That, it seems to me, is what the apostle is exhorting us to do here. He prays that the eyes of our understanding may be enlightened that we may try to measure the immeasurable and try to scale these heights, the topmost level of which can never be reached. We are attempting to measure, to compute, to assess what God has really done. This is how He is going to display the exceeding riches of His grace in all those future ages 'by his kindness toward us'". Yes, but—the way He did it—'through Christ Jesus'!

What does it mean? I speak carefully for this reason, that we are obviously looking into the mystery, not only of God's love, but into the mystery of God's being. It is here that we cease to understand, and so must 'take off the shoes from off our feet' (Exodus 3: 5). But let us observe what the Scriptures say. If you want to measure the unsearchable riches, or the exceeding riches of the grace of God in Christ Jesus, you can start by *looking at the problem from the standpoint of the Father Himself*. Here is the question: Can God suffer, does God suffer? The theologians have argued on this great and important question: 'The Passibility of God or the Impassibility of God'; is God passible, or is God impassible? A tremendous subject! We can never decide it, we cannot fathom it. At this point our minds begin to boggle and we begin to speculate. We do not understand and are obviously not meant to, partly because of our finite, and still more because of our sinful, condition. And yet it seems to me that we must be careful, on the other hand, that we do not ignore scriptural statements, or in addition, that we do not detract from them. There are certain things which are stated in the Scripture which we should study and consider, think about and meditate upon, with the greatest possible care. At any rate we surely must say this, that what God has done for us through Christ Jesus was not done without cost to God.

Look at the matter from the standpoint of God as Father. These are the terms that are used: 'When the fulness of the times was come, God *sent forth* his Son, made of a woman, made under the law'. I am interested in the 'sending forth'. Oh, you may say, it is an anthropomorphism, that is, a condescension to our human inability, that God should represent Himself in that manner. Yes, but there is a truth in the representation, there *was* a sending forth. The Son, the Lord Jesus Christ, was in the bosom of the Father from all eternity, dwelling eternally with God, co-equal and co-eternal. God the Father sends Him forth. I do not understand fully what it meant to God, but I do know that we are meant to think of it in these human terms, that God did send Him forth. And that is where we ask the question: What did that mean to God the Father? It is through Christ Jesus that He is going to show the unsearchable riches of His grace, it is through this action that all the principalities and powers in the heavenly places are going to admire the manifold wisdom of God; not only what they see in the Church, but also in the way God has brought the Church into being, 'through Christ Jesus'.

Take some other terms. 'God so loved the world that he *gave* his only begotten Son' (John 3: 16). What a pregnant word—He 'gave'! He gave His only Son! Now we are familiar with these terms. We talk about people giving their lives for their country, we talk about parents giving their children to be foreign missionaries; they give them, they send them forth, they let them go. Giving—but it costs! These are the terms that are used about God. But take another, a still more striking expression: 'He that *spared* not his own Son, but delivered him up for us all, how shall he not with him also freely give us all things?' (Romans 8: 32). Look at that great statement and notice the terms: He did not 'spare' Him. Is God passible or impassible? What does that word 'spare' mean? God the Father knew what was necessary before the way of salvation could be made, what was necessary before He could still 'be just and the justifier of him that believeth in Jesus' (Romans 3: 26). He knew what it would involve for the Son in suffering, and He did not spare Him, but delivered Him up to all that was meant in that death, that cruel, agonising death. He knew it all, He did not spare Him, He delivered Him up, for us all. Now these are the terms with which we have to grapple as we consider this great question of the passibility of God. But there are others. 'He hath *made him to be sin* for us, who knew no sin, that we might be made the righteousness of God in him' (2 Corinthians 5: 21). God the Father has made His own Son to be sin—not a sinner, He has made Him to be sin, with which He was going to deal—for us, that we might be made the righteousness of God in Him. And that of course points back to some of those extraordinary statements in the fifty-third chapter of the Book of the Prophet Isaiah: 'The Lord hath laid on him the iniquity of us all'. Did God do that without feeling? Did God do that without suffering? It is a great mystery.

But if we want really to understand what happened on that first Christmas Day when Christ was born in Bethlehem, we must look into these things. We take it so much for granted, we take it so easily. 'God sent His own Son; John 3: 16; we all know all about it.' Do we? Do we know anything about it, I wonder? We talk so glibly about the love of God. Have we ever considered what it meant to God? 'He hath laid on him the iniquity of us all.' 'It hath pleased the Father'—we read again—'It hath pleased the Lord to bruise him'; it was His pleasure; not that it gave Him pleasure, but it was His pleasure, His will, that He should bruise Him. He bruised His own Son, for us. That is where you get a measure of the exceeding riches of His grace. 'He hath put him to grief.' Verily He, God, has put Him, His only begotten Son, to grief, in order that you and I might become His children, and in order that we might enjoy the exceeding riches of His grace. But you do not begin to measure that grace until you take these three words, 'through Christ Jesus'. That is how God has done it. There we have just a glimpse of it, from the standpoint of the Father, the event itself which has taken place as it was and is in God Himself. The unsearchable riches of His grace! Who can measure this? Who can understand this? That is our gospel, that God the Father has sent Him forth and has given Him, and has laid upon Him the iniquity of us all. 'Through Christ Jesus!'

But let us *look at it for a moment from the standpoint of the Son*, the One who came and to whom all this happened. Here again we are involved in what Carlyle would call 'infinities and immensities', which baffle us and cause the brain to boggle. How can we measure this? Well, the apostle teaches us something of it, particularly in writing to the Philippians in the second chapter, verses 5–11. We know that it meant this for the Son: there is the One who was in the eternal glory, in the bosom of the Father, co-equal, co-eternal, sharing the glory of God in all its fulness—in '*the form of God*'. Do you know what your salvation meant inevitably to the Son? It meant a decision not to hold on to all the privileges and the signs of that eternal glory. 'Though He was in the form of God, He counted it not robbery to be equal with God,' says the Authorised Version, or, according to a more accurate translation, He did not regard that as a prize to be held on to at all costs. He did not say to the Father: I am not going to leave all this behind in order to save those people who have rebelled against You. I am anxious to help them, and to do anything I can, but I cannot do this; I cannot lay aside for the time being, the insignia of My glory, the marks of My eternal Godhead; I cannot do that. I am prepared to do anything, but I cannot do that. He said the exact opposite! 'He thought it not robbery to be equal with God'. He regarded the insignia of His Godhead not as a prize to be held on to, to be clutched. He deliberately decided that He would for the time being lay them aside. Not lay the Godhead aside—He could not do that—He did not lay the Godhead aside, but He did lay the signs of the Godhead aside.

Then after that first initial decision the second followed, and of necessity. '*He made himself of no reputation.*' How superior the Authorised Version is here to the Revised Version and others, which say here 'He emptied himself'! No, He did not empty Himself, He did not empty Himself at all. He 'made himself'—still remaining what He was—'of no reputation'. There is no 'kenosis' in the sense of evacuating Himself of His Godhead, for that is impossible. It is something much more wonderful than that. It is that He decided to 'make himself of no reputation'. Though still the eternal Son of God, He came down to earth, and He was born as a babe and He lived as a man. He was still the same but He made Himself of no reputation. We read stories of great kings putting on ragged clothing and going to work with their hands; nobody knew them, nobody recognised them. What had happened? The king had made himself of no reputation, he pretended to be an ordinary man, he did not take with him the trappings and the insignia of his regal position; in other words, he made himself of no reputation. Or you can think of it in terms of a king travelling incognito. That is the very thing that happened in the incarnation. That is what happened when the Son of God came down on earth to dwell amongst men. Though He remained exactly what He always was, He came as a Man and took upon Him the form of a servant.

There, we are beginning to measure the exceeding riches of God's grace. That is what your salvation and mine has meant and has cost. We are interested in the exceeding riches of His grace, and we are just measuring something of it. How easy it is to sentimentalise about the Babe of Bethlehem! But as you look at Him, go back, go back into eternity, consider what it meant for Him to come here, and what it involved! How vital it is to be theological and doctrinal in all our thinking concerning Him! You think with your mind, and only then do you feel with your heart. You do not start with your heart, you start with your head, with your mind, with your understanding. The apostle has already prayed that the eyes of our understanding may be enlightened! You are Christians, he says, but have you realised what has happened, what was involved, what it has meant? 'He made himself of no reputation'. He had to arrive at those two decisions initially before the incarnation could take place. And then it did take place. And so He came and was born of the virgin's womb—in a stable, in a little place called Bethlehem. He had taken unto Himself human nature. As I have said, He had not evacuated the Godhead out of Himself in order to become Man. Remaining still Very God of Very God, He took unto Himself human nature. So that He was now really Man as well as really God. And there we see Him lying in the manger.

As I understand this statement of the apostle, God in all this was showing forth 'the exceeding riches of his grace', and even causing the principalities and the powers and the angels in the heavenly places to be amazed—I imagine that when the angels looked down over the ramparts of heaven they said something like this:

> *Who is this so weak and helpless,*
> *Child of lowly Hebrew maid?*

That is what they said, 'Who is this?' You remember that we saw in the preceding message that these same powers will look at the glorified Church and at people like ourselves with our white robes and the palms in our hands, and say 'Who are these'? But there in Bethlehem the question was:

> *Who is this so weak and helpless,*
> *Child of lowly Hebrew maid?*

There is one answer, and one answer only ' 'Tis the Lord, the King of glory'. That is the wondrous story of the first Christmas. Or let Charles Wesley answer the question. Looking into that manger, what do we see? According to Charles Wesley:

> *Veiled in flesh the Godhead see;*
> *Hail, the incarnate Deity!*

What paradoxes! There are your measures; there are the 'immeasurable riches of God's grace'; there are the exceeding riches, the unsearchable riches—'veiled in flesh' (there is the one end) 'the Godhead see' (there is the other end). Can you measure it? 'Hail, incarnate' (yes, He is a Child, He is a Babe, He is crying like every other child; He is incarnate, He is in the flesh—but) 'Deity' (there is the other end). The immeasurable riches of God's grace! It is 'through Christ Jesus', through sending His own Son into this world in that way, that God has blessed us and shown His kindness toward us.

Then go further and *look at His life*. Have you ever stopped to think and to meditate about this? What must it have been like for the eternal Son of God to live in a world like this, a world of sin? Have you not sometimes felt a feeling of utter disgust as you have walked about the streets of London, and seen certain manifestations of sin? The ugliness, the foulness, the bestiality of it all! You have felt a sense of physical revulsion, you have been revolted—and there is nothing wrong in feeling that, for it is foul, it is terrible. But multiply that by millions, by eternity, and try to understand what it must have been like for the Son of God to have lived and dwelt in a world like this, and to have mixed with our fallen race—the One who is described as 'the friend of publicans and sinners'. This is a part of the measure of God's grace 'through Christ Jesus'. That is where you see 'the unsearchable riches of his grace'. 'He endured the contradiction of sinners against himself' for thirty-three years. And while He was here He never possessed a home of His own. 'Foxes have holes, and the birds of the air have nests', He says, 'but the Son of man hath not where to lay his head'. And then that other statement in the Gospel of John: 'Every man went unto his own house; Jesus went into the Mount of Olives'. He never had a house, He never owned a home. The One through whom all things were made, and without whom nothing was made that is made, had not a place where to lay His head, had not a home of His own. 'Through Christ Jesus!' Then think of all the plotting against Him, the buffeting, the spitting in His face, the arguing, the attempts to trip Him.

These are all facts, and we must concentrate on the facts, we must come right back to them. We are not saved by a philosophy, not by some beautiful idea, not by some marvellous fantasy or some poetic conception. No, these are literal, hard, solid facts. He came down to earth and He went through all this for us men and for our salvation. It is all literal fact. See Him in the garden of Gethsemane, sweating in an agony 'great drops as it were blood'. 'The unsearchable riches of his grace, through Christ Jesus.' *And then the cross— the pain and the suffering*! 'We may not know, we cannot tell what pains He had to bear.' But we know that He was there again in a great agony. He cried out saying, 'I thirst'. And then towering over all other suffering, the sense of desertion—'My God, my God, why hast thou forsaken me'. 'The exceeding riches of his grace in his kindness toward us through Christ Jesus.' Bearing the crushing . load of the world's sin; bearing the wrath of His holy Father; being made sin! That is the measure. And while He was enduring it all

He was still the eternal Son of God as well as Son of man. Such suffering we cannot imagine; but He suffered enough to bear the full penalty of sin. It is 'through Christ Jesus' the blessings come to us.

He dies, and they take Him and *they bury Him in a grave*. You remember how Peter put this in his address to certain unbelieving Jews, in a perfect manner, when he said, 'You put to death the Prince of life'—which means the Author of life. There, again, you have the absolute measure: 'death'—'the Author of life'. The Author of life was put to death. There is the measure of the exceeding riches of God's grace. They put Him to death, they took down His body and they buried Him in a grave and rolled a stone over the grave. That is the measure of it all. And then *God raised Him*, as Paul tells us here, and brought Him forth from amongst the dead, and took Him into heaven, and glorified Him and *exalted Him*. There is the whole movement, from the glory of eternity down to earth and the grave, and back to the glory again. That is the measure of 'the exceeding riches of His grace'.

The apostle's point is that God has done all this in order that He might show forth to all future ages His own glory and greatness, and especially the exceeding riches of His grace. And let it be emphasised again, to show it not only to men. It is indeed the theme of men, but not only of men: it is the thing that amazes angels. A hymn which we sometimes sing puts it perfectly:

> *Angels from the realms of glory,*
> *Wing your flight o'er all the earth.*
> *Ye who sang creation's story,*
> *Now proclaim Messiah's birth!*

The angels that sang on the morning of creation sang again on the morning of His birth. Never had heaven seen such a thing as this. Never had heaven such a theme as this, as this astounding event. That Babe that was born, whom they knew as the Lord, the only begotten Son of the Father, the One through whom all was created, is lying as a helpless Babe in a manger. It is not surprising that they sang and hailed Messiah's birth. And they continue to be surprised, because the apostle Peter tells us in his first Epistle that not only had the prophets under the old dispensation prophesied of these things, namely, the sufferings of Christ and the glory that should follow; and been surprised and astonished by them, but that it is also true to say, 'which things the angels desire to look into' (1 : 12). What an amazing statement! These 'things' are the 'sufferings of Christ and the glory that shall follow', the whole movement of the incarnation, the life, the atoning death, burial, the resurrection, the glorification—'which things', says Peter, 'the angels desire to look into'. He uses a very interesting word there. That word 'desire', means a very intense and a very strong desire. Indeed it includes a further idea which is that they stooped down in order to look into it. 'Which things the angels are stooping down to look at!' The incarnation of the Son! The death of the Author of life! The burial of the Creator! It is the most astonishing thing. The angels are amazed, and they worship and they praise God as they see this manifestation, this display, this showing of the exceeding riches of His grace. What amazes them is not only the fact that rebels, miserable sinners such as you and I, should be quickened with a new spiritual life and raised again and made alive unto God, and be ultimately glorified and spend our eternity in His presence—that is amazing, and they are marvelling at that—but when they consider the way in which God has done it all, even their power of expression fails and becomes inadequate. This is something surpassing everything, that God should have so loved the world as to give, even to the shameful, cruel death of the cross, His only begotten Son, that whosoever believes in Him—without any works or merit—should not perish, but have everlasting life. 'That in the ages to come He might show the exceeding riches of His grace in His kindness toward us through Christ Jesus.'

12

BY GRACE THROUGH FAITH

For by grace are ye saved through faith; and that not of yourselves: it is the gift of God: Not of works, lest any man should boast. For we are his workmanship, created in Christ Jesus unto good works, which God hath before ordained that we should walk in them. Ephesians 2: 8–10

In these three verses the apostle summarises the great argument which he has been conducting in the first seven verses of this chapter. He brings it all to a focus. I suppose that in certain respects we can say that there is no more important doctrinal statement anywhere in the Epistle. Of course it is all packed with doctrine, as we have seen; but certainly from our standpoint, and in order to have a true and a clear understanding of what it is that makes us Christian, there is nothing that is more important than this particular statement. And therefore, obviously, it is equally important in a practical sense.

Here is a statement, surely, that must be determinative in all evangelism. In the same way it must determine our entire practice of the Christian life, because belief and practice cannot be separated. You cannot separate finally a man's view of these things from his whole relationship to them. That is why I say that we are here face to face with one of the most crucial statements that is to be found anywhere in Scripture, and that is obviously why the apostle puts it in this particular form. For the same reason also he has already prayed in the previous chapter that the eyes of our understanding may be enlightened. We can never repeat that too frequently. This great Epistle, perhaps the greatest of all the Epistles in some senses, packed as it is with profound theology and doctrinal statements, nevertheless was written primarily in order to help people in a practical and pastoral manner. In other words, we must not think of it as being first and foremost an attempt on the part of the apostle to write a theological treatise. The apostle was not a professional theologian—I wonder whether there ever should be such a thing? The apostle was a preacher and an evangelist. Such a man, of course, must be a theologian—if he is not he cannot be a true evangelist—but it was not a professional matter. The apostle's approach is not academic, it is not theoretical; he was concerned to help these people to live the Christian life. That was why he wrote to them. But he knew that no person can live this Christian life unless he first of all has a true understanding of what it is that makes us Christians at all. Therefore as Paul writes to them he must start with this great doctrine and then go on to its application.

That is what he is doing here, and his prayer for them is that the eyes of their understanding might be enlightened, that they might know the hope of God's calling, the riches of the glory of His inheritance in the saints, and, perhaps most important of all, the exceeding greatness of His power to us-ward that believe. That was their trouble; they did not realise that power. And this is our trouble—our failure to realise the exceeding greatness of the power of God in us who believe. So he has gone on to unfold it and expound it and to put it clearly before them. He has stated it in great detail: the negative description in verses 1 to 3; the positive in verses 4 to 7. Having stated it in detail he says: Now then, it all comes to this . . . You notice that he starts with the word 'For'—'For by grace ye are saved'. It is a continuation; he is looking back to what he has been saying, and then he puts it all once more in a manner that we should never forget.

This is a description of what it really means to be a Christian. More and more am I convinced that most of our troubles in the Christian life really arise at that point. For if we are not right at the beginning we shall be wrong everywhere. And it is because so many are still confused at that very first step that they are always full of problems and difficulties and questions, and do not understand this and cannot see that. It is because they have never been clear about the foundation.

Well, here it is for us—and, as I have said, there is no clearer statement of it anywhere in the Scripture. Why then the confusion? The confusion often arises because people turn these great statements of the apostle into matters of controversy. And they do that because they will insist on bringing in their philosophy, by which I mean their own ideas. Instead of taking the plain statements of the apostle they say: But I cannot see this. If that is so, then I do not understand how God can be a God of love. In other words, they begin philoso-phising, and, of course, the moment you do that you are bound to be in trouble. We either accept the Scriptures as our only foundation, or else we do not. Many say that they do accept them, but then they bring in their inability to understand. Now the moment you do that you have left the Scriptures and you are introducing your own ability, your own understanding, and your own theories and ideas. That has constantly been the trouble, and especially with these three verses that we are considering. What I propose to do, therefore, is just to put these statements before you, and ask you to consider them and meditate upon them. Here is the whole foundation of our position as Christians. It is here we are told exactly how we have ever become Christians.

What does the apostle say? He says that we are Christians entirely and solely as the result of God's grace. Now surely no one can dispute that. 'For by grace are ye saved through faith; and that not of yourselves: it is the gift of God.' Notice the apostle's method here. The whole statement is in three verses, and in a sense we can take the three verses as our divisions, our headings. He first of all makes a positive statement, in verse 8. He follows it with a negative, in verse 9; and the purpose of the negative is to reinforce the positive. It is just saying the same thing negatively. And then in the tenth verse he seems to combine the two, the positive and the negative.

Let us look first at the positive statement. Here is his assertion positively, that *we are Christians entirely and solely as the result of the grace of God.* Let us remind ourselves once more that 'grace' means unmerited, undeserved favour. It is an action which arises entirely from the gracious character of God. So the fundamental proposition is that salvation is something that comes to us entirely from God's side. What is still more important is this, that it not only comes from God's side, it comes to us in spite of ourselves—'unmerited' favour. In other words, it is not God's response to anything in us. Now there are many people who seem to think that it is—that salvation is God's response to something in us. But the word 'grace' excludes that. It is in spite of us. The apostle, as we have seen, has already been very much concerned to say this. You notice the interesting way in which he, as it were, slipped it in in the fifth verse. He interrupted himself, broke the symmetry of his statement, and was guilty of a serious blemish from the standpoint of literary style. But he was not interested in that. Listen to him: 'Even when we were dead in sins, he hath quickened us together with Christ', and then, instead of going on to the next step—in parenthesis '(by grace ye are saved)'. Here, he puts it a little more explicitly. Salvation is not in any sense God's reponse to anything in us. It is not something that we in any sense deserve or merit. The whole essence of the teaching at this point, and everywhere in all the New Testament, is that we have no sort or kind of right whatsoever to salvation, that the whole glory of salvation is, that though we deserved nothing but punishment and hell and banishment out of the sight of God to all eternity, yet God, of His own love and grace and wondrous mercy, has granted us this salvation. Now that is the entire meaning of this term 'grace'.

We need not stay with this because we have been dealing with it in the previous seven verses. What is the point of those verses? Is it not just to show us that very thing negatively and positively? What is the point of that horrible description of man by nature as the result of sin in the first three verses, if it is not just to show that man, as he is in sin, deserves nothing but retribution? He is a child of wrath by nature, and not only by nature but by conduct, by his behaviour, by his whole attitude to God—living according to the course of this world, governed by the prince of the power of the air. That is the sort of creature he is; dead in trespasses and sins, a creature of lusts, lusts of the flesh, 'fulfilling the desires of the flesh and of the mind'. There is no more appalling description possible than that. You cannot imagine a worse state than that. Does such a creature deserve anything? Has such a creature any right at all in the presence of God? Can he come forward with a plea or with a demand? The whole point of the apostle is to say that such a creature deserves nothing at the hands of God but retribution. And then he works it out in his great contrast—'but God'—which we have already considered in detail. And the whole purpose of that, surely, is to exalt the grace and the mercy of God, and is to show that where man deserves nothing at all, God not only gives him, and gives him liberally, but showers upon him 'the exceeding riches of his grace'.

That, therefore, is the first principle, that we are Christians solely and entirely and only because of the grace of God. I have referred to that fifth verse because it is extremely important in this whole argument. Notice the way the apostle inserted it there, slipped it in, as it were, insinuated it. Why did he do so? Notice the context. He says that it was even 'when we were dead in sins' that God quickened us. Then at once—'(by grace ye are saved)'. If you do not see it at that point you will see it at no point. What he has been saying is this. We were dead, which means without any life at all; without any ability, therefore. And the first thing that was necessary was that we should be given life, that we should be quickened. And he says that that is the very thing that God has done to us. Therefore, he says: Can you not see it? it is by *grace* you are saved. So he puts it in at that particular point obviously for that reason. It is the only conclusion one can draw. Creatures who were spiritually dead are now alive—how has it happened? Can a dead man raise himself? It is impossible. There is only one answer, 'By grace ye are saved'. We come, therefore, to this inevitable conclusion, that we are Christians at this moment only and entirely by the grace of God.

The apostle was never tired of saying this. What else could he say? As he looked back on that blaspheming Saul of Tarsus, who

hated Christ and the Christian Church and did his best to exter-
minate Christianity, breathing out threatenings and slaughter; as
he looked back at that and then looked at himself as he now was,
what could he say but this, 'I am what I am by the grace of God'?
And I must confess it passes my comprehension to understand how
any Christian looking at himself or herself can say anything different.
If when you get on your knees before God you do not realise that
you are 'a debtor to mercy alone', I confess I do not understand
you. There is something tragically defective, either in your sense of
sin or in your realisation of the greatness of God's love. This is the
running theme of the New Testament, it is the reason why the saints
of the centuries have always praised the Lord Jesus Christ. They
see that when they were utterly hopeless, indeed dead and vile and
foul, 'hateful and hating one another' as Paul puts it in writing to
Titus, then God looked upon them. It was 'while we were yet sinners',
more, it was 'while we were enemies' that we were reconciled to
God by the death of His Son—at enmity; aliens in our minds,
utterly opposed. Surely we must see that it is by grace and by grace
alone that we are Christians? It is utterly undeserved, it is only as
the result of the goodness of God.

The second proposition, as I have indicated, is put by the apostle
in a negative form. He says that *the fact that we are Christians gives
us no grounds whatsoever for boasting*. That is the negative of the
first proposition. The first is that we are Christians solely and entirely
as the result of the grace of God. Therefore, secondly, we must say
that the fact that we are Christians gives us no grounds whatsoever
for boasting. The apostle puts that in two statements. The first is,
'that not of yourselves'; but he is not content with that, he must put
it still more explicitly in these words, 'lest any man should boast'.
There we have two vitally important statements. Surely nothing
could be stronger than this, 'Not of yourselves': 'lest any man
should boast'. This must always be the crucial test of our view of
salvation and of what makes us Christians. Let us then examine
ourselves for a moment. What is your idea of yourself as a Christian?
How have you become a Christian? What is it dependent upon?
What is the background, what is the reason? That is the crucial
question, and according to the apostle the vital test. Does your idea
of how you have become a Christian give you any grounds whatsoever for being proud of yourself, for boasting? Does it in any way
reflect credit upon you? If it does, according to this statement—
and I do not hesitate to say it—you are not a Christian. 'Not of
yourselves: lest any man should boast.' In the third chapter of the
Epistle to the Romans the apostle puts it still more plainly. He asks

his question. Here, he says, is God's way of salvation, and then he asks in verse 27, 'Where is boasting then?' He answers by saying, 'It is excluded', it is put out through the door and the door locked on it; there is no room for it here at all.

It is not surprising that the apostle Paul is so fond of putting it in that particular way, because before his conversion, before he became a Christian, he knew a great deal about boasting. There was never a more self-satisfied person or a more self-assured person than Saul of Tarsus. He was proud of himself in every respect— proud of his nationality, proud of the particular tribe into which he had been born in Israel, proud of the fact that he had been brought up as a Pharisee and had sat at the feet of Gamaliel, proud of his religion, proud of his morality, proud of his knowledge. He tells us all about it in the third chapter of the Epistle to the Philippians. He would boast. He would stand up and say, as it were: Who can challenge this? Here I am, a good and a moral and a religious man. Look at me in my religious duties, look at me in my life, look at me in every respect; I have given myself to this godly, holy living, and I am satisfying God. That was his attitude. He was boasting. He felt that he was such a man, and had lived in such a way, that he could be proud of it. It was one of his great words. But he came to see that one of the biggest differences that becoming a Christian made to him was that all that was put out and rendered irrelevant. That is why he used rather strong language. Looking back on all that in which he had boasted so much, he says, 'It is dung and loss'! He is not content to say that it was wrong; it is vile, it is filthy, it is foul. Boasting? Excluded! But the apostle knows the danger at this point so well that he does not content himself with a general statement; he indicates two particular respects in which we are most liable to boast.

The first is this question of works. 'By grace are ye saved, and that not of yourselves, it is the gift of God; not of works lest any man should boast.' *It is always in connection with works that we are most liable to boast.* It is at that point that the devil tempts us all in a most subtle manner. Works! That was why the Pharisees were the greatest enemies of Jesus Christ; not because they were mere talkers, but because they really did things. When that Pharisee said (Luke 18: 9)—'I fast twice in the week', he was speaking the truth; when he said 'I give tithes of all that I possess', it was strictly accurate. The Pharisees were not merely talkers, they really did these things. And it was because of this that they so resented the preaching of the Son of God and were most responsible for His crucifixion. Is it going too far to say that it is always more difficult to convert a good person than a bad one? I think the history of the Church proves that. The greatest opponents of evangelical religion have always been good and religious people. Some of the most cruel persecutors in the history of the Church have belonged to this class. The saints have always suffered most acutely at the hands of good, moral, religious people. Why? Because of works. The evangelical gospel always denounces reliance upon works and pride of works and boasting about works, and such people cannot stand it. Their whole position has been built up on that—what they are and what they have done and what they have always been doing. This is their whole position, and if you take that from them they have nothing. They therefore hate such preaching and they will fight it to the last ditch. The gospel makes paupers of us all. It condemns us every one. It strips us all naked. There is no difference, Paul argues everywhere, there is no difference between the Gentile who is outside the pale and the religious Jew, in the sight of God—'there is none righteous, no not one'. So works must go out, they must not be boasted of. But we tend to boast of them—our good living, our good deeds, our religious observances, our attendance at services (and particularly if we do so early in the morning), and so on. These are the things, our religious activities, these make us Christian. That is the argument.

But the apostle exposes and denounces all that, and he does so very simply in this way. He says that to talk about works is to go back under the law. If you think, he says, that it is your good life that makes you a Christian, you are putting yourself back under the law. But that is a futile thing to do, he says, for this reason. If you put yourself back under the law you are condemning yourself, 'for by the deeds of the law shall no man be justified in his sight; for by the law is the knowledge of sin'. If you want to try to justify yourself by your life and by your works, you are walking straight to condemnation, because the best works of man are not good enough in the sight of God. The law has condemned all—'All have sinned and come short of the glory of God'. 'There is none righteous, no, not one.' So do not be foolish, says Paul; do not turn away from grace, for in so doing you are turning to condemnation. No man's works will ever be sufficient to justify him in the sight of God. How foolish, therefore, to go back under works!

But not only that, he explains further in the tenth verse that it is to put things the wrong way round. Such people think that by their good works they make themselves Christian, whereas Paul says, it is exactly the other way round. 'We are his workmanship, created in Christ Jesus *unto* good works, which God hath before ordained that we should walk in them.' The tragedy is that people think that if only they do certain things and avoid certain things, and live a good life and go out and help others, in that way they will become

Christian. What blindness! says Paul. The way to look at good
works is this. God makes us Christians in order that we may do
good works. It is not a question of good works leading to Christianity,
but Christianity leading to good works. It is the exact opposite of
what people tend to believe. There is nothing, therefore, that is
such a complete contradiction of the true Christian position as this
tendency to boast of works and to think that, because we are what
we are, and are doing what we are doing, we are making ourselves
Christian. No; God makes Christians, and then they go on to do
their good works. Boasting is excluded. 'Where is boasting? It is
excluded. By what law? by the law of works? Nay, but by the law
of faith.' We see that works are excluded in the matter of becoming
Christian. We must not boast of our works. If we are in any way
conscious of our goodness, or if we are relying upon anything that
we have done, we are denying the grace of God. It is the opposite
of Christianity.

But alas, it is not only works and deeds that tend to insinuate
themselves. There is something else—faith! *Faith tends to come in and
to make us boast.* There is great controversy about this eighth verse—
'For by grace are ye saved, through faith, and *that* not of yourselves;
it is the gift of God'. The great question is, what does the 'that'
refer to? And there are two schools of opinion. 'For by grace are
ye saved through faith, and that (faith) not of yourselves; it is the
gift of God,' says the one school. But according to the other view
the 'that' does not refer to the 'faith' but to the 'grace' at the beginning of the sentence: 'For by grace are ye saved through faith, and
that (this position of grace) not of yourselves; it is the gift of God'.
Is it possible to settle the dispute? It is not. It is not a question of
grammar, it is not a question of language. You will find, as usual,
that the great authorities are divided between the two schools, and
it is most interesting, and almost amusing, to notice the sides to
which they belong. For instance, if I were to ask you what was the
view of John Calvin on this, I am sure you would reply at once that
Calvin said that the 'that' refers to faith and not to grace. But actually
Calvin said the exact opposite, that it refers to 'grace' and not to
'faith'. It is a question that cannot be decided. And there is a sense
in which it really does not matter at all, because it comes to much
the same thing in the end. In other words, what is important is
that we should avoid turning faith into 'works'.

But there are many people who do that. They turn their faith into
a kind of works. Indeed there is quite a popular evangelistic teaching
at the present time which says that the difference which the New
Testament makes can be put in this way. In the Old Testament
God looked at the people and said: Here is my law, here are the

Ten Commandments, keep them, and I will forgive you and you will be saved. But, it goes on to say, it is not like that now. God has put all that on one side, there is no longer any law, God simply says to us, 'Believe on the Lord Jesus Christ', and if you do you will be saved. In other words they say that by believing on the Lord Jesus Christ a man saves himself. But that is to turn faith into works because it says it is our action that saves us. But the apostle says 'Not of yourselves'. Whether the 'that' refers to faith or to grace, it does not matter; 'you are saved', says Paul, 'by grace, and that not of yourselves'. If it is my belief that saves me I have saved myself; but Paul says that it is not of yourself. So that I must never speak of my faith in a way that makes it 'of myself'. And not only that. If I become a Christian in that way, again surely it gives me some grounds for boasting; but Paul says, 'Not of works, lest any man should boast'. My boasting must be entirely excluded.

As we think of faith we must be careful, therefore, to view it in this light. Faith is not the cause of salvation. *Christ* is the cause of salvation. The grace of God in the Lord Jesus Christ is the cause of salvation, and I must never speak in such a way as to represent faith as the cause of my salvation. What is faith then? Faith is but the instrument through which it comes to me. 'By grace are ye saved, through faith.' Faith is the channel, it is the instrument through which this salvation which is of the grace of God comes to me. I am saved by grace, 'through faith'. It is just the medium through which the grace of God bringing salvation enters into my life. We must always be extremely careful, therefore, never to say that it is our believing that saves us. Belief does not save. Faith does not save. Christ saves—Christ and His finished work. Not my belief, not my faith, not my understanding, nothing that I do—'not of yourselves', 'boasting is excluded', 'by grace, through faith'.

Surely the whole point of the first three verses of this chapter is to show that no other position is at all possible. How can a man who is 'dead' in trespasses and sins save himself? How can a man who is an 'enemy and alienated in his mind', whose heart is 'at enmity against God' (for that is what we are told about the natural man), how can such a man do anything that is meritorious? It is impossible. The first thing that happens to us, the apostle has told us in verses 4 to 7, is that we have been 'quickened'. New life has been put into us. Why? Because without life we can do nothing. The first thing the sinner needs is life. He cannot ask for life, for he is dead. God gives him life, and he proves that he has it by believing the gospel. Quickening is the first step. It is the first thing that happens. I do not ask to be quickened. If I asked to be quickened I would not need to be quickened, I would already have life. But

I am dead, and I am an enemy, and I am opposed to God, I do not understand, and I hate. But God *gives* me life. He has quickened me together with Christ. Therefore, boasting is entirely excluded, boasting of works, boasting even of faith. It must be excluded. Salvation is altogether of God.

That brings us to the last principle, which I summarise in this way. *Our being Christians is entirely the result of God's work.* The real trouble with many of us is that our conception of what it is that makes us Christian is so low, is so poor; it is our failure to realise the greatness of what it means to be a Christian. Paul says: 'We are his workmanship'! It is God who has done something, it is God who is working; we are *His* workmanship. Not our works, His work. So, I say again, it is not our good life, and all our efforts, and hoping to be a Christian at the end, that makes us Christians. But let me go further. It is not our decision, our 'deciding for Christ', that makes us Christians either: that is our work. Decision does come into it, but it is not our decision that makes us Christians. Paul says we are *His* workmanship. And thus, you see how grievously our loose thinking and our loose speaking misrepresent Christianity! I remember a very good man—yes, a good Christian man—whose way of giving his testimony was always this: 'I decided for Christ thirty years ago and I have never regretted it'. That was his way of putting it. That is not Paul's way of describing becoming Christian. 'We are his workmanship!' That is the emphasis. Not something I have gone in for, not something I have decided, but something that God has done to me. He might better have put it like this: Thirty years ago I was dead in trespasses and sins, but God began to do something to me; I became aware of God dealing with me; I felt God smashing me; I felt the hands of God re-making me. That is Paul's way of putting it; not, *I* decided, not, *I* went in for Christianity, not, *I* decided to follow Christ, not at all. That comes in, but that is later.

We are His workmanship. A Christian is a person in whom God has worked. And you notice what kind of work it is, according to Paul. It is nothing less than a creation. 'Created in Christ Jesus, unto good works.' The apostle is very fond of saying this. Listen to him saying it to the Philippians: 'Being confident of this very thing, that he which hath begun a good work in you will perform it until the day of Jesus Christ' (1: 6). GOD! He has begun a good work in you! It is God's work! He came when you were dead and He quickened you, He put life into you. That is what makes a man a Christian. Not your good works, not your decision, but God's determination concerning you put into practice.

It is here we see how our ideas of what the Christian is, fall hopelessly short of the biblical teaching. A Christian is *a new creation*. He is not just a good man, or a man who has been improved somewhat; he is a new man, 'created in Christ Jesus'. He has been put into Christ, and the life of Christ has come into him. 'We are partakers of the divine nature', says the apostle Peter (2 Peter 1: 4). 'Partakers of the divine nature'! What is a Christian? A good man, a moral man, a man who believes certain things? Yes, but infinitely more! He is a new man, the life of God has come into his soul— 'created in Christ', 'God's workmanship'! Had you realised that that is what makes you a Christian? It is not attending a place of worship. It is not doing certain duties. These things are all excellent, but they can never make us Christians. (They could make us Pharisees!) It is God who makes Christians and He does it in this way. He created everything out of nothing at the beginning, and He comes to man and He makes him anew and gives him a new nature, makes a new man of him. A Christian is 'a new creation', nothing less.

If you are interested in works, says Paul, I will tell you the sort of works that God is interested in. It is not the miserable works that you can do as a creature in sin by nature. It is a new kind of work— 'created in Christ Jesus unto good works, which *God* hath before ordained that we should walk in them'—*God's good works!* What does he mean? He means that our trouble is not only that our notion of Christianity is inadequate, our notion of good works is still more inadequate. Put down on paper the good works that people think are good enough to make them Christian. Get them to put them all down on paper, all those things on which they are relying. Put them on paper, and then take them to God and say, This is what I have done. The thing is laughable, it is monstrous. Look at what they *are* doing! They are not the good works in which God is interested. What are God's good works? Well, the Sermon on the Mount and the life of Jesus Christ provide the answer. Not just a little negative goodness and morality, not perhaps doing an occasional kindness and being very conscious of it. No, disinterested love! 'Let this mind be in you which was also in Christ Jesus, who, being in the form of God, thought it not robbery to be equal with God: but made himself of no reputation, and took upon him the form of a servant, and was made in the likeness of men; and being found in fashion as a man, he humbled himself, and became obedient unto death, even the death of the cross'—giving Himself for others without counting the cost. Those are God's good works. 'Loving God with all the heart and soul and mind and strength, and our neighbour as ourselves!' Not doing him an occasional good turn, but loving him as yourself! Forgetting yourself in your concern for him! Those are God's good works. And those are the works for which He has created us.

A Christian, according to this definition, is one who has been made anew after the image and the pattern of the Son of God Himself. The apostle puts it in the fourth chapter of this Epistle in verse 24 thus, 'And that ye put on the new man, which after God is created in righteousness and true holiness'. Not a little bit of goodness, but true holiness, 'holiness of the truth', and utter, absolute righteousness! And already in the first chapter Paul has put it like this in the fourth verse: 'According as he hath chosen us in him before the foundation of the world, that we should be holy and without blame before him in love'. In writing to the Romans he puts it like this: 'Whom he did foreknow, he also did predestinate to be *conformed to the image of his Son*'! What is a Christian? Just a good man? Somebody who is just a little bit better than somebody else? Not at all! He is like Christ! Conformed to the image of God's Son! How can a man who is dead in trespasses and sins raise himself to that? It is impossible. 'By grace ye are saved;' 'not of yourselves', 'no boasting'. No man can attain to this, no man can raise himself to this. It is God's work, and God's work alone. The Christian is one who is meant to be like Christ. He has the life of Christ within him. 'I live, yet not I, but Christ liveth in me.' What is Christianity? It is 'Christ in you, the hope of glory'; 'Made after the image of God's own Son'. Thank God it is of grace! If it were not of grace we would all be hopeless, we would all be undone, we would all be condemned. But because it is by grace, because it is God's work, because I am God's workmanship, I know that, in spite of myself, in spite of the sin that yet remains within me, I shall be made perfect. If it were left to us there would be no hope at all. Who are we to face the world, and the flesh, and the devil? But thank God it is 'by grace'. We are His workmanship. We are in His hands—and if He has started working in us He will go on with the work until it is complete. If you will not submit readily and willingly, He will chastise you, He will knock those corners off you, He will chisel them away. If you are in His plan, if He is making you after the image of Christ, He will go on with His work until every 'spot and wrinkle and any such thing' shall have been removed, and you will stand in the presence of God 'faultless and blameless' and 'with exceeding joy.'

Thank God it is not of works; thank God it is not my believing; thank God there is nothing of which I can boast. 'God forbid that I should glory save in the cross of our Lord Jesus Christ, by which the world has been crucified unto me and I unto the world.' 'By grace, through faith!'

13

HIS WORKMANSHIP

For we are his workmanship, created in Christ Jesus unto good works, which God hath before ordained that we should walk in them.

Ephesians 2: 10 .

We have glanced at this great statement previously when we took it in its context in connection with the two previous verses, 8 and 9. These three verses together, as we saw, are a composite statement, therefore before we come to take this verse on its own, it was right that we should have taken it as a part of the argument which the apostle puts before us in the three verses together. The argument is that our salvation is entirely of grace; it results from the grace of God. There is no boasting; that is excluded altogether. We must not even boast of our faith, we must not turn even faith into 'works'. 'We are saved by grace, through faith.' Faith is the instrument and the channel, it is not the determining cause. Now that is the great argument, you remember, that it is all by grace and of grace. The apostle puts it in a negative and in a positive manner. And in this tenth verse he brings out what is in many ways his final argument. He says it is entirely of grace; it is not of yourselves, it is the gift of God, not of works, lest any man should boast, 'for we are *His* workmanship'—any other view is impossible, is quite inadequate and ridiculous. And indeed, he says, this can finally be clinched by the fact that the good works that we ought to perform as Christians are works that are already before ordained that we should walk in them. Even the very works that we do as Christians are prepared beforehand by God that we might walk in them. So far then, we have looked at this statement in a general and, chiefly, negative way.

It is, however, such a profound and such a glorious statement that it would be very wrong to leave it just at that. It is a part of the argument, but it is also a statement in and of itself, a positive statement, and one of the most important and vital statements that we can ever consider. Here we are given one of Paul's definitions of what it means to be a Christian. And there is, I suppose, no more exalted statement of it than just this, that we are God's workmanship. That is the truth about us all as Christians, and that is the truth about the Christian Church. It is our business to learn to think of ourselves in that way; and it is only as we do so that we shall truly function as Christians.

It seems to me, more and more, that all our troubles really come from our failure to realise the truth about ourselves and our position as Christians. The central trouble with us—and it is an astounding thing to realise—is our initial failure to have the true view of these matters. We are so much the creatures of tradition. We start off with the wrong ideas—the natural man ever starts with a wrong conception of Christianity. We persist in thinking of it as just being good or doing good, or some such thing; and it is extremely difficult to shed that idea. But that is something which falls hopelessly short of this great New Testament concept. These New Testament Christians are constantly being exhorted to realise the privilege of their position. Though they are but a handful of people in a great pagan society they are always being told to rejoice, to consider their wonderful destiny; they are being reminded of who they are and what they are, and they are told to lift up their heads and to go forward in a triumphant manner. All that is done, of course, in the light of what the New Testament expounds as the true doctrine concerning the Christian.

This matter can be put in the form of a question. Are we filled with a sense of privilege and of joy? What is our understanding of being Christian? What is our view of the Church? Is it not true to say that, speaking generally, we always tend to think of it in merely human terms? We tend to think of the whole Church of God as a human institution and society, we think in terms of the activities of men and what men are doing and not doing, and of committees and gatherings and organisations and the like. All these things are undoubtedly a part of it, and they are essential, but they do not constitute the Church. That is not what makes the Church the Church. And again, it is exactly the same with regard to the individual Christian. Are we confident, have we got assurance, as we think of ourselves and consider the complete Christian life and all that belongs to that life? Do we think of it solely in terms of ourselves and of what we are doing and proposing to do, or do we see ourselves as part of a great process? Do we realise that we have the privilege of being brought into a great scheme and plan? Now that is the idea and outlook the apostle is putting before us here, in a positive manner. Let us therefore, come immediately to a consideration of the terms he uses.

Paul's first proposition is this: *we are God's workmanship.* That is the first thing we have to realise about ourselves as Christians.

Negatively, as we have already seen, that means that *we do not make ourselves Christians.* We are not what we are as the result of anything that we have done. Nothing whatsoever!—boasting is excluded. 'Not of works.' 'Not of yourselves.' But we do not stop with the negative, we must go on to look at it positively like this. We are God's handiwork. That is the meaning of the term. We are, so to speak, a thing of His making. This is to me a most remarkable and thrilling thought, that we are something that is being made and fashioned by God. We can think of this individually, of ourselves as Christians; and we must think of it as being true of the whole Church. Once again let me put the matter in the form of a question. Do we habitually think of ourselves in that way? Is it not, alas, true to say of most of us that we persist somehow in thinking of God as being entirely passive? Our idea of God is that He is there in the heavens entirely passive and waiting for us to approach Him. We think: Of course if I go to God He will listen to me, He will answer me, He will bless me. But in that way, we think of the real activity always as being on our part. God has a great treasure house, a great storehouse; He has great gifts to give, yes, but He does nothing about it, He just waits until *we* do something, and then when we take action God responds.

Let us examine ourselves again in the light of that. Is it not our tendency to think of it in that way? I decide for Christ, and therefore I am justified. I may go on like that for years. Then I decide that I want to be sanctified, so I apply for that also, and God gives it me. But God is passive the whole time; it is *my* activity that matters, it is what I decide, it is what I do. All that is, of course, altogether contrary to the teaching of the apostle, which reminds us, and puts tremendous emphasis upon the fact, that Christianity is entirely the result of the activity of God. 'His workmanship are we.'

It is God who is the Workman, it is God who is active. It is astounding that anyone could ever fall into the particular error I have just outlined, because the Bible is nothing but the record of the activity of God. How is it possible that anyone can read an open Bible, starting with the words 'In the beginning God', and then go on to think of the whole thing as the activity of man? It is God who acts everywhere. He made man, He made the world. Man sinned— God went after him. It is God who called Abraham; it is God who created the kings; it is God who called the prophets; it is God who gave the law; it is God who gave the instructions about building the tabernacle and the temple; and it was God, who, in the fulness of the times, sent forth His own Son. It is God's workmanship, God's activity, from beginning to end. And yet, even we who are Christians tend to forget that, and to think often of our Christian life, and of our being Christians at all, in terms of something we have done, or something we have attained. Even if we start in the right way we tend to insinuate the other idea later on. We will persist in thinking of God as being more or less passive and simply ready to respond to what we do and what we desire. But the very term the apostle uses here should make such thoughts quite impossible. God is the Workman. God is the One who is fashioning. It is a wonderful picture of God as a kind of Artist, as some kind of Artificer. The picture invites us to think of God as in some great workshop, and asks us to watch Him forming and fashioning and bringing something into being.

Now this is characteristic biblical teaching with regard to God. Take the pictures which we are given in the Scriptures, of God as a Potter. You get it in the Old Testament, you get it in the New Testament. This same apostle, in writing to the Romans, uses that very metaphor. Here is a lump of clay; the workman, the potter, comes along and takes hold of this shapeless mass of clay, and begins to work on it. He begins to round it off and to get rid of angles and corners; he has certain lathes, and he puts it on the lathe. He is fashioning, he is making a vase or some kind of vessel. That is the picture that is given—the potter and the clay, and that is precisely the idea that the apostle has here, that God is the Workman, and we are the clay that is being formed and fashioned. The work is His, not ours. He is the Workman, the Artist, who is producing a piece of work.

Indeed, the apostle uses another term that is still more explicit: 'We are his workmanship, *created* in Christ Jesus'. That takes us right back, of course, to the original idea of creation. 'In the beginning God created the heaven and the earth.' What is creation? The very idea, the essential idea of creation, is that something is made out of nothing; it was not there before, but it is now brought into being. That is the precise way in which the apostle thinks of the Christian. So we must say farewell for ever to all ideas of improvement, and of self-improvement especially. The most important fact about the Christian is that he is a new creation, a new creature. God the Creator, God the Potter, the Artificer, God the great Maker, the great Workman, has brought something into being in my life that was not there before—that is what makes me a Christian. And I am not a Christian apart from that. So that to talk about Christian nations and a man being a Christian because he belongs to a Christian nation is simply, of course, a blank denial of the whole biblical teaching. It is God's action, a specific action, a new creation. The God who at the beginning (as Paul puts it in 2 Corinthians 4: 6) 'commanded the light to shine out of darkness,' that same

God, in the same way 'hath shined in our hearts, to give the light of the knowledge of the glory of God in the face of Jesus Christ'. That is what it means to be a Christian. Nothing less than that! How can one put it more clearly? What concerns me is not simply that we should have the right idea, but that we should all come to see that there is no greater travesty of Christianity than the idea that we are Christians because of something that *we* are, or something that we do. We must realise that we are the workmanship of the great Workman, the great Artist. There is nothing more wonderful than this, that I, such as I am, am something that has been brought into being, something that has been fashioned by God Himself, that I am like clay in the hands of the potter. As I think of my Christian life in this world I must stop thinking of it simply in terms of what I do and am doing, but rather think of it in terms of what God is doing to me, that I am in the hands of the great Maker, in the hands of the Creator, and that He is working in me and upon me. That is the apostle's conception and teaching here.

Let us now consider it a little more in detail, because the more we understand this great truth in detail the more it will amaze us and thrill us. *How does God do this work?* The first thing we have to emphasise is that *it is in and through the Lord Jesus Christ*: 'created in Christ Jesus'! That is always the case. We have already seen it in verses 4 to 7 where we have been told that we have been quickened with Him, raised together with Him, seated with Him in the heavenly places. In other words, God makes us Christians by applying to us, by mediating to us, that which He has done for us in Christ. It is all in Christ, therefore. It is in Him, in His Person. It is 'of his fulness that we receive, and grace for grace'. We receive the benefits of His death, we receive the benefits of His life; we receive His very life itself. All good comes to us from Christ. That is how God does it. He has sent forth His Son, then He brings us to the Son. Or, to use another scriptural term, He forms the Lord Jesus Christ in us. That is what He is doing: He is forming Christ in us. 'My little children', says Paul to the Galatians (4: 19), 'of whom I travail in birth again, until Christ be formed in you'. That is the New Testament idea of being Christian. It is a great mystical conception, it is a vital conception. We are at this point altogether outside the realm of our little works and decencies and moralities. Christ is being formed in me!

How does God do that? Look for a moment at *the means that God employs* to form Christ in us. Take my illustration of the workshop, or the factory. You can go to a shop and there see a finished article for sale, a beautiful bowl, a beautiful vase, or whatever it is. How has it come into being? You may be fortunate enough to be taken on a visit to the factory. Have you ever been to a glass factory or some such place? I remember once visiting one in Venice, and there we saw men actually making the wonderful things which we had seen previously in a finished form. We were rather amazed when we saw the first beginnings. Well, it is something like that that we have to think of now. How does God produce this finished article, the Christian? Go to the workshop, and there you will discover exactly how it is done. That is what we are told in this very Epistle.

The first thing we become conscious of is *the work of the Holy Spirit*. You have noticed the striking order in Scripture—God the Father, God the Son, God the Holy Spirit. The Father plans salvation; He sends the Son to work it out; and then He and the Son send the Spirit in order to apply it. God works in us and God makes Christians of us, and fashions us according to the image of Christ, or forms Christ in us, primarily by the work of the Holy Spirit. 'Know ye not that your bodies are the temples of the Holy Ghost?' says the apostle in writing to the Corinthians. The Holy Spirit is in us if we are Christians; we cannot be Christians without having the Holy Spirit in us. And He works in us. We shall consider later exactly how He works. I am simply introducing you at the moment to the means that God employs. There is this constant activity of the Holy Spirit in the individual Christian, in groups of Christians, in the Church. The Holy Spirit is in the Church, and He is working and He is doing God's work; God is working through Him.

Then the next thing we have to mention is the Word, *the Scriptures*. You remember our Lord's great high priestly prayer in which He says, 'Sanctify them through thy truth, thy word is truth'. How are we born again? According to the Epistle of James we are 'begotten by the word of truth' (1: 18). Peter says, 'Being born again, not of corruptible seed, but of incorruptible, by the word of God which liveth and abideth for ever' (1 Peter 1: 23). God uses the Word in order to give us life. The Word is preached and the Word becomes life to us. There is a seed of life in it, and God puts the life into us through putting the Word into us. You get that same idea in the fifth chapter of this Ephesian Epistle, where we are told about 'the washing of water by the word'. As we think of this process which God is working out in us we have to think of this Word. That is where the importance of reading the Scriptures comes in. It is the means that God Himself uses. God could have done it without means, but He has chosen to do it in this way. So He gave the Holy Spirit to enlighten these writers, to give them understanding, to open their minds to the truth, and to enable them to convey the truth. And the Spirit led them and guided them. It is all designed to this great end—God as the Workman, producing Christians and perfecting Christians! How tremendously important is the Word!

Not only that, however, but *the preaching of the Word* also. You will find in the fourth chapter of this Epistle to the Ephesians that Paul puts it like this: 'He gave gifts unto men; and He gave some, apostles; and some, prophets; and some, evangelists; and some, pastors and teachers'. What for?—'for the perfecting of the saints, for the work of the ministry, for the edifying of the body of Christ, till we all come in the unity of the faith and of the knowledge of the Son of God unto a perfect man, unto the measure of the stature of the fulness of Christ'. Do you understand? Do you see what is happening in the factory where Christians are being made? Look at the benches, look at the lathes. What do you see there? Apostles, prophets, pastors, teachers, preachers—all put there by God, and He is doing His great work by them and through them. He is using all these men to fashion Christians. That is the New Testament idea of Christianity!—not a man hesitating in his bed on Sunday morning as to whether he will go to a place of worship or not; or whether he will read the Bible, or pray. It is not *our* work; 'not of yourselves'. God is doing this, and this is how He does it. It is God who calls men to preach the gospel. Preaching is not a profession—alas, it often is, but then it is of no value. It is God who calls and who places men in their different offices. He has planned it all. It is His design, it is His blueprint, and it is all being put into operation. The preaching and the teaching, the gifts that God gives to men, and the gifts that He gives to the Church are all a part of the process. None of them are given for their own sake, they are simply given in order that God may use them, in order to bring to pass His great purpose.

What else? We find another element put before us in the twelfth chapter of the Epistle to the Hebrews. *Circumstances and chastening!* What is the teaching in the twelfth of Hebrews? These Hebrew Christians were tending to grumble and to complain because they were having trials and troubles and tribulations; and the argument that is put before them is that it is all happening to them because they are children. 'Whom the Lord loveth he chasteneth!' He uses an illustration. Take our earthly parents, he says. They correct us; but why do they correct us? They do so because they are concerned about our well-being, because they are concerned about our development. The good parent chastises the child, not simply to relieve his pent-up emotions but because it is in the best interest of the child, because he loves the child, because he is considering the child's future. And his argument is that God as our Father does exactly the same thing with us. That does not mean that every time something goes wrong with us we are of necessity being chastened by God. We are living in a world of sin, we are living in a world where secondary causes operate, and oftentimes our illnesses and diseases and trials happen to us merely as the result of secondary causes; but there is very clear and explicit teaching in the Scripture that God does chastise His own children. And He does that in order to perfect them. In other words, if we will not listen to the teaching of the Scripture, if we will not accept it positively, if God has started working in us and making us and fashioning us, He will produce the ultimate result by this other method. It may involve chastening, chastisement—the potter's use of the lathe suggests this; certain angles have to be removed and certain corners have to be got rid of. God puts us on the lathe, as it were. Or, to use the very illustration of that twelfth chapter of Hebrews, He puts us into the gymnasium, He makes us go through these exercises in order that we may be perfect. He intends us to develop. Indeed, I would refer you to the teaching in the eleventh chapter of the First Epistle to the Corinthians in connection with the Communion Service, where the apostle teaches very explicitly that some members of the church at Corinth were sick, and weak, simply because of their sin, their refusal to judge and to examine and to correct themselves. God was dealing with them by means of sickness. And he adds: 'Some indeed even sleep'. A great mystery that, but the teaching clearly is that some may even die because it is a part of God's way of dealing with them. We do not understand that fully, but there is the teaching. And all I am concerned about at this moment is that we may see that that is a part of the process in the great factory. If there is a resistance in this mass of clay, if there is some obduracy, if there is some difficulty about it, God has His method, He has His machinery, He has His way. He is producing a perfect article and He uses all these various means and methods. We are His workmanship!

If those are the means that God uses, what is *the actual work itself*? What does He actually do to us, what does He do in us? Again I am simply picking out certain things that are of greatest importance. One of the first things a man becomes conscious of when God begins to work in him is that he is *disturbed*, he is *convicted*. Look back into your own experience and I am sure that you will find that to be true. You were living your life in a certain way and going along in a certain direction. Thousands of others were doing the same thing. Suddenly (or gradually, it does not matter which) you were conscious of a sense of disturbance. Somehow or another you were not as happy as you had been before. Questions began to arise in your mind. You notice, I do not say that you sat down and said to yourself, 'Now I am going to start thinking'. Not at all—questions arose in your mind. Is not that it? Where did they come from? They came from God. That is the work of the Holy Spirit—conviction of sin. A man is arrested, he is pulled up, he is disturbed; he does not understand it, he is annoyed about it; indeed, he tries to shake it off. He may take to drink, he may plunge into business, anything to get rid of it. But there it is, something is happening to him. God is in pursuit of the man. As the poet put it:

> *I fled Him, down the nights and down the days;*
> *I fled Him down the arches of the years;*
> *I fled Him down the labyrinthine ways of my own mind.*

But from the Hound of Heaven there is no escape.

Do you know what I am talking about? His workmanship! Conviction of sin! Disturbances! These curious interferences and interruptions, this sense that we are being dealt with. No man can be a Christian without knowing something about that. If you do not understand, to some small extent at any rate, the feeling of the Psalmist in Psalm 139, when he cries out saying, 'Whither shall I flee from thy presence?' you are just not a Christian at all. The very sense of resistance to God is a proof that God is dealing with you and doing something to you. That is the first thing always—disturbance, conviction of sin, being arrested, being pulled up, being caused to think, questions, queryings. They are all the work of God through the Holy Spirit. That is how He begins when He first takes hold of this amorphous mass of clay. He takes hold of it; that is the first step. Before He has taken it to that lathe, before He has chiselled off any portions, before He begins to smooth it and to glaze it, the first step is just taking hold of it. Has God taken hold of you? Or are you in charge of yourself still? If you are still in charge of yourself, just manipulating yourself and trying to make yourself something, you are not a Christian at all. The first thing that is true about the Christian is that He is aware that God has taken hold of him. The Potter has taken hold of the clay.

The next step is an *enlightening of the mind* to see truth. What a wonderful process it is! A man to whom these terms meant nothing, though he had heard them all his life, suddenly begins to see something in them. He sometimes read the Bible and he was bored by it: he now sees that it is a living Word, and he wants to read it. That is God; God in the Spirit working in the man and opening his mind increasingly to a perception and an understanding of the truth. It is He who is doing it—putting in the thought; the light and the power of the Spirit, God opening things out, the Word opening before us; our eyes, our understanding being enlightened. And then in turn that leads to a desire for truth, and a thirst for it. 'As new born babes,' says Peter, 'desire the sincere milk of the word. . . .' How can you if you are not born? if you have not got life? But if you have life you will desire it, as the babe desires the milk. And, still more important, joy in the truth and rejoicing in the truth, finding pleasure in the truth. This is God's work, this is how He does it all.

And it leads in turn to this, that *we become aware of the new nature* that God has placed within us, the new principle of life. In spite of ourselves we find that we have got a new outlook. Again, I say, we may dislike that, but it is a fact. I find that I am not any longer what I was. I may say to myself: Would to God I had never heard of this so that I could go with my companions as before! But I cannot. I may make myself go but I am not happy with them, I find I am different. I have a new outlook; I have new desires; and I have new powers. We are His workmanship! He is the Potter and we are the clay. That is the thing the apostle is teaching us here.

Let me say just a word about *the design*. There is a definite design, of course. 'Created in Christ Jesus unto good works which God hath before ordained (or prepared) that we should walk in them.' Now this is the remarkable thing, that there is a design for the Christian, and God has planned it and designed it all. What is it? It is that we are to conform to the life of our Lord and Saviour Jesus Christ. We are to live in this world and in this life as He did. As I put it before, we are to live the Sermon on the Mount. We are to carry out the ethical instruction of these New Testament Epistles—to 'love one another', to 'put filthy communications out of our mouths', and avoid all 'foolish talking' and 'jesting'—it is all to go. 'Be ye therefore followers of God as dear children, and walk in love as Christ also hath loved us and hath given himself for us; but fornication and all uncleanness or covetousness let it not be once named among you, as becometh saints; neither filthiness nor foolish talking nor jesting which are not convenient; but rather giving of thanks.' That kind of life! We have been formed for that. That is what we are fashioned unto. That is the design, that is the shape, that is the mould, that is the image. God is making us for that.

And all that is in this life. Would you like to know what the ultimate design is? This is *a process*. You do not become perfect in a moment. Sanctification is a process, and God puts us through the process by the means that I have already indicated. Do you want to know the result of it all? Well, this is the ultimate, this is what will be true of us in glory, in eternity, when the work is really finished. He has given the apostles and the other ministries for 'the perfecting of the saints, for the work of the ministry, . . . till we all come in the unity of the faith and of the knowledge of the Son of God, unto a perfect man, unto the measure of the stature of the fulness of Christ.' That is going to be the end. You and I, as certainly as we are Christians at this moment, are going to attain to that, 'unto the measure of the stature of the fulness of Christ'. Listen to Paul stating it in the fifth chapter about the Church in general: 'That he might sanctify and cleanse it with the washing of water by the word, that he might present it to himself a glorious church, not having spot or wrinkle or any such thing, but that it should be holy and without blemish'. Christian people, we are in that process as certainly as we are Christians. God has taken hold of us, He is fashioning us, and He is going to keep on working in us, and with us, until we have come to this—without 'spot or wrinkle or any such thing'. No blemish will remain, every vestige of evil will have gone, and we shall be entirely perfect. That is the design, that is the pattern.

The only other thing I would say is this, that in the light of this doctrine it is absolutely certain that *we shall come to perfection*. 'He which hath begun a good work in you will perform it until the day of Jesus Christ.' (Philippians 1:6.) Nothing outside us can ever prevent it. I will go further; nothing inside us will ever prevent it. God never starts a work only to give it up half-complete. That is utterly incompatible with His majesty and His glory. When God begins God continues. If God has taken hold of you and has started fashioning you according to the image of Christ, Christian friend, as certainly as the sun is shining in the heavens He will go on with it until you attain 'unto the measure of the stature of the fulness of Christ'. He will go on with it until there is 'no spot or wrinkle or any such thing', no blemish at all, and you will stand before Him perfect and faultless with exceeding joy. What a glorious doctrine! Yes, but in certain respects what a terrifying doctrine! If you are a Christian and you in any way resist God's will for you, be prepared for what is coming to you. Be prepared for chastening, chastisement. Be prepared perhaps for severe and harsh dealing. Because He will perfect you. He has set His love upon you, and you are in His hands. There are no rejects out of His factory. God's work is always perfect, and it is always complete. What a blessed ground of assurance!—in spite of my waywardness and sinfulness and imperfection. My only hope is this, that I am in His hands, that He is the Workman and I am the clay, and that I know that He will bring to pass His perfect will. If it depended upon me, or any one of us, the whole thing would long since have been a hopeless failure. But, we are His workmanship!

I close by leaving you with three or four questions as tests. Is this happening to you? Can you say that you are God's workmanship? Have you got that subjective feeling of being dealt with by God? Are you aware of the Presence and of the hands? Are you conscious of being moulded and fashioned? Do you agree with this doctrine, or are you fighting against it? That is a very good test. Are you desiring the sincere milk of the Word as a newborn babe? But, still, the best test of all is this: Are you desiring holiness? 'Created in Christ Jesus *unto* good works, which God hath before ordained that we should walk in them.' It is a part of His plan. If you do not desire to be holy I do not see that you have any right to think that you are a Christian. It is a part of God's design that we be prepared unto good works. If you think that you can abstract forgiveness only from the plan of salvation, you completely misunderstand the plan. When God looked upon you and loved you and began to work in you to make you a Christian, He had already prepared the works which you should live and perform. There is no such thing as justification without sanctification. If there is no beginning of sanctification in you, you are not justified. Do not delude yourself, do not mislead yourself. There is no such thing as faith without works. 'Faith without works is dead.' The proof of faith is works. There is no value in a profession of Christianity unless it is accompanied by a desire to be like Christ, a desire to be rid of sin, a desire after positive holiness. According to this verse it is essential. 'We are his workmanship, created (by him) in Christ Jesus unto good works.' He is making us for that. God works in us to produce this result. So the final test of whether God is working in us is that we desire to be more and more like Christ, holy and pure, separate from the world and from sin, hungering and thirsting after righteousness, that we may please the God who has thus begun to work in us.

14

JEW AND GENTILE

Wherefore remember, that ye being in time past Gentiles in the flesh, who are called Uncircumcision by that which is called the Circumcision in the flesh made by hands.   Ephesians 2:11

This verse is the beginning of a statement which is continued in the twelfth verse: 'That at that time ye were without Christ, being aliens from the commonwealth of Israel, and strangers from the covenants of promise, having no hope, and without God in the world'. But I call attention now to the eleventh verse only.

Here we come to a new section in the statement which the apostle Paul makes in this second chapter of this Epistle. There is a definite break here, and the apostle takes up a new idea and a new thought. It is important, therefore, that we should be clear in our minds as to what his argument is, and what he is setting out to do.

The great object of the Epistle is to explain and to expound God's grand purpose during this present age. It is put in summary form in the tenth verse of the first chapter—thus, 'That in the dispensation of the fulness of times he (God) might gather together in one all things in Christ, both which are in heaven and which are on earth, even in him'. That is God's great purpose during this present dispensation, God's great purpose in our Lord and Saviour Jesus Christ. Christ came into the world, ultimately, in order to reunite, to head up again, in Himself, all things both in heaven and in earth. The apostle is concerned to expound that and to explain it to the members of the church at Ephesus and to the other churches to which this circular letter was to be sent. We have seen also that the apostle goes on at once to say that this great ultimate purpose of God is already being put into operation, that the Church is herself an illustration of this wonderful thing, in that the Ephesians, together with other Gentiles, had been brought into the Church as well as the Jews. Having said that, the apostle goes on to tell these Ephesians that the most important thing for them was to have the eyes of their understanding enlightened.

He wants them to know particularly 'the exceeding greatness of God's power toward them'. So in this second chapter he proceeds to expound and to show to them that great power. He illustrates it

to them. It is an amazing and an astonishing thing that these
Ephesians, these Gentiles, should be members of the Christian
Church, side by side with Jews. And there is only one thing that has
made it possible, that is, this exceeding greatness of God's power.
It is the same power that God manifested in raising the Lord Jesus
Christ from the dead.

How is it shown? In this way. There were two main obstacles
standing between these Ephesians and their coming to God and
being Christians and members of the Church. The *first obstacle was
their state and condition in sin.* The apostle deals with that in the first
ten verses of this chapter. We have already been dealing with that;
let us not forget it. He reminds them of what they were. But now
they are Christians. What has changed them, what has brought
them from that to this? There is only one answer: it is God's power—
nothing less. There stood that awful obstacle—and it is still the
great obstacle that stands between all men and God—death in sin.
Nothing but the power of God could have dealt with such a
situation.

But there was a *second obstacle*, something further, standing between
these Gentile Ephesians and membership of the Church of Christ
and knowledge of God. What was that? *It was their position, or status,
in the economy of God,* and especially in terms of their relationship to
the law of God. That is the subject which the apostle takes up here
in this eleventh verse, and which continues until the twelfth verse
of the third chapter.

Here, obviously, is another vitally important matter. As that first
obstacle still operates, so this second obstacle still operates. We are
not engaged, therefore, in some academic, purely objective study
of something that was true two thousand years ago. It is as true
today as it was then. Scripture is always relevant and contemporary,
it speaks about us and all others. So that it is of vital interest to us
to understand the apostle's teaching at this point.

I propose to deal with it in general only for the moment, as I
want to give a general introduction to the whole section. The
apostle is anxious that these Ephesians should truly grasp and
apprehend what a tremendous thing it was that they should ever
have become Christians, and that they should be members of the
Christian Church. His second way of getting them to see that, is
this: '. . . remember', he says, 'that . . . in times past'—then follows
the description. That is how he introduces it. It is only as they
remember that, and only as they realise what the truth about them
is, that they can really begin to understand the greatness of God's
power. You will never realise the greatness of God's power until you

realise the greatness of the obstacles which that power has overcome. There are many people today who see nothing in the Christian salvation, who are not amazed at it, and who think that Paul was probably psychopathic because he goes off into ecstasies as he contemplates its glories. They see nothing at all in it; there is nothing amazing in Christianity to them, nothing astounding. Why? Because they have never realised the problem, because they are ignorant of sin, and know nothing about the wrath of God. They do not realise the nature of these obstacles and problems. The apostle did; and he wants the Ephesians to do so too. His method to that end is to remind them of what they were, and to get them to see how God had overcome this second obstacle. This, in a sense, is as marvellous and as wonderful as the way in which He overcame the first.

What is this second obstacle? Let me put it like this. *The world in those ancient times was divided into two main groups, the Jews and the Gentiles.* The division seemed absolute, and any talk about reconciliation seemed monstrous and impossible. Jew and Gentile! Jews and 'dogs'! But on the other hand the Gentiles had their classification, and particularly the Greeks. The whole world, for them, was divided up into Greeks and Barbarians—the knowledge-able people, the philosophers, the Greeks on the one hand; the ignoramuses, the illiterate, the Barbarians on the other. That was the position, and it seemed utterly impossible that these two sections, these warring sections who despised each other so heartily, could ever be brought together and reconciled, still less that they should ever be found on bended knee together worshipping and adoring the same God and the same Lord. But it has happened, says Paul. The astounding thing is that it is true. These Ephesians have been brought in, and are likewise in the membership. This is the astounding thing that nothing less than 'the exceeding greatness of God's power' could ever have brought to pass.

Now that is the message. The way in which the apostle puts it is extremely interesting. Take this eleventh verse that we are considering. Here he introduces the subject. Have you noticed the way in which he does so? People often find this to be a difficult verse, and it is so until you see exactly what it means. At first reading it seems impossible. Look at it again. 'Wherefore remember that ye (you Ephesians), being in time past Gentiles in the flesh'—then this long statement, 'who are called Uncircumcision by that which is called the Circumcision in the flesh made by hands'.

It means this. Paul starts by reminding them that they actually were 'Gentiles in the flesh'. It was just a fact of history, a literal, solid fact, that as Gentiles they had not been circumcised. So they were 'Gentiles in the flesh'. 'In the flesh' is not here a contrast with 'in the spirit', because if that were so the apostle would seem to be saying: It is true that you were Gentiles in the flesh, but of course in the spirit you were all right. That is not what he means at all. What he means is this: it is a hard fact that you were Gentiles in the flesh; you had not the mark, the sign, the symbol of being Jews— you had not been circumcised. But he does not leave it at that. He might have done, but he goes off into a kind of digression which terminates at the end of the verse, and then comes back to the original point at the beginning of verse 12. But the digression is full of interest. 'Wherefore remember that ye, being in time past Gentiles in the flesh', who are called Uncircumcision by the self-styled or self-called Circumcision which is in the flesh made by hands. The trouble was that the Jews had taken hold of this, which really was a fact, and had turned it into a problem. Through misunderstanding the teaching of their own Scriptures, they had come to think that the only thing that really mattered was the sign in the flesh. They were regarding it in a material manner, in a fleshly way, and to them nothing mattered but circumcision *qua* circumcision. To them that was everything, that was all-important and nothing else mattered. They had misunderstood the entire purpose even of circumcision itself; and thereby they had created this great barrier and obstacle in the ancient world. The apostle puts it in these words: You were Gentiles in the flesh. Yes, and by these people who talk of themselves as The Circumcision, or The Concision, you were dubbed and described as The Uncircumcision. These people who speak only in terms of the flesh and that which is done by men's hands, thinking only along that level, hold themselves apart and say, 'We are the Circumcision' and those others are the 'Uncircumcision'.

This is a very important point to observe as you read the New Testament Epistles. Take, for instance, what Paul writes to the Philippians (3.3) 'For we are the Circumcision'—we, Christians!— 'who worship God in the spirit and rejoice in Christ Jesus and have no confidence in the flesh'. It is exactly the same point. In other words, to have a true understanding of these Pauline Epistles we must understand the point that he is making in this verse. Not only was it a fact and a truth that the Gentiles had not been circumcised; unfortunately the Jews had exaggerated that fact, and had made it a wall of division which seemed to be quite irremovable.

Now that bit of exposition is vital to an understanding of everything that we have to say. There were two aspects to this second obstacle which God had to overcome before the Ephesians could ever become Christians. First of all there was the Jews' attitude towards the Gentiles. And then, secondly, there was God's attitude towards the Gentiles. God's attitude must arise because after all they had not been circumcised, they were not of the seed of Abraham. But before we come to that we must look at this Jewish attitude, this 'Concision and Uncircumcision', this division. There is, I believe, an element almost of sarcasm in the way in which the apostle puts it here—'which are called the Uncircumcision by that which is called (which means the self-called, the self-styled) Circumcision in the flesh made by hands'. You notice his emphasis. His great point is that God has overcome this dual obstacle. Both these difficulties have been overcome by Christ and by what He has done. The attitude of the Jew to the Gentile has been put right if the Jew has become a Christian; and God's attitude towards them has also changed. So the whole question of the law has been solved by our Lord and Saviour. That is the actual argument of the apostle.

Let me now show you *the relevance of all that today*, because it is still true. We are living in an age and at a time when there is a great deal of thought and concentration upon this selfsame problem. The world is full of divisions and full of strife. We are all aware of it; we see it as between nations—there is tension between the Arab States and Israel, between East and West, and all the various subdivisions and ramifications. Divisions!—Iron Curtain, Bamboo Curtain, and so on! But not only is this true in the realm of nations and international relationships; it is equally true within the nations: classes, groups and various other divisions. The world, in a sense, is full of this very thing. As the ancient world was divided in the way that we have seen, so the modern world is divided up in these various ways. And, alas, the same thing is true of the Christian Church: sects, denominations, groups and divisions, and barriers. And all this is occupying a great deal of thought and attention at the present time. There is endless talk about this, there is endless writing about it. Everybody is concerned about producing understanding, obtaining unity, and about dealing with this problem in these various realms. And yet does it not seem to be the case that much of the talk and the writing and the busying is utterly vain and futile? It does not seem to lead to anything; and the question is, Why? The answer lies in what the apostle teaches here; for his claim at this point is, as it is in the whole of his Epistle, that the only unity worth talking about is possible only on certain conditions. The early Church, consisting of Jew and Gentile, was the demonstration of true unity. They had been brought together, they went together by one Spirit to the same Father in prayer, they were in the same Church, they were fellow citizens, indeed members of the same family. That is the only way, and every other way that may be tried will lead to nothing. To me one of the major tragedies of the hour, and especially in the realm of the Church, is that most of the time seems to be taken up by the leaders in preaching about unity instead of preaching the gospel that alone can produce unity. The time is spent in talking and in conferences, endlessly—conferences in which they 'explore their difficulties'. You will never get unity that way. It is the gospel alone that will produce unity. And while there is disagreement about the gospel it is a waste of breath and of energy to be talking about any other possible way to unity. That is the message of this section, as I see it; and it applies not only to the Church but also to the world that is outside.

What then is the teaching? Let me summarise it like this. The apostle would have us see that there are two main matters that must be considered before there is any hope of unity and the resolving of the problems and the difficulties. What are they?

The first is that we must realise the cause of the trouble. This needs to be stated constantly and endlessly at the present time! Most of the vain talking and writing about unity and understanding today is entirely due to one thing, namely, that they have never faced the cause of the trouble. You must have diagnosis before treatment. A man who rushes to treatment before he is certain of the diagnosis simply does not know his work. And he is a positive danger. To medicate symptoms at the expense of the disease, the root cause, is sheer lunacy. It is because people simply will not acknowledge the cause as it is taught here that all their attempts at unity prove utterly futile.

Here, the apostle tells us about the cause, the disease. Look at this case of the Jews as he puts it in the eleventh verse. We can express it like this as a principle. The division in the ancient world was due to one thing, and that was that *differences had been turned into barriers*, differences had become a 'middle wall of partition'. There are differences, and it is folly to minimise differences. Differences are facts. And even when you have true unity, differences will still remain. But the tragedy is that men exaggerate differences and turn them into barriers, into obstacles, into 'curtains', middle walls of partition. That is the very thing that these Jews had been doing. It was God's ordination that there should be Jews and Gentiles. It was God who had made the nation of the Jews. There was a real difference. The Jews were circumcised, the others were not. But that was not to be a barrier. God did not create the nation of the Jews in order to have nothing to do with the others; He created the nation of the Jews in order that through them He might speak to the whole world. But the Jew had misunderstood. He had turned this difference into a barrier, and he held himself aloof and despised the others. The Circumcision—the Uncircumcision!

How does this work out? According to the apostle it seems to work out like this. First of all it leads to *pride*. Actually, of course, it is due to pride, it is due to self. That is ultimately the cause of every division and every barrier and every obstacle. That is the cause of every middle wall of partition. It is the ultimate cause of everything that divides people. Pride and self! Pride is blinding, pride is a powerful spirit that controls us and dragoons us and dominates us. Under the influence of pride a man cannot think straightly, he becomes prejudiced. He cannot see anything truly as it is. Prejudice is one of the greatest curses in life, and it is generally grounded and rooted in pride. It is an utterly blinding force. How does it work? It first of all prevents our seeing that there are two sides to a question. To the man who is governed by prejudice there is not a second side, there is only one, there is not another. He is absolutely blinded. Now that was the attitude of the Jew: 'the Circumcision', 'the Uncircumcision'! He would not recognise the Gentiles, he turned his back upon them. Is not that the essence of all disputes?

Then another way in which prejudice works is this. It always leads us to take a *false view of ourselves*. The prejudice, and the pride that leads to prejudice, not only prevent a man seeing that there is another side; they also produce in him an entirely false view of himself. In this way, prejudice always exaggerates what is true of him. It was God's ordinance that the Jew should be circumcised, but the Jew had exaggerated that into saying that there was only one real nation on earth, the Jewish. The others were 'dogs'. He exaggerated what was true of himself. He thought that merely because he was a Jew he was of necessity right with God, and that he needed nothing more. That was why the Jews crucified the Son of God, because He showed them that that was not true.

Another thing it does is to render us *incapable of seeing and realising that whatever we may be, and whatever we may have, is not due to us but to God who has given it us*. The Jew had quite forgotten that circumcision was the gift of God to him. 'We be Abraham's seed and were never in bondage to any man' (John 8:33), said the Jews to Christ on one occasion. Poor blinded fools! As if they were responsible for themselves! We all tend to do the same thing. Look at men boasting about their own ability. What right has a man to boast of his ability? Has he produced it? Has he generated it? No, he was born with it, it was given to him by God. All these gifts are given to us by God. A man is proud of his appearance. Is he responsible for it? Did he produce it? But that is what pride does, you see. It exaggerates what we have, and it claims that we have generated it. And it does not realise in humility that it is all God-given and comes from His bounteous hands. These are the seeds of disunion and of war and of bloodshed.

Further, it makes us take an entirely *false view of others*. As it makes us exaggerate what we have, it makes us detract from what they have. You recognise it working in your own life, do you not? How we always add to our side and take off from the other side! We are reluctant to recognise goodness when it is there in others: we do not want to do so. And because we do not want to, we will not. Indeed, we subtract, we take away until there is nothing left. The Jew was convinced that there was nothing of value in the Gentiles; they did not seem even to be human beings; they were 'dogs'. In exactly the same way the Greek with his learning regarded others as Barbarians, illiterates. Prejudice not only detracts and subtracts from what is true of others; but it proceeds to despise them. Think of Kipling's 'lesser breeds without the law', and terms like 'non-British', 'foreigners', 'Herrenvolk', 'natives'. There you have the source of many disputes and problems. It is because that mentality so tended to predominate in the last century that the world is confronted by so many problems today, and this country of ours perhaps, in particular. But it is also true of the individual. It is true of all who are governed by pride and self. That is how it works out—exaggeration of what is complimentary to us, detraction from others and despising of others. 'That which is called the Uncircumcision by the (self-styled, self-called) Circumcision in the flesh made by hands!' It is not surprising that Paul was somewhat sarcastic. He wanted to ridicule the thing, so he painted it like this in order that all may see what a horrible, foul thing it is.

But there is *a second great cause of division, namely, a wrong sense of values*. Having already referred to this in principle, let me now give the details. The whole tragedy of the Jew at that time was that he had missed the real point. He was lacking in a real sense of values. He thought that it was circumcision in the flesh that mattered. What Paul and others had to teach him was that it was circumcision in the spirit that really matters; that you can be circumcised in the flesh, but be damned and lost at the same time; that the man who is right with God is the man who has been circumcised in his spirit; and that that is as possible to the Gentile as to the Jew. But the Jew had stopped at the flesh; his sense of values was wrong, he had misinterpreted circumcision. Circumcision was merely an external sign of a spiritual, inward state. That is what it was meant to be, but the Jew had been blind to it.

Notice the two things Paul emphasises: 'in the flesh', and 'made by hands'. 'Uncircumcision by that which is called the Circumcision in the flesh made by hands'. By 'the flesh' here he means the *emphasis upon externals* and upon that which is purely physical. Nationality! That is purely of the flesh. It is a complete accident that a man should be born into one nation rather than another. It is a fact, certainly, that there are different nations and nationalities; but we tend to do exactly what the Jews did, we turn these things into barriers. Because I happen to be born of a certain nation, that is *the* nation. The other man says exactly the same thing about his nation. It is just taking something that is true in the flesh but exaggerating it until it becomes a tremendous thing. Nationality! People will fight for it, they will give up their lives for it, they will kill others because of it. Nationality! Birth! Family! Blood! How we exaggerate these things and inflate them! How we despise others! How these things create barriers! People attach more significance to the mere pedigree of men than to their spirits, to their souls, to their characters, to their understanding. These are literal barriers in life; people are ostracised for these reasons. The colour of one's skin! Purely a matter of the flesh, but, alas, it is the kind of thing that leads to that horrible phrase—'lesser breeds without the law'. The soul, the mind, the spirit, are not considered. The assessment is purely in terms of the flesh. Ability, money, school and training, position in life—these are the things which are causing division and dispute and misery and wretchedness in the world today, and they all belong to the flesh.

Unfortunately, when you come to the realm of religion you find the same thing. Nothing causes so much division as concentration upon the mere *externals of religion*. The people who persecuted our Lord most of all and who finally were responsible for His death were the Pharisees and the Sadducees. Why? Because they were only interested in the externals, the forms, the ceremonies and the ritual, and missed the spirit completely. And it is still the same. Concentration on forms, beautiful services, liturgies, ceremonial, dress, and things of this kind in connection with the worship of God are dividing people. It is simply the old practice of the Jews repeated in modern form; that which is of the flesh taken hold of and exaggerated until it becomes a barrier.

But look at the other phrase for a moment. Not only 'the flesh', but 'made with hands', says Paul, that is, *purely human*. What are the things that are causing division in the Church today? Why will not all meet together at the same communion table? Ah, says one, you shall not come to the table and take of the bread and the wine unless you have been confirmed, unless certain hands have been put upon your head. 'Made by hands,' you see! It does not matter that a person has been born again and has the Spirit of God in him and that he is living the Christian life as a saint. He shall not come and partake because he has not been confirmed. What is the value of talking about unity and reunion, what is the point of having great conferences and giving them such publicity, if the very leaders in such conferences still act in terms of such barriers? It is unreal, I would almost say it is dishonest. But others say: You shall not come to the table unless you have been baptised in a particular manner. It is the way in which you have been baptised that matters, and you are excluded from the table of the Lord simply because of the amount of water with which you have been baptised. 'Made by hands!' And there are other circles which will not admit you to partake of the bread and the wine because of similar details and minutiae. It is a repetition of the outlook of the Pharisees and Scribes, the Sadducees and the doctors of the law. These things belong merely to the periphery. We are prepared to grant that there are differences of opinion about these matters, but they should never come to the centre, they should never become barriers, they should never be middle walls of partition. You should not refuse to come to the Lord's table with another for any one of those reasons.

You find similar traditions in matters of Church government and Church order also. There are people who are much more loyal to the tradition of their particular denomination than they are to the Lord Jesus Christ. It is generally an accident that they belong to the denomination, it is simply because their parents did, and that they were brought up in it; but they will fight for it, they will quarrel about it. This becomes the important, the vital thing. Christ and His truth are somehow forgotten entirely and are not mentioned. 'Made with hands,' human traditions, loyalty to forms, traditionalism! These are the things that lead to the separations and disunities.

These, then, are the causes. *What of the cure?* The apostle puts it quite plainly here. Christ alone can cure, and for the reason that what is needed is a change of heart. It is not enough just to appeal for goodwill and for kindness and for friendliness and for brotherliness. It simply does not work, and it will not work; in fact it never has worked. Neither is it sufficient merely to appeal in general to men and women to apply the teaching of Christ. That is the popular appeal today. Come, they say, let us take the teaching of Christ, let us apply it. Some people think that if you did that, if this country did that, somehow even war would be banished and there would be no more trouble. The answer to that, again, is that it is not true, simply not fact. It has been tried already. It has been tried in schools where they no longer believe in discipline. It has been tried in the prisons, where again we no longer really believe in discipline. And you see the results, you see the increasing lawlessness and godlessness. But more important than that, it is unscriptural, it is not biblical, it is not God's teaching, which is, that until a man comes 'under grace' he must be kept 'under law'. Man's nature is wrong and it will always express itself, therefore you must curb it, you must control it. While there are wild beasts about you must be ready for them. The idea that, if you go and talk sweetly to people of the Hitler mentality, they will listen to you and they will cease to be aggressive, is almost too pathetic and fatuous even for consideration.

No, *there is only one way: it is Christ's way*. He tells us the truth about ourselves. He makes us face ourselves. Face to face with Him I see my utter worthlessness, my wretchedness, my woe. When I look into the face of Christ I have nothing to boast about, I forget all that I have exaggerated, all the things to which I have trusted. Here, I am nothing, I am a pauper. He makes me see the truth about myself. You will never get unity amongst men until they see the truth about themselves. He also makes me see that the same thing is true of everybody else; that it is true of the other man whom I have disliked, or the other nation; that we are all the same, that we are one in sin and one in failure; that we are together under the wrath of God; that the things we have exaggerated are trivialities. 'There is none righteous, no, not one'; we are all condemned felons before a holy God. He brings us down together to the dust. He has demolished most of the differences already.

Then He shows us that we all need the same grace, the same mercy, the same love. And we receive them together and we all share in them together. We worship the same Person, and rejoice in the same salvation. Having realised all this, my loyalty henceforth is not to myself but to Him; and the other man's is not to himself but to Him. So we have forgotten one another and we are no longer jealous and envious and quarrelling; we go together to Him and join in singing His praise together.

That is Christ's way of doing it. It is not the application of the spirit of Christ by man. It is the putting of the Spirit of Christ into man. Unregenerate man cannot apply the principle and the spirit of Christ; he does not want to. A man may persuade himself for a while that he wants to, but others will not, and there will be divisions and distinctions and wars. There is only one hope—that men and women be born again, that they be reconciled by the blood of Christ, that God should forgive them, that God should give them a new nature and a new heart, and implant a new Spirit within them. And as they share this Spirit together they will worship

Him and praise Him and boast in Him; now they will not boast in themselves or in their nations, or in anything save in the fact that the Lord Jesus Christ has been crucified for them, and that by Him they have been crucified unto the world and the world has been crucified unto them.

This is the only basis of unity. Not organisation, not anything else, but the humility of the new man in Christ, the Christ-dominated, the Christ-centred life. Every middle wall of partition is broken down by this, 'of twain he makes one new man' in Christ. May God open our eyes to this in all our personal relationships. May He open the eyes of the Church to it. May the world see that there is only one hope of true peace, and that is, to come and lie together at the feet of the Prince of peace, the King of righteousness.

15

WITHOUT CHRIST

*That at that time ye were without Christ, being aliens from the common-
wealth of Israel, and strangers from the covenants of promise, having no
hope, and without God in the world.*   Ephesians 2: 12

We now come in this twelfth verse to look at, and to deal in detail
with, the second aspect of this problem, namely, how could these
Ephesians who were Gentiles, uncircumcised—how could they
possibly be brought into the Christian Church and be joined with
Jewish Christians to form one new body, the Christian Church?
That is the question with which the apostle deals here. The distinction between Jew and Gentile was a very real one. We must not
minimise it, or detract from it, or make light of it. After all, it was
God Himself who introduced the sign of circumcision. It was God
who commanded Abraham to circumcise himself and his children,
and that this should be done in perpetuity. Therefore we must not
underestimate that distinction between Jews and Gentiles. But
though we recognise the distinction, we must be clear in our minds
as to what it means and what it represents. It was at that point
that the Jews had gone astray. To them the external sign alone
meant everything. It was something in the flesh, it was something
external. Is a man circumcised? Then he is all right, he is one of
God's people. Is he uncircumcised? Then he is all wrong and has
no hope. They had completely misunderstood the point, the purpose,
and the spirit of circumcision.

The apostle Paul deals with this question in many of his Epistles.
He puts it, for instance, in a particularly clear manner in his Epistle
to the Romans, in the second chapter in verses twenty-eight and
twenty-nine, where he says: 'For he is not a Jew which is one outwardly; neither is that circumcision, which is outward in the flesh;
but he is a Jew, which is one inwardly; and circumcision is that of
the heart, in the spirit and not in the letter, whose praise is not of
men but of God.' In other words, the Jews had completely failed to
see and to realise that the whole object of this was something spiritual in the mind of God. The apostle is very concerned about this.
Some people, when they hear that there is no longer circumcision
or uncircumcision, Jew or Gentile, and so on, are prone to say:

Well then, we need pay no attention to these things. Some Christians have been foolish enough to say that because we are Christians we do not need the Old Testament. But that, says the apostle again in the Epistle to the Romans, is quite wrong. 'What advantage then hath the Jew, or what profit is there of circumcision?' And he replies 'Much every way; chiefly because that unto them were committed the oracles of God'. Then in the ninth chapter of the Epistle to the Romans he works out the same argument again. He says he has great heaviness and sorrow in his heart—'I could wish that myself were accursed from Christ for my brethren, my kinsmen according to the flesh; who are Israelites'. What does that mean? He goes on to give the answer, 'to whom pertaineth the adoption, and the glory, and the covenants, and the giving of the law, and the service of God, and the promises; whose are the fathers, and of whom as concerning the flesh Christ came, who is over all, God blessed for ever'. There was a very real purpose and object in the distinction between Jew and Gentile. It was not as the Jews misinterpreted it, but it was there and it was a tremendously important matter. Here, now, in this twelfth verse of Ephesians 2 Paul gives the true view of it. In the eleventh verse he gives the false view of circumcision; in the twelfth verse the true view of circumcision and the absence of it.

The apostle presents his teaching in a most interesting and extraordinary and, at first sight, surprising manner. This is how he puts it: 'That at that time ye were without Christ'. Now that is a strange way of putting it—'*without Christ*'. It can be translated as 'apart from Christ', 'outside of Christ', 'not in fellowship with Christ', 'not in relationship to Christ', or even 'living apart from Christ'. Then having put it like that in general, he goes on to put it in particular in *five separate points*: being 'aliens from the commonwealth of Israel', 'strangers from the covenants of promise'; 'having no hope', 'without God', 'in the world'.

This surely demands our careful attention. Paul is obviously referring to *the position which obtained before Christ*, under the old dispensation, under the Old Testament. The world was divided into Jews and Gentiles, those who as Jews had been circumcised, and the uncircumcised, the Gentiles, the other nations. Yet you notice that he refers to the Gentiles at that time and in that condition in these terms, 'without Christ', 'outside Christ'. Here he is referring to a position which obtained before the Lord Jesus Christ ever came into the world; and yet he puts it in terms of being 'in Christ' or 'outside Christ', living apart from Christ. Why does the apostle describe that state of affairs in terms of a relationship to Christ?

The answer is, of course, that in a sense he is doing something which he is bound to do, and unless we understand and grasp clearly what he is doing here we must have read our Old Testament in vain. He is here making a general review of the Old Testament. What characterises it? The answer is: 'the commonwealth of Israel'; 'the covenants of promise'; the hope that God gave to the people; their relationship to God; their separation from the world. That is a summary of the condition and the position of the Israelites under the Old Testament dispensation. All the other nations were outside these blessings, and yet he describes it all in terms of being 'in Christ', or 'outside Christ'.

How are we to understand this? The answer is that everything God did to and for the Jews under the old dispensation was done with an eye to Christ. *Everything in the Old Testament looks forward to Christ.* We must never look at any of those things in and of themselves. Everything that God did to those Jews, those Israelites, He did in preparation for the coming of the Lord Jesus Christ. The apostle puts it in a phrase in Galatians 3: 23 in this way: he says that God's purpose was to 'shut us up unto the faith which should afterwards be revealed'; 'the law was our schoolmaster to bring us to Christ', it was never meant to be anything in and of itself. That is where the Jews went wrong. They thought the law was something in and of itself, and that they were saved because they possessed the law while others had not got the law. No, says Paul, the law is our schoolmaster, our pedagogue, to bring us to Christ. The purpose of all those things was to shut us up to the faith that should yet be revealed.

We can look at it like this. God made man in His own image, and man lived in correspondence and in fellowship with God. But alas, he sinned and fell away from God. After that he gave birth to progeny, the earth became filled with people, and until the call of Abraham the whole world and all its peoples and its nations were in the one relationship to God. There was no division in an important sense until you come to the call of Abraham. There is a kind of division already between the line of Cain and the line of Seth, but God dealt with all nations and all peoples in the same way until the call of Abraham. Then God did something new. He told Abraham that He was going to make of him a nation, that out of his loins a great nation would come, a people special and peculiar to the Lord God Himself. He was going to create a new nation, a special nation. He was going to set them apart from all the other peoples and He would be in a peculiar relationship to them. That is the formation of Israel, that is the genesis of the commonwealth of Israel, the people of God. Then with that people He made certain covenants. He gave certain promises to them, He pledged Himself to them. He took this man Abraham aside and he said 'In thee and in thy seed shall all the nations of the earth be blessed'. God covenanted with Abraham, He pledged Himself to him, He took an oath—that is the meaning of covenants. These promises were often repeated—the one great covenant repeated in various forms— repeated to Isaac and to Jacob, to Moses at Sinai, again to David, and preached by the prophets. That is what is meant by these terms 'the commonwealth of Israel', 'the covenants of promise', and so on. They were all looking forward to the coming of the Messiah, the great Deliverer. In other words, the thing we must grasp is this, that God now looked down upon the world and its people in two ways: He looked upon these covenant people in one way: He looked upon the others in another way. And the covenant people were known by the sign and the mark of circumcision. Every boy that was born into Israel was to be circumcised on the eighth day because he belonged to this covenant people, this nation of Israel, God's people. There on the one hand are God's people: here on the other hand are the Gentiles.

That is the thing of which the apostle is reminding these Ephesians, and his object in doing so is this. He wants them to realise the greatness of their salvation. He wants them to realise that the fact that they have now become fellow citizens, fellow-heirs with the saints and of the household of God, is the most astounding thing that could ever have happened. The only way in which they can understand it is to experience something of 'the exceeding greatness of God's power to us-ward who believe'. It is not only the power that raises us from the death of sin, it is a power that overcomes this tremendous question of how those who are outside the covenant relationship can ever be brought into it. So he goes on to explain it and to expound it to them. No man will ever rejoice in Christ as he should unless he realises what his position was before he became a Christian. The trouble with all professing Christians who are not rejoicing in Christ is that they have never realised what they were in sin. It is of no help to say that you must 'always be positive'; you must start with your negative. If you do not realise what you were before God took hold of you, you will never praise Him as you ought. So Paul goes into it in great detail. There are many people who have never seen any need of Christ. Why? Because they are self-satisfied and think all is well with them as they are. That is the trouble. Paul is anxious that his readers should understand this matter. He has prayed that God would 'open the eyes of their understanding' that they might do so. You were afar off, he says, but now you have 'been brought nigh by the blood of Christ'—can you not see what God has done? Can you not see the measure of His love and grace and mercy, and His almighty power?

That is his argument. Let us look further at it in order to *apply it to ourselves*. Do you know in your heart as well as in your head this wonderful love of God? Are you thrilled as you think of it and conceive of it? Are you filled with a sense of wonder, love and praise? If not, it is because you do not realise what God has done for you in Christ. The way to understand this is to look at what it means not to be a Christian—'without Christ' 'outside Christ'. In other words, the first principle we lay down is that the one thing that matters in this life and in this world is to be related to God in Christ. There is nothing more terrible that can be said about any-body than this—'without Christ', 'living apart from Christ'. When the apostle looks for a term in which he can show these people how far away they were, and the utter hopelessness of their position, this is the term he chooses, 'without Christ'. 'Living apart from Christ'. 'In no living relationship to Christ'. There is nothing worse than that. But on the other hand there is nothing more wonderful than to be 'in Christ'. These are the New Testament terms—'in Christ', 'outside Christ'.

Those are the *only two positions that matter*. We are all of us either 'in Christ' or else 'outside Christ'. Do you know exactly where you are? This is not theory, this is actual fact and experience. This is the thing that is going to determine our eternal destiny. It is because they do not know what is meant by being 'outside Christ' that there are millions of people in the world today who always spend their Sunday morning reading newspapers and the filth of the law courts instead of looking into the Word of God. They do not realise what a terrible position they are in 'outside Christ'. So Paul tells them in detail what it means in the five terms, as I have already mentioned. They can be classified under two headings.

First let us consider: *what it means to be without Christ as regards our relationship to God.* Here the apostle says two things, the first two of the five terms. The first is that we are in the state and condi-tion of being '*aliens from the commonwealth of Israel*'. A commonwealth means a community of citizens or of people definitely constituted a polity. At least it means a number of people who are definitely constituted into a community. They are something separate and distinct, which can be recognised. What we are told therefore is that God, in the way I have indicated, formed a community for Himself. This is God's way of salvation; He forms a people, He forms a community. He sets them apart, and He is in a particular relationship to them. A detailed description of all this is given in the nineteenth chapter of the book of Exodus. The apostle Peter quotes it in his first Epistle, the second chapter, verses nine and ten. God gathered those people together before He gave them the Ten Commandments, and He said, 'Ye are a peculiar treasure to me,' 'Ye are a chosen generation, a royal priesthood, a holy nation, a people for my peculiar possession.' He set them apart for Himself, He divided them off from everybody else. But it does not stop at that. He did that because He was going to take a special interest in them. They are a people for His own 'peculiar possession.' So later on God said through the prophet Amos of this nation of Israel: 'You only have I known of all the families of the earth' (Amos 3: 2). Obviously, that does not mean that He was not aware of all the others. Of course He was. To 'know' in the Scripture means to take a very special personal interest in, to be concerned about, to care for, to look upon with a father's eye and with a loving gaze. 'You only have I known of all the families of the earth'—that was Israel. God saw all the other nations, but He did not know them, He did not take this particular interest in them; they were outside the commonwealth of Israel, they were aliens. Indeed, the word used here by Paul is very interesting. It reads here 'being aliens'; it should be translated 'having been made aliens', or 'having become aliens'. In other words no one was ever meant to be in this position; it is all the result of the Fall and the result of sin. Man has become an alien, outside the peculiar interest of God.

The first thing, then, that is meant by being 'without Christ', is that you are outside that circle in which God is peculiarly interested. You do not belong to the covenant people. You are just one of a great mass somewhere; there is not this special interest, this special object of concern. 'Aliens from the commonwealth of Israel!' Today it is the Christian Church that corresponds to the commonwealth of Israel. The most terrible thing about a man who is not a Christian is that he is outside that circle and does not belong to the people of God. Are you an alien from the commonwealth of Israel? Do you feel strange in a Christian service? Do you say to yourself: What is that man talking about? What is all this? It does not seem to be very practical, he does not seem to be preaching about international conferences and the making of atomic bombs or current political issues. It is not relevant, it is not up-to-date. Is it strange and alien to you? Or do you feel you belong to it? It is a terrible thing to feel that you are an outsider, that you have no part in these things, that somehow they have nothing to do with you. Are you in? Do you love the brethren? Have you a part in these things? It is a terrible thing to be 'outside Christ', an 'alien from the commonwealth of Israel'.

The next thing the apostle tells us is that the Gentiles were *strangers from the covenants of promise*'. I have reminded you of the covenants that God made. He took hold of Abraham. Not because there was anything peculiarly good about Abraham; he was a pagan amongst other pagans. God called him out and said: I have set My eye on you, I am going to bless you, I pledge Myself to you. As the author of the Epistle to the Hebrews reminds us, He did it with an oath (6: 13–18). He pledged Himself and gave an oath, that it might be sure to Abraham and to his seed. The promises of God! Read your Old Testament and you will see them one after another. God calls these men apart, He gives them a revelation, a vision, He addresses them, He sends a word to them. This is the thing that keeps them going. That was the secret of the people who are described in the eleventh chapter of the Epistle to the Hebrews—the promises. God looked upon them and said, Have no concern; let the other nations envy you and try to destroy you; let men rise up against you; it does not matter; you are My people, I will never let you go ,'I will never leave thee nor forsake thee'; hold on to My covenant word and My promises, look forward to their fulfilment.

The covenant promises! But the Ephesians were strangers to them. The Gentile nations knew nothing about them. While the peculiar people of God, the Jews, were receiving these great messages and rejoicing in them, the others knew nothing at all about it—strangers, absolute strangers, who had not heard of the promises, knew nothing about them, and were not interested in them. That is still true of all who are 'outside Christ', those who are not living in relationship to Christ. They can read their Bible and it does not move them. They can look at these 'exceeding great and precious promises' and say: To whom does this apply, what is all this about? They are strangers, they are like people from another country, they do not understand the language. Does the Bible speak to you? Is it intelligible to you? Do you feel it is but gibberish and a jargon? Or does it speak to you, and speak words that lift you on your feet and make you praise God? Are you a stranger to the covenants of promise, or do you know that they are speaking to you and that you are a member of the company, that God is addressing you as you read His holy Word? What a terrible thing it is to be 'outside Christ', not in a living relationship to Christ, and strangers from the covenants of promise!

Let us go on to consider the *second* heading: *the inevitable con-*

sequences of being 'outside Christ'. The apostle mentions three. The first is, *without hope*. Surely that is one of the most terrible statements in the whole of Scripture, if not the very worst. 'Having no hope!' There is nothing worse than that! 'While there is life there is hope;' yes, but when hope goes there is nothing. Hope is the last thing that goes, and when hope goes 'chaos is come again'—as Othello put it. But a man who is without Christ is without hope.

This means first of all that he has no hope in this life. Had you realised that without Christ there is no hope in this life, in this world?—none at all! Is that an exaggeration? In answer, I ask you to consider the statements of the profoundest thinkers the world has ever known, and you will find that they are invariably pessimists. The greatest works of Shakespeare are his tragedies. All religions, apart from the Christian faith, are profoundly pessimistic. The only comfort they give you is that you escape from this world some time; you may have to go through a whole series of reincarnations— but there is no hope here, you must get out of it and somehow or other be lost in some Nirvana. They have no hope for man in this world. It is the flesh, the body, they say, that causes all our troubles, and there is no hope for you while you are in it. So you have got to get out of this world. Hinduism, Buddhism, and the rest are all completely hopeless. They are the products of profound thinking without revelation; and they are all hopeless. This is something that you find in all the great philosophies, in all the great religions. You find it in all great literature. Have you noticed that our greatest poets are pessimists? Wordsworth tells us that he has been listening to the 'still, sad music of humanity'. Of course, if you are flitting about from dance hall to dance hall and cinema to cinema you will not hear it, because there is such a clatter and a noise that you cannot hear it; but the poet sits, listens, and meditates, and what does he hear?—Isn't life wonderful?—No, what he hears is the 'still, sad music of humanity'. 'Life is real, life is earnest.' It is not a giddy round of pleasure after pleasure. There is no hope found in this life and in this world.

All this is summarised very perfectly for us in the Book of Ecclesi- astes, where the author says, 'Vanity of vanities, all is vanity'. That is not said superficially at a moment of disappointment; it is the conclusion arrived at by a profound thinker who has tried all the possibilities, considered all the things that are offered, and who has found that all together they come to nothing. 'The thing that hath been, it is that which shall be; and that which is done is that which shall be done; and there is no new thing under the sun.' (1: 9). There is no hope for the world, it is not going to get better and better. All the futile idealism of the last hundred years is utterly condemned by all the great thinking of the centuries—and, of course, it is utterly discredited today by facts and events. There is no hope in this life and in this world apart from Christ. 'Vanity of vanities, all is vanity' can be written over it all. Not only is there no hope that things will be better, but there is no hope that man himself will get better. He is no better than he was under the Old Testament dispensation. He is still committing the same sins, he is still guilty of the same faults; there is no evidence of spiritual improvement in man. Man today is as rotten as he was the moment he fell in the Garden of Eden. Moreover, there is nothing whatsoever to look forward to. We are all getting older, our powers are failing, death must come, inevitably. Do what you will you cannot get away from it. That is life without Christ. Let Shakespeare sum it up for us in his inimitable manner. He puts it perfectly towards the end of his life in one of his last dramas, *The Tempest*.

> *The cloud-capp'd towers, the gorgeous palaces,*
> *The solemn temples, the great globe itself,*
> *Yea, all which it inherit, shall dissolve,*
> *And, like this insubstantial pageant faded,*
> *Leave not a rack behind: We are such stuff*
> *As dreams are made of, and our little life*
> *Is rounded with a sleep.*

That is life without Christ. No hope! Absolutely none! This is not pessimism, this is realism, this is facing the facts. There is no hope in this world, it is not getting better. Look at your newspapers, look at the facts: man is not improving, and there is nothing before him but death. The cloudcapped towers, the gorgeous palaces, the great globe itself—everything is going to dissolve.

As there is no hope in this life, in this world, there is certainly no hope beyond it for the man who is outside Christ. Death is but the journey's end to him. As Horatius Bonar puts it in his hymn, 'Men die in darkness at your side, Without a hope to cheer the tomb'. They look forward, but what do they see? Nothing! They cannot see through death, they have not 'the faith that sees through death'. What lies beyond? They do not know. They either say there is nothing, or else there is torment, or else a series of reincarnations. They do not know; and as they arrive at the end and are leaving everything, the palaces and towers are collapsing, and there is— nothing. Without hope! That is life without Christ. That is the life that is being lived by millions of people in this country today, who think that we are fools because we sit in chapels listening to this old gospel. They think that they have life and freedom—but that is their position, 'having no hope!'

But even worse: '*without God*!' What does Paul mean by this? He means obviously without a subjective experience of God. God is still there, of course, but these people do not know that, they are not aware of that; and they are not enjoying Him. Let me summarise it in this way. They do not know God and they are not in fellowship with God; therefore they are without all the help and all the peace and all the joy that comes through the knowledge of God and faith in Him. Their world is collapsing, everything is going wrong, they are left alone. In their utter isolation and desolation they have nothing, because they do not know God. Christians too have troubles in this life, accidents take place, things go wrong; in his circumstances the Christian may be identical with the other man. But there is this great difference: the other man is without God; the Christian *has* God and knows God.

How different from the psalmist is this other man without God! The psalmist, you remember, said this: 'When my father and my mother forsake me, then the Lord will take me up'. His father and mother have left him, friends and companions have all gone, everything has gone. It is well, says the psalmist, 'when my father and my mother forsake me, then,' even then, 'the Lord will take me up'. Listen to him again: 'I laid me down and slept'—he was surrounded by enemies at that point; 'I laid me down and slept: I awoke'— why?—'for the Lord sustained me'. Listen to him at another time: 'Out of the depths have I cried unto thee'. He was down in a horrible pit and all seemed to have gone; but he looked up, God was still there; 'I cried unto the Lord out of the depths'. 'The Lord is my shepherd, I shall not want.' 'Though I walk through the valley of the shadow of death, thou art with me, thy rod and thy staff they comfort me.' I can see nothing else now but I still see Thee. The other man does not know this; he is 'without God'. 'The Lord is my light and my salvation, whom shall I fear? The Lord is the strength of my life, of whom shall I be afraid?' With God!—not 'without God'. But listen to him putting it again in one amazing statement: 'From the end of the earth will I cry unto thee, when my heart is overwhelmed. Lead me to the rock that is higher than I.' There he is, almost drowning in an ocean of trouble, with enemies and everything against him; he cries unto God, 'Lead me to the rock that is higher than I', knowing that there he will be safe. But this other man does not know this, he is without Christ, and therefore without God. How unlike the apostle Paul, who tells us: 'At my first answer, no man stood with me, but all men forsook me; I pray God that it be not laid to their charge. Notwithstanding, the Lord stood with me, and strengthened me.' Paul was on trial, all his friends had left him, 'no man stood with me, all men forsook me'. 'Notwithstanding, *the Lord* stood with me, and strengthened me.' And again, he writes to Timothy from prison when everything was going against him, and says, 'Nevertheless, I am not ashamed; for I know whom I have believed, and am persuaded that he is able to keep that which I have committed unto him against that day' (2 Timothy 1:12). Hear the author of the Epistle to the Hebrews quoting the Old Testament, 'The Lord is my helper, and I will not fear what man shall do unto me.' Why? Because God has said, 'I will never leave thee nor forsake thee'.

But this other man does not know that; he is left to himself when his world has collapsed and everything has gone wrong. He is not only 'without hope' but he is 'without God' also, and he cannot look forward to the day which is coming when, according to the book of Revelation, 'God shall wipe away all tears from their eyes' and there shall be sorrow and sighing and weeping no more. A man without Christ does not know these things. How unlike our Lord Himself he is! Hear the Lord Himself saying it: 'Behold, the hour cometh, yea is now come, that ye shall be scattered, every man to his own, and shall leave me alone; and yet I am not alone, for the Father is with me' (John 16:32). He was not 'without God'. God was with Him when all had forsaken Him and had fled. 'And yet I am not alone, the Father is with me.'

What a terrible thing it is to be 'without hope', and 'without God', and '*in the world*'—belonging to this passing world that is under the wrath of God, under condemnation, and to be destroyed. 'The world passeth away and the lusts thereof, but he that doeth the will of God abideth for ever.'

Are these words coming to someone who is 'without Christ?' If so, do you realise where you are? You are outside the commonwealth, the special interest of God; you have no promises to sustain you, 'no hope', you are 'without God', 'in the world'! If you see that, and if you realise what that means, there is only one thing for you to do—fly to Christ. The Ephesians had been once in that position —'but now in Christ Jesus, ye who sometimes were far off are made nigh by the blood of Christ'. You need not remain an outsider. You need not continue to feel that these things do not belong to you. God is speaking to you. Believe Him, listen to Him, act upon what He says, go to Him, confess all that is true of you, and cast yourself upon His love and grace and mercy and compassion. And He will receive you, and He will tell you that He has sent His Son to die and to shed His blood for you that you might be reconciled to Him, and might become His child, and might become a 'fellow-citizen with the saints and of the household of God'. You will find that you have a new life and a new hope, and you will know God, and you will know that He will never leave you nor forsake you. Fly to Him.

If you are already there, rejoice in Him. To be 'in Christ'! There is nothing beyond it. It is heaven on earth. It is the foretaste of eternal bliss.

16

MADE NIGH

But now in Christ Jesus ye who sometimes were far off are made nigh by the blood of Christ. Ephesians 2: 13

These words are obviously a continuation of the statement which begins at verse eleven. They are, at the same time, the complement, as it were, to that statement which we have previously considered. The apostle is setting out here the greatness of this Christian salvation. He wants us to realise that it is so great that nothing less than the power of God Himself could ever have achieved it. That is his whole argument. The power that makes us Christians is precisely the same power that brought the Lord Jesus Christ from the dead and from the grave, showed Him in glorious resurrection, and then raised Him into the heights, into the heavenly places, where He is seated at the right hand of God's power. That is the theme. We must not miss the wood because of the trees. The trees are glorious, but the wood is still greater and still better. So let us hold the two things together in our minds as we proceed.

It is 'the exceeding greatness of His power to us-ward who believe' that the apostle is writing about and wants us to comprehend. We shall need the aid of the Holy Spirit to do so because our minds are so small and so feeble and so inadequate. We pray, therefore, as Paul prayed for the Ephesians, 'that the eyes of our understanding may be enlightened', that we may really know this. The apostle writes his letter in order to help us to do so. *Two things, he says, are essential if we would understand the greatness of Christian salvation: the first is the realisation of our condition apart from it; and the second is the realisation of our condition as the result of it.* Previously we have looked at our condition apart from salvation, as described in the twelfth verse of this chapter: 'At that time ye were without Christ, being aliens from the commonwealth of Israel, strangers to the covenants of promise, without hope, and without God in the world'. It is only as we realise this, in the first instance, that we shall realise how wonderful it is that anybody at all should be a Christian. And after all, that is the amazing thing—not that so many are not Christian; the amazing thing is that anybody is a Christian. Nothing but the power of God in Christ accounts for it. We only grasp this when we realise what man is by nature, when we realise what he is as the result of sin. But we must go much further. If we are to measure this great power, we must not only measure the depth out of which we have been raised, we must also measure the height to which we have been exalted and elevated.

Here are the two poles which represent the extremes in which all who are Christian have found themselves: first of all, outside Christ; then, in Christ. That is what the apostle is doing here in verse thirteen. Having given the negative he goes on to show the positive. You recall that in the first ten verses he was doing exactly the same thing but from a different angle. There he was concerned with our actual spiritual condition—dead in trespasses and sins—and showing how we had been raised to the heights. Here, as we have seen, he is putting it mainly in terms of law, and in terms of our status and standing in the sight and in the presence of God. Once more I assert that it is essential that we should realise the two sides.

Nothing is clearer to all who have any pastoral experience than this, that when people are unhappy about their salvation, and are lacking in assurance, and when there is no joy in their Christian life, it is generally due to one of these two things, or quite frequently to the two together. They are in that condition either because they have never truly been convicted of sin, because they have never really seen their hopelessness, or else because they have never seen their true position as Christians, and the heights to which they have been raised. So the two things must always be taken together. And in the New Testament they always are—and invariably they are taken in that order: the negative first, then the positive. We have already seen it in this chapter.

The apostle always starts with a *negative*. You remember how, when he was on his way up to Jerusalem, and was bidding farewell on a great and lyrical occasion to the elders of this very church at Ephesus—he had not got time to go up to Ephesus himself, so they sent the elders down to meet him. They met in Miletus and in one of the most moving bits of literature I know, the apostle talks to them, and says in effect: I would remind you how when I was with you I ceased not night and day with tears to bear my testimony to the gospel and to preach it. And what was the preaching? 'Repentance toward God, and faith toward our Lord Jesus Christ' (Acts 20: 21). You will never find the apostle Paul saying that people can come to Christ first and afterwards repent. He made that impossible because he always preached repentance first. And that is what he is doing here: that is what you were, this is what you are. And it is only as we grasp the negative and the positive that we shall truly appreciate this great salvation and rejoice in it as we ought.

Let me ask a simple and obvious question at this point. Do we realise the greatness of our salvation? Or let me ask a more sensitive, delicate question. Are you rejoicing in your salvation? Are you prouder of the fact at this moment that you are a Christian than of anything else in your life? I do not hesitate to say that, unless we are prouder of this, and glory more in this, than in anything else, then, to put it at its lowest, our understanding of it is seriously defective. When a man truly sees this, he has only one thing to say; it is what the apostle says: 'God forbid that I should glory save in the cross of our Lord Jesus Christ'. If we truly see this, it is everything. There is nothing comparable to it. So that is a very good test as to whether we really have understood these things or not. Do we realise our privilege? Do we realise the glory of our position at this moment, as Christian people? Let us help one another to come to that place.

We have considered the negative, let us now look at the *positive*. Here it is in one phrase—the apostle again follows his invariable method. He first states his whole theme in one sentence; then he breaks it up and takes it bit by bit. That is what he does in the rest of the chapter. In this thirteenth verse, once more we are face to face with one of these glorious and moving summaries of the whole of the Christian faith. It is all here in the one verse. I sometimes have a feeling that if I could only say this as I should say it, and as the Holy Spirit can enable one to say it, there would be no need to say any more. Here it is: 'But now, in Christ Jesus, ye who sometimes were far off are made nigh by the blood of Christ'.

That is the whole gospel. But let us look into it; it is the very essence of the Christian message. I take it, for the moment, as a whole and look at it in general; and then, God willing, we shall follow the apostle as he himself proceeds to break it up into its various component parts. The matter divides itself up quite inevitably. There are three things here. The first is the contrast between what we were and what we are; the second is what we are, and the third is how we have become what we are.

Firstly, the contrast between what we were and what we are. The apostle puts it in his usual manner—but! He first puts the dark picture, he gives us the negative, and presses it home. Then having done that he says 'But'! You remember the other striking example of it we had in the fourth verse. Having given us that appalling account of ourselves as we were dead in trespasses and sins, suddenly he says, 'But God who is rich in mercy, for his great love wherewith he loved us . . .'. Here again he does it. These 'buts', these blessed 'buts', cannot be repeated too frequently. The whole gospel comes in here. 'But now'!—you see the difference. It is all in the word 'but'. However, he adds these other terms, 'now', 'sometimes'. The word 'but' contrasts; 'now' contrasts with 'then', 'former times', 'times past', 'sometimes'. These are his great words, his contrasts. And what is the effect of these words? You can tell whether you are a Christian or not by just answering this question: Do you feel at times that the greatest word in the entire language of humanity is the word *but*? If you do not, your understanding of Christianity is very defective. There you were! But—and immediately you lift up your head and you begin to sing; a window is opened, a light has flashed, suddenly the gloom has gone. 'But now!' What does it tell us? It is the 'but' of hope, the 'but' of relief, the 'but' that says there is an end to despair and darkness and gloom, that all is not lost, that God is yet with us. We lift up our heads. 'The people that sat in darkness have seen a great light.' 'God who commanded the light to shine out of darkness, hath shined in our hearts, to give the light of the knowledge of the glory of God in the face of Jesus Christ.' That is what we have here in other language.

I want to emphasise especially that these words bring out in a very striking manner the *sharpness of the contrast*, the completeness of the separation, the absolute quality of the difference. This is emphasised everywhere in the New Testament. The difference between a Christian and a non-Christian is an absolute difference, it is a complete contrast. It is clear, it is definite, it is distinct. There should never be any difficulty about telling whether we are Christians or not. The contrast between a Christian and a non-Christian is as extreme and as definite as this: 'now'—'then'; the 'but'; the complete difference; the extraordinary change. There are no shades of difference between being 'not Christian' and being 'Christian'. It is not that you go from black to white through various shades of grey, and you cannot quite tell where you are—the black is beginning to be affected by a little white, and then there is a little more, and a little more, and at last, you say: Ah! this is white! It is not that. That is thoroughly false; that is a complete contrast to what the apostle is teaching here. It is either black or white, he says, and there are no intermediate almost imperceptible stages. It is not like those subtle changes in the colour of the spectrum where you cannot quite tell at any given point where one colour ends and another begins. Not at all. This contrast is clear and definite.

Many are in trouble about their whole position as Christians because they have never understood the teaching of Scripture on this matter. This contrast between the non-Christian and the Christian *is true of all*. I say that for this reason, that I can imagine

someone saying: Ah! wait a minute, of course I can understand
the contrast in its extreme form as the apostle puts it there, because
after all he was writing about those Ephesians, who had not even
believed in God, who were pagans, right out in the world, living
the typical life of a pagan—and, of course, when a pagan like that
becomes a Christian the contrast obviously is extreme and striking.
And they go on to say that it is still the same at the present time.
Some people who have become Christians were once upon a time
drunkards and wife-beaters and almost murderers—they could not
have been more ungodly. Of course when such a person becomes a
Christian you have this astounding contrast and you are justified in
emphasising your 'but'; and saying 'now' and 'then'; 'times past',
'formerly', and so forth. But, they say, surely that does not apply
to people who have been brought up in a nice and respectable
manner, in a Christian country, people who were sent to Sunday
School when they were children and were taken to services by their
parents, and who have never done any of these violent and foul and
extreme things? Surely they have just 'grown' into Christianity and
what change there is must be almost imperceptible. Surely, they
argue, you do not emphasise this extreme contrast in the case of
such people?—it may be true for pagans and outsiders, but not,
surely, for anybody brought up nicely in a Christian country. My
reply is, that it is as extreme in their case as in the other; that the
difference between non-Christian and Christian is always equally
great.

What decides whether we are Christian or not *is neither what we
do nor what we are: it is our relationship to God.* 'Made nigh', says Paul.
He does not say 'have now improved', or 'are now living a better
life'. No, the thing that makes you a Christian is that 'you who
were far off are made nigh'; you are near to God whereas formerly
you were far from God. So the distinction and the difference are
to be drawn not in terms of our morality or conduct or behaviour
but in terms of our relationship to God.

Let me give an illustration to show what I mean. It is a matter
of relationship, I say, not of one's moral condition primarily—that
follows. Look at it like this. Take the state of marriage. Think of a
man who got married yesterday. You can say this about him, can
you not?—'Until yesterday he was a single man, now he is a
married man'. Now when you are thinking of the particular
relationship of the married state it is entirely beside the point and
a complete waste of breath to indicate various things that were true
about that man. You may tell me that he drank rather heavily or
that he gambled a great deal. But I am not interested in that at this
point; I want to know whether the man was married then or

whether he was not married. If you are thinking in terms of the married state and the married relationship, it is a sheer irrelevance to tell me about the man's moral life or conduct or behaviour. The vital matter is, that he was not married but now he is married. All those other things at that point and in that connection are pure irrelevancies.

Now it is exactly the same in this whole matter of being a Christian. I am not really interested as to whether you have been living in the gutters of life or in the most respectable tenements of life. The one question I ask is this: Are you near to God? Do you know God? Have you entered into the 'holiest of all'? That is the one question: the others are irrelevancies. As regards respectability and goodness and morality and ethics, you can be a paragon of all the virtues, and yet not know God. Judged by that test of personal relationships, according to the Scriptures there is no difference between the vilest and the foulest sinner on the one hand and the most respectable sinner on the other. '*All* have sinned and come short of the glory of God'. 'There is none righteous, no not one.' They are all outside the door, they are not given entrance into the audience chamber, into the presence of the Monarch, they are all shut outside. But you say: Ah! they are very different; look at their clothing, they are not dressed the same. I say I am not interested. The only question is this: Are they outside the door, or are they inside the door?

The trouble invariably in this matter is that, instead of considering it in terms of this personal relationship to God, people will persist in considering it in terms of goodness and behaviour. I remember someone once saying to me (and I use the illustration because I think it puts the matter perfectly): You know, I sometimes almost wish that I had lived a foul and a violent and an extremely sinful life. Why? I said. Well, she replied, in order that I might know this great change that such people know when they are converted. You see the fallacy, the misunderstanding? That person was looking at the matter entirely in terms of conduct and behaviour, negatively. If she had only looked at it in terms of knowing God and rejoicing in Him, she would have seen that there was no difference between her and the foulest and the vilest sinner. The test is a positive one. This 'but'; 'now'—'formerly', 'times past', this contrast, is extreme. It can never be over-emphasised.

Let us move on to the *second* principle, which is to consider *what we are as Christians*. That will serve to emphasise the contrast still more as we bear in mind the message of verse twelve. Paul puts this in these wonderful words: '*made nigh!*' The 'made nigh', of course, is the contrast to 'aliens', 'strangers', 'without God', 'outside

Christ', not in living relationship to Christ. But now, 'made nigh!' This is the whole truth about the Christian. The apostle obviously had an illustration in his mind. He was thinking of the temple. The temple at Jerusalem was divided into different places or courts. The most important place was the 'holiest of all,' the inner-most sanctuary, where the presence of God was revealed in the Shekinah glory over the mercy seat. And into that 'holiest of all', into the very presence of God, only one man was allowed to go. That was the high priest, and he only went in once a year. Then there were the courts. The outermost court of all was called the 'Court of the Gentiles'. They were the furthest away from God! They were not even allowed into the 'Court of the People', the Court of the Jews. The ordinary Jews were not allowed to go where the priests were allowed, and even the priests could not go where the high priest went. But the furthest away were the Gentiles, the outsiders. The apostle will work out that point in greater detail towards the end of this chapter. But here it is already in this par-ticular form. What he says is that they who were furthest away have been brought in, have been made nigh, in a most amazing manner have an entry, as it were, into the holiest of all. This is the position of all who are Christian, and this is the truth that we must empha-sise. The non-Christian is without God, without Christ; he has no access, he has no knowledge, he has no entry.

What is the truth about the Christian? The first thing that is true about the Christian is, not that he has had some experience, but that now he is made nigh, has this entry, this access, and *is able to go into the presence of God*. And of course he is able to do so with all others who are doing the same thing. So that Paul carries on this other contrast. Before, the Jews were a separate people. They went to God through their burnt offerings and sacrifices, through their priesthood. The Gentiles could not. But now the Gentiles can not only go into the presence of God; they go in with the Jews who have become Christians—they all go in together. He will say that also later in these words, 'Through him (Christ) we both have access by one Spirit unto the Father'.

But now I am concerned with this in general. It is the most wonderful thing in life. Look at it like this. Do you remember what happened when Adam and Eve had sinned in the garden of Eden, in Paradise? They were driven out of the garden, and there at the eastern end of the garden, at the gate, God set up 'the flaming sword, and cherubim'. What for? To prohibit the re-entry of the man and the woman into Paradise, into the garden of Eden. That is the effect of the Fall and of sin. Man is shut out of the presence of God. 'Without Christ!' 'Without God in the world!' And 'without hope!' And he cannot get back because of the flaming sword, and the cherubim. 'But now, in Christ Jesus', the gate is open, and man, in spite of the fall and of sin and shame, and all that is true of him, can come back and enter in, has access into the presence of God. He is reconciled to God, he is restored to God's favour, the enmity is removed, the wrath of God against sin is appeased and satisfied. There has been an at-one-ment—an atonement; they have been brought together again; man is made nigh, introduced into the audience chamber, presented to the King of glory.

Or we can put it like this. Paul in the previous verse has been saying that all who are not Christians are strangers to the covenants of promise. He means the one great covenant of grace that God repeated several times with slightly different emphases. God has pledged Himself, God has covenanted with man, God has said, 'I will do this; I will make a new covenant'. What Paul is saying here is that the Gentiles, though they were so far away, *have been brought into the covenant* and are now beginning to enjoy the full blessings of God's new covenant with man, in and through our Lord and Saviour Jesus Christ. What are these blessings? There is a perfect description of the new covenant in the eighth chapter of the Epistle to the Hebrews (v. 10–12). It is a quotation from Jeremiah 31: 'This is the covenant that I will make with the house of Israel after those days, saith the Lord; I will put my laws into their mind and write them in their hearts, and I will be to them a God, and they shall be to me a people: And they shall not teach every man his neighbour, and every man his brother, saying, Know the Lord, for all shall know me, from the least to the greatest. For I will be merciful to their unrighteousness, and their sins and their iniquities will I remember no more.' That is the new covenant. When a man is not a Christian he is a stranger to that covenant. What is it to be a Christian? It is this—to be made nigh, to be brought into the covenant, to be told, 'All this applies to you'.

Let us look again at the meaning of all this. It means that *we know God*. That is Christianity, to know God! You can be religious and know certain things about God, and believe certain things about God, and be interested in God, and read books about God, and listen to lectures and arguments about God. Yet you may not be a Christian. To be a Christian is to know God. Says the new covenant, 'They shall no longer teach one another saying, Know the Lord, for all shall know me, from the least to the greatest'—the least as well as the greatest. To know God! 'I will be to them a God, and they shall be to me a people.' That is what it means to become a Christian. Formerly you were not a people, you were aliens from the commonwealth of Israel (God's people), and you were strangers from the covenants, without God in the world; but now you have been made nigh, you are with the people of God, you know God.

What else? Now, because we know God, *we come with boldness to the throne of grace*. That is the argument again of the Epistle to the Hebrews (4: 16), where we read, 'Let us therefore come boldly unto the throne of grace, that we may obtain mercy and find grace to help in time of need.' Have you been made nigh! When you get on your knees to pray, do you pray with confidence, with this boldness? Do you know you are going to the throne of grace? And do you know that you are given mercy? And do you get that grace to help? That is the position of the man who has been made nigh: he is near, he is in the audience chamber. Listen to the author of the Epistle to the Hebrews in the nineteenth verse of the tenth chapter: 'Having, therefore, brethren, boldness to enter into the holiest of all by the blood of Jesus, by a new and living way which he hath consecrated for us, through the veil, that is to say, his flesh; and having an high priest over the house of God, let us draw near with a true heart, in full assurance of faith, having our hearts sprinkled from an evil conscience and our bodies washed with pure water'. That is what it means to be a Christian. 'Sometimes'—'but now, are made nigh'! 'Entering into the holiest of all!' Are you there, have you been there, do you know this way? The Christian is a man who can enter into the presence of God, into the 'holiest of all'; there is nothing to stop him.

What else? We come into His presence *with full assurance of faith*. What a terrible thing it is to be on your knees, and to be filled with doubts and uncertainties, and to say: I don't quite know whether I have a right or not—can I ask God?—I have no right, I am a sinner, and I have done this and that. That is not praying. The way to pray is to go into the 'holiest of all' with full assurance of faith, knowing God and knowing His relationship to you and His attitude towards you through 'the blood of Jesus'.

See the truth also in the words of the prologue of the Gospel according to John. He says that to 'as many as received him gave he power (or authority) to become the sons of God'. Do we understand that clearly?—that the Christian is a man who not only has access into the presence of God but who knows God as his Father? Christ has given him authority to be a child of God. He has been adopted. And though he is going into the presence of the holy and eternal God, he goes with the confidence of a child. He has an authority, the authority of the Lord Jesus Christ, to say that he is a child, and there is no porter that can prohibit him, there is no enemy that can hold him back. He holds his birth certificate in his hand and he says, I am going to my Father. 'Made nigh!' He not only knows that he is a child of God because he has the certificate in his hand—the certificate is the Word, the Scripture—he has another form of assurance also. 'For ye have not received the spirit of bondage again to fear, but ye have received the Spirit of adoption, whereby we cry, Abba, Father', says Paul in Romans (8: 15). That is the Christian's position. He is not praying to some distant God, he is not concerned about forms and appearances and beauty of language. He goes as a child to his Father: 'Abba, Father!' He knows God as his Father, he has a filial spirit, his whole heart is going out to God and he knows that God's heart is opened out to him. That is true Christianity. Is it surprising that the apostle emphasises the contrast between what these people were and what they now are?

And, of course, because the Christian knows that God is his Father and that he is a child of God, *he knows God's love to him*. He knows that 'the very hairs of his head are all numbered'. He knows that God is taking a personal interest in him, that nothing can happen to him apart from God; that though God is so great, and eternal in His majesty, His might, His glory, and His power, He like a Father is interested in His every child, knows all about us, is deeply concerned about our welfare. The Christian knows that there at His right hand is One who came from heaven to earth and identified Himself with us, took His place alongside of us, took our sin upon Him, and died for our sins. So this man goes into the presence of God knowing these things. That is what it means to be 'made nigh'.

In the fourth chapter of the Epistle of James in the eighth verse, there is this extraordinary statement: 'Draw nigh unto God, and he will draw nigh unto you.' But how can I draw nigh unto God unless I know the way? How can I draw nigh unto God unless I know that I am in the covenant, that I am no longer a stranger, no longer an alien, no longer afar off and outside? The only way to draw nigh unto God is the way in which the apostle puts it at the end of this glorious verse, the full consideration of which I must leave until later. There is only one way to draw nigh, there is only one way of entering into the 'holiest of all:' 'by the blood of Jesus'. 'But now ye who sometimes were afar off are made nigh, by the blood'—the blood!—'of Christ'. The blood of the lamb on the lintel and the door-posts of the houses of the Israelites in Egypt saved them and spared them; and the one sign that is looked for on all who would approach and draw nigh unto God is the mark of the blood of the Son of God. Is it on you? If it is, you have a free right of entry (and no one can stop you) into the 'holiest of all,' into the very presence of God Himself. Are you there, have you been there? Do you pray with confidence and assurance? Do you know God? Are you enjoying fellowship with Him?

To be 'nigh unto God' is to experience all those blessings of the new covenant in Jesus Christ.

17

THE BLOOD OF CHRIST

But now in Christ Jesus ye who sometimes were far off are made nigh by the blood of Christ.

Ephesians 2: 13

The trouble with us Christian people always is that we fail to realise the greatness of our salvation. That is why these New Testament Epistles were written. They were written to Christians, and they were necessary because these people, like ourselves, being still in the flesh, and being subject to the temptations and the trials that are inevitable in a world of sin, were constantly looking at themselves apart from Christ, and failing to realise what exactly was true of them in Christ Jesus. And the apostles set out to show that to them. That is the only way whereby we can ever understand the greatness of this salvation; and as we do so it will lead to joy and rejoicing, to praise and thanksgiving; to an assurance and a confidence in Christ which nothing can shake. But in order to come to that we have to realise two things. We have got to see what we were without Christ. Then we have to realise what is now true of us in the Lord Jesus Christ.

Here we have the positive side of this great measurement of the love and the power of God toward us in Christ. We saw that there are three things here, and now we come to the third and last of them.

The *third* thing then, is this: how all this comes to pass, how this great change takes place, what it is that entitles us to say 'sometimes afar off' and 'now . . . made nigh'—*what it is that brings us 'nigh unto God'*. The apostle deals with that at the end of this verse: 'But now in Christ Jesus ye who sometimes were far off are made nigh—by the blood of Christ'. Here is the statement which will always be found everywhere in the New Testament in this connection. We have already seen it. The apostle has already told us in the first chapter in the seventh verse—'in whom (in Christ) we have redemption through his blood, the forgiveness of sins, according to the riches of his grace'—and he goes on repeating it. And he will go on repeating it. The remainder of this chapter, in a sense, is but an elaboration and an exposition of this thirteenth verse. He brings it all out in detail and he keeps on repeating his phrases. It is the whole story of the New Testament, it is the very heart of the Christian message and the Christian faith. How is it that we are made nigh unto God? The only answer is 'in Christ Jesus', and especially 'in' or 'by His blood'.

Here is the very foundation of the Christian faith. If we are not clear about this we cannot be right anywhere. Let the critics say what they will, this is surely the New Testament message. It is *in Christ Jesus*, and it is *by His blood*. Our gospel is a gospel of blood; blood is the foundation; without it there is nothing. Therefore we must look into this and emphasise the things which the apostle is so concerned to emphasise in writing thus to the Ephesians.

How do we draw near to God, what right have we to seek God's face and to come near unto God? Well, we start with negatives. First and foremost, *it is not because of what I am by nature.* It is not because of any goodness that is in me. My right to go to God is not based upon the fact that I live a good life or try to live a good life, or that I am moral. That is no reason for coming near unto God; that is not the thing that brings me nigh unto God. There are many moral people in the world who are not even interested in God; and even if they were interested in God their own morality alone is never sufficient. We need not stay with that, the apostle has already been emphasising it in the previous verses: 'not of works'! So that if in any sense we are relying upon ourselves and our goodness and our morality, we are denying the gospel. There is no greater denial of the Christian faith than to think that because you are a good person you have a *right* to go to God in prayer. That is an utter, absolute denial of it all. If that were true Christ need never have come into the world at all—still less need He have died upon the cross on Calvary's hill. And yet I think you will agree that it is essential to emphasise this. There are large numbers of people sin, who go into the presence of God exactly as the Pharisee went till as described in our Lord's picture of the Pharisee and the publican who went up into the temple to pray (Luke 18: 9–14). The Pharisee went right to the front and stood up and said: 'I thank thee, O God, that I am not as other men are, and especially like this publican; I fast twice in the week, I give tithes of all that I possess'. That man, says our Lord, does not go down to his house justified; he is not heard by God, he is not nigh unto God. There is a sense in which there is no one further from God than the man who thinks that his goodness is of the slightest value in the presence of that burning fire, that consuming fire, the holiness of God.

Secondly, our right to draw near to God *is not because of good deeds that we do to others.* There are many who take up that position. They say, Well, of course I admit that I am not perfect, but after all I am trying to make up for that, I am trying to atone for that by doing good; I am engaged in philanthropic activities, I try to help others, I go out of my way to do that. You will agree that here again is a large group of people. They admit that they have nothing whereof to boast, they are honest enough to know that there are hideous, foul, vile things within them. Ah yes, they say, but surely if one tries to compensate for that and make atonement for it by doing good, that will admit us into the presence of God? Here are your idealists, your public benefactors, the people who talk about 'reverence for life' and of doing good. They sometimes make great sacrifices; they may give up a great profession, they may sacrifice home comforts and go to the distant parts of the world. They certainly are doing great good, but if they think it is the doing of that good that admits them to God and makes them acceptable with God, they are denying the gospel, exactly as the first group did.

But I would go even further. We draw nigh unto God *not even because we are religious* and because we are interested in worship, and because we are interested in God. Here is something which is on a higher plane than the previous two claims. The other two are looking at self only. But here is a person who really is concerned about religion, and about relationship to God. He desires to worship God. But if he relies alone on his religious practices it will avail him nothing. And yet again, you will agree, there are large numbers of people who belong to this group. They attend services, they are careful about forms. They may sacrifice in order to do this, and rise up at a very early hour in the morning because they think that there is some peculiar merit in that. They will do this and that, and observe forms and follow the ritual, and they rely upon that as the way of approach. But even that is a denial of the Christian message. The apostle Paul was a highly religious man before his conversion. Martin Luther was a highly religious man before his conversion. John Wesley was a highly religious man before his conversion. You can be fasting and sweating and praying, but that may be the greatest obstacle to coming 'nigh unto God'. That is not the way.

And lastly under this heading of negatives, I would indicate that the way to draw nigh unto God *is not the way of mysticism*. This again must be emphasised, because mysticism in various forms is always with us. It is not always found in its classic form as it was taught and practised in the Middle Ages, and in the later Middle Ages especially, by some of the great masters of the so-called mystical life, and as it is still practised by many who follow that teaching in the Roman Catholic Church and in various other branches of the

Christian Church. But mysticism in its various subtle forms ever tends to be with us. (There is, of course, a true Christian evangelical mysticism, but I am dealing with what is generally regarded as mysticism.) Now mysticism is based on the claim that the way to draw nigh to God is to look into yourself. The mystic would probably agree with everything that I have said so far in my negatives. If you want to know God, says the mystic, if you want to draw nigh unto God, you must turn to yourself and look into yourself; you must sink into yourself. God, says the mystic, is within you. So you must shut yourself off from all externals and external activities and you, as it were, sink into God. And that, they say, is the way to draw near to God. The way of renunciation, the way of contemplation, the way of rest, the way of letting go, relaxing, and just sinking into the ground of existence, sinking into God!

Or perhaps we can characterise it in this way. The essence of that teaching is that one can really approach God and find God and draw nigh to God directly, without any mediator. This takes certain popular forms. There are people, for instance, who teach it by saying, If you are in trouble about your life, if things are not going well with you, if you do not quite know what to do with yourself or in your circumstances, the thing to do is quite simple. Start listening to God, just where you are and as you are; you need do nothing else; you just sit down and relax and begin to listen to God. You have only got to let go, as it were, and thus, in this relaxed state, just wait upon God, and God will speak to you; you can arrive at Him directly. But, says someone, where does Christ come in? That, they say, is something that follows later. The first thing you have to do is to get to God and to get contact with God, and later you will be taught how to come to Christ. It is taught quite specifically that, without even mentioning the name of Christ at all, any man, whenever he desires to do so, can draw nigh to God and immediately get into contact with Him. So they claim to 'bring people to God first', asserting that, if it is so desired, they can then take them on to Christ. But surely it is obvious that this is an utter denial of what the apostle teaches here. We are made nigh. How? 'In Christ Jesus', 'by the blood of Christ'.

How can I go into the presence of God? One thing is clear. I cannot do it in and of myself, in any of the ways I have indicated. Whether I am active or passive, whether I am highly religious or not, whatever I do I can never bring myself into the presence of God. Quite right, says the apostle: the truth about you is this, that now in Christ Jesus ye who sometimes were far off are *made* nigh. *It is something that is done to you*; you have been made nigh, brought nigh. It is not your activity, it is Another's activity, it is something that has been done to you, that has happened to you. It is because that is true, of course, that this is a gospel. Hear the apostle Paul, putting it in writing to the Corinthians: 'God was in Christ reconciling the world unto himself'. It is not the world that reconciles itself unto God. That is not the message. The new message is, that whereas men had failed completely, God was in Christ reconciling the world unto Himself. Or take the words of the Lord Jesus Christ. Is it not astounding that, having open Bibles in front of us, we can still go on trying to discover God and to draw nigh to Him in the ways I have been indicating, when the Son of God Himself said: 'I am the way, the truth, and the life; no man cometh unto the Father but by me'? You would have thought that that was enough once and for ever. It is the most categorical statement imaginable. 'No man cometh unto the Father but by me.' And yet here are men saying: I am going in the strength of my own goodness, I am going to sit down and relax and I will find God speaking to me. And Christ is not even mentioned, does not seem to be needed!

And this passes as Christianity. Is it surprising that Christendom is as it is, that our churches are as they are, that we are not experiencing the presence of God and mighty revival and re-awakening? We are insulting the Son by forgetting Him and by feeling that He is not necessary; we are denying the specific statements of the apostle and of the Son of God Himself. There is no way of drawing near to God except *in and through the Son of God*, our blessed Lord and Saviour Jesus Christ. 'There is one God, and one mediator [one only!] between God and men, the man Christ Jesus.' The teaching therefore is that no man is nigh unto God unless he is in Christ. The apostle has already been expounding that. It is all 'in Christ'. And let us be clear about this. If I am not in Christ I have never been near God. The only way that I can ever be nigh unto God is by being in Christ; but in Him I am near God, made nigh to God. But in particular, 'by His blood'! That is the thing that the apostle emphasises. He is not content just to say: 'But now in Christ Jesus ye who sometimes were far off are made nigh'. He must add, 'by the blood of Christ'. This is absolutely essential. I know that this 'theology of blood' is hateful to many people today. People not only dislike it, they hate it, they abominate it. I well remember how some two years or so ago I was called in to help in a discussion that was taking place between a businessman who had become a Christian, and a professional man who was not a Christian. They were having a great discussion, and this is what I heard the professional man saying as he stated the case: Of course, I have great respect for my friend here, he is a good man; I can see what has happened to him: that is all right, and he does a lot of good and I agree with that; but you know, he said, what I can't stand is this blood and thunder business that he keeps on talking about. The blood of Christ! People have referred to it as 'this butchery', 'this wallowing in blood.' By all means let us live a good life, they say, let us worship God, but must you drag in this blood perpetually? It seems a scandal to them, it seems something hateful. And yet the apostle goes out of his way to bring it in. It is by the 'blood of Christ'. And the blood of Christ means the death of Christ, the life poured out.

In other words, we are made nigh in Christ Jesus; *but not primarily by His teaching.* He did teach. He taught men how to live—witness the Sermon on the Mount—but if He had left it at that I should be as far away from God as a man could ever be. The Lord Jesus Christ, by His teaching and His telling me how to live, does not bring me near to God. In a sense He drives me further away. The Pharisees thought—in their interpretation of the law—that they really were drawing near to God by keeping the law. But when Christ expounded what the law truly meant, they began to see that they were very far from God. When you realise that God is interested in a desire as much as in a deed, in a motive as much as in an action, that the look is as bad as the act in God's sight, then you realise that Christ's teaching condemns you completely. He does not bring me to God by teaching me how to live. Still less does He bring me to God by giving me an example to follow. Whatever I may feel about myself, when I look at Him I want to hide myself in shame. The lives of His servants are more than enough to make me feel how poor my life is. When I read the lives of the saints I realise how poor and shoddy my best efforts are. But when I look at the Son of God! People talk about the 'imitation of Christ' and how they are going to follow Christ; but they have never realised what they are saying. Christ utterly condemns us. Who can follow Him? No one left to himself can follow Him; it is impossible, it is too exalted. It is not His example that brings me nigh.

Neither does He bring me nigh simply by telling me that God is love. Now this, I suppose, is the most popular misunderstanding of the gospel today. People say, What Jesus Christ does is this—and this is how He brings us to God—He tells us that God is love. All we really need is to be assured that God is love. They say that that is the only thing that men and women really need, that they have the wrong idea of God; that if they only knew that God is a God of love they would rush into His presence and they would spend the rest of their lives there. What a fatal underestimate of sin, and of the effects of the Fall! Would men be more interested in God if they knew that He is a God of love? Of course they would not! They would trade on it. They would say, Ah well, if God is a God of love I can do what I like, the love of God will forgive me. And that is the very thing they are saying. So the Lord Jesus Christ does not bring us nigh to God simply by telling us that God is a God of love and that He is ready to forgive. The Old Testament had already told us that: 'Like as a father pitieth his children . . .' and so on. The Old Testament is full of the love of God. Did that succeed? It did not. It never has done, and never will. That is not the way.

There is only one way whereby even Christ can bring me nigh unto God, and that is by His blood, by His death; by His broken body, by His shed blood, by His life poured out. That is why He instituted the Lord's Supper with the broken bread and the poured-out wine, as a perpetual reminder that His death is the only way to God. We see there the wondrous foreknowledge of God in Christ. Knowing how ready men are to fall into error and into heresy, He established, He commanded, He ordained the Lord's Supper—bread, wine; broken bread, poured-out wine—that it might perpetually preach the fact that that is the only way into the presence of God. The veil is His own body—it must be rent. The death of Christ! It is only by the death of Christ, by the blood of Christ, that one can be made nigh unto God.

How does the death of Christ accomplish this work? There are two main ideas here. I shall put them before you briefly. The *first* is what is commonly called 'expiation.' The blood of Christ *makes expiation for our sins*. You remember that momentous statement made by John the Baptist at the very beginning of our Lord's ministry? 'Behold', he said, look at, 'behold the Lamb of God that taketh away the sin of the world' (John 1 : 29). There it is in a single phrase. The Lord Jesus Christ, what is He? He is the Lamb, the paschal Lamb, the Lamb of sacrifice. He is the One who sums up all the Old Testament ceremony and ritual. The Lamb of God, the Lamb that God has provided—not the lambs that men had provided. But why is a lamb necessary? Why should there be a sacrifice? The answer is that 'the wages of sin is death'. God decreed and pronounced that man, sinning, should die. And the wages of sin, therefore, is death. And God has likewise stated and decreed that only a sacrificial and atoning death can cover this. So that we read, 'Without shedding of blood there is no remission' of sins. God's punishment for sin is death, spiritual death, separation from God to all eternity. And whether we like it or not, it is a fact. Ignorance of the law is no excuse in law. That you do not agree with the law makes not the slightest difference when you are arraigned in the court. And this is God's law. 'The wages of sin is death'. And we are all sinners. And the punishment must be meted out—otherwise God is no longer just, and God is no longer righteous and holy. Why did Christ, therefore, come into the world? He came, says the author of the Epistle to the Hebrews, 'to taste death for every man' (Hebrews 2:9). He came, says Peter, for this reason: 'who his own self bore our sins in his own body on the tree, that we being dead to sins should live unto righteousness' (1 Peter 2:24). That is why He came. What is happening on the cross? 'God hath made him to be sin for us, who knew no sin,' says Paul 'that we might be made the righteousness of God in him' (2 Corinthians 5:21). 'God was in Christ, reconciling the world unto himself, not imputing their trespasses unto them.' God takes my trespasses—He took my trespasses, I should say, and He imputed them to Jesus Christ; He put them on Him; He took my debt and put it on Him; He demanded the penalty from Him; and it was paid. That is God's way of salvation in Christ and by the death of Christ. Why did Christ die? The answer is that 'God hath laid on Him the iniquity of us all'; it is 'by his stripes we are healed'. God smote him in order that I might not be smitten. That is why He died, that is why His blood was shed. This is the only way to atone for sin; it would never have happened otherwise. Peter pulled out his sword on one occasion to defend our Lord. Put it back, Peter, said Christ in effect, do you not know that I could command twelve legions of angels if I desired, and I could be wafted to heaven without suffering at all; but I have come in order to suffer and so fulfil the Scriptures (Matthew 26:51-4). 'He set his face steadfastly to go to Jerusalem'. He could have escaped it all. But then, if He had escaped it all, you and I would die in our sins. He had to die; it is God's way of forgiveness. By His blood! By His life poured out! You see now why the apostle must bring it in. Without this there is no forgiveness. I cannot draw nigh unto God without it, expiation is absolutely essential. Before I can draw nigh unto God, something has got to be done about my sins. I can do nothing about them; they are condemned by the law of God, and that law must be satisfied; and Christ has satisfied it. He kept the law perfectly; He bore my punishment meted out by the law. The obstacle of the law of God has been removed. The way is now open, the barrier of my sin has been taken out of the way. That is what is meant by expiation.

But the blood of Christ does a *second* thing. And this is vitally important in our context. Paul says that we were 'aliens from the commonwealth of Israel' and 'strangers from the covenants of promise'—the covenant! God has made a covenant with man as we saw when we considered the new covenant. Read the eighth chapter of the Epistle to the Hebrews, and there you will find the full terms of the new covenant. 'I will put my laws into their mind, and write them in their hearts: and I will be to them a God, and they shall be to me a people. And they shall not teach every man his neighbour . . . saying: Know the Lord: for all shall know me, from the least to the greatest. . . . Their sins and their iniquities will I remember no more.' That is the new covenant. These Ephesians were strangers to all that. But now they have been made nigh by the blood of Christ.

How does this come to pass? Here is the explanation. Every covenant was ratified and sealed by blood. As you read the Old Testament you will find it everywhere. When God made a covenant with man it was always ratified and sealed by blood. An animal was killed, the blood was taken and sprinkled on the document. Indeed, you will find that the temple was sanctified and consecrated in the same way—the vessels of the temple, the books and the book of the law. You will find that the priests were set apart by blood being sprinkled upon them. You will find that when a leper was cleansed blood was placed upon him. That is God's way, that is the way it is settled and sealed. Every covenant of God is ratified and sealed by means of the sprinkling of blood. And *the new covenant has been ratified* in the same way but, this time, by the blood of Jesus Christ. No longer the 'blood of bulls and of goats or the ashes of an heifer sprinkling the unclean'. It is the blood of Christ. He has ratified the new covenant. Listen to the terms used, especially in the Epistle to the Hebrews. We read that Jesus is 'the mediator of the new covenant'. You will find it clearly in the twelfth chapter. In the same way in the thirteenth chapter we read about 'the God of peace, that brought again from the dead our Lord Jesus, that great Shepherd of the sheep, through the blood of the everlasting covenant' (verse 20). The blood of the everlasting covenant! Have you noticed how the Lord Jesus Christ, when He instituted the Lord's Supper, took the cup when He had supped and said, 'This cup is the new testament in my blood'—the new covenant in my blood. Have you noticed how Paul reminds the Corinthians of that, in 1 Corinthians, chapter 11, 'After the same manner also he took the cup when He had supped, saying, This cup is the new covenant in My blood; this do ye, as often as ye drink it, in remembrance of me'. Those are the terms. The covenant is ratified by blood. In other words, the new covenant between God and man would not be sure for us unless Christ's blood had been sprinkled upon it. That is the seal that guarantees it. The bearing of our sins away was not enough. Before I can draw nigh unto God and be made nigh unto God, I must be a beneficiary under the new covenant; and Christ is the Mediator of the new covenant. It is He that stands between God and man. He is the Daysman that brings us together. He is the One that stretches out a hand to God and a hand to us. He is God; He is Man; yes, He is the complete Mediator. It is therefore by means of the blood of the covenant that I can draw near to God.

Someone may say at this point, I have listened to all you have said, but I feel I am such a terrible sinner, so that when I begin to pray I am troubled about that; how can I draw near to God? The answer is, that you must believe this teaching, you must realise what it says, and you must come nigh with boldness unto God by the blood of Jesus. The first thing you have to do is to *listen to what the blood of Christ says*. Did that ever occur to you, that the blood of Christ speaks? Do you remember what we are told in Hebrews 12: 22–24: that we are come to the heavenly Jerusalem, to Mount Sion, and so on, 'and to Jesus, the mediator of the new covenant', and last of all, 'to the blood of sprinkling that speaketh better things than that of Abel'? Blood speaks. The blood of Abel spoke. What did it say? Listen to Genesis 4: 10. God addressed Cain after he had murdered Abel and said, 'What hast thou done? The voice of thy brother's blood crieth unto me from the ground.' The spilt blood of Abel was crying out to God for vengeance. That is how the blood of Abel speaks. It speaks of judgment, it speaks of vengeance, it speaks of cursing, the curse that descended upon Cain. But the blood of Jesus 'speaketh better things than that of Abel'. What does it speak? It speaks of pardon, it speaks of expiation, it speaks of peace with God. It is shouting out, it is crying out to you: I have died; you can live. The punishment has been borne; you are free. Have you listened to the blood of Jesus? It is speaking, and speaking better things than the blood of Abel. Listen to the blood of Christ as it tells you that He has tasted death for you, and borne your punishment, that the law of God is satisfied, and that the way into the presence of God is open.

Or take it in a second way. Listen to this in Hebrews 9: 14: 'How much more shall the blood of Christ, who through the eternal Spirit offered himself without spot to God, purge your conscience from dead works to serve the living God? And again, Hebrews 10: 22: 'Let us draw nigh unto God with a true heart, in full assurance of faith, having our hearts sprinkled from an evil conscience and our bodies washed with pure water'. What does it mean? It means that when you get down on your knees before God and your conscience accuses you and reminds you of what you are and what you have done, and resurrects your sins, you should turn upon it and say: I am sprinkled with the blood of Christ, you cannot condemn me; 'there is therefore now no condemnation to them that are in Christ Jesus'. Answer it. *Have your conscience sprinkled with the blood of Christ* and it will be cleansed from all your dead works.

I understand, you say, I see now how I can come into the presence of God, because I see that my sins have been dealt with. I am therefore in the presence of God. But what if I should fall into sin again, what if I should do something wrong? Here is your answer, in the First Epistle of John: 'If we walk in the light as he is in the light, we have fellowship one with another, and the blood of Jesus Christ his Son cleanseth us from all sin' (1: 7). You will sin: but *the blood of Christ will still cleanse you from your sin.* You have been brought nigh to God, you are walking with Him in fellowship, but you fall into sin. You think, It is all finished, that is the end I have sinned against the light. No, go back! The blood of Christ is still able, it will cleanse you from all sin and from all defilement, and you can continue walking with God, enjoying your fellowship with Him. 'You who sometimes were far off have been made nigh by the blood of Christ.'

I want to ask you a question. Have you been made nigh? I can tell you, very simply, how to know whether you have or not. If you are still talking about being good enough, you have not been made nigh. If you are still relying on yourself in any shape or form, you are still afar off. If you are still talking of *not* being good enough, you also have not been made nigh. Because as long as you keep on talking of not being good enough, what you really are saying is that you think you can make yourself good enough. But you never can. You will never be nearer than you are now. Never! If you lived a thousand years you would be no nearer. You will never be good enough to come into the presence of God. So if you are still saying: Ah, that is wonderful, but I am not good enough, I am a sinner, that means you are not made nigh. The one who is made nigh is one who says: I know that I am a sinner, I know the sins of the past, I know that I still have a sinful nature within me; but though I know that, I know that I am in the presence of God, because I am in Christ. I have listened to the voice of the blood of Christ and it has spoken to me of forgiveness, of reconciliation, of expiation, of God being satisfied, of God being 'just and the justifier of him that believeth in Jesus'. The blood is sprinkled on my conscience. Let hell try to denounce me, I know that God accepts me; I am relying only, utterly, entirely, upon

Jesus Christ and Him crucified. 'His blood can make the foulest clean, His blood avails for me.' In His merits alone I know that I have access to God and that God receives me, that I have been 'made nigh by the blood of Christ.' Let us then 'have boldness to enter into the holiest by the blood of Jesus'; but still 'with reverence and godly fear'. Boldness, confidence; and yet still knowing that 'our God is a consuming fire'. Not glibly, not lightly, not loosely, not flippantly, not boisterously, not carnally. 'With reverence and godly fear'—yet knowing, yet certain, yet sure, because I enter in, 'by the blood of Jesus'.

18

HE IS OUR PEACE

For he is our peace, who hath made both one, and hath broken down the middle wall of partition between us; Having abolished in his flesh the enmity, even the law of commandments contained in ordinances; for to make in himself of twain one new man, so making peace; And that he might reconcile both unto God in one body by the cross, having slain the enmity thereby.
Ephesians 2: 14–16

Here we have another of those great statements, majestic and all-inclusive, which we find so regularly and constantly as we work our way through this chapter. It is a part of the paragraph which begins at verse 11 and which runs on right into the third chapter. And again it is important, as we come to this fresh step which is taken by the apostle, that we should be bearing the general argument in our minds. You can never truly see the parts of the apostle's argument unless you are carrying the whole in your mind at the same time. There is no meaning, there is no true existence to a part, apart from the whole. Let us, therefore, refresh our memories.

The apostle is demonstrating 'the exceeding greatness of the power of God to us-ward who believe'. That is what he wants these Ephesians and all Christians to know. He prays that the eyes of their understanding may be enlightened in order that they may know this and grasp it. This is not ordinary human knowledge; this is not something that falls into the same category as history or philosophy, or something like that: it is a special type and kind of knowledge. And it can only be grasped and apprehended as we are enlightened by the Holy Spirit. So the apostle has to start with that prayer. To a man whose mind is not enlightened by the Holy Spirit all this argument is quite irrelevant. And that is the position of the world and the attitude of all who are not Christian. They say they want something practical, something relevant. That is because of their blindness, for if they had eyes to see, they would see that this alone is relevant. But the apostle has prayed that they might know, in particular, 'the exceeding greatness of God's power to us-ward who believe'. And he demonstrates it, you remember, in two main ways. In the first he shows that they were dead in trespasses and sins; and nothing can raise the dead but the power of the Creator. It is God alone who can raise the dead—and He has raised these people out of spiritual death, with Christ, into newness of life; they are even seated with Him in the heavenly places.

But there was a second thing, and that was the division in the ancient world between Jews and Gentiles. Before people like these Ephesians who were Gentiles, pagans, could ever have become members of the Church, somehow or another God had to deal with that radical division. And what the apostle is dealing with in these verses, beginning with verse 11, is how God has done that. The general statement is that they were in times past Gentiles in the flesh, they were 'without Christ, being aliens from the common-wealth of Israel and strangers from the covenants of promise, having no hope, and without God in the world; but now, in Christ Jesus, ye who sometimes were far off are made nigh by the blood of Christ.' That is the statement, that is the proposition, that is the astounding thing.

The apostle felt, however, that it was not enough merely to leave it like that. It is such a marvellous thing, such a wonderful thing, that he must divide it up, split it up into its component parts, in order that they might see more in detail how this truly staggering thing has ever come into being.

He starts this detailed exposition in verse 14 with the striking statement: '*He (Christ) is our peace*'; 'For He is our peace'—the 'for' connecting it up with what has gone before. He is working out an argument, he is continuing the theme. '*For* he is our peace'— this One by whose blood we have been made nigh is our peace. Now that is one of the most glorious things that is said about the Lord Jesus Christ anywhere. Of all the terms and titles applied to Him there is none more wonderful than this. He is our peace. This conception is one which is used very frequently, in the Old Testament and the New, with regard to this whole question of salvation. There is no more beautiful expression of it than that in the Epistle to the Hebrews in the thirteenth chapter and the twentieth verse: 'Now the God of peace, that brought again from the dead our Lord Jesus, that great Shepherd of the sheep, through the blood of the ever-lasting covenant, make you perfect in every good work to do his will, working in you that which is well-pleasing in his sight'. There it is! God is 'the God of peace'. That is a very good way of thinking of salvation; we are saved, we are Christians, simply because God is a 'God of peace'. Everything is really the result of that.

But the message of the Bible is that *God is a God of peace, and produces the peace and makes peace, in and through His only begotten Son, our Lord and Saviour Jesus Christ.* The result is that you find that the Lord is described in some such terms throughout the Old Testament, in prophecy. You find such a man as Jacob, for instance, at the end of his long and changeful life, blessing his sons and the various tribes that were going to develop out of those sons; and when he comes to Judah he says, 'The sceptre shall not depart from Judah until Shiloh come'. What is Shiloh? Shiloh is peace, the Author of peace, the Prince of peace. Jacob was given to see it. He did not understand it fully, but these men, inspired by the Holy Spirit, had been given an understanding of God's great purpose, and Jacob had seen that it was out of Judah that Shiloh should come. Shiloh! 'He is our peace.' It is said of Him again, that He is not only 'the King of Righteousness' but also 'the Prince of Peace'. Those are titles that are ascribed to Him. Let me remind you also, that when, eventually, in the fulness of the times, the Son of God was born, the shepherds watching their flocks by night heard a great angelic anthem. This was its message, 'Glory to God in the highest, and on earth peace, goodwill toward men'. And so it is everywhere. 'He is our peace.'

This is the very essence of salvation. The apostle puts it thus, in order to show us still further what an astounding and amazing thing our salvation is. I must remind you again that that is the great theme, the kind of 'leit motif' running parallel with the great, grand, central 'motif' itself. The apostle wanted these Ephesians to realise the glorious nature of their salvation. This he brings out in different ways in verses 1 to 13, and here in verse 14 it is taken even a step further. As we have seen, in verses 1 to 10, we are shown that *sin is that which produces death*. It is only as we realise truly the nature of sin that we shall realise truly the nature of salvation. That is why there is nothing that is so unscriptural, and so foolish, as to say, We only want the positive. Don't worry about the negative, don't talk so much about sin; we want to know about the love of God and the positive. But you will never know that unless you realise the negative. The apostle constantly emphasises that. In order to measure the love of God you have first to go down before you can go up. You do not start on the level and go up; we have to be brought up from a dungeon, from a horrible pit; and unless you know something of the measure of that depth you will only be measuring half the love of God. In the first ten verses the apostle shows us that God has to overcome sin as it leads to spiritual death.

Then having done that, he goes on to show us in verses 11 to 13 how *sin always leads to separation*—the separation between the Jews and the Gentiles, 'who are called Uncircumcision by that which is called the Circumcision in the flesh made by hands'. Separation! Aliens from the commonwealth of Israel and strangers from the covenants of promise! Sin separates man from man as well as from God.

But in this fourteenth verse we are shown that sin does not stop at separating men, it goes further; *sin puts men at enmity*; and not only at enmity with one another but at enmity also with God. That is the ultimate of sin, that is the horrible aspect of sin; that is where you see the real ugliness of sin. Sin not only separates men from God and from one another, it produces *a state of enmity* against God and enmity against one another. That is why the great problem in the world today is the problem of peace. That is why all the conferences are being held. That is the great concern of everybody—is there not some way of banishing war, of reconciling men to one another, making a durable and a sure and a lasting peace? How can men be reconciled? We are aware of these divisions, these quarrels, all over the world, in the nations, in the groups within the nations as well as between nation and nation. The whole world seems to be in a state of strife and of enmity. Why is it? It is here that you see the relevance of the Scriptures. And it is at this point that one sometimes finds it difficult to be patient, as a Christian. And yet we must be patient. We see the world and its men, and its great men so-called, apparently wasting their time in attempting the impossible. It is difficult to be patient at times. It is even more difficult to be patient when one sees men, even in the Christian Church, completely misunderstanding and misinterpreting the Scriptures, and, as it were, standing before the world and saying: You have only to do what we tell you, and the peace you are looking for and longing for will come to pass at once. That is tragic; it is nothing but sheer failure to understand a statement such as this which we are considering.

Sin is the cause of the trouble; it puts man at enmity against God and it puts man at enmity against man. The explanation is quite simple. Sin is essentially pride, self. Clearly, we must go back to the book of Genesis. People who think that you can cut out the early chapters of Genesis and still have a Christian gospel are just displaying their ignorance. It is there you get the fundamental explanation of all that obtains today. *The root cause of all the enmity is the pride of man*; man interested in himself; man setting himself up as an autonomous being even face to face with God, and ready to listen to the question 'Hath God said?'—Who is God to tell you what you may or may not do? Man, said Satan to man, you do not realise how big you are, how great you are. God is keeping you like a slave and using you like a servant. Why do you not stand up for yourself, why do you not assert yourself, why do you not stand on your dignity and demand your rights? Do not be put down, stand up! And he stood up. I do not want to be paradoxical, but it was because man stood up that he fell. He was standing in a way in which he was never meant to stand; he was trying to stand in a way that he could not stand; and it led to the Fall and all its appalling consequences. It is all due to pride, self-interest, self-concern. Man sets himself up as a god. He thinks he is an autonomous being, that he has a right; he talks about his rights and his demands. That is simply a manifestation of self-interest, self-adulation, self-love, self-praise. He is constantly turning in upon himself and revolving round himself. He is the centre. Yes, but unfortunately, all men are doing the same thing. And that is where the trouble comes in. If I alone existed there would be no trouble, but every other 'I' is exactly the same as I am. The result is that the world is peopled by a number of gods, all asserting themselves and demanding their rights and claiming the same things. It is inevitable that there should be clashes. It is a war of the false gods. They are all together in enmity against God; but that does not mean that they are all agreed amongst themselves. Oh no! Do you not see how this is the pattern for all the problems in the world today? You get all the workers combining together against the masters; and all the masters against the workers. But does that mean that they are all very happy and agreed amongst themselves and all helping one another and all sacrificing for one another? Of course it does not. They divide amongst themselves—worker against worker, master against master, in rivalry, competition, jealousy and envy. The trouble exists everywhere. Mankind combines in enmity against God, but is full of internecine strife—man against man quite as much as man against God.

That is the only adequate explanation of the world as it is today. And *the supreme tragedy is that the world does not see it*, has not begun to see it. And that is because it starts with the supposition that, whatever the explanation is, it has nothing to do with God. We are too clever to believe in God, we have started by shutting God out. It cannot be that. Whatever it is, it is not religious. It has nothing to do with God and Christ. We are adult now, we are no longer children, so it is not that, that must not even be considered. So we try to find some other explanation and cure. But the appalling failure is evident on all hands. And of necessity it will continue while man will not see the true explanation. He does not see that it is because he is in a wrong relationship to God, that he is in a wrong relationship to his fellow man.

The Lord Jesus Christ put that very clearly once and for ever. Somebody came to Him one day and said, 'Master, which is the first, the chiefest, the greatest of all the commandments?' And this was His reply: 'Thou shalt love the Lord thy God with all thy heart and with all thy soul and with all thy strength and with all thy mind. That is the first and the greatest commandment. And the second is like unto it; Thou shalt love thy neighbour as thyself'. Now the important thing there is to notice the order: First, the relationship to God; second, the relationship to your fellow man and woman. The whole tragedy of the modern world is due to the fact that the first is entirely left out and men think you can start with the second. But you cannot, because you are to love your neighbour as yourself, you are to love your neighbour as you love yourself. The problem therefore is, how am I to love myself? And according to the Bible, I shall never love myself in the right way until I see myself as I am in my relationship to God. So I cannot possibly carry out the second commandment unless I am already clear about the first. It is impossible. And man today, not recognising God, and not starting with God, and not submitting himself to God, is trying to reconcile himself to his fellow man. And of course he is not succeeding, he never can succeed. He is violating the law of his own nature. He has been made by God, he has been made for God; and he does not see himself truly, he does not see anybody else truly, until he sees himself and all others in the light of God's law, face to face with God Himself.

That is the background to the apostle's statement here: 'He is our peace'. *Christ alone is our peace.* There is no peace apart from Him. The world can go on developing intellectually and in every other respect, it can add to its knowledge of science and of sociology and of psychology and all else, it can multiply its institutions, it can train us in this respect and that respect, but it will all lead to nothing because the problem can never be solved except in, and through, our Lord and Saviour Jesus Christ. It is almost incredible that it is still necessary to say this. But it is necessary. Modern history proves that to the very hilt. This twentieth century should have been the best and the greatest century that the world has ever known, according to human understanding. But look at it. It is one of the worst, one of the most appalling. That is very depressing, says someone, I do not need to be depressed like that. The answer is that it is not a question of depression, it is a question of facing facts. If you really are concerned about the problem of man and of the world, as well as about your own problem, you have got to face it radically. And here are the facts. If you try to start with the second commandment it will lead to disaster, because man is not merely an intellect, he is not merely a social being. According to Scripture, there is an evil principle at work in him; he is infected by sin, he is in a diseased condition. And before you begin to train him you must heal him. He needs new life. The apostle puts it as a general statement, which is of course the whole case for Christianity—'He (and He alone) is our peace.'

Now that means a number of things. First and foremost it means that *He Himself is our peace*. What I mean by that is, that the Lord Jesus Christ not only makes peace—He does make peace, as I hope to show you—but He Himself is the peace. He is our peace. Which is just another way of saying that we must be in Christ before we can enjoy the blessings of God as the God of peace. It is only as we are related to Christ, it is only as we are incorporated in Christ or, to use a biblical term, grafted into Christ, it is only as we are members of Christ and parts of His body, and sharing the life of Christ and drawing from the life of Christ—it is only as all this is true of us that we shall really enjoy the blessings of peace. Once more, as we realise that, we see the unutterable superficiality of so much that is being said at the present time. I do not want to be misunderstood, or to say anything disrespectful about those who are called Pacifists, but the real trouble with that teaching is its lack of theological understanding, and its failure to realise the problem of sin. And it not only applies there, but to all the glib talk of men and women who say that the problem is so simple, that all you need do is just to call people together to a meeting and talk pleasantly to them, and you all end by shaking hands, and all will be well. There were statesmen who believed quite sincerely and genuinely that if only they could meet Hitler, one each side of the table, and talk to him, the whole thing would be settled. 'Peace in our time', they said, 'we have met him, we have made a gentleman's agreement.' But it was not long before they discovered that the man with whom they had shaken hands was not a gentleman. And that is still the trouble. How superficial, how pathetic it is, that men still think that by catch phrases you can solve the problems of sin in man. No, '*He* is our peace'; He, the Eternal Son of God, who had to be born as a Babe in Bethlehem. It is that that was essential to solve this problem. And yet they say that just being nice and pleasant and friendly, and talking across a table, can put it all right. If it were as simple as that, the incarnation need never have taken place, the death on the cross would never have happened: but before there can be peace these have had to happen. He Himself, the blessed Person, is our peace. And it is only as we understand something of this mystical doctrine of the Christian as a member of the body of Christ that we can truly participate in that peace and enjoy it.

But *He also makes peace*, says the apostle. This is a point about which we must be perfectly clear. How does Christ make peace? We must interpret it scripturally and not sentimentally. Notice the terms: 'He is our peace'; and then, He has made peace—'so making peace'. What does this mean? The superficial, sentimental interpretation of the Scripture to which I have referred, seems to think that it works out like this: that the Lord Jesus Christ teaches us how to make peace. They say, 'You read your Scriptures and then, in the spirit of the Scriptures, and of what you have understood from the Scriptures, go to your enemy, put the teaching into practice, and you will win him over'. The argument on the international level is, that if one nation simply disarmed completely it would have such a staggering effect upon all the other nations that you would never have another war.

I once heard a man in a meeting who spoke, I think, for some thirty-five minutes and who during that time took us, as he thought, through the entire Epistle to the Ephesians with no difficulty! He told us that its message was delightfully simple. He was a well-known pacifist who suffered a lot for his pacifism; an honest man, a sincere man, and a good man. His understanding of our text was that it was simply a question of applying the teaching of Christ and the Christian spirit. The climax of his address was a story he told us, and which to him proved the entire matter. He said he happened to be the governor of a certain girls' school, a public school, and he told us that a number of the governors had long been unhappy about the fact that there were punishments and rewards in the school. The children who did wrong were punished in various ways, and he and others felt that that was not the way of Christ, not the Christian way. There should be no punishment, no discipline in that sense; but instead, the children should be appealed to, should be put on their honour and should be told that they would in future be treated as adults, and that the headmistress and the mistresses would trust them. So, he said, after many years they persuaded their colleagues on the board and the staff to agree to this, and in that particular school all forms of punishment were abolished. He said, Some of our friends, of course, had been prophesying that that would lead to disaster, but you know, he continued, the very first year after we did it, the number of scholarships obtained for Oxford and Cambridge was higher than it had ever been before. That, he said, is what happens when you put the love of Christ into practice and into operation. There it was! it was so simple, you simply applied the teaching. Do that individually, do that in communities and in groups and divisions; do it between countries and there will never be any trouble any more!

What a travesty of the Scripture! Was it really necessary for the Son of God to leave the courts of heaven if that is the answer? Was the death of the cross ever necessary, if it is just a question of applying some teaching? That is not what we are told here. He, Christ, has *made* peace. It is not that He tells me to do something— He does that, of course, but I can only do what He tells me because He has first done something Himself. He has made peace. He is our peace. He is the Prince of peace. It is the God of peace who makes peace. It is not primarily men applying a certain teaching, it is something fundamental that is done by God in Christ that creates an entirely new situation. That is why I am never tired of saying that it is not the business of the Christian Church merely to give advice to statesmen and others, and to tell them how to solve their problems; for you cannot have peace amongst men until men are made Christians. It is impossible. That is why the gospel is necessary, that is why Christ came. You cannot apply teaching intended for Christians to non-Christians. To do so is rank heresy. These Epistles were not written to the world, they were written to Christians. We must be born again, we must be made anew, before this can possibly apply to us. Christ makes peace. That is the fundamental proposition. He is our peace, and He has made peace; it is something which He brings into being.

The apostle tells us in these verses *how He brings peace into being.* Two things are essential before there can be true peace. Men must be reconciled to God and men must be reconciled to one another. The apostle takes up both problems. He starts with men being reconciled to one another. He does that, I take it, because what was prominent in his mind at the moment was this: he was looking at the Christian Church and there he could see Jews and Gentiles. So he starts with the concrete fact of the Church. There together, praising God, are men who were once bitter enemies. What has brought them together? He starts with that question and deals with it in verses 14 and 15. Then in verse 16 he shows how they both together have been brought to God and how the enmity between them and God has been abolished.

How then does Christ reconcile men to one another? How does He bring men to one another in love? How does he destroy the enmity that is between men? First Paul puts it negatively. He says that Christ has 'broken down the middle wall of partition between us'. At this point let me indicate that the Authorised Version here, and indeed the Revised also, are not quite as good as they might be. At this point the Revised Standard Version is surely better. Here is the translation of the Authorised and (with slight variation only) of the Revised: 'He is our peace, who hath made both one and hath broken down the middle wall of partition between us, having abolished in his flesh the enmity, *even*' (that word is supplied, it is not in the original and so it is put in italics) '*even* the law of commandments.' That is not very good and it is better to take it like this: 'He has broken down the dividing wall of hostility (or of enmity) by abolishing the law of commandments.' He has broken down the middle wall of partition; of enmity. How?—by abolishing the law of commandments in ordinances. That is the better way of looking at it. What does it mean then? What has brought Jew and Gentile together in the Christian Church? The answer is that *the Lord Jesus Christ has broken down the enmity*. There used to be a kind of middle wall of partition between them. The apostle is using there as a figure what was true of the temple. In the temple the Court of the Gentiles we saw was furthest out. Gentiles were not allowed to go into the Court of the People, the Jews. There was a wall dividing them, a middle wall of partition. Indeed, that old temple was full of partitions. There was in addition the Court of the Priests, the Holy Place, and then the 'holiest of all' into which nobody was allowed to enter but the high priest once a year only. It was a place of partitions. But in Christ, says Paul, the partitions have been flattened, they have been knocked down, brought to the floor, and the way into the 'holiest of all' is open. But he is particularly interested here in the fact that the first partition between the Gentiles and the Jews, the enmity, has gone.

But why does he call this an enmity? Because, after all, it was God who had appointed the details concerning the construction of the temple, it was God Himself who had given the law to the children of Israel. And yet Paul says that it was this law of commandments contained in ordinances that really produced the enmity. That is a very important and a very subtle point, and it is there that we see exactly what sin does to man. God, as we have already seen, had divided the human race into two groups. He created for Himself a special people from Abraham. They are the Jews, the commonwealth of Israel, God's people. They were really apart from all others, and they were meant to be apart. God gave them special laws, these 'laws of commandments in ordinances', as Paul describes them. He means the ceremonial law, the law about burnt offerings and sacrifices, the meal offerings, and all the others which you read about in the book of Leviticus and elsewhere. God appointed them. Those were the ways in which the children of Israel were to come to God and to be blessed by God; and unless they observed them, God would not meet with them and God would not bless them. God gave them the law. They were not to eat certain types of animals, and so on. They were all God's laws, the ceremonial law, the law of commandments expressed in ordinances, in dictates. Well, you say, if that is so, where does the enmity come in? That is precisely where sin comes in. God did divide up the world into two groups, and He did give these commandments. But He did not do it in order to create enmity; He did it in order that the children of Israel might bear witness to Him and to His holy laws and to the way of salvation. But they, because of the principle of sin and of self and of selfishness, interpreted God's act in such a manner as to say, We, and we alone, are the people, and those others are dogs, they are scarcely human beings at all.

The Jews turned the commandment of God into a middle wall of partition; into a matter of hatred and of enmity. And the Gentiles looked on and said, Who are those Jews? What are these claims that they are making for themselves? So they hated them. And the Jew hated the Gentile. But that was never God's intention. The law was a part of God's revelation, a part of God's way of salvation. But man in sin turns the very gifts of God into causes of enmity. That is how the middle walls of partition come in. This is not a purely academic point. The world today is full of such partitions. Look at the gifts that God gives to men. They are all manifestations of His bounty and of His graciousness. He gives the gift of ability and understanding, He gives business acumen to certain men and they prosper and they succeed. He showers His gifts in these ways. But do all men get down on their knees together and thank God for His gracious gifts to men? Do they all with humility ascribe the glory and the honour to Him, and thank Him who is 'the Giver of every good and every perfect gift'? We know well that they do not. They are still doing what the Jew and the Gentile did. The man with ability says, Of course I have a brain, I have understanding. Look at that other fellow, he knows nothing. And so he despises him. And the other man looks up at him and says, Who is he? Who does he think he is? Enmity! And it is all because of the gifts of God. And so it is with every other gift that God gives. They are gifts of God, they are wonderful, and if we all but realised that and were humble, we would all enjoy them together. The man without the talent would say, How marvellous to see that man! how wonderful is God to have endowed that man with such capacity! But it is not so; these things lead to jealousy and rivalry, enmity and hatred and malice, bitterness and scorn, and everything that poisons life.

There will never be true peace until all that is broken down. Christ, says the apostle here, has broken it down in this matter of religion once and for ever, for '*He has abolished the law of commandments contained in ordinances.*' That is how He did it. Which means that the way to God now is no longer the way of burnt offerings and the sacrifices and the things that were peculiar and special only to the Jew. It is through Christ and through Him alone. So the thing that had led to the enmity and the jealousy and the rivalry, has been taken away by Christ. The cause of the enmity has been removed. And as men see that in Christ, the enmity disappears. The Jew who really understands the doctrine of Christ no longer separates himself in terms of the ceremonial law. He says, That is finished in Christ, I therefore am now in the same position as a Gentile. And the Gentile sees also that there is no longer that peculiar distinction between him and the Jew, and that the way is in Christ for him as for the Jew. So they all come together to God in the same way, in and through our Lord and Saviour Jesus Christ.

You see the point we have now reached. Christ has broken down the middle wall of partition, the enmity. And that is how He has done it. 'Christ is the end of the law for righteousness to everyone that believeth.' There is no need any longer for the ceremonial and the ritual of the Jew; it has been finished. Christ is the fulfilment of it all. They were but types pointing to Him. Men should never have stopped at them, they should have been led by them to Him. But He has put an end to them. So that in this whole matter of access to God, the old distinction, originally made by God Himself, has been abolished by God Himself in Christ, and the way is now open, to Gentile as well as Jew, to come into the presence of God. Not through an earthly, human priesthood, not with material offerings and sacrifices, but through the one and only Mediator between God and men; the Man Christ Jesus, by the sacrifice of His life and His precious blood. The middle wall of partition has been broken down, and it is only as men learn that truth, that they will be delivered from the enmity.

19

CHRIST'S WAY OF MAKING PEACE

For to make in himself of twain one new man, so making peace.

Ephesians 2: 15

As we come to consider this particular statement we must remind ourselves that it is a part of the great argument which the apostle works out in these verses. He is dealing with the amazing phenomenon presented by the Christian Church. He is looking at the Christian Church, and there he sees as fellow members—Jews and Gentiles, people who had belonged to that commonwealth of Israel, together with those who had hitherto been aliens from it and strangers from the covenants of promise. And what he is doing here is to explain how this had come to pass. It is the power of God that has done it. Nothing else could do it, nothing else could bring Jew and Gentile together in a common act of worship. And that is the power which brought Christ from the dead, nothing less than that! That is the thing he is expounding, and he does so in detail. The argument is a subtle one; in the whole range of Scripture there is no more closely-knit argument than in this particular section. Every phrase is important, every word is significant, if we are to grasp the mighty statement and appreciate its full richness and glory. He adds statement to statement, and each one follows the other with a logical precision that is quite remarkable. The mind of the great apostle is revealed here in a most amazing manner. The thing was so clear to him, and it will become clear to us if we take the trouble to look at his phrases one by one and observe the connection of each one with the previous one, and how it inevitably leads to the next one. But in addition to that, we need the enlightening which the Holy Spirit alone can provide. So the apostle, before he ever embarked on this moving demonstration of the wondrous grace of God, had already prayed for these Ephesians who were to read the letter, that 'the eyes of their understanding' might be enlightened. Without that we can do nothing. A very good way therefore of testing whether the Holy Spirit has enlightened the eyes of our understanding is to ask ourselves whether we are following the argument as we proceed. More, are we rejoicing in it, are we thrilled by it, do we see that we are looking at the most astounding thing in the world?

Here is the essence of the argument: Christ Himself is our peace. 'He is our peace'—it is all in Him. And it is also true to say that He makes peace: 'For to make in himself of twain one new man, so making peace'. He Himself is peace; He makes peace. And we have seen that the apostle tells us that the Lord Jesus Christ makes peace between man and man, and between man and God. He is the peace in every respect. The apostle puts them in that order, he puts man and man first, then he goes on in verse 16, which we shall consider later, to show how both are reconciled together in one body to God. The order, of course, is interesting. Theologically the order is the other way round, but the apostle is dealing with it in a practical and pastoral sense. He is starting with the concrete fact of the Church, with Jews and Gentiles on their knees together worshipping in the same way; he starts with that, man and man, and then he shows how they both go together to God. At the moment we are looking at the way in which He reconciles man to man. The apostle tells us that this is done in two ways: first of all negatively, and then positively. We have already considered the negative aspect as it is expressed in the words 'He hath abolished the law of commandments in ordinances'. He has removed the middle wall of partition —the enmity—which was between Jew and Gentile.

But that is only negative, and it is not all; indeed, it is not enough. This is the point I am anxious to emphasise now. *To abolish middle walls of partition alone does not produce peace.* That is the tragedy of so much thinking today, it seems to me, that so many have not a true conception of peace. Peace, according to the Scripture, does not merely mean the cessation of hostility. Neither does peace merely mean the prevention of actual hostility. But as the word 'peace' is used currently today it is obvious that that is what many mean by peace. Peace is regarded as merely a state in which you are not actually fighting. Peace becomes just an absence of war. That may be man's idea of peace: it is not God's idea of peace. That is not the scriptural notion of peace. Merely to cease fighting is not peace, merely to prevent future hostilities is not peace. You see how grievously the gospel is being misused, misinterpreted and misrepresented today by people who teach that we merely have to apply 'the teaching of Christ' to the international situation to solve the problem of world tension. We shall discover further reasons for saying that as we proceed. God is not content merely with the absence of outward and aggressive enmity and the manifestation of that enmity. When God makes peace, He does something inward, something vital. God is not content merely that men should not be at one another's throats; God's idea of peace is that men should embrace one another and love one another. That is Christian peace, nothing less than that. Not merely that we should not fight each other but that we should love one another, that there should be unity and oneness, that we really become one and love one another as we love ourselves. That is the truth that is emphasised in this particular bit of argument we are now considering. Peace must be thought of in terms of heart, of attitude; it is a matter of essential, vital, inward unity and love. What Paul tells us is that Christ has produced that peace. How has He done so? Here is the answer: 'To make in himself of twain one new man, so making peace'.

The apostle introduces here the profound New Testament doctrine of the Christian Church, the nature of the Christian Church. The new man, the new body, is the Church. *Christ's way of making peace is to form, to make, to bring into being the Christian Church*; therefore any attempt to understand the Christian way of peace must immediately introduce the idea of the Church. Or consider it in this way. According to this argument, peace amongst men is only possible as they all together belong to the body of Christ and are Christians. So, patently, it is not something that can be applied to nations. Therefore, to preach the Christian message as if it were something which can be applied to and by nations which are not Christian, which do not think in Christian terms, and which do not belong to the body of Christ, is rank heresy, and a complete denial of the teaching of the apostle. And yet that is the very thing that is being done. There are people who say that all the statesmen and the nations have to do is to apply this teaching. No man can apply this teaching unless he is a Christian, and no man will apply it unless he is a Christian. Indeed, as I shall show, even Christians are very defective in their application of it. But it demands, it postulates, a Christian character. Let us now observe how the apostle works that out.

You see the immediate relevance of all this, how important it all is. This is not dry-as-dust theology and doctrine. The thing that is uppermost in the minds of men today is the desire for peace—but they must see it in the right way. But apart from this general application, I know of nothing more edifying, nothing that is so strengthening to one's faith, nothing, therefore, that is so comforting, as to realise the truth of what the apostle tells us here. The Church, he tells us, is a new creation: 'For to make in himself of twain one new man'. Now this word 'make' here is much too weak. The word means 'to create in Himself'. A creation! A well-known hymn puts it well:

The Church's one foundation
Is Jesus Christ her Lord;
She is His new creation
By water and the Word.

That is the truth: *the Church is something absolutely new* that has been brought into being, something that was not there before. It is comparable to what happened in the very beginning when God created the heavens and the earth. There was nothing there before God created. Creation means bringing into being something that was previously not there, non-existent; it is making something out of nothing.

That is the phrase that is used here. Its implications in this matter of producing peace are obvious. How does God make peace between Jew and Gentile? It is not by a modification of what was there before; it is not even by an improvement of that which was there before. God does not just take a Jew and do something to him, and take a Gentile and just do something to him, and thereby bring them together. Not at all! It is something entirely new. Creation! Now this is vital to the whole position. As we enter the Christian Church we do so as new creations, we enter into something that is entirely new. There is a sense in which it has no relationship at all to what existed before. Let me try to illustrate this. The Church must not be conceived of as a coalition of a number of parties. No, it is the abolition of the old and the creation of something entirely new. Or let me try another illustration. The point which needs to be illustrated here is seen very clearly in the difference between the United States of America and the United Kingdom, similarly in the difference between the United States of America and the British Commonwealth of Nations. In the United Kingdom or the British Commonwealth of Nations, you have an association of a number of nations, nationalities, peoples and tribes. They all belong to the same Commonwealth, but they still exist as separate nations—their nationality is not demolished, is not destroyed. They still remain separate nations, but they have chosen for certain reasons to work together. That is the real characteristic of the British Commonwealth of Nations, at one time held together by force and power, now held together by common interests and common purposes. The idea of individual nationhood still remains, but voluntarily they come into an association. It is therefore an association which can be broken, because they have not ceased to be these particular elements. It is the same in the United Kingdom—English, Welsh, Scots and Irish. The nationality has not been abolished, it is still there, but they have chosen to work together and to do certain things in common. But in the United States of America the position is very different. The United States of America is not a number of united nations, it is not a gathering of separate nations. In other words, men have gone out to that country from the various countries of Europe and elsewhere, and in order to be true citizens of the United States they have to finish with their past. It is a new nation. It is not a collection of Germans and Swedes and Finns and Norwegians and British and French and Italians and Greeks. Not at all! They are all doing their utmost, and quite rightly, to forget all that. They are Americans; they have finished with the old alignment, the old national ties. There is a new nation. Now that is the kind of thing we have here. The Church is not a sort of coalition of Jews and Gentiles; something absolutely new has come into being which was just not there before. Creation!—'for to create in himself of twain one new man'. This is a most important principle.

Let us turn now to a second proposition. *The Church is formed in Christ*: 'For to create *in himself* of twain one new man, so making peace'. The Church is formed in Him, it happens as the result of her relationship to Him. We have already seen something of this in the first chapter. We have also seen it hinted at and suggested in the first ten verses of this chapter. But here it is once more. The Church is the body of Christ, and He is the Head; the Church derives her life, her sustenance, her power, everything, from Him. 'To create in himself of twain one new man.' How does He do this? As members of the Church we are members of the body of Christ, In 1 Corinthians 12: 27 Paul puts it in this way: 'Ye are the body of Christ and members in particular.' We are all particular individual members of this one body. There is an essential unity in a body. A body is not a collection of parts, it is not a mere loose attachment of fingers and hands and forearms and arms and legs and toes. Not at all! It is an organic whole, a vital unity with individual parts; but the whole is greater than the sum of the parts. There again you have the same idea. You must not think of a finger in isolation, it is always a part of the whole. So He has 'created in himself of twain . . .;' it is all 'in himself'. We must grasp this idea, therefore, of the Church as the body of Christ, with Christ as the Head, and the organic unity of all the parts, each one supplying something, as the apostle will tell us later in the fourth chapter.

So I go on to the third proposition which is, that *the Church, as the result of this, is a new man*: 'for to create in himself of twain *one new man*'. Here he is not using the term the 'new man' in the same sense as he uses it elsewhere when he talks about the new and the old man in the individual Christian. The one new man here, the one body, is the Church, consisting of these various parts, all as a representation of the body of Christ. Indeed we can call it *a new humanity*. And that, it seems to me, is the best way of looking at it. In Jesus Christ, and as the result of His perfect work, something entirely new has come into being. What is it? It is a new humanity. We can think of the Church not only as a body, but as a humanity! The comparison and the contrast that at once suggest themselves to us amount to this. Formerly we were all in Adam. We were all one in Adam, the whole of humanity was in Adam, so what Adam did the whole of humanity did. 'As in Adam all die'—that is the statement. We were all in Adam, he was the head and the representative of the entire human race. There was a unity; humanity was one body in Adam. Adam was the head of that humanity which consisted of Adam and his seed. Now this is what has happened, and this is where the encouragement and comfort and consolation of the gospel come in. As a Christian, I have finished utterly and absolutely with that old humanity. I no longer belong to Adam. The old man has been crucified with Christ. The old man has died. Christ is the second man. Christ is the last Adam. The first Adam! The last Adam! The beginner of one humanity, which went wrong and which went into sin and failed; the Beginner of the new humanity, that can never fail because it is in Him! The Second Man! Paul refers to Him elsewhere as 'the first-born of many brethren'. That is precisely the same idea! When we look at Christians, when we look at the Christian Church, we are looking at a new race, a new humanity, which is altogether different from the old. It is not that the old is taken and improved a little. It is a new creation, it is a new humanity coming out of Christ as that other humanity came out of Adam. It is absolutely new, it is a 'new creation'; no other term is adequate.

It amounts to this. In our new birth, in our regeneration, in our being 'born again', *we are born into this new race*, into this new body, into this new family. That is how Christ makes peace. He does not produce a conglomeration of different people; he produces a new people, a new family, a new household, a new race. The apostle explains that in detail towards the end of the chapter; but here it is in principle. That is how Christ makes peace. To persuade nations not to fight one another is not peace in this sense. Peace is only made in God's way, and in Christ's way, when we all belong to the same family, have the same blood in us, as it were, are members of the same humanity, members of the same body, in this living vital relationship to God. That is the only peace the New Testament is interested in. How monstrous it is, therefore, for the Church to say to the statesmen, All you have to do is to apply our teaching and you will produce peace amongst the nations. It is a denial of the whole doctrine of the Church. It is a denial of the doctrine of regeneration. It is indeed a complete misrepresentation of the teaching of our blessed Lord.

There, then, is the argument as such; but there are certain things which we must emphasise. For instance, *the old is entirely done away with*. That follows of necessity from all that we have been saying. The Jew has been done away with as such, even as the Gentile has been done away with, in Christ. If you believe in this new creation, you must realise that all else has been entirely done away with, put aside. 'There is neither Jew nor Greek . . ., for ye are all one in Christ Jesus' (Galatians 3: 28). Another obvious principle is that nothing that belonged to the old state is of any value or has any relevance in the new state. If that seems startling to us we have but to read what Paul says in Galatians 6: 15: 'In Christ Jesus neither circumcision availeth anything, nor uncircumcision, but a new creature'. What a tremendous statement! In Christ Jesus circumcision is irrelevant, it 'availeth nothing'. But uncircumcision is equally irrelevant, it also 'availeth nothing'. In Christ Jesus, in the realm of the Church, in this matter of relationship to God and peace amongst men, there is only one thing that matters—a new creation. So that Jew has gone, Gentile has gone; all that belonged to Jew, all that belonged to Gentile, is irrelevant henceforward. It is the new creature that matters. There is no more comforting or consoling thought than that. It tells me that all that was true of me in my old life does not matter any more. The sins I once committed have been dealt with, they no longer matter. They matter as little as circumcision and uncircumcision. If I am in Christ, I am a new creature. That old man has been dealt with, he is dead, he is gone. 'There is therefore now no condemnation to them that are in Christ Jesus.' 'I have been crucified with Christ.' I am dead! 'No longer I, but Christ liveth in me.' That is what this means. What a glorious, what a blessed doctrine! Christian people, are you still foolish enough to listen to the devil when he makes you look back on your old life? You should not do so, you should reject him, you should resist him, you should tell him that is finished with, that that old man you once were is dead, and that you have nothing whatsoever to do with him. This is something which is absolutely and entirely new.

A third principle is that *we are all the same in this new relationship* because we have all become something new. How does Christ form the Church, how do the Jew and Gentile come together? It is not by the Gentile becoming a Jew or a Jewish proselyte. There were

many in the early Church who thought it was that. But that is not
the way; it is not that the Gentile has to become a Jew, that he has
to submit to circumcision and take up all the ceremonial. But on
the other hand the Jew does not have to become a Gentile. The glory
of this way is that the old is entirely done away with. It is not a
modification of the Gentile and a modification of the Jew; it is not
a meeting round a conference table and the two opposing sides
agreeing to compromise and to meet half way on a fifty-fifty basis.
Not at all! Something absolutely new is brought into being. The
Jew does not become a Gentile, the Gentile does not become a Jew.
It is a new man, a new creation.

Our fourth principle takes us yet further. *The unity of this new
body is an absolute unity.* I use the term advisedly. There is no such
thing as a Jewish section of the Christian Church. There is no such
thing as a Gentile section of the Christian Church. And there never
will be. The old has been done away with. The Lord Jesus Christ
Himself put it like this once and for ever in a most important statement from this standpoint, Matthew 21 verse 43. Addressing the
Jews He said, 'Therefore I say unto you, the kingdom of God shall
be taken from you and given to a nation bringing forth the fruits
thereof'. That new nation is the Church. The Jews as such have
ceased to be the special people of God. There is a new nation. And
there will never be a Jewish section in the Church in a different
position from the Gentile section. All that is finished. That is the
statement of the Lord Himself. You remember how the apostle
Peter says the same thing in 1 Peter 2: 9 and 10: 'Ye', he says
(using of the Church, consisting of Jew and Gentiles, the very words
that God spoke to the nation of Israel just before the giving of the
law), 'Ye (the Church) are a chosen generation, a royal priesthood,
an holy nation, a peculiar people'. That is the new nation. And it
is not a mixture of Jew and Gentile, but a new man; Jew finished,
Gentile finished, a new creature. There is no more, says Paul,
Jew nor Gentile, Barbarian, Scythian, bond nor free, male nor
female. Thank God all that is finished, there is but one new man,
in Christ Jesus.

The way in which He makes peace can be put finally like this.
You and I have peace and enjoy peace with one another, and
there is peace in the Church, only on condition that we realise and
put into practice the principles we have just been enunciating. There
are ultimately but two big principles. *We must cease to think of ourselves in the old way and in the old terms in every respect.* As Christians,
as members of the Church, we must cease to think of one another
in terms of nationality. Politically we still do so. In the Christian

Church we must not do so. We must forget all that. We must cease
to think of people in terms of their natural birth, or in terms of their
ability. All these things divide: nationality, birth, upbringing, caste,
all these things divide. Ability, lack of ability, divide; wealth and
poverty divide. In the Church and as Christians, we must not think
of ourselves any longer in those terms, because the moment we
begin to bring in those categories there is no longer peace; there is
division, separation, enmity. Not only that, we must not even think
of one another any longer in terms of our former life and behaviour
—our previous goodness or badness, our previous morality or
immorality. It does not matter, it does not count in the Church.
In the Christian Church a highly respectable man must not look
at another man and say: I remember what he once was, I remember
where he has come from; has such a man an equal right in the
church? That is the very antithesis of peace. That is the attitude of
that elder brother condemned by our Lord in the parable of the
Prodigal Son. All those categories have gone.

I will go further. In the Christian Church, you even forget your
former religion. It does not matter whether you were highly religious
or not, the question is whether you are a Christian now. You may
have been very devout; it does not matter—you can be devout
without being a Christian. All that is finished with. The old terms
and categories no longer apply, and in the realm of the Church you
do not ask any one of those questions about a man. You simply
look at him and you see the marks of Christ in him. You may
remember the immortal story connected with old Philip Henry,
the father of the commentator, Matthew Henry. Philip Henry as a
young man fell in love with a young lady, who came from a very
much higher position in life than himself. She was also in love with
him. Then the question came of getting the consent of her parents.
And the parents turning to their daughter said, 'This man, this
Philip Henry, where has he come from?' And she said, 'I do not
know where he has come from, but I know where he is going'.
That is the thing. It is not where he comes from that matters. Where
is he going? Is he destined for glory, for God, for eternity in the
presence of Christ, does he belong to Him? That is the only question.
Nothing else matters in this realm, because the moment you bring
in other considerations you bring in division.

So I put it positively in this way. *We must always actively think
and conceive of ourselves in this new way.* Always! Failure to do these
two things always leads to trouble. There are remarkable illustrations of this in the New Testament itself. Do you remember how our
Lord caught His own closest apostles and disciples one day quarrelling amongst themselves? What were they quarrelling about?

Which of them should be greatest in the kingdom! And He turned to them and said: You do not understand; in My kingdom things are absolutely different from the kingdoms of the world. In the kingdoms of the world your great men are served by others; in My kingdom greatness consists in service. 'The Son of man', He says, 'came not to be ministered unto but to minister, and to give his life a ransom for many.' 'And whosoever will be chief among you, let him be your servant.' It is a complete reversal; but they did not grasp that.

There is an account of a similar thing in the sixth chapter of the book of the Acts of the Apostles, when the Church had only just come into being. This is what we read: 'In those days, when the number of the disciples was multiplied, there arose a murmuring of the Grecians against the Hebrews because their widows were neglected in the daily ministration'. These people had been converted, were saved, and had become Christians, but they had not learnt this lesson. Grecians, Hebrews! It isn't fair, they said; they were dividing up in terms of cultural differences, and the peace had gone immediately.

Another striking illustration is found in Acts 15: 'And some days after, Paul said to Barnabas'—Barnabas was a very nice man, you remember, 'the son of consolation'; he and Paul had been travelling together—'Paul said to Barnabas, Let us go again and visit our brethren in every city where we have preached the word of the Lord and see how they do. And Barnabas determined to take with them John, whose surname was Mark. But Paul thought it not good to take him with them, who departed from them from Pamphylia and went not with them to the work'. John Mark had deserted on a previous journey, and Paul said, No, it is not right to take him. 'And the contention was so sharp between them that they departed the one from the other: and so Barnabas took Mark and sailed unto Cyprus; and Paul chose Silas and departed, being recommended by the brethren to the grace of God.' Why was it, do you think, that Barnabas wanted to take John Mark with them? They were relatives! And this excellent, noble Christian man, Barnabas, just forgetting the doctrine for a moment, said: I say we take Mark with us. And his only reason for saying it was that Mark was his relative. In the Christian Church you must forget that. You do not take your relative with you if he has already failed and if there is a better man; you do not give preference to a man because he belongs to your family. No, neither Jew nor Gentile; the old has gone. It is something new! So you do not drag your family relationships in. How often has that been done! I see it so frequently. A man is called of God to start a work, undoubtedly called of God, and then when he comes to die he appoints his own son as his successor. Sometimes it may be right; very often it may be wrong, and you will find the work will begin to droop and to dwindle, and it will eventually die. Why? Because the son was not really called. It is very natural, I agree, but it is not Christian. Paul and Barnabas separate because the question of family relationships comes in.

This danger of allowing the past to intrude is found everywhere. Do you remember how Paul had to withstand Peter to the face over this very matter? Certain people came down from Jerusalem, certain Jews, and told Peter, You should not eat with the Gentiles. Peter listened to them, and division came in. The whole effort of the Judaisers was based on this. They said, You know it is not enough to believe in Christ, you have got to be circumcised as well. And thereby they caused a division. They did not realise that the old had gone. Circumcision no longer matters. The Jew does not matter *qua* Jew.

In many ways the most perfect illustration of what I am trying to say is found in the First Epistle to the Corinthians. The church in Corinth was in great trouble, and Paul had to write a letter to them. They were dividing up in a wrong way, first of all about men. 'I am of Paul. I am of Apollos. I am of Cephas.' Which is the best preacher? which is the most eloquent? which is the one you like? Worshipping, following men; putting men before Christ! That is the old, that is carnality, that is what the world does. That should not happen in the Christian Church. What else? They were going to law against one another, they had certain disputes and they took them to the open courts. Paul says, But you are not behaving as Christians. If you had some conception of the Church you would appoint the humblest member of the church as judge and umpire; you would take your case to him, and if he decides against you, you would say, I submit, I am happy to do it for the sake of the body of Christ. That is the new! What else? The strong and the weak brethren! The matter is dealt with in 1 Corinthians 8. The strong brother had a clearer insight into truth than the other, and they quarrelled about it. The strong brother was despising the weak and the weak was thus being caused to stumble. Paul says, Do not destroy with your meat a brother for whom Christ died. Realise the new relationship. You are brethren in Christ, do without your meat for the sake of peace and concord and for Christian happiness. 'Wherefore if meat make my brother to offend, I will eat no flesh while the world standeth, lest I make my brother to offend (1 Corinthians 8: 13). Indeed, in Corinth, they were divided even on the question of spiritual gifts. The people with the flashy, spectacular gifts were boasting, and despising the others; the eye was saying 'I have no need of thee' to the foot, and so on. It was all because they did not grasp the doctrine of the Church as the body of Christ. Failure to do so will always lead to division.

I mentioned just now that wealth should not come into this realm. James deals with that, you remember, in the second chapter of his Epistle. He says, In the church, in your assembly, if a man comes in with a great gold ring, you do not lead him right to the front because he is a very wealthy man; and if another man comes in in rags you do not say to him: You sit there at the back. We do not do that sort of thing in the church, says James; we do not recognise such distinctions, we do not assess men by their clothing or by their appurtenances. You must look at the soul, the relationship to God and to Christ; and there, all are one. The old has been done away with. All has become new.

To sum it up in a positive word, we turn to Colossians 3: 15. Paul has been dealing with quarrellings and disputings. This is, he says, the thing to remember: 'Let the peace of God (or the peace of Christ) rule in your hearts, to the which also ye are called in one body'. Do you know what he means by that phrase 'Let the peace of Christ rule in your hearts'? It means this: let the peace of Christ act as arbitrator; let the peace of Christ act as umpire amongst you. You all, with your rival positions and differences, say, 'Let the peace of Christ decide this. I am not going to decide it; it is not a question of my rights, my demands; I am prepared to agree to anything that promotes the peace of Christ amongst us as well as the peace of Christ in my own heart.' Set that up as umpire, says Paul, and peace shall reign among you.

We are called into one body. 'For to make in himself of twain one new man, *so* making peace.' And it is the only way. It is as I know I am in Christ, and look at another and know that he is in Christ, that I can forgive and forget, I can join hands and humble myself with him. We are all one in Christ, and we are going to spend our eternity in glory together. It is as we remember that, and only as we know that that is true of us, that there can be a true, a real, a lasting peace.

Blessed be God for the new creation in Christ Jesus!

20

THE ONE MEDIATOR

And that he might reconcile both unto God in one body by the cross, having slain the enmity thereby. Ephesians 2: 16

In these moving and glorious words, the apostle continues his great statement of God's way of reconciling men, and shows how yet another obstacle to that desired result is removed. The Ephesians, pagans as they were, Gentiles, were not only separated from the Jews, the commonwealth of Israel, they were also separated from God. And obviously there can be no true unity between man and man until there is this other unity; because the original division into Jew and Gentile was all in terms of relationship to God. So the apostle now goes on to show how this second matter also has been dealt with, and in the same way as before, by our Lord and Saviour Jesus Christ. But you notice that the apostle puts this in a very interesting manner. Instead of simply stating how the pagan Ephesians had been reconciled to God, he says 'And that he might reconcile *both* unto God in one body by the cross, having slain the enmity thereby'—both, Jews and Gentiles. Then he shows us exactly how this has taken place.

The teaching here is fundamental and vital, and especially as regards this whole question of unity and of peace. In its general form we can put it like this. *All the minor and secondary divisions and separations and quarrels among men are ultimately due to the fact that all men are separated from God.* Now that is a fundamental and a universal proposition. The world is full of divisions and distinctions, countries, nations, blocs, groups, curtains, one side and the other side; in the nation, classes, industrial groups, capital and labour, master or employer and servant, and so on; and within all these groups again, divisions, rivalries, envies. The world is full of divisions and separations. But according to the teaching of Scripture the really significant thing is that all these minor and secondary, third-rate, fifth-rate, tenth-rate divisions and separations and quarrellings are due to one thing only, namely, that all men are separated from God and are in the wrong relationship to Him.

That is the whole case of the Bible. There would be no trouble in life at all were it not that man has rebelled against God and has fallen away from God. All the troubles are due to that. Conversely therefore, we are entitled to say that unity among men is only possible as men are reconciled together to God. The importance of that statement is obvious. There are people who talk glibly about the application of Christian teaching to the problems, and who tell us it is all quite simple. But according to this teaching it is impossible until men and women are reconciled to God. It is a sheer waste of energy and of breath and of time to try to get Christian behaviour from people who are not Christians. They cannot respond. A man has to be right with God before he can be right with his fellow men and women. I would remind you of how our Lord answered a question that was put to Him when He was asked which is the first and the greatest commandment. His reply was, 'Thou shalt love the Lord thy God with all thy heart and with all thy soul and with all thy strength and with all thy mind'; and then, 'The second is like unto it, Thou shalt love thy neighbour as thyself'. But you cannot do the second until you have done the first. This is a basic, foundational principle.

Let us see how the apostle works this out. In a sense he is going on to a new theme. In another sense he is continuing the old one. The fact is, the two themes cannot be separated. That is why he connects them with this word 'and', which really means here 'in addition'. What is he saying? The best way, perhaps, to approach the matter is to look at this great world 'reconcile';—'And that he might *reconcile* both unto God'. The word the apostle actually used and which is translated 'reconcile' is most interesting. It is only found in one other place in the entire Bible, and that is Colossians 1, 20 and 21. He there uses the identical word—but nowhere else. You find the word 'reconcile' in a number of places in the Authorised Version. You will find it in Romans 5: 10. You will find it in 2 Corinthians 5: 18, 19 and 20. But in all those cases the word used by the apostle was not the same word as is used here. It is the same root; in a sense it has the same essential meaning; but here he used a very special word, he put a prefix on to the word which he uses in the other places. And therefore in expounding this we must take the word as he used it, prefix as well.

What, therefore, does the word 'reconcile' mean? Let me suggest that it includes the following ideas and conceptions. It means *first* of all a change from a hostile to a friendly relationship. That is the simplest meaning, the basic meaning. But it means more. In the *second* place, it does not merely mean a friendship after an estrangement, a mere doing away with the estrangement. It is not merely that it brings people into speaking terms again who formerly passed one another without even looking at each other. It means more; it means really bringing together again, a reuniting, a re-connecting. It carries that meaning. In the *third* place it is a word also that emphasises the completeness of the action. It means that the enmity is so completely laid aside that complete amity follows. And the emphasis here is on the completeness of the action. It is not the patching up of a disagreement. It is not a compromise, the kind of thing that happens so often when a conference has gone on for days and there has been a deadlock and somebody suddenly gets a bright idea and suggests introducing a particular word or formula, which just patches up the problem for the moment. It is not that. It is a complete action, it produces complete amity and concord where there was formerly hostility.

But in the *fourth* place, it also means this. It is not merely that the two partners to the trouble or the dispute or the quarrel have decided to come together. This word that the apostle uses implies that it is *one* of the parties that takes the action, and it is the *upper* one that does it. A part of this word indicates an action from above. It is the Greek word 'kata'; it suggests an action that comes down from above. It is not that the two sides come together as it were voluntarily; it is the one bringing the other into this position of complete amity and concord. And finally, in the *fifth* place, the word carries the meaning that it is a restoration of something that was there before. Now our word 'reconcile, which is really a transliteration of the Latin word, in and of itself suggests that. Re-concile! They were conciled before, they are now re-conciled, brought back to where they were. The word carries all those meanings, and it is this last point especially that is introduced by the special prefix found in the word used by the apostle here, the prefix, *apo*, a bringing back again, the *re*. That is the thing that is emphasised here.

What then is the apostle's teaching? Let me put it to you in a number of principles. The first thing, obviously, taught here is that *sin separates from God*. All our troubles are ultimately due to the fact that we are not clear about sin. The apostle has already said it in verse 12; he repeats it here. It can never be repeated too often: 'That at that time ye were without Christ, being aliens from the commonwealth of Israel, and strangers from the covenants of promise, having no hope, and without God in the world'. The opposite is, being 'made nigh', being drawn nigh. The terrible thing about sin, but the thing we all are prone to forget, is that sin is not mere transgression of the law—it *is* that; sin is not only disobedience—it *is* that; sin is not only missing the mark—it *is* that;

the most appalling thing about sin, the devastating thing about sin, is that it means *breaking fellowship with God*. It means that we are cut off from God, that we are out of relationship to God, that we are without God. Now that is the thing the apostle is emphasising here. But it does not even stop at that. Sin also produces enmity between man and God. And that, according to this teaching everywhere, is the condition of man in sin. It happened at the beginning of history. God made man for Himself, and man was in fellowship with God. If only we would hold on to that idea as we ought! We were made for God, we were meant for God; we were never made for the world, and the flesh, and the devil. Man was made for God, he was meant for fellowship with God, he was meant to enjoy God. And that was his original condition. But, alas, sin came in; and the terrible thing about sin was not simply that Adam and Eve ate of the forbidden fruit—that was true, that was an action, that was rebellion, that was arrogance, that was breaking God's commandment and ignoring His law—but the terrible thing was that it broke fellowship. Man was walking with God, and suddenly he turned his back on Him. That is the awful thing about sin. That, therefore, is the problem, that is the thing that needs to be put right. It is not just a question of our being forgiven for particular actions. That is not the only problem. The basic problem is, How can this fellowship be restored? How can it be brought back again?

It is just here that so many go wrong in their thinking about these matters. That is why they do not understand the meaning of the death of Christ, and the cross, and why they see no meaning in a Communion Service. They say, Surely there is no great problem; when a child does something wrong a parent forgives him and all is well; is it not like that with God?' If I confess my sins, if I say I am sorry, will not God just forgive me? And the answer of the New Testament is, that it is not as simple as that. If it were as simple as that the Lord Jesus Christ would never have come into the world; He certainly would never have gone to the cross. No, the problem is one of fellowship; the problem of how fellowship can be restored. And this is not only of importance in our initial coming into the Christian life; there is nothing that is more vitally important for Christians at all stages. The sooner we begin to think of sins, not in terms of bad actions simply, but in terms of our relationship to God, the better Christians we shall be.

All this is set out perfectly in the First Epistle of John in the first chapter. There you have a picture. *The Christian is a man who is in fellowship with God* and walking with God. 'Our fellowship is truly with the Father, and with his Son Jesus Christ,' says John. He says that the apostles are in this fellowship and that they want others to be enjoying it also. But then the question arises, How is this possible? 'God is light, and in him is no darkness at all;' and I am sinful and I keep on falling into sin. The moment I fall into sin I break my fellowship with God. It is not only that that sinful action is wrong, but I am insulting my Companion. I am doing something in the presence of the holy God, who is light, that is to Him hateful and abhorrent. How can we walk in fellowship? That is how John puts it. I am emphasising it for this good reason, that in my personal experience and in my experience as a pastor, there is no more important discovery that a Christian can make in his battle with sin, with particular sins, than just this very thing. What I tell people always is this: Stop praying about that particular thing that gets you down; make your praying positive; think of it in terms of your fellowship with God. Do not think of it merely in terms of your falling, and of that particular thing; turn your back on it, begin to think of yourself as a companion of God and of Christ, and say, Now I am with Him and I must do nothing in His presence that He will dislike and that will hurt Him. Think positively! Remind yourself that Christ is always with you, and then you will begin to hate the thing and it will become unthinkable. But that is what we tend to fail to do, is it not? We forget that the terrible thing about sin is that it is a violation of fellowship and that it separates us from God. The term 'reconciliation' at once brings us face to face with the fact that we have been out of fellowship and that we need to be restored to fellowship.

When God called Abraham and formed the nation of Israel, *He was already taking a great step to bring that reconciliation to pass.* The whole world had sinned in Adam and had fallen away from God, so all were by nature estranged from God. Man did nothing and could do nothing about that. But God did something, He took action. Out of all the mass of mankind He formed a new nation for Himself, a people for His own peculiar possession, a people with whom He could have fellowship and who could have fellowship with Him, a new nation, a new creation. That is the commonwealth of Israel. All the rest were outside that commonwealth, they were still not in fellowship with Him. These were in fellowship, the rest were not. Now if we do not grasp this truth there is a sense in which we do not understand the Old Testament at all. This is the sum and substance of the Old Testament, the story of God's forming this peculiar people for Himself, and the relationship between them.

But unfortunately that was not sufficient, for the apostle tells us here that *the Jews as well as the Gentiles needed to be reconciled to God.* Jews as well as Ephesians needed a reconciliation. Why? The New Testament supplies the answer. All the Levitical sacrifices, the burnt offerings and the sacrifices, the killing of the paschal lamb and the daily lamb, and the presentation of the blood, and all the rest of this rich and elaborate ceremonial was really not sufficient; it was merely a shadow of something that was to come, it was merely a covering over of the sins of men. 'For it is not possible that the blood of bulls and goats should take away sins'; it covered over the sin but it did not really deal with the problem. It was sufficient for the time being. But according to this same apostle Paul, in the third chapter of the Epistle to the Romans, it was necessary that God should justify such dealing with sins, and He did justify it on the cross of Calvary. He had to justify Himself for the remission of sins that were past, and there He does it.

But not only was that a problem. The Jews, alas, needed to be reconciled for this reason also, that they had so completely misunderstood what God had done in Abraham, and in the nation, that they thought that the mere fact that they were physical descendants from Abraham in and of itself saved them. John the Baptist knew that, because when he began to preach to those Jews he said, 'Begin not to say within yourselves, We have Abraham to our father, for I say unto you that God is able of these stones to raise up children unto Abraham'. But that is what they were saying. On one occasion the Lord Jesus Christ said to them, 'If ye continue in my words then are ye my disciples indeed, and ye shall know the truth and the truth shall make you free'. But they resented it, saying, 'We be Abraham's seed and were never in bondage to any man; how sayest thou, Ye shall be made free?' (John 8: 33). The Jews had misunderstood it all; they thought that because they were Jews they were right with God, but thereby they brought condemnation on themselves. They needed to be reconciled. And furthermore, as we have seen on a previous occasion, their attitude to the Gentiles was terribly sinful. They regarded them as dogs, they despised them as outsiders. For these various reasons they needed to be reconciled to God.

That brings us to our next principle, which is, that *both Jew and Gentile are reconciled to God together in exactly the same way*, not separately. 'And that he might reconcile both unto God in one body'—that is the point, that is the emphasis here. Now the 'one body' does not mean the physical body of the Lord Jesus Christ. The 'one body' is the Church. So what he teaches is that the Jew and the Gentile are reconciled to God in exactly the same way; there is no longer any difference between them. There is only one way of being reconciled to God. 'There is one God and one mediator (only) between God and men, the man Christ Jesus.' (1 Timothy 2: 5.)

There are no separate ways into the kingdom of God for Jew and Gentile; there is only one way, and this is it, the 'one body' again. I emphasise this for this reason, that there is a teaching which is quite popular, but which seems to me in the light of this verse and others to be terribly, dangerously, unscriptural, which says that now during this dispensation it is in Christ and by His grace and by His death that men are saved, but that in a future time the Jews will then be saved by the keeping of the law. To them will be preached not the gospel of the grace of God but 'the gospel of the kingdom', and the law, and they will keep the law and they will enter into the kingdom by the keeping of the law. I say again, quite deliberately, that that is a denial of the fact that there is only one way to be reconciled with God, namely, through Jesus Christ and Him crucified. There is no access into the presence of God except through the one and only Mediator; 'that he might reconcile *both* in one body', and it is the only body, the only way. It is in this one body, the Church; and no man ever has been or ever will be reconciled to God save in this way. Abraham and the Old Testament saints, all whose sins had been covered, are really reconciled to God in Christ. All in all future ages will be reconciled in the same way. It is by the grace of God and that alone that any man can be saved.

So I go on to the next principle, which I put like this. *The reconciliation is achieved and produced by the Lord Jesus Christ.* 'And that he'— He, the Lord Jesus—'might reconcile both unto God in one body'. He! Oh that we all might be clear about this! There is no hope for man apart from Him. He came into the world because it was the only way. No man, I say again, ever can or ever will save himself by his own efforts or striving, no matter what is preached to him. Neither can the law save him; as Paul says: 'What the law could not do in that it was weak through the flesh . . .'. Christ had to come. 'God was in Christ reconciling the world unto himself', and there is no other way. Here the apostle puts the emphasis upon the Lord Jesus Christ. It was God who sent Him, but it was Christ by coming and by all His active and passive obedience who has done it. 'He is our peace', and He alone is our peace. I say again that unless we ascribe all the praise and the honour and the glory to the Lord Jesus Christ we are not Christians. *It is His action;* it is God's action in and through Him. Man is dead in trespasses and sins, he is an enemy and alien in his mind by wicked works, he is a God-hater, he does nothing and can do nothing good. How is reconciliation possible? We found the answer in the definition of the word: it is an action from above, it is a move on God's part, the God against whom we have rebelled and on whom we have turned our backs.

It is He who initiates the great movement. He began it in the Old, He continues it in the New; it is perfect in Christ. It is His action. It is all in Jesus Christ. It is all the grace of God in Christ. 'God was in Christ, reconciling the world unto himself.' That is the message.

But in particular you notice the apostle says it is *by the cross*. 'And that He might reconcile both unto God in one body—by the cross.' I would again call your attention to the way in which the apostle keeps on repeating these things. 'But now in Christ Jesus', he has said in verse thirteen, 'ye who sometimes were far off are made nigh by the blood of Christ'. He does not stop here at saying 'that He might reconcile both unto God in one body'; he adds—'by the cross'. He brings it in because he must bring it in. There is no reconciliation apart from the cross. And what does the cross mean? The parallel passage in Colossians 1: 20, puts it perfectly: 'Having made peace by the blood of his cross'. It is the death, the life laid down, it is the blood-shedding, the life poured out. That is how God makes peace, that is how Christ makes peace, that is how reconciliation comes about.

There is no possibility of reconciliation apart from the death of the Lord Jesus Christ upon the cross on Calvary's hill. Why? Well that is the last point. '. . . having slain the enmity *thereby*'—therein, by that. Here we come to the question people are so fond of asking. Why was the death of Christ upon the cross essential, and how does it reconcile us? You will find that strange answers are given to that question which seem to me to be quite incapable of being reconciled with the apostle's statement. Some say that what happens is that 'God forgives the cross'; that cruel men put our Lord to death but that God forgives them even for doing that. They say that we were all there—'Were you there when they crucified my Lord?' Yes, they say, you were, you were in one of the groups—the soldier, the Pharisee, or one of them, and you crucified Him; ah, but this is the message. God forgives even that. But that is not making peace *by* the cross. That is making peace in spite of the cross, which is the exact opposite. But what the apostle teaches everywhere is that God, Christ, makes peace *by* the cross, through, by means of, the cross. Yet another explanation given is that God always produces good even out of evil. Joseph, in his day, saw it. Joseph said to his brothers, '. . . ye thought evil against me; but God meant it unto good . . .'; you sold me in a wrong way, you meant something wrong: ah yes, but God turned the evil into good, and He always does. The supreme illustration of that, they say, is that God even turned the evil of the cross into good. Men performed an evil action, but God turned it into something marvellous. Is that saving us and reconciling us *by* the cross? No! I say again that it is just a way of

saying that He saves us in spite of it. That is not saving *by* the blood
of the cross. That is not making peace by, through, or by means of,
the blood of the cross. Still others say that it means that as I look
at Christ there dying innocently on the cross my heart will be
broken as I realise the sinfulness and the enormity of it all. But that
will not do either, because that again is not a making of peace by
the blood of the cross. According to Paul it has happened, it has
been done; it is not something that only happens when I realise
what has happened on the cross; it was done once and for ever, the
action was complete on Calvary—God *was* in Christ reconciling
the world to Himself. He has done it once and for ever. It is something much more profound than any of these explanations.

The true teaching is that *before reconciliation is possible something has
to happen on God's side* as well as on our side. Sin has brought enmity
between man and God. God hates sin. God's wrath is manifested
against sin. And before there can be reconciliation, before God can
again bless men, this enmity has got to be removed. And the
teaching is that it has been removed by the blood of the cross.
Why does he mention the blood, why the cross, why the death?
Because that is the explanation of all the Old Testament teaching
about sacrifices. That was God's own method, it was God who
ordained it all, as a picture of that which was going to be done in
Christ. Is not this how they did it? They took the animal, then they
put their hands on the head of the animal. What did that mean?
They were taking their sins and the sins of the people and symbolically transferring them to the animal. Then the animal was
killed, its blood was shed; and the blood was presented as an
offering; the animal was offered as a sacrifice. That is the teaching.
And that is precisely the New Testament teaching about the death
of Christ on the cross. 'God was in Christ reconciling the world unto
himself, not imputing their trespasses unto *them*.' Why not? Because
He imputed their trespasses unto *Him*! God took your sins and mine
and He put them on the head of Christ, and then as the Lamb of
God He slew Him. Not imputing their trespasses unto *them*! Because
'he hath made *him* to be sin for us who knew no sin, that we might
be made the righteousness of God in him' (2 Corinthians 5: 21).
By the blood of His cross! By the cross He did it! The enmity—
man's enmity against God was put on to Christ and there was taken
away. He slew it there. That is the teaching. That is the meaning
of the cry of dereliction, 'My God, my God, why hast thou forsaken
me.' It is because Christ's blood, the blood of the Lamb of God,
was shed on Calvary's hill that the way of reconciliation is open.
The enmity has been removed, and God can look on man with

benignity and is ready to bless him and to receive him and to restore him. The Jews needed that, the Gentiles needed it, and together in Christ they have received it. In Christ, by His blood, they can enter together into the 'holiest of all.' What a wonderful gospel, what an amazing statement! What happened on Calvary? Christ was slain. Yes, but by being slain, He slew the enmity. He was slain—He slew the enmity! He made an open show of principalities and powers, He nailed the law to the cross, and man is reconciled to God. And all are reconciled in the same way, in Christ. Whether you are Jew or Gentile, Barbarian or Scythian, bond or free, male or female, good or bad, high or low, you have got to come this way. Christ died for the Church. Or, as the apostle Paul puts it in his farewell address to the elders of the church at Ephesus: '. . . the church of God which he hath purchased with his own blood' (Acts 20: 28). One body! The only way to reconcile God and man, and man and God, is by the cross, by Christ's death, which slays the enmity, which takes away *all* sins. 'The blood of Jesus Christ his Son cleanseth us from all sin.'

21

PEACE WITH GOD

*And came and preached peace to you which were afar off and to them that
were nigh.* Ephesians 2: 17

The apostle, in this particular verse, takes another step forward in
his great statement concerning salvation. His theme is that God in
Christ has brought the Jews and the Gentiles together in the Church,
by making of them one body, so reconciling them to Himself by
our Lord's death upon the cross. He has told us how the Lord Jesus
Christ, by dying upon the cross, has broken down the middle wall
of partition. It was at Calvary that the middle wall of partition was
broken down once and for ever. On the cross; not before then, not
until then. The veil of the temple was not rent until our Lord died
upon the cross. It is the cross that does that. Our Lord did not do
that in His teaching or in His miracles. It was at the moment of
his death that the veil was rent. The law of commandments in
ordinances has been abolished. Not only that, He has also 'made
of twain one new man'; a great unity is made possible. And finally
he has told us how it was by Christ's dying upon the cross that
God thus reconciled Jew and Gentile to Himself.

But that, obviously, is not sufficient in and of itself. Think of
mankind in sin. God has sent His Son to make a way of salvation.
The Son has done everything which He was sent to do. He has
obeyed His Father in all things; He has kept the law positively,
actively; He has borne the law's punishment of our sins, passively,
in His own body on the cross. We have emphasised all that—I
repeat it because it is obvious that it still needs to be repeated,
because people still preach on the cross without even mentioning
the bearing and the punishment of sins. However, we have gone into
that in great detail.

But now the question arises, *How has all that which has been done,
which has been prepared, come to us?* This verse which we are looking
at now answers that question. 'And came and *preached* peace to you
that were afar off and to them that were nigh.' In other words,
having made the way and the possibility, the Lord now comes to
us and tells us that He has done so, proclaims it, heralds this good

news to us, that the peace between man and God which man so sadly needs, is available.

There is a good deal of disagreement as to what exactly our verse means, and what exactly it says. It refers to the Lord Jesus Christ. He is the One who has been doing all the things we have been considering, 'that *He* might reconcile both unto God in one body by the cross, having slain the enmity thereby'; and '*He* came and preached peace to you which were afar off and to them that were nigh'. The Lord Jesus Christ is the One of whom Paul is speaking; it is His action. The two possible views are as follows:

First, there are those who say that this verse is a reference to what our blessed Lord did while He was here in the world. The words we have to consider are these: 'and came and preached peace'. A better translation is this, 'having come, he preached peace'. What does this 'having come' mean? The one group would have us believe that it is a reference to the incarnation, to the first coming of our Lord, and to His ministry here on earth as described in the pages of the four Gospels. The *second* view is that which says that this is a reference to the preaching of the Lord Jesus Christ through the apostles; not His own preaching in person, but His preaching through the Church, through the apostles—that which happened after His death and resurrection and ascension and subsequent to the sending of the Holy Ghost upon the Church on the day of Pentecost.

While it is an interesting point, it is not, fortunately, a vital one in an ultimate sense. Yet it is of interest, and therefore we must glance at it in passing. There are certain considerations which seem to me to militate very strongly against the first view. As you read the Gospels you will find that our Lord's ministry was confined to the Jews. He said of Himself that He had not come 'except to the lost sheep of the house of Israel'. He specifically said to His disciples 'Go not into the way of the Gentiles'. His ministry was confined to the Jews. You remember the incident of the Syrophenician woman. When she came and asked a blessing for her daughter, His reply was, 'It is not right to take the meat of the children and to give it to the dogs'. This was His attitude everywhere. But yet it is not quite as simple as that, because we find that now and again in His teaching He did indicate that He really had come for all, for Gentiles as well as Jews. I believe there is a hint of that even in the great statement in Luke 4: 18, with its quotation from Isaiah 61, where He seemed to be preaching a gospel for all peoples, and especially as He continued His discourse. He also said on one occasion, 'Other sheep I have which are not of this fold'—clearly a reference to the Gentiles. And then you remember that though He had refused the request of Andrew and Philip to see the Greeks that had come saying, 'Sir, we would see Jesus', He nevertheless did go on to say, 'And I, if I be lifted up, will draw all men unto me'. That was clearly a prediction that He was going to do something by His death which would open the door of entry even to Greeks, to Gentiles, to those who were 'afar off'. It seems to me, therefore, that a fair examination of the four Gospels leads us to the conclusion, that while our Lord deliberately confined His ministry and that of the disciples during His life on earth to the Jews, He gave indications now and again that there was to be something wider and greater after He had accomplished on the cross the work which He had been sent to do.

I would therefore decide that on the whole the second interpretation is better; that what the apostle is really saying here is that *Christ, through the apostles, through His servants, preached this gospel of peace with God*, that He had made possible by His perfect work upon the cross. There is a sense in which He could not have done that during His life on earth because men could not understand the meaning of the cross; even the apostles could not, they always stumbled at it. It was necessary that the work should be finished, that He should have risen again, that the Spirit should have been given, before this could happen. And so it did happen. You notice that the first verse in the book of Acts tells us that the writer, Luke, reminds Theophilus 'of all the things that Jesus began to do'. He is now going to tell him about the things that Jesus continued to do. And that is the meaning of the book of Acts—it is a record of the acts of the risen Lord through the Church. You remember how Peter and John, having healed the man at the Beautiful Gate of the temple, said, '. . . why look ye so earnestly on us, as though by our own power or holiness we had made this man to walk . . . His name through faith in his name'—referring to Christ—'hath made this man strong . . .' 'In the name of Jesus Christ of Nazareth'; He is the doer, as it were, through the apostles. This is something with which we must all be familiar. The apostle Paul says in writing to the Corinthians, 'We are ambassadors for Christ . . . . we beseech you in *Christ's* stead, be ye reconciled to God.' And of course there is the tremendous fact that it was Peter on the day of Pentecost who said 'The promise is unto you (speaking primarily to Jews and proselytes) and to your children, and to as many as are afar off'. There is the first great, unmistakable, explicit pronouncement that the gospel is indeed to be preached to all. And I would argue that the next verse in our very section, namely verse 18, where the apostle immediately refers to the Holy Spirit, is a confirmation of that. The statement he makes in this seventeenth verse makes him think of the Spirit at once, and that leads him on to his next statement. But to me the clinching, final proof is found clearly in 1 Timothy 3: 16, where the apostle issues a remarkable statement. He says this: 'Without controversy, great is the mystery of godliness. God was manifest in the flesh, justified in the Spirit, seen of angels, preached unto the Gentiles, believed on in the world, received up into glory'. You notice the sequence. 'Preached unto the Gentiles' follows not only 'being justified in the Spirit' but also 'seen of angels', which to me is an unmistakable reference to His death upon the cross. There is a sense, therefore, in which it is clear that that was the sequence in the mind of the great apostle.

That, then, is more or less the mechanics of our text, interesting and important, and worthy of further study. But the important thing is that the apostle is asserting a fact. Whether it began with the Lord Himself in His earthly ministry or not, the fact is that the Christian message is a proclamation to Jews and Gentiles, Gentiles and Jews, that the way to peace with God has been opened by Jesus Christ and Him crucified. That is the message. And that is the thing the apostle is anxious that these Ephesians should lay hold of. That is the thing he wants them to be amazed at, that this is possible, that this has happened, and that Christ Himself is thus preaching it, offering it to them, holding it before them, inviting them to act upon it. And that is still the message which the Christian Church must preach; this is her message to the world now. Our business, therefore, is to discover the teaching, the doctrine, of this tremendous statement. It is one of the most glorious in the whole of Scripture. 'And preached peace to you that were afar off and peace to them that were nigh.'

What is the teaching? Let us summarise it like this. The first great statement, obviously, is that *man's fundamental need is peace with God*. That is the peace our Lord preaches, peace with God. It is a continuation, you see, of the statement of the previous verse, 'That he might reconcile both unto God in one body by the cross, having slain the enmity thereby'. Then He will go on in the next verse to say, 'Through him we both have access by one Spirit unto the Father'. That is the peace, therefore. It is not so much peace between Gentiles and Jews here; He has finished with that, it is now the peace that both need with God. That is why I like that other translation which says, 'And came and preached peace to you which were afar off and peace to them that were nigh'. The Jews need the peace as much as the others.

I say, again, the fundamental proposition is that man's supreme and primary need is the need of peace with God. Man out of relationship with God, *man in sin, is restless and wretched and unhappy*. There is a wonderful statement of all this in the fifty-seventh chapter of the Book of the Prophet Isaiah. I have no doubt but that the apostle had this passage in his mind as he was writing these words. It is, 'Peace, peace, saith the Lord, Peace to them that are far off and peace to them that are near' (verse 19). But then the prophet goes on to say this: 'The wicked are like the troubled sea when it cannot rest, whose waters cast up mire and dirt'. There is the picture, there is the explanation—'like the troubled sea'. We are all familiar with that picture of the restless sea. Why is the sea always restless, always in motion? why are there waves, why is there ebb and flow? The scientists tell us that the answer is that the sea is being acted upon by two opposing forces. There is first of all the moon. The moon partly controls the movements and the motions of the sea. On the other hand there is the magnetic force in the heart of the earth, a tremendous magnetic pull. On the one hand is the pull and the influence of the moon, and the converse influence of the magnetic powers in the centre of the earth on the other. And the result is that the sea is in constant motion; you have the waves and the billows, the ebb and flow; and then occasionally there comes a gale, the wind rises and begins to blow upon the sea and raises the billows, and you have a terrible storm. 'The wicked are like the troubled sea when it cannot rest, whose waters cast up mire and dirt.' Have you ever walked along a beach after a storm, and seen the mud and the dirt and the bits of wood and the various other things cast up? They are the flotsam and the jetsam, the filth and the mire left upon the sea shore after the ending of the storm. What a perfect description it is! Well, says Isaiah (and it is in the mind of the apostle here undoubtedly), the wicked are like that.

The picture is of man apart from God, restless like that sea. What is the cause of this? It is exactly the same explanation in a spiritual sense as that of the state of the sea. It all began in Eden. Man was made by God and placed in Paradise. There was no motion there, there was no restlessness in Paradise, for there was only one force working upon man—God! God made man in His own image, he was in correspondence, in communion with God, he was enjoying God, and his life was a life of unmixed peace and bliss. There was no unhappiness, there was no problem, there was no trouble, there was no anxiety. Man was in a state of innocence and of entire peace and quiet and freedom. But man fell. Man listened to another power and to another force, and in listening became subject to it. The force of the devil, the force of evil, the force of hell began to play upon him, and from that very moment man's life has been one of restlessness and of conflict. Man, out of relationship with God, is exactly like the sea. There is still in him a recollection, a memory, of his original righteousness. He does not know that, he cannot put it like that; he does not believe the Bible, he does not believe in theology; nevertheless, it is a fact. There is in man a factor called the conscience. Oh, how many a man has wished he had not got one; but he has it, and it will go on speaking, and pulling; it is an influence in his life. What is it? It is the memory, the partial recollection of his original righteousness. Man knows in his heart of hearts that he was meant for something better. He has a sense of justice, of right and wrong, of good and evil. I go further, he has a sense of God. He does not like it, but he has it; and it disturbs him. That is one side—the power that comes from above. But there is another power pulling in the opposite direction—man's fallen nature, lust, passion, desire, jealousy, envy, all these horrible foul things. The apostle has put it once and for ever in the seventh of Romans 'For I delight in the law of God after the inward man: but I see another law in my members, warring against the law of my mind, and bringing me into captivity to the law of sin which is in my members'. The two are antagonistic, and the result is that man is restless and like the waves of the sea, the troubled sea when it cannot rest. And then occasionally the storms come. I mean some ferocious onslaught by the devil! There is always a slight movement in the air, but you do not always call it a gale. When the movement is magnified it becomes a gale. The devil is always there and he is always troubling us, but there are times when he makes an onslaught and we are attacked violently, thrown hither and thither, and dashed about like a storm at sea. The devil and his forces seem to be unleashed and our little lives are as turbulent and as tossed about as the sea in the mightiest storm. And not only that—circumstances! Wars come, illnesses come, a loved one is taken ill, something goes wrong, and our whole life is upset. We do not know where we are; our foundations, we say, are shaking. They are all together rocking like the sea. You see how perfect the description is. That is man out of relationship with God, that is man as the result of the fall. He has no peace, he is restless.

The result of all this, of course, is that *man is never satisfied*. There is nothing so characteristic of the sinful life as its restlessness. Do you not see it in the world today? Has the world ever been so restless as it is at the present time? Look at the modern pleasure mania. What is it due to? Restlessness! People say, Let's go out, let's go and do something; we can't stand it if we stay at home, we shall go mad; let's go out, let's forget it, let's get away from it. Pleasure! Trying to run away from the restlessness! Some new excitement, a craving for something fresh! Excapism is the term that is used for it today, and the word is true to the fact. The world is excited and it is trying to excite itself still more. It must take a stimulus in the form of drink or entertainment. It must have something to keep it going. It is all an expression of this fundamental restlessness, this dis-ease, this lack of peace, this lack of the quiet mind. Man in sin does not know peace of mind, he does not know peace of heart. He is as unstable, says James, as the waves of the sea. He is double-minded—this pull, that pull; he feels he ought to be better, but he likes something that is bad; and there he is torn between the two. All his life and all his ways are indeed like the restless waves of the sea. No satisfaction!

The analogy is perfect, is it not? The mire and the dirt that are thrown up by it all! Millions spend their Sundays reading about it. The mire and the dirt! It is in all the papers, it is everywhere, it is in people's conversation; it is becoming very obvious. Respectability is disappearing, sin is becoming open again. The storm has been blowing for some time and the mire and the dirt are becoming increasingly evident. That is man in sin; no peace, no rest, no quiet; like the troubled waves of the sea, his life throws up mire and dirt and filth. The horror and the ugliness of it all! And the tragedy is that man in his ignorance and blindness does not realise all this. He does not know, he does not understar d; he feels his troubles are due to his circumstances, or to his environment and he is always trying to find peace and produce rest. But he cannot; try as he will he fails. It all points to the fact that the supreme need of man, the fundamental need of man, is the need of peace and rest, the quiet mind, the tranquil heart.

But let us go on to the second point. *Peace is the need of all men, not only of some.* 'He came and preached peace to you that were afar off, *and* peace to them that were nigh.' The Jews needed the message quite as much and in exactly the same way as did the Gentiles that were so far off. Now this is the apostle's great point here. He has got to establish that the Jews need the message quite as much as the Gentiles. But the Jews could not see it. That was their problem. Of course, Gentiles might need this!—although they did not even like that because they felt that God was not interested in any people but themselves. But *they* certainly did not need it! That was why the Pharisees so hated our Lord. Our Lord's preaching made the Pharisees feel that even they were sinners, and they did not like the feeling. They said, We are godly, we are religious, we are the good people, we have got the law! And so the apostle Paul had to write chapters two and three of his Epistle to the Romans just to show

them that they needed the message of peace as much as did the
Gentiles. The Jews thought that, because they had the law, this somehow meant that they had kept it; that because they knew there was
a law, that that put them right with the law. And so Paul has to
say, 'By the law is the knowledge of sin'; it does not save you from
it, it does no more than give the knowledge. But they could not see
that. They felt that their privileges—and they had privileges, as
Paul shows—automatically saved them. They had the oracles of
God, the Old Testament Scriptures; the law was given to them, the
fathers belonged to them; and so on. That was true. But because
they relied on these privileges and their possession of them, they were
outside the kingdom. But they could not see that. So the message
has to come to them as it has to come to all others. But this is still a
problem to many people. There are many people who think that the
gospel in an evangelistic form certainly needs to be preached to
certain people, but not to all. They think that that is surely not
necessary for people who were brought up in Christian homes and
who were taken to Sunday School in their youth and have always
gone to a place of worship. You do not need to preach evangelistic-
ally to them, they say; surely they are already there, they are nigh.
They cannot see that those who are nigh need the same message as
those who are afar off. But they do, says Paul—'preached to them
that were afar off and to them that were nigh'.

Notice further that *far off and near are only relative distinctions, not
absolute distinctions*. Let me give you an illustration. Take the case of
two men who figure in the New Testament, one the apostle Paul,
the other the Philippian jailer. Consider them. Look at Saul of
Tarsus, a Hebrew of the Hebrews, of the tribe of Benjamin, trained
as a Pharisee, one who had sat at the feet of Gamaliel, one who
knows the law, and revels in it. He is serving God, he thinks, with
all good conscience. A godly, good, moral man, a religious man!
On the other hand, the Philippian jailer, a Gentile, a violent fellow,
a man who is ready to commit suicide when things go wrong. As
you look at those two men what do you say about them? One's
instinct is to say: the apostle Paul is very near the kingdom of God;
the Philippian jailer is far away. And yet, what the apostle himself
tells us is this, that in reality the two men were identical in their
need, that he himself needed the gospel of peace as much as did
the Philippian jailer. 'It is a faithful saying, and worthy of all
acceptation', he says, 'that Christ Jesus came into the world to
save sinners'—people like the Philippian jailer and the members
of the church at Corinth who were adulterers, fornicators, abusers
of themselves with mankind, the refuse of society? No, no, not only
them, Christ Jesus came into the world to save sinners;—'of whom I

am the chief'! Does it not sound monstrous, does it not sound quite
ridiculous, that this godly young man, this good Pharisee, is in the
same position as the Philippian jailer? But he says it is so. There
was no difference, for 'there is none righteous, no, not one'. We are
all in the same position. And it is still the same today.

Let us be quite clear about this. There are some people of whom
it is obvious, that they are as far away from the kingdom of God
as it is possible for a man to be. The people to whom I was making
reference just now, whose idea of happiness and of joy is to get drunk
and to become worse than beasts, the people who live in sinks of
vice and iniquity with never a thought about God or morality but
just living according to their animal nature, are, you say, as far off
from the kingdom of God as it is conceivable for anyone to be.
But here are other people, nice, quiet, respectable, never doing
outwardly evil things, hating them, trying to do good, striving
morally, trying to uplift the race, full of good works and deeds and
actions, full of intellectual interests and pursuits, interested in the
things of the mind, and so on, attending a place of worship, members
of a church perchance. At first, and on the surface, the two positions
seem to be diametrically opposed, and you tend to argue that there is
nothing at all in common between them. And yet the whole purpose
of the gospel is to say that before God they are identical, and that
they need exactly the same message. The second type needs the
message of peace as much as the first. Peace to them that were
nigh as well as those that were afar off! These people seem at the
very door of the kingdom, but they are not *in* the kingdom. And
the moment you begin to analyse it you see how true this is. Your
intellectualists and moralists and idealists are as restless as the other
people, and as unhappy. They can no more find peace than the
other people. Of course, they may not throw up as much dirt and
mire. It is not a filth that is obvious in their case, but the wreckage
is equally obvious. It is not mud and dirt, it is bits of stick perhaps,
or bits of ornaments or something like that. In the case of the
wretched people who are living the life of the gutter, it is obvious,
it is open, it is outward; everybody can see it. The condition of a
man blind drunk or a man in a rage is obvious, everybody can see
it. But the fact that you do not see much motion on the surface of
the lives of the others does not mean that there is not any motion.
I can demonstrate that there is tremendous motion. Beneath the
apparently calm equable surface there is a riot going on, there is a
tremendous raging. How do I know it? In this way. The great
disease of mankind, of civilised man particularly, is what is called
neurosis. Neuroses, we are told, are due to repressions. What is a
repression? Something you keep down, you do not let it come to

the surface, you do not go out and get drunk or commit adultery. No, but there is a fight, it is raging within, it is a tempest, a veritable torrent of lust and passion, kept down as it were, but it is there. There is no rest, there is no peace. Repressions and neuroses!— manifesting themselves perhaps in gastric ulcers, coming out in sleeplessness and having to live on phenobarbitone. That is the disease of modern man and of civilisation. The first people I have been describing never have to take these drugs; the restlessness takes a different form with them; but these others repress it, and nature protests. The struggle is so great that the nerves give way, and so these drugs become necessary to them. The two positions are really identical. It is not the symptoms of a disease that matter, it is the disease itself that matters; and so you find that these people who seem so near the kingdom, who are so nice and good and who are always talking about moral uplift and trying to improve the lot of man, and who go in for culture, are as restless and as much at dis-ease as the violent, open sinner. They need peace as he needs peace.

But perhaps I can prove my point more conclusively if I ask you to look at the types, the two kinds, experimentally. The test of our position, as I said under my first principle, is whether we know God. It is not whether you believe things about God. There is no peace without *knowing* God. Your learned, intellectual, highly moral and good person, who may always be reading books on theology and perhaps the Bible, may not know God at all. Because of that he is restless and unhappy. He cannot find God, he is always seeking, searching, going to lectures, hoping something is going to happen; but he has not got it. He has not got it any more than the other person. That is the test. They are worried about some past sin. They are afraid to die. They do not know where they stand, they do not know that their sins are forgiven. They do not know what awaits them in the future. They have not the faith that sees through death, they have not an assurance of heaven, they do not know that they are the children of God; and the result is that they are restless, ill at ease, and unhappy. Am I making my principle clear? Is not this the trouble with them? They are so near, and yet so far. 'Afar off' and 'near', as I have said, are relative terms. The question that matters is this, Are you *in* the kingdom? And if you realise that that is the question you will realise that to be near gives no final advantage over being afar off.

May I offer you an almost ridiculous illustration? You want to go on a journey, so you go and join a bus queue. The bus comes along, and you are about the tenth in the queue. People begin to board the bus. You say, 'It is all right, I am getting on'. The ninth man goes on, and then the conductor says, 'No more. Full up'.

Does it help you at all that you were to have been the next if there had still been room? The fact is you are not on the bus, and the fact that you were the very next man to get on does not help you. Or it is the same thing as a man going to catch a train, and just as he goes to the barrier to show his ticket the whistle is heard and the train has gone. He says, I nearly got it!—but does that help him? Such illustrations may be amusing, but I trust that those who laugh will ask themselves this solemn question, 'Am I in the kingdom of God, or simply near it?' You may have been standing on the doorstep for many long years. Cannot you see that will not help you? I am asking, Are you in? Do you know God? Do you know that your sins are forgiven? And when you go to pray to God when you have some problem, do you know that you find Him and that you are speaking to Him? Have you access with confidence and boldness? Do you enter by the blood of Jesus into the 'holiest of all'? That, I say, is the question, and there is no other question. So near, and yet so far! To be an inch outside the kingdom is no advantage over the man who is a thousand miles away from being in the kingdom. 'Peace to them that are afar off, *and*, peace to them that are nigh.' It is needed by all. 'There is no peace, saith my God, to the wicked.' 'There is none righteous, no, not one.' 'All have sinned and have come short of the glory of God.' Or, as Augustine put it finally in his own experience, 'Thou hast made us for Thyself, and our hearts are restless until they find their rest in Thee'. Moral intellectualists, are you at rest? Is all quiet within, is there peace in your soul, and peace between you and God? It is needed by all.

That brings me to my last principle, which is this. *Christ, and Christ alone offers and is able to give this peace to all who see their need of it.* That is what the apostle is glorying in. Christ has made and opened up the way. No man can find out God by seeking. No man can reconcile himself to God. But, as we have seen, Christ has made peace between man and God by the blood of His cross. It was there He abolished the enmity, and He did it by taking it upon Himself. Not only the vile, foul, open, flagrant sins, but the sins of self-righteousness, self-satisfaction, smugness, moralism doing duty for spirituality. He has taken all upon Himself. 'Who his own self bear our sins in his own body on the tree, that we being dead to sins should live unto righteousness; by whose stripes we are healed.' And it was because of that that He could say 'Peace I leave with you, my peace I give unto you; not as the world giveth, give I unto you. Let not your heart be troubled, neither let it be afraid.' Have you received His peace? He reconciles you to God; and the peace of God that passes all understanding can keep your heart and mind if you but go to Him. 'In *nothing* be anxious, but in all things, with prayer and supplication and thanksgiving, let your requests be made known unto God, and the peace of God that passeth all understanding *shall* keep your hearts and minds through Christ Jesus' (Philippians 4: 6 and 7). Take it to Him. Christ has opened the way for you to go to God with your troubles, your problems, whatever they are.

> *O what peace we often forfeit.*
> *O what needless pains we bear,*
> *All because we do not carry*
> *Everything to God in prayer.*

And the way is open for you to do so, for Christ has opened it. The sin has been taken away, the enmity, the antagonism, has been destroyed, and you can go confidently into the presence of God.

And having taken your problems and troubles to Him, leave them with Him, leave them there. 'Thou wilt keep him in perfect peace whose mind is stayed on thee.' Stay it on Him!—you have an abundant, open, free entry, by the blood of Jesus Christ. Go in, look on Him, stay your mind upon Him, and begin to enjoy His blessed peace. Christ gives peace with God, peace with others, peace within. 'He came and preached peace to them that were afar off and to them that were nigh.' Someone may read these words who has been living as it were in the very jaws of hell. My friend, you can have this peace, *now*. But if your position is that you have always been interested and have been very near always, you also can have it, *now*. You can have it together. It is the free gift of God through Jesus Christ our Lord. Have you got it? Are you rejoicing in it? It can be yours now, and evermore.

22

ACCESS TO THE FATHER

For through him we both have access by one Spirit unto the Father.
Ephesians 2: 18

Here, in this statement, the apostle reaches the grand climax of the
mighty argument which begins in the eleventh verse of this second
chapter of his Epistle. There is nothing beyond this; this is the very
top, the acme. This is the quintessence of the Christian faith and the
Christian position. There is no doubt, therefore, that we are looking
at and considering one of the greatest and most glorious statements
that is to be found in the whole range of Scripture. To me it has been
a thrilling experience to take these steps with the apostle, step by
step. Each time we climb higher and higher and higher. But at last
we have reached the top, we are standing on the summit, we have
arrived at the grand plateau, and we are just looking, looking and
gazing, with astonishment and amazement at the height to which
we have been brought. Indeed to me the statement before us is
not only stupendous, it is staggering. 'Through him, we both have
access—access!—by one Spirit, unto the Father.' Our chief trouble,
and the whole trouble with the Church, is that we do not realise the
meaning of a statement like this. Were we to do so the Christian
Church would be revolutionised. Were we to do so we should be
lost in 'wonder, love and praise'. We should realise that the most
marvellous, wonderful thing that can ever happen to anybody in
this world is simply his becoming a Christian. If only every Church
member, every Christian in the Church, realised the truth of this
statement, the Church would be so different that we should scarcely
recognise her. But oh, how different is the Church from what we find
here! How many think of Christianity and of the Christian Church
simply as a place which they attend now and again, and that
perhaps in a perfunctory manner, hesitating, and doubtful whether
they will or not, and as a matter of duty; or as a place in which
they may exercise certain gifts that they have, and be busy—a kind
of club, an institution, a human society. What a contrast to what we
have here! This is Christianity, this is what makes one a Christian.
The Christian Church really consists of people who realise that this
is the whole object and purpose of everything—access by one Spirit

unto the Father. We must meditate upon this, we must pause with this, we must look into it and we must take time to do so; for, as I shall try to show you, we find gathered together in this one verse the most stupendous things that we can ever be told or can ever realise about ourselves.

There are certain things that stand out on the very surface of this verse. For instance, we are brought at once by this verse face to face with *the mystery of the blessed, holy Trinity*. Through Him (the Son, the Lord Jesus Christ) we both have access by one Spirit (the Holy Spirit, spelt quite rightly with a capital S in all the versions because it is a reference to the Holy Spirit) unto the Father. Here is one of the great Trinitarian verses of Scripture, and we pause for a moment before this ineffable mystery. Do we realise, I wonder, as we should, that the doctrine of the Trinity is in a sense the essence of the Christian faith? It is this doctrine which, of all others, differentiates the Christian faith from every other faith whatsoever. We believe in one God. And yet we assert that the one God is three Persons, Father, Son, and Holy Spirit or Holy Ghost. A great and inscrutable mystery! We do not understand it, we assert it. It is taught here, it is taught in other places in the Scriptures. The Bible teaches clearly that the Lord Jesus Christ is truly God, and likewise that the Holy Spirit is truly God, and yet it says that there is but one God: God is one, and there is only one God, subsisting in three Persons. Do not ask me to explain it. But you do not begin to understand your Bible, you cannot possibly understand the Christian faith, unless you accept it, believe it, and bow before it, and humble yourselves, and say, I worship, I adore, I praise Thee 'Great Jehovah, Three in One'. It is vital, therefore, that we as Christian people should be constantly reminding ourselves of this. And as we do so, our services will be filled with reverence, with worship, with a sense of awe, with a sense of glory, and with a sense of praise, true praise. Whenever we pray, whenever we come together to worship, we are worshipping this Triune God. We cannot conceive of the glory and of the majesty and of the greatness, but we must try to do so. We must prepare our spirits, we must meditate, we must ponder this matter, we must search the Scriptures for it, we must see it; and having recognised it, like the men of whom we read in the Scriptures, who have come near to God, we shall take our shoes from off our feet, we shall feel that we are men of unclean lips, we shall be conscious of the ineffable glory.

Let me go on to a second observation. *The three Persons in the blessed, holy Trinity are interested in us and are engaged together in our salvation.* Now you see what I meant when I said that this is a staggering verse. That is exactly what it says, that the three Persons, eternal in their glory and their holiness and their might, the three Persons in the blessed holy Trinity are interested in you if you are a Christian, and are interested in your salvation, and are working out your salvation. The world talks about honours, and it is interested in honours and in privileges and in getting admission to clubs and positions and in being introduced to great people. Here is a fact: the three Persons in the Trinity are interested in *you* and have done something about *your* salvation! What if every Christian realised that!

How are They engaged in our salvation? This Epistle has been telling us. The apostle took up practically the whole of the first chapter to tell us that it is *the Father* who thought of salvation and who initiated salvation. Do you remember that recurring phrase, 'according to the mystery of his will', 'according to the good pleasure which he had purposed in himself, that in the dispensation of the fulness of times he might gather together in one all things in Christ'. The Father, 'worketh all things after the counsel of his own will'. The theologians used to talk about the 'Economic Trinity'. This great work, this great business of salvation, has been divided up between the three Persons. The Father conceived and planned salvation. He thought it out, He purposed it, He decided on it, He determined it. The everlasting and eternal God! It is His plan and purpose. Let us never represent the Christian faith and the Christian position with regard to salvation as if it were something that the Son has to extort from the Father. It is the Father who sent the Son. You notice in the high priestly prayer, in the seventeenth chapter of John's Gospel, how plainly our Lord says, 'I have finished the work which *thou* gavest me to do; I have glorified thee on the earth'; He came 'to give eternal life to as many as God has given him'; 'Thine they were, thou gavest them me'. All His references are to the Father. The Father is the One who conceives and initiates, and sets moving this great and glorious plan and way of salvation.

Then *the Son* volunteered to do the work. There is no question but that a great council was held in eternity before time began, as the Scriptures tell us: 'before the foundation of the world'. All that has happened was foreknown and foreseen. The Father conceived the plan and the Son offered and volunteered to come to execute the plan. The Father gave Him the people, the Father gave Him the work to do, and He came and He did it. And there, just before the cross, He was able to say that He had done it. We are familiar with the great facts; but let us never forget them. Let us remind ourselves constantly of what it involved for the Son, who though He was 'equal with God' and 'counted it not robbery to be equal with God', yet 'humbled himself, and made himself of no reputation'. He came in such a lowly manner; He knew what it was to be poor and to suffer the privations of poverty; He mixed with ordinary people and lived an ordinary life. Can we conceive what it meant to Him? He suffered against Himself 'the contradiction of sinners'; He bore their malice and their spite and their envy. But above and beyond it all, He took upon Himself our sins, suffered Himself to be made sin by the Father for us, though He Himself knew no sin; suffered to have laid upon Him the iniquity of us all; went there to the cross 'to bear our sins in his own body on the tree'. That is what He did. He kept the law actively, He lived under it as a man, 'made of a woman, made under the law', put Himself deliberately under it, went to be baptised by John the Baptist, identifying Himself with the sinner, and all that is involved in that, and died and was buried. The Prince, the Author of life, died and was buried in a grave; but rose again. There are the mighty facts. That is the part of the Son— coming out of the bosom of the Father, coming out of eternity. He was in the beginning with God, nothing was made without Him; but He leaves that glory, He lays it aside—'Mild, He lays His glory by'—and goes through with His great task. Through Him, this blessed Son! That is the work of the Son.

Then there is the work of *the Holy Spirit*. It is He who works out the salvation in us, one by one. That is His work. You notice that the Son voluntarily subordinates Himself to the Father. And the Holy Spirit subordinates Himself to the Son and to the Father. They are co-equal, they are co-eternal, they are equal in every respect; and yet for the sake of our salvation there is this subordination of Son to Father, and Spirit to Son and Father together. And the Spirit comes and He applies the work. He applies it to me, applies it to you. It is He who mediates Christ to us, it is He who brings us to see our need and all the other things that we hope to consider later; it is He who applies the grand redemption that has been worked out by the Son. And not only does He do it in the individual, He does it in the Church. He builds up the Church, He fills the Church with His life and with His presence. That is the work of the Holy Spirit. 'He shall not speak of himself'. He simply speaks of Christ. 'He shall glorify me,' says our Lord; and He has done so, and still does.

Thus on the very surface of this verse we have these two tremendous statements: that we are looking at the three Persons in the blessed Trinity; but still more amazing and astounding, that the three Persons are interested in us and are concerned about our salvation, and have worked to bring our salvation to pass.

We must reflect further before we leave such mighty matters.

First, *the problem of sin, your sin and mine, was and is as great as that.*
There is nothing that surprises and astonishes me more about so
many people, even within the Church, than the way in which they
so dislike the doctrine of sin, and say, Why must you always be
stressing sin? Here is the answer: sin is a problem as great as this,
that it necessitated the action of the three Persons in the blessed holy
Trinity to deal with it. It is the only explanation. Sin is such a
profound problem that it involved all that. It is not a simple
problem; it is not a problem that God can deal with simply, because
He is God and because He is love. No! Sin is as profound a problem
as this, that because of it a council was held before time, and the Son
had to come into the world, out of eternity, and go through all that
I have been describing. That is what sin necessitates. It needs also
the presence of the Holy Spirit in the Church. Or, to put it in
another way, salvation is not just a matter of our coming to realise
that God is love and then of God forgiving us. How often is it
misrepresented in some such terms, as if the only thing that was
meant to take place at the cross was a demonstration that God is
love, and that the only problem is to bring us to see and to know
that God is love. That is not the teaching here. We have emphasis
here upon the blood of Christ, upon His flesh, His body, His cross,
His dying. No, salvation is not just a matter of realising that God is
love and receiving forgiveness: salvation is something that involves
these particular activities of the three Persons: nothing less could
do it. 'There was no other good enough to pay the price of sin.'
There was a price involved, there was a righteousness, a justice in
God, involved. The cross had to be, it was the only way. So here the
apostle is showing us something of the real nature of salvation.

But I suppose that the thing that is most staggering of all is to
grasp and to realise, if we can, the amazing fact that *the three
Persons in the blessed, holy Trinity so loved us as do all this for us.* Self-
subsistent, eternally existing in that ineffable unity and glory,
yet concerned about us! The Father Eternal has His eye on you and
He knows you, and He is interested in you. The Son of God has so
loved you that He has given Himself for you. And the Holy Spirit
so loves you that He comes into you to apply all this and to work
it all out. If you do not agree with me that this is the most stupendous
thing you will ever hear in time or in eternity, well then I despair
of you. Is there anything beyond this?—that I am told that these
three Persons have not only loved me but have acted in this way in
order that I might be redeemed. If we but realised this as we ought,
its effect upon us would be tremendous, it would revolutionise our
whole conception of Christianity. We would not think of it in terms
of duty or anything else, we would think of it in terms of glory and

of privilege and of wonder. It would be the most thrilling thing in the world to us. We would revel in it and would say with Paul, 'God forbid that I should glory save in the cross of our Lord Jesus Christ'. We should be filled with a sense of 'wonder, love, and of praise'.

But let us go on to a third statement. We see that here we are held face to face with the doctrine of the Trinity, we are told that the three Persons in the Trinity are interested in us and in our salvation and are working it out in us. And then we are told that the end of salvation, the ultimate goal of salvation, *the object of salvation, is that we might know God as our Father*. 'For through him we both have access by one Spirit unto the Father.' Now that is the chief end and object of salvation. It is the thing the apostle is especially concerned to emphasise here, the fact that all Christians come together to the Father. Jews and Gentiles come together as one body and as one spirit into His presence. This is the climax. The apostle has already been telling us how the Lord Jesus Christ has removed the barriers and the obstacles and the hindrances between the Gentile and the Jew, how He has removed this common enmity between me and God, and indeed he has even gone so far as to tell us in verse sixteen that he reconciles both Jew and Gentile unto God 'in one body by the cross, having slain the enmity thereby'. Well surely, says someone, you cannot go beyond that. Is there anything beyond reconciliation? There is! That is why I say that this eighteenth verse is the climax. Reconciliation is amazing. But this is more wondrous and more amazing. Reconciliation is not the end. Beyond reconciliation, we have access to the Father. You can in a sense be reconciled to people and still not have much intimacy with them. You can cease to be at enmity; the barriers, hindrances, and obstacles may have been removed; but that is not all, there is this further thing.

The apostle, it seems to me, tells us three things here. The *first* is that *we have access* by one Spirit unto the Father. Now this word 'access' is an important and an interesting word. It can also be translated by the word 'approach' or better still, I think, by the word 'introduction': 'For through him we both have an introduction by one Spirit unto the Father'. It means that the relationship is restored, that friendly relationship with God whereby we are acceptable to Him and have assurance that He is well disposed towards us. Now the important thing to realise here is that the Lord Jesus Christ does not merely prepare or open the way to this. He actually effects it, He actually produces it Himself. It is He who introduces us to the Father, brings us, takes us by the hand and ushers us into His presence. I am anxious to emphasise the fact that this is really the grand end and object of salvation. And I suppose there has never been a time when this needs to be emphasised more than today. We have all become so subjective, and are so much interested in our own moods and states and feelings and conditions, that when we give our testimonies we say that what salvation has done is to make us happy, or to take away this or that; and there we stop. But the grand object of salvation is to bring us into the presence of God—nothing less, nothing short of that. You notice how our Lord Himself said this same thing in the third verse of the seventeenth chapter of John: 'This is life eternal'—people say, I have received eternal life, I am saved, I have got eternal life. Yes, but what is eternal life? It is not just that you are no longer what you once were; it includes that, but that is comparatively a very small matter. The great thing is this—'This is life eternal, that they might know thee, the only true God, and Jesus Christ whom thou hast sent'. Or listen to it in Hebrews 10: 19: 'Having, therefore, brethren, boldness to enter into the holiest by the blood of Jesus'— that is what the blood of Jesus has done, it has enabled me to enter into the 'holiest of all'. You see the imagery, you catch the idea in Paul's mind. Under the Old Testament ceremonial the common people were not allowed to enter into the 'holy place,' still less the 'holiest of all'. Into the holy place the priests alone were allowed to go. But even the priests were not allowed to go into the 'holiest of all.' One man only was allowed in there, and that was the high priest, and he was only allowed in once a year, and then 'not without blood'. He went in once a year. And it was such a tremendous thing that while he was there, hidden from view, the people waited apprehensively for his return. In the Old Testament, we read in great detail, about the kinds of vestments and clothing that were to be worn by the priests and the high priest; and you will find in the case of the high priest that round the hem of his great robe bells were to be placed. Have you ever asked yourself what was the purpose of the bells, the pomegranates and the bells? What was the object? It was just this. The people knew that it was a tremendous thing and a staggering thing for anybody to go into the 'holiest of all', into the presence of God. 'Who shall dwell with the devouring fire? asks Isaiah. 'God is a consuming fire,' His holiness is such that everything tends to shrivel out of His presence. The high priest goes in once a year to represent the people and make an offering for their sins. The question is, Will he come out alive? And how delighted the people were to hear the jingling of the bells on the hem of his vestment! They knew then that he was still alive, that his sacrifice, the offering that he had presented, the blood that he had taken, was sufficient, that God had accepted it and that their sins were forgiven.

As he came out they heard the jingling of the bells louder and louder. He had been into the 'holiest of all'. But what we are told here is this, that through Christ, by the Holy Spirit, we ourselves can enter into the 'holiest of all'. We have access to the Father: no longer in the outer court, no longer merely amongst the priests, the 'veil' has been rent, we go right in. We have access unto the Father. Peter says the same thing in 1 Peter 3: 18. 'For Christ also hath once suffered for sins, the just for the unjust. . . .' Why? That I might not go to hell? that I might be happy? that I might no longer fall to a particular sin? All perfectly true; but that is not what Peter says; what he says is this—'Christ suffered the just for the unjust, that he might bring us to God'. 'These things I write unto you,' says John as an old man nearing the end of his life, 'that you might have fellowship with us; and truly, our fellowship (as apostles) is with the Father, and with his Son, Jesus Christ.' My friends, this is the grand end and object of salvation, that we enter into the presence of God and have fellowship with Him. We are no longer afar off, we have been made nigh, we are brought right in, we are face to face with Him, we have fellowship with God. To know God, and Jesus Christ whom He has sent! Have you got the access, have you realised it? Are you exercising your right to it?

But let us go on to the *second* emphasis. The second thing he tells us is that we have access *to the Father*. Now you notice the change in the term. What he says in verse sixteen is this: 'And that he (Christ) might reconcile both unto God in one body by the cross'. Why does he not say here therefore, 'For through him we both have access by one Spirit unto God'? But he changes it, he says 'unto the Father'. That is not an accident. The apostle deliberately changes his term. Why? Here again is something that is staggering in its immensity and overwhelming if we but realised it, that God in Christ by the Spirit becomes to us our Father. That is why the Lord, when He gave His model prayer, taught us to say 'Our Father, which art in heaven'. That is why, again, the Lord Jesus Christ, when He was talking to the woman of Samaria about worship used the same term. She, with her ignorant ideas of worship, talks about 'this mountain' and 'Jerusalem'. But our Lord changes the whole course of the conversation, and lifts it right up and says: 'The Father seeketh such to worship him'; 'God is a Spirit, and they that worship him must worship him in spirit and in truth'; these are the people that the Father seeks to worship Him. Or take again the way Christ puts it in John 14: 6: 'I am the way, the truth, and the life; no man cometh unto the Father but by me'. There are people who may believe in God but they will never know Him as Father except in Jesus Christ and by the Spirit. 'No man cometh unto the Father but by me.' And listen to Peter putting it again in his first Epistle: 'And if ye call upon the Father, who without respect of persons . . .' (1 : 17). It is the Father that we call upon. And again, John says, 'Truly, our fellowship is with the Father'—not, 'with God', 'with the Father'; he uses the word Father here. This is obviously the teaching of the whole of the New Testament, and it is again the differentiating thing about the Christian position. A Christian is one who is brought into the same relationship with God as the Lord Jesus as Son of man. That is Christianity, that is salvation. You notice how He prays. 'Father', He says, 'the hour is come,' and again, 'Righteous Father', and 'Holy Father.' Not a God afar off, but Father! So that we realise—and this is what it means—that He is ready to receive us, that He is ready to hear us.

To know this is to know that God has a loving interest in us. 'We have known and believed the love that God hath to us', says John again in 1 John 4: 16, and we confide in it, we rest in it. 'We have known and believed the love that God hath to us;' that is what you say when you realise that you have come to the Father. If you know God as your Father you know that the very hairs of your head are all numbered. Do you know that? The Father—it is to the Father we are coming. Did you notice that most amazing statement of our Lord's in His high priestly prayer, recorded there in John 17: 23? I suppose that of all the statements concerning the Christian there is nothing beyond this: 'I in them and thou in me, that they may be made perfect in one, and that the world may know that thou hast sent me, and hast loved them as thou hast loved me'. If we are truly Christian, and if we have come to the Father, then we know that God loves us as He loves His own Son. We therefore know that He will never leave us nor forsake us. We therefore know that whatever happens, underneath are always the everlasting arms.

That brings me to the *third* and final point, which is, that we *have* this access: Through him we both *have* access by one Spirit unto the Father.' We have it, says Paul. Shall I put this as a number of questions? Have we this? Are we enjoying the access? Are we resting on it? Are we enjoying the peace that results from it? Do you know God's love to you? Do you know that He really loves you? Do you know Him as your Father? Do you really know that 'all things work together for good to them that love God'? But come, let me take you higher, and ask this question: Do you know what it is to be in the 'holiest of all?' We have access, introduction, by one Spirit unto the Father. We are taken by Christ, by His blood, into the 'holiest of all', through the Holy Spirit. Is that true of you? Have you known and felt and realised the presence of God? That is what Christ has come to do, says the apostle. It is an advance on reconciliation, you see. It is not merely forgiveness, it is not merely that the enmity has gone. We have access, we have the right to go in. Do you approach God with full assurance of faith? Do you heed the exhortation of the Epistle to the Hebrews when it says, 'Let us therefore come boldly unto the throne of grace'? (Hebrews 4: 16). Do you go to God with the instinct and the assurance and the confidence with which a child goes to his father? It is to the Father that we are going, says the apostle. You know how a child behaves. He is in trouble, he has his little problem, something is grieving him tremendously, and he rushes to his father or mother. He tells them all about it, and he is confident that they can deal with it, and he is then quite happy. That is the kind of thing the apostle means. 'Except ye be converted and become as little children, ye shall not enter into the kingdom of heaven' says our Lord (Matthew 18: 3). Do we therefore go to God instinctively as to our Father? Do we take to Him all our cares and problems and worries and anxieties? Do we go to God with them, and, like the child, having told Him all about them, leave them with Him, confident and assured that He will deal with them all, and that we therefore can enjoy that peace of His which passes all understanding?

Shall I ask it all and sum it all up in a final question? Are we enjoying God? What is the chief end of man? runs the first question in the *Shorter Catechism* of the Westminster Assembly. And the answer is given: 'The chief end of man is to glorify God and to enjoy Him for ever'. And according to the apostle here, the enjoyment begins now, in this life, in this world. We do not have to wait until we go to heaven. We are meant to enjoy God here on earth, to know Him as our Father, and to rest in that knowledge, to enjoy the knowledge, and to enjoy God Himself in fellowship with Him.

That is but the beginning of what this verse tells us. It assures us that the love of God to us is so great that the three Persons in the Trinity have taken part in dealing with us, in such a way and manner that you and I, lost and condemned and hopeless in sin, might, even while left in this world of sin and of woe, enjoy the companionship of the Father, walk with Him in fellowship and communion, and enjoy Him. We are to look forward increasingly to seeing Him as He is, without any veil to conceal Him from our sight, and we are to enjoy Him in fulness throughout eternity. Do we enjoy God? It is all possible, it is open, through Christ and by the Holy Spirit.

23

LORD, TEACH US TO PRAY

For through him we both have access by one Spirit unto the Father.

Ephesians 2: 18

We continue our study of this great and wonderful verse, than which, there is surely no greater in the entire range of Scripture. It holds us face to face with the most exalted and sublime truth that a human being can ever confront. There is no doctrine higher than the doctrine of the blessed holy Trinity. And here we are face to face with it. But still more remarkable is the statement that the three Persons in the blessed holy Trinity are concerned about us and have worked and are working in the matter of our salvation. But above all I remind you that the *end* of salvation is to bring us to God as our Father. This is the purpose of salvation, this is the grand end and object of it all; and our whole conception of Christianity and of salvation is incomplete and imperfect unless we realise that it was designed above everything else to bring us to God, to give us 'access unto the Father'.

But the question arises at once as to *how we have that access.* That being the end and the goal and the object of our salvation, the great question is, how do we arrive there? In other words, we are brought face to face here with the great question of prayer. I do not propose to deal with the question of prayer in its entirety or in its fulness. I am concerned to deal with it only as it is dealt with in this particular verse, which concentrates our attention upon the most important thing of all in connection with prayer, namely, our knowledge of how we obtain the access, the way of 'drawing nigh unto God'.

As we approach the subject let me repeat certain questions which I have already asked. They are the obvious questions. Do we know God? Do we know God as Father? Are our prayers real to us? Do we enjoy freedom in prayer? Or perhaps the most searching question of all, I sometimes think, is this: *Have we confidence in our prayers?* I like to put it like that for this reason, that we all know, alas, from experience, what it is to pray when we have some difficulty, some problem, or some crisis in our lives; when we do not know what to do and we have exhausted our own reasoning. We have listened to others and consulted them, have read the Bible, and still are no nearer to a solution. So we say, There is nothing for me to do but pray. But even then we still feel uncertain. We have no real confidence in our prayers and they seem to be more or less useless. And of course such prayers really are useless; because unless we have true confidence in them it is not real prayer, as I think this verse will show us very clearly. It is important therefore for us to start with those preliminary questions. 'We have access', says Paul, 'to the Father'—'we' being all Christians and not only the apostles. He is talking about these Ephesians, these people who until very recently had been pagans, outside Christ, without God, without hope in the world, strangers, foreigners, far away, aliens in their minds. 'But now', says Paul, 'we'—you and I, and all who are Christian—'have access (introduction, entry) unto the Father' Himself. It is one of the things in which the apostle rejoices more than anything else. He repeats it many times in this Epistle, as he does in all his other Epistles. In the next chapter he says, for instance, 'For this cause I bow my knees unto the Father of our Lord Jesus Christ', and goes on to pray for them.

There is nothing which is more important than this. Are we enjoying the benefits of our Christian faith? This is the point at which that can best be tested: if our Christianity does not help us when we are in trouble, then, to say the very least, it is very defective. If it does not help us and sustain us and make all the difference in the world to us at our moments of crisis, what is the value of it? There are other things which seem to be very wonderful when the sun is shining and when everything is going well; the world and its ideas, all seem quite satisfactory then. It is when things go wrong that the testing time comes. And when everything seems against us 'to drive us to despair', the question is, can we go on to say 'I know one gate is open, one ear will hear my prayer'? That is the question. 'There hath no temptation taken you', says the apostle Paul to the Corinthians, 'but such as is common to man; but God is faithful, who will not suffer you to be tempted above that ye are able, but will with the temptation also make a way to escape . . .' (1 Corinthians 10: 13). Do we know that? Are our prayers effective, efficacious? Have we confidence in them? Do you feel when you have prayed that the burden is lifted? When you go to God in prayer, do you really leave the matter with Him? The child and the father are the perfect illustration at this point. The little child in trouble goes to the parent and at once he is happy because he has a feeling and a belief and a consciousness that the parent is able to deal with it all, and so he relaxes and is at ease and happy again. We are

meant to be like that with God, we have access to the Father.
Are we enjoying this access? Do we know what it is to enter in?
Are we availing ourselves of the introduction?

That is inevitably the question that faces us as we consider this
great statement. There are many who fail to enjoy the benefits of
salvation; there are many who do not avail themselves of this access
to the Father and to whom prayer, therefore, is not real, for the
reason that they ignore or have never grasped clearly the teaching
of this particular verse. Yet here we have the key to true prayer.
They fail because they have either ignored it altogether, or else
they have never grasped it in its fulness, and therefore have never
acted upon it. Prayer is not a simple matter; there is no greater
fallacy than to think that prayer is simple. There are many people
who contrast prayer with teaching, with doctrine, with theology.
Their attitude is: I cannot be bothered about doctrine and so on,
but prayer is everything to me; it does not matter what you believe,
it is praying to God that matters. Now that, of course, is a complete
denial of the teaching of this verse.

This verse shows us very clearly, not only that prayer is not as
simple as that, but that *prayer is something which is based upon teaching*,
upon a true understanding. Let us look at it like this. You remember
how the disciples on one occasion went to our Lord and said,
'Master, teach us to pray as John taught his disciples'. Have you
ever felt like that? I make bold to say that unless you have felt the
need of being taught how to pray, it is because you have never
prayed. We need to be taught how to pray. Those disciples had
observed their Master, they saw Him arising a great while before
dawn, going up the mountain to pray, and praying for hours,
praying right through the night sometimes. They said to each
other, How does He do that?—because I find that five minutes
seem to be an eternity. I cannot pray for five minutes, He prays for
hours. How does He do it? 'Master, teach us how to pray.' They
were right: we need to be taught how to pray. You remember
again that our Lord, in speaking to the woman of Samaria, puts it
like this to her when she talked glibly about worshipping God. She
said, You Jews say that it is in Jerusalem that one ought to worship;
our fathers say that you should worship in this mountain—as if
she knew all about worship and prayer. And our Lord said to her,
'The hour cometh when ye shall neither in this mountain nor yet
in Jerusalem worship the Father . . . Ye worship ye know not what;
we (Jews) know what we worship, for salvation is of the Jews. God
is a Spirit; and they that worship him must worship him in spirit
and in truth' (John 4: 20-24). The trouble with the Samaritans
was that their whole idea of God was wrong. They localised Him

to a particular mountain, and indeed many of the Jews were guilty of the same thing, for they would localise God to the temple. But our Lord says, You cannot worship with those wrong ideas, 'God is a Spirit, and they that worship him must worship him in spirit and in truth'. We must know certain truths before we can worship God. And the moment I say that, we see how inevitable it is that so much of what we call praying and prayers, must of necessity be useless. So often we rush into prayer because we are desperate and almost, as it were, in the words of the poem, we cry to 'whatever gods may be.' We do not know the God to whom we are praying. Teaching is therefore essential to prayer, because I must know to whom I am praying and I must know how I can enter into His holy presence. Now that is exactly the subject that is dealt with in this verse.

There are two things which are absolutely essential to prayer, according to the apostle's teaching at this point. There are two truths we have to grasp, two doctrines to lay hold of—'*Through him*': '*by one Spirit*'. That is the apostle's teaching—not only here, it is the teaching of the whole of Scripture. There is no such thing as praying to God unless we are clear about these two doctrines, these two principles. Both are essential; not one, or the other, but both, and both always together. I want to emphasise this because there is a great deal of confusion about it. There are those who do not hesitate to teach that this whole matter of approaching God, and of prayer to God, is something which is supremely simple and easy. According to them there is no need of any teaching at all, but you can go immediately into the presence of God as you are. They say, Are you in trouble? Are you in difficulties with regard to your future? Do you need guidance? and so on. Well, they say, it is all perfectly simple. All you need to do is to sit in a chair and relax and begin to listen to God; it is as simple as that; nothing more is necessary. God is there waiting to speak to you, and all you have to do is to down tools, as it were, and listen to Him. You have immediate contact with God, you get directly into the presence of God, and nothing more is necessary. Such is their belief and indeed it is a very common teaching. It is the sort of thing we all tend to assume and to take for granted. But if the teaching of the apostle in this particular verse is right, then that is not only wrong, it is dangerously wrong, it is tragically wrong.

But then there are others who tend to go astray at a different point. They emphasise one of these two principles and leave out the other. They emphasise the correct doctrine concerning the Lord Jesus Christ His atonement, and so on, quite rightly; but they neglect the absolute necessity of the operation of the Holy Spirit. And according to Paul's teaching their prayer is equally useless. You can be entirely orthodox and at the same time spiritually dead. You can say all the right things and still not know God and have no confidence in your prayers. Alas, I have known such people. They were certainly orthodox, but they did not know God, they never realised the vital importance of this doctrine of the Spirit in this matter of prayer. And so their prayers were mechanical, correct, but useless.

On the other hand, there are those who put their whole emphasis on the Holy Spirit and completely ignore our Lord and His work. This is the peculiar danger of all mystics. The mystics have discovered that there is a very definite teaching about the Holy Spirit. They have discovered, and they are quite right, that Christianity is something alive, vital, real. They say, All this orthodoxy is good in its way, but so many people are orthodox but utterly dead. The great thing about Christianity is that it is alive. Take, for instance, the case of George Fox, the first Quaker, the real founder of the Society of Friends. That was his great message. He would look at the places of worship in his day, 300 years ago, and he would say, Look at those people; they are saying all the right things, but look at their lives; talk to them and you will find that they are dead. He said that the great thing about Christianity is that it brings one into a living knowledge of God; it is something within, a power, a light within. Up to a point he was, of course, emphasising a vital truth. The work of the Holy Spirit is absolutely essential. But the tragedy of subsequent Quakerism—I am not speaking of George Fox himself at this point because he did hold the true doctrine—the tragedy is that in the following centuries, the Quaker movement has tended to put its exclusive emphasis upon the Spirit and has been ignoring and forgetting the doctrine concerning our Lord and Saviour Jesus Christ. According to the apostle's teaching here, that is equally wrong. Any teaching that bypasses the Lord Himself is of necessity wrong. 'Through him—by the Holy Spirit.' The two are essential.

I must go a step further and say that not only are these two principles absolutely essential, but *nothing must ever be added to them.* This is all, this is exclusive. My reason for saying this is that Catholic teaching—Roman, and other forms of Catholicism that imitate Romanism without believing in the Pope—is keen to make additions. The Roman Catholic church puts alongside the Lord Jesus Christ and the Holy Spirit, the Virgin Mary. She is brought in as an additional mediator, as an additional medium, as one who is vital in our coming to God. But to add anything or anyone to the Lord

Jesus Christ and to the Holy Spirit is not only to deny the Scripture, it is again to go tragically astray in the whole matter of prayer. It is wrong, and a denial of Scriptural teaching, to pray to the Virgin Mary, or to the 'saints' who have lived in the past—'saints' of whom it is claimed that they were so saintly that they are able to exercise the function of what the Catholics call 'supererogation'— they have such an abundance and an over-plus of righteousness that they can give a little of it to us and thereby help us! We must add nothing and no one to what is plainly indicated here. 'Through Him we both have access by *one Spirit* unto the Father.' So you see the importance of teaching. You see what our Lord meant when He said 'in spirit and in *truth*'. You see how vital it is that before we begin to speak in prayer we should stop and think, and be guided by the plain teaching of Scripture in what we are about to do. Let us next look at our two principles separately.

The *first* thing is '*Through him*'. That is what the apostle puts first here, that is what he puts first everywhere. This, of course, is a reference to our Lord and Saviour Jesus Christ. It is still necessary to emphasise this, and to say again that *there is no access to God except in and through our Lord and Saviour Jesus Christ*. 'I am the way, the truth, and the life; no man cometh unto the Father but by me' (John 14: 6). And yet people rush into the presence of God and think He is their Father without even mentioning the Lord Jesus Christ at all, in spite of His plain, explicit statement. Or listen again to this apostle putting it in 1 Timothy 2: 5-6: 'For there is one God, and one and only mediator (that is what it means)—one God and one mediator between God and men, the man Christ Jesus, who gave himself a ransom for all . . .' What could be plainer? Or again: 'Other foundation can no man lay than that is laid, which is Jesus Christ' (1 Corinthians 3: 11). Or take again that great passage in the tenth chapter of the Epistle to the Hebrews: 'Having therefore, brethren, boldness to enter into the holiest by the blood of Jesus' (v. 19)—the only way. Not by the blood of bulls and of goats, not through an earthly human priesthood. That, says the author, arguing it out in detail, obviously was inadequate and insufficient. The very fact that they had to go on repeating their ministrations day after day was a proof that it was not enough. The fact that the high priest had to keep on going into the 'holiest of all' every year, to make a fresh remembrance of sins, is sufficient proof that he could not do it finally and fully. 'But this man, after he had offered one sacrifice for sins for ever, sat down on the right hand of God; . . .' Could teaching be plainer? Could anything be more explicit? And yet how obvious and evident it is that all this teaching is being bypassed, and men and women talk of having contact with God, and of knowing God, and being blessed and led by God, without even mentioning the name of the Lord Jesus Christ at all, as if He had never been in the world, and as if He had never died upon the cross. Do you feel that I am labouring a point needlessly? I would ask you to consult your own experience, and to listen to what is being said, and to read what is being written. Do you always remember, when you pray to God, that apart from the Lord Jesus Christ you could have no access at all?

Let me make this very plain and clear. There is a verse in the First Epistle of Peter that seems to me to show it very explicitly. It gathers up into itself the great teaching of this second chapter of the Epistle to the Ephesians. Peter puts it like this: 'For Christ also hath once suffered for sins, the just for the unjust, that he might bring us to God; being put to death in the flesh, but quickened by the Spirit' (3: 18). There, it seems to me, is a perfect statement of this doctrine. Christ, you notice, 'has once suffered for sins, the just for the unjust'—with what end and object? 'To bring us to God'; 'being put to death in the flesh, but quickened by the Spirit'. Or again you will find the apostle Paul in Romans putting it equally clearly. Referring to our Lord, he says: 'Who was delivered for our offences, and was raised again for our justification' (4: 25). He means that it is through Christ, it is in Christ, it is by Christ and what He has done, that we have this access unto God; and apart from that we have no access unto God at all.

In the same way you cannot read the Old Testament without seeing clearly that there is need of instruction about our approach to God. The Old Testament is full of it. That is the meaning of the burnt offerings and the sacrifices and the meal offerings, and all the rest of the ceremonial. God had told and taught these people that that was the way to approach Him. He appointed a high priest called Aaron, told him exactly what to do, gave him all these instructions. Aaron had to go in bearing the blood of a slain animal. Why? Because God is thereby teaching us that it is only in His way, the way He has prescribed, that we have access into His presence.

Now, it is in and through the Lord Jesus Christ we have our access to God. The Lord Jesus Christ admits us into the presence of God because *He is our great Sin-bearer*. That is what we must put first as the apostle does. 'But now in Christ Jesus ye who sometimes were far off are made nigh by the blood of Christ.' Have you noticed the repetition of the terms? His blood, His flesh, His body, His cross? That is what must ever come first. Spurgeon used to say, and I am increasingly convinced of the rightness of his dictum, that the ultimate way to test whether a man is truly preaching the gospel or not, is to notice the emphasis which he places upon 'the blood'. It is not enough to talk about the cross and the death; the test is 'the blood'. 'But now in Christ Jesus ye who sometimes were far off are made nigh by the blood of Christ'. We have seen that there are people who, though they will agree that sinners are made nigh by the death of Christ, by the cross of Christ, yet are very unsatisfactory in their explanation of the How? They regard it as a great demonstration of the love of God in forgiving men in spite of the fact that they crucified His Son. God, they say, still brought victory out of the apparent defeat, and you can trust a God who does a thing like that. That is their interpretation of the death and of the cross; the blood of Christ does not come in. But Paul says salvation is 'by the blood of Christ' And the author of the Epistle to the Hebrews says the same thing. It is the blood of Christ that is essential in the first instance. And for this reason: our Lord Jesus Christ is 'the Lamb of God that taketh away the sin of the world'. 'The blood', you see, makes you think of necessity in terms of sacrifice, in terms of atonement; and if people do not mention atonement they are not preaching the death of Christ truly. 'The blood' fixes it to sacrifice and to atonement. The sins of men were placed symbolically upon the head of an animal and the animal was slain; the body was burned and the blood was then presented. Christ is 'the Lamb of God that taketh away the sin of the world'. The sins of men have been placed on Him, they have been dealt with in Him; He has been smitten because of them, His blood has been shed. And that is how we have our entry: He has 'borne our sins in his own body on the tree'. We must start with that. 'Without shedding of blood there is no remission of sins.' You cannot throw away the Old Testament. The Church, the early Church, was led by the Holy Spirit to keep the Old Testament and to incorporate it with the new literature, because it is an essential part of the teaching. It is God who has taught that without this offering, without the sacrifice, He cannot forgive, He cannot have dealings with men.

So any view of the cross and of the death of Christ which does not bring 'the blood' to the very centre and make it an absolute necessity is a misrepresentation of the cross. Christ is our Sin-bearer. He died on Calvary's hill for our sins, to receive the punishment of our sins. The just and holy God had to punish sin, and He punished it there. A preaching of the cross which does not mention the righteousness and the justice of God, and the absolute necessity of punishment, is a complete misrepresentation of the doctrine of the death of Christ. Here it is, you see, it is open before us: 'by his blood', 'his body', 'his death', everywhere repeated. It is the central theme of the New Testament. Read on to the book of Revelation and you will find that those people who are arrayed in white robes are said to have 'washed their robes in the blood of the Lamb'. 'Unto him that loved us and washed us from our sins in his own blood.' It is everywhere. How can men try to explain their entry to God without this most wonderful thing of all, that the Son of God was put to death by His own Father through the law because of our sins, and in order that we might be reconciled!

But it does not stop there. He is first of all our Sin-bearer, but in addition *He is our great High Priest*. 'Put to death', says Peter, 'in the flesh, quickened by the Spirit.' 'Delivered for our offences' says Paul, 'raised again for our justification.' And this is wonderful. Or again take it as it is put by the author of the Epistle to the Hebrews in the fourth chapter, verses 14-16—this is apostolic preaching—'Seeing then that we have a great high priest, that is passed through the heavens, Jesus, the Son of God, let us hold fast our profession; for we have not an high priest which cannot be touched with the feeling of our infirmities, but was in all points tempted like as we are, yet without sin. Let us therefore come boldly unto the throne of grace, that we may obtain mercy and find grace to help in time of need.' After the high priest in Israel had killed the animal and collected the blood, he then took this blood and went in through the veil into the 'holiest of all'. And the atonement was finally made when he presented the blood of sacrifice. The Lord Jesus Christ died upon the cross, His blood was shed, His body was buried in a grave. Ah, says someone, that is the end therefore, even He was defeated. Not at all! He rose again. And having risen and having manifested Himself, He entered into the 'holiest of all'. He has passed through the heavens into heaven itself. He has gone immediately into the presence of God, and He has presented His own blood. He has not presented the blood of bulls and of goats. He does not try to cleanse with the ashes of an heifer. He has taken in 'his own blood'. It is by the blood of Jesus! He has entered in and God has accepted Him and His offered blood. God has said, in other words, that He is satisfied with His work. God pronounces that the death of Christ is sufficient, that His justice is satisfied. He admits the High Priest right into His own presence, and He bids Him to sit down at His right hand. The result is that the throne of God, which is a throne of judgment, becomes a throne of grace. 'Let us therefore come boldly unto the throne of grace,' is the message of Hebrews 4: 16. And how do I know that it is a throne of grace? My only way of knowing that is that the Lord Jesus Christ is seated by the side of God. My Representative! One who came and took my nature upon Him and who has borne my sins! He has been accepted of God, He is the great High Priest. He knows me, He has suffered temptation as I have, He knows my weakness and my frailty. He is there with God, and the fact that He is there assures me that it is a throne of grace. God is eternally righteous and holy, but because of Christ and what He has done for us and for our sins God smiles upon us in His grace and receives us as His children. Christ saves us then not only by shedding His blood but by entering into the heavens as our great High Priest.

There is also another way in which He helps me to have access to the Father. You may say, Very well, I can see that my sins are forgiven in that way, but still, when I think of God in His eternity of power and of majesty and of might, when I think especially of His holiness and His absolute purity, I feel that I am unclean. I believe my sins are forgiven, but oh, there is still unrighteousness left within me; How can I appear before God? How can I draw nigh unto God? I read in the Scriptures that Isaiah, when he saw a vision of the Lord, said: 'Woe is me! for I am a man of unclean lips', and how can I draw near unto God? The answer is still 'in Christ'. And in this way, that He has not only been delivered for our offences and raised again for our justification; but more than that, *He has been made our righteousness.* 'But of him', says the apostle Paul to the Corinthians, 'are ye in Christ Jesus, who of God is made unto us wisdom, and righteousness, sanctification and redemption'. Or listen to him putting it again like this: 'He hath made him to be sin for us, who knew no sin, that we might be made the righteousness of God in him' (2 Corinthians 5: 21). Let me use a simple illustration. Here is a great banqueting chamber, with wonderful people inside it and a great ceremony taking place. There am I out in the street; I would like to go in, I am invited in, but I feel that I am in rags, that my clothing is unworthy. If I go in everyone will look at me and I shall feel that I am an odd person and I shall be unhappy, and I shall not enjoy it. What can I do? The answer is that I am given a new robe, a robe of righteousness. I am clothed with the righteousness of Jesus Christ. That is what the Scripture teaches: His good, perfect life, His life of holiness, is given to me, is attributed to me, is imputed or reckoned to me. As my sins were attributed and imputed to Him, His righteousness is attributed to me. He kept the law perfectly; God regards that as done for me, He puts it to my account. I am clothed with the righteousness of Christ. It was because of that, that Count Zinzendorf was able to say in the hymn that John Wesley has translated:

Jesus, Thy blood and righteousness,
My beauty are, my glorious dress;

Midst flaming worlds in these arrayed,
With joy shall I lift up my head.

Clothed with the righteousness of Jesus Christ! Is this dry-as-dust doctrine? It is as vital as this to you, that if you do not believe it you cannot pray. It is only as you are conscious that you are covered by the righteousness of Christ you can go into the presence of God with confidence and with assurance. But with this you can, as that hymn puts it so perfectly. No one can bring a charge against me; even God cannot, for it is God that justifies me and gives me the righteousness of His own Son.

Finally, I would put it like this. We have this access through Christ because we are not only given His righteousness, *we are given His life.* We are born again of Him, we become 'partakers of the divine nature', He is the 'first-born among many brethren'. Indeed, Paul has been saying it at great length already in this chapter. He says it, you remember, in those wonderful steps: 'Even when we were dead in sins hath quickened us together with him, and raised us up together, and made us sit together in the heavenly places in Christ Jesus'. Christ, having finished His work, has passed through the heavens, has taken His place, is seated at the right hand of God; and, in a marvellous way, 'in Christ', I am also there. That is how I have my access into the presence of the Father. If Christ had not died for my sins, God would not receive me; I will go further, God could not receive me. It is an absolute necessity. Do you imagine that the Heavenly Father would ever have sent His only begotten, dearly beloved Son into the world to endure such suffering and agony unless it was absolutely essential? Would the cross ever have happened unless it was an utter necessity? It is unthinkable.

There was no other good enough to pay the price of sin,
He only could unlock the gates of heaven and let us in.

It is through Christ. You are absolutely dependent upon Him. Were it not that He has gone in with His blood, you could never go in. But because He has entered you can enter.

And remember that He is there, a sympathising High Priest, because He has been here in this world, and because of all He has suffered. He transmits our prayers with His holy incense to the Father. It is but natural, therefore, that these various authors should end always with exhortations: 'Having boldness, therefore, brethren, to enter into the holiest by the blood of Jesus'; and again, 'Let us therefore come boldly to the throne of grace'—with confidence, with assurance, with certainty. 'Therefore'—in the light of the doctrine of Christ as the Sin-bearer, as the High Priest, as our Righteousness, as the One in whom we are incorporated, the One with whom we have been crucified, the One with whom we have died, died to the law, died to sin, risen again in newness of life—'Reckon yourselves therefore to be dead indeed unto sin, but alive unto God, through'—and only through—'Jesus Christ our Lord' (Romans 6: 11).

Have you realised your utter dependence upon the Lord Jesus Christ and His perfect work? If you have not, it is not surprising that your prayers have seemed vain and futile and empty. Henceforward, when you go to God, start with Christ. Thank the Lord Jesus Christ for what He has done for you, thank God for sending Him to do it; tell Him that you realise that you are entirely dependent upon Him, but that believing it you know that He is waiting to receive you. Call Him your Father, and tell Him that you know that He is your Father because He is the Father of your Lord and Saviour, Jesus Christ—'Through him, we have access by one Spirit unto the Father'.

24

PRAYING IN THE SPIRIT

For through him we both have access by one Spirit unto the Father.
Ephesians 2: 18

We come back once more to this all-important verse in which the great apostle shows the Ephesians what cause they have for rejoicing that they are Christians, and therefore fellow-heirs of the kingdom of God with the Jews. It is a crucial verse. We have seen that we are reminded here that the three Persons in the blessed holy Trinity are concerned in our salvation, and play their part in our salvation. That is, I take it, the most glorious fact which we shall ever know. There is nothing beyond that, even in heaven. It is there we shall know in its fulness what God the Father, God the Son, and God the Holy Ghost have done for us and our salvation. We have also seen that, immediately here in this life, the greatest benefit of all that we derive from this great fact of salvation is that we have access to the Father. That is the end of salvation, that is the grand object behind everything that God has done in and through our Lord and Saviour Jesus Christ—He died 'to bring us to God', and His blood was shed in order that we might be able to enter into 'the holiest of all'. To stop, therefore, at any point short of this is not only to ignore the Scriptures, it is indeed to go against the Scriptures, because, what matters ultimately is not what you and I think we need or desire, it is what God has provided. And this is the end and object of salvation, that we might have access to the Father, that we might go into the presence of God and enjoy communion with Him.

In view of the fact that that is the highest privilege and the greatest blessing that we can ever know, it is not surprising that it is at this very point that most of us, indeed all of us, have often found great difficulty, and may still be in great difficulty. I suppose that in the last analysis, *the most difficult thing we ever try to do, because it is the greatest thing we ever do, is to pray*. And there are problems in connection with prayer which often agitate the minds and the hearts of God's people. This is not surprising, as prayer is the greatest thing of all. The adversary of our souls, therefore, is particularly concerned to attack us at this point. That is something which we all have learned from experience. There is nothing, in a

267

sense, which is so difficult as to pray. Let me just remind you of some of the many difficulties in order that we may see the object which the apostle has in his mind in stating what we have in this verse.

There is the difficulty of realising the presence of God. God is Spirit, God is unseen. That in itself at once constitutes a difficulty for us. We are accustomed to seeing people or to hearing their audible voices as we have fellowship and communion with them. But God is unseen. 'No man hath seen God at any time.' To put it another way, often one is aware of a sense of unreality in one's prayer. And there are voices that come to us, suggestions sent by Satan, to the effect that really we are merely going through some psychological procedure, that we are just persuading and deluding ourselves, virtually speaking to ourselves and encouraging ourselves. There is this general sense of unreality which people so often complain of.

Then there is the problem of concentration. If you are reading a book it is not so difficult to concentrate. If you are talking to somebody else there is no such problem. But have we not all found oftentimes that, when we begin to pray, our minds wander in every direction, our imaginations travel the whole world, and though we are on our knees with the intent of speaking to God, we tend to be thinking about problems—something that happened yesterday, something that is going to happen tomorrow. How difficult it is to gather together one's mind and one's thoughts and to concentrate truly so that our prayer becomes a living and a true and a vital act! Then, too, there is the sense of unworthiness, the reminder of our sinfulness, and the feeling that we have no right to approach God. This awful sense of unworthiness militates against us. Again, doubts come, doubts insinuated into the mind, questions and queryings. I need not elaborate; we are all familiar with these things and they happen because prayer is the supreme activity of the human soul, it is the highest point we ever reach in this life—communion with God. So that as we engage in it, all the forces of hell, as it were, are playing upon us and are doing their utmost to spoil our efforts. I say that, not only as a matter of fact, but also partly by way of encouragement. Do not be discouraged by the fact that you have found prayer difficult. Indeed, the thing to fear is that prayer may be too easy; because, if we realise exactly what we are doing, we shall see that inevitably we become the special target and victim of the great adversary of our souls, and our praying correspondingly difficult.

For all these reasons then it becomes very necessary that we should be taught how to pray and that we should know how to pray.

Nothing is so fatal as to engage in prayer without thinking. The first act in prayer always should be what the Fathers used to call 'recollection'. There should always be an act of recollection. It is so wrong to rush into the presence of God with petitions, without realising what we are doing. We must stop, pause, and meditate, and remind ourselves of what we are doing. There are many ways in which this point can be made clear. If you are to have an audience with the Queen you will probably find it wise and expedient to discover something about Court etiquette. Now, multiply that by infinity, and there you have a soul going into the presence of God. It is not something that we can do lightly and thoughtlessly, not something we can rush into; we must realise what we have to do. Here the apostle, in giving a list of the amazing things that have happened to these Ephesians, brings us to this tremendous height, 'In him we both have access by one Spirit unto the Father'. Not only are you no longer strangers and foreigners and aliens, you come into the presence of God. How did you get there? He tells us, you remember, that there are two essentials; and we have emphasised the fact that there are only two. There are only two things about which we must be absolutely clear and certain. One is the Lord Jesus Christ Himself; and the other is the Holy Spirit. There is nothing else to add to that list. You do not add the Virgin Mary, you do not add the Church, you do not add a priesthood, you do not add the saints. You add nothing. All that is essential to prayer is that you go through the Lord Jesus Christ; and we have considered how we do so.

The *second* thing is that we realise that it is '*by one Spirit*'. As we come to consider this, the first thing we have to emphasise is that this means the Holy Spirit Himself. The apostle is not saying here that, now that the Jews and Gentiles share the same ideas and have the same outlook and have a common spirit, they can therefore pray together. That, of course, is true, but there is something much bigger here. This is not a reference to human spirits which have now come into unity or unison. He refers to the Holy Spirit; so very rightly in our Bibles the translators have indicated this by writing 'Spirit' here with a capital S. It is a reference to the Holy Spirit Himself. And what the apostle is teaching is that *the Holy Spirit is as essential to prayer as is the Lord Jesus Christ Himself.* Not One without the Other, but Both together.

Once more we must ask ourselves certain questions. Have we in our prayer lives up till this very moment realised the vital place and importance of the Holy Spirit? Have we realised that without Him we really cannot pray truly, and that true prayer is always prayer *by* the Holy Spirit *through* the Lord Jesus Christ? As Christian people we have realised how essential the Lord Jesus Christ is, the one and only Mediator between God and man. But here, according to the apostle, it is equally essential that we should realise our dependence upon the Holy Spirit and His own peculiar work and activity in us. And this is not an isolated statement; the apostle repeats this. For instance in the last chapter of this Epistle to the Ephesians in the eighteenth verse, where he has been talking about putting on the whole armour of God, he winds up by saying, 'Praying always with all prayer and supplication in the Spirit' (again with a capital S)— in the Holy Spirit. That is his conception of prayer. And if you go on to the Epistle to the Philippians you will find that he says the same thing again in the third chapter in the third verse, where he tells them to 'Beware of dogs, beware of evil workers, beware of the concision. For', he says, 'we are the circumcision who worship God in the Spirit' (again capital S); or you might translate it 'we who worship God by the Spirit' and who realise that we are utterly dependent upon Him. The Judaizers—'the concision'—did not worship God in the Spirit or by the Spirit; theirs was a mechanical form of worship. And what differentiates Christian worship and prayer from every other type and kind of prayer is that it is in the Spirit. There are many other people who pray, but they do not pray 'in the Spirit'. This is the peculiar thing, the differentiating thing about Christian prayer. The apostle Jude says exactly the same thing in his letter in verse twenty: 'But ye, beloved, building up yourselves on your most holy faith, praying in the Holy Ghost, keep yourselves in the love of God'. There it is, quite explicitly. You are praying, he says, in the Holy Ghost.

These expressions are not used at random by the New Testament writers. 'In the Spirit' was to them of the very essence of prayer. And, indeed, in saying all this they are just showing how the word of Zechariah has been fulfilled, where he prophesies that the 'Spirit of grace and of supplications' shall be sent upon the people in this age of the Messiah (12: 10).

It is of vital importance, then, that we should understand the part that the Holy Spirit plays in this question of prayer. In a sense we already have our exposition in the fourth chapter of the Gospel according to John. There, in speaking to th ewoman of Samaria, our Lord puts this thing clearly once and for ever. She talks glibly about worship—'Our fathers worshipped in this mountain; and ye say that in Jerusalem is the place where men ought to worship.' Our Lord corrects her, and puts this matter plainly and clearly: 'God', He says, 'is a Spirit, and they that worship him must worship him in spirit and in truth'. What is prayer? What are the true characteristics of prayer? What is this praying in the Spirit?

Let us take the *negatives* first. It is obviously not *a matter of place* and not a matter of ceremony as such. Our Lord at once puts His finger on that fallacy in the mind of the woman of Samaria—'this mountain'. If you want to worship, the Samaritans said, you must worship here. The Jews, on the other hand, said that you must do so in Jerusalem in the temple, that God was confined to the temple— as they, the Samaritans, thought He was confined to their mountain. Places! Ceremonies! There are people who only pray when they are in a place of worship, and who know nothing about private prayer, about secret prayer. Prayer to them is something that only happens on certain set occasions, in particular places. Now true prayer in the Spirit is the very antithesis of that. It is not confined to any particular place, or to any particular kind of ceremony.

There are, again, some people to whom the very essence of prayer seems to be *the question of posture*. How concerned they are about being able to kneel! Indeed I have known people who have seriously suggested that you cannot possibly be praying unless you are on your knees. We cannot go into all these points, interesting as they are. I am simply trying to emphasise the great central principle, that there is no one posture that is essential to prayer. It is right to kneel in prayer, it is equally right to pray standing, it is equally right to fall prostrate on your face on the floor. All these things are in the Scriptures. In other words, it is not the posture that matters. And if you find a tendency within yourself to say that the posture is the great and the central and the vital thing, it is no longer praying 'in the Spirit'. You are attaching significance to an inci- dental. Of course you can pray in the temple, you can pray on a mountain, but not only in the temple or on a mountain, and not only in any given posture.

Then there is the whole question of *forms of prayer*. Here is another complicated subject. Should we have set prayers? should we have formal prayers? should we have liturgies? What a vital subject this is. Three hundred years ago this was partly responsible for the Puritan movement. Some said that there is no freedom in prayer while you are tied to liturgies and to set forms and to read prayers. They felt that that was a relic of Roman Catholicism. They said that prayer must be free, and must be under the guidance and inspiration of the Holy Ghost. So the emphasis must not be placed upon beautiful phrases, perfect diction, and particular forms. Do not misunderstand me, I am not saying that a written or a read prayer cannot be a true prayer; but always in this matter of prayer we have to be very careful that we keep the balance between the freedom of the Spirit and the form. The two things, up to a point, are essential. But clearly the teaching of our Lord Himself is that the vital thing is the Spirit; the control, the inspiration, the freedom of the Holy Ghost. And so you will always find in every great period of revival in the long history of the Church that when revival comes people begin to shed the forms and the liturgies and to indulge in extempore, free prayer. But that again can become mechanical, and the fact that you are not using set forms does not of necessity mean that you are always free. There is a greater danger in forms than in the extempore prayer, but even the extempore does not guarantee that you will not become mechanical and tied. The great principle is this: do not put your emphasis upon form or beauty or perfection of diction, or anything like that, but upon the fact that true prayer is in the Spirit. In other words, prayer, according to this teaching, is never something merely formal, it must always be vital.

Again, I do not say that you should not have *set times of prayer*; but the moment you start doing that you have to be careful. There will be the danger that you are praying because it is 12 o'clock or 7 o'clock, or some other time of day or night, rather than because you are longing to be in communion with God. All these things may become dangers. That is why, it seems to me, there are *certain phrases and expressions* which we should never use. This teaching about the Spirit in prayer means that we should never talk about 'saying our prayers', or use that other glib phrase that is so often on the lips of some people, 'saying a prayer'. People talk about going into a building and 'saying a prayer'. What they mean by that is that they are reciting a phrase. You cannot 'say a prayer' when you are having communion with God. Where is the Holy Ghost? Where is the living element? Repeating phrases is not praying. No, says our Lord, you have got to get rid of all that; prayer is a spiritual matter. 'God is a Spirit, and they that worship him must worship him in spirit and in truth'. The Holy Ghost is absolutely essential; and without Him we cannot truly pray, for prayer means a living and a vital and a real communion with God who is Spirit. God is Spirit. And prayer really means my spirit is in communion with God. It is personal. It is this fellowship, this immediate fellowship, and nothing less than that. Thus the apostle is reminding the Ephesians that in this matter the Holy Spirit is absolutely essential. You can read your prayers without the Holy Ghost. You can repeat phrases without the Holy Ghost. You can be on your knees speaking without the Holy Ghost. But you cannot make contact with God, you cannot really commune with God who is Spirit, without the activity of the Holy Ghost. Let me even go so far as to say this, that without Him even the Lord Jesus Christ Himself and His work, alone, cannot bring us into this vital relationship to God. 'The hour cometh and now is when the true worshippers shall worship the Father (neither in this mountain nor yet in Jerusalem, but) in spirit and in truth.' That, He says, is what is coming. And that is what is produced and made possible by the Holy Ghost. Without the Holy Spirit prayer is mechanical, lifeless, difficult, prayer is an awful task: but with Him everything is changed and it becomes free and glorious and the supreme enjoyment of the soul.

That leaves us now with the question, *What exactly does the Holy Spirit do in this matter of prayer?* And the answers are almost endless. I am simply going to give certain headings. We might in a sense sum it all up by saying that it is He who mediates to us, and makes actual and living and real for us, all that has been done by our Lord and Saviour Jesus Christ. But let us divide it up in this way.

Why do I pray, why should I ever pray, why do I ever want to pray? The answer is that it is the Holy Spirit who *creates within me a spiritual mind*. Man by nature, as we have seen at length in this chapter, has not got a spiritual mind or a spiritual outlook. And without that, prayer is a complete impossibility; we simply cannot pray at all. Of course we may have been taught to say our prayers, and we may go on mechanically doing that throughout our lives. And oh, how many of us remain children in this matter until our very graves! Taught to say your prayers morning and evening— and you will see adult men, intelligent men, men of business and of professions, who are rather pleased and rather proud that they are still saying the prayers they learnt as children. They have remained children in this matter; they have not remained children in other matters, but in this they are simply doing still what they have always done. And it is as thoughtless now as it was then. That is not praying. The first thing that is absolutely essential is that we should have a spiritual mind, a spiritual outlook. We were dead in trespasses and sins; and though we have become Christians the deadness still tends to remain and to afflict us. Is it not difficult at times to rouse ourselves? We do not feel inclined to pray, we feel lifeless, lethargic and dull, and spiritual things are not real to us. We cannot pray in that state. Now the Holy Spirit enlivens us, quickens us, disturbs us, moves us, stimulates us, moves our carnal minds to think spiritually. That is always the first essential in this matter of prayer. We become aware of the spiritual realm and we are reminded that we ourselves have a Spirit within us. And the moment we begin to realise that, in a sense we are already beginning to pray. But of course it does not stop there.

It is the Spirit who shows us our need, it is He who *reminds us of our sin*. There is nothing that is so likely to lead a man to prayer as his consciousness of his sin and of his need. And this is the peculiar work of the Holy Spirit. You see the difference between merely rushing into the presence of God with certain petitions, and truly having fellowship and communion. You say to yourself, I am going to have this audience with the King eternal, immortal, invisible. Who am I to go in? What kind of a creature am I? How am I clad, how am I shod, what is my appearance? In other words, the Holy Spirit is making you see your sin, He is convincing you and convicting you of your need, He is creating within you a godly sorrow, a true repentance. That is most conducive to prayer. He is preparing you.

That leads to the next thing, which is that He *shows us our need of God* and of God's mercy and God's blessing. At once you are taken out of the realm of generalities and you realise that you are an isolated soul. You are not interested any longer in things nor merely in events or happenings; you have been brought by the Holy Spirit to realise that God has given you this special gift, the soul, the spirit. You came into the world an individual, and though you are one of millions of people in this world you are still a separate, distinct, isolated being, and have a relationship to that God who is Spirit and personal also, and you are going on to meet Him. So you begin to feel the desire to know Him and to make contact. The Holy Spirit does that. Now this is of the very essence of prayer; it becomes personal at that point, and is no longer interested only in forms and appearances, and things of that kind.

All this is still somewhat vague. But it is a vital step when a man begins to feel his need of God. I do not know about you, but more and more I find myself these days looking for this one thing in all people. The people to whom I am drawn, the people I like, are those who give me the impression that they are hungry for God, that they have a longing in their souls for the living God. I put them before all others. This is the vital thing, a hunger, a thirst, for God. There is nothing, in a sense, beyond that. You can be very busy and active without this. You can be so busy that you become almost impersonal, outside yourself, and you do not realise your own soul's condition and your need of God and your relationship to God. The Holy Spirit produces that felt need of God.

Then the Holy Spirit goes on to *reveal God in His glory to us*. This is something again that is absolutely vital and essential. I take it that ultimately all difficulties in prayer spring from our failure to realise the truth about God. Oh, what a difference it would make! We are all like Moses, are we not? And like Joshua after him? We want to rush into the presence of God. You remember how Moses at the burning bush did not quite understand. He was going to investigate, he was rushing in. The voice came and said, Stand back!

'Take off thy shoes from off thy feet, for the place whereon thou standest is holy ground.' That is the ground you and I are standing on when we engage in prayer. We are going into the presence of God. And the Holy Spirit reveals Him to us in His glory and in His majesty. But not only that, He reveals Him to us as our Father. And so He creates the desire within us to know Him and to have communion with Him. It was something like this that made the psalmist say, 'As the hart panteth after the waterbrooks, so panteth my soul after thee, O God', 'My soul thirsteth for God, for the living God.' The living God! He no longer merely wants to pray to God, he wants the living God and a real, live act of communion, the knowledge that he is with God. Now the Holy Spirit alone does that. And when this kind of thing is taking place prayer is entirely different. It becomes the most exciting thing in the world, it becomes the most thrilling thing. It is no longer formal and set and difficult, and we no longer have all these problems.

Furthermore, He does the work which our Lord Himself says is His most special and peculiar work of all, namely that He *keeps our eyes on the Lord Jesus Christ*. The Lord said that the Holy Spirit would glorify Him: 'He shall glorify me'. That is His supreme task and purpose. And that is exactly what He does. Having shown us our utter sinfulness and helplessness and smallness. and the glory of God, He leads us to the Lord Jesus Christ. He makes us see Him in all the glory and wonder of His Person, in all the glory and the wonder of His work. We see Him as the Mediator. Let me put that in the form of a question. Do we always realise, when we pray, our utter, absolute dependence upon the Lord Jesus Christ and His atoning work? Are we always mindful of the fact that apart from the blood of Jesus we cannot have access into the presence of God? We would all have to confess, surely, that thousands of times as we have prayed, we have 'taken it for granted'. This is what we take for granted. The most glorious fact in history we take for granted. We do not thank God for it, we do not meditate upon it, we do not think of it until our hearts are ravished. We assume it. Is there anything more terrible, or, in a sense, verging more upon the blasphemous, than to assume the blood of Calvary and the death of Christ? The Holy Spirit will never allow us to do that. He will reveal the Lord Jesus Christ to us in all His glory, and, thank God, in His all-sufficiency. So that as you are there in the presence of God, and terribly conscious of your sinfulness, your unworthiness, your uncleanness, your vileness, and your weakness, the Holy Spirit will reveal to you that it was 'when we were yet without strength, in due time Christ died for the ungodly'; it was 'while we were enemies' we were saved by the death of the Lord Jesus Christ. It is then that the Spirit will remind you that Christ said 'I came not to call the righteous, but sinners to repentance'. It is then you will see the procession, the Mary Magdalenes and all the others coming, led by Him, to God. The Holy Spirit will show it all to you. And you will realise that, in spite of your unutterable vileness, you nevertheless have an access into the presence of God. You will say with Charles Wesley,

> *Just and holy is Thy name,*
> *I am all unrighteousness;*
> *Vile and full of sin I am,*
> *Thou art full of truth and grace.*

He reveals, He unfolds, the Lord Jesus Christ. When you engage in prayer, have you those exalted views of the Person and the work of the Lord Jesus Christ? That is the test of whether you are praying 'in the Spirit'. You cannot pray in the Spirit without being led to see Him and to realise Him in a manner that you have never done before.

It is the Holy Spirit likewise that *leads us to an understanding of all the promises of God.* We know what it is to be hemmed in by trials and tribulations and problems, and to be aware of our own weakness and ineffectiveness. Indeed we are tempted to cry out to Him, What shall I do, what can I do? And there the Holy Spirit begins to reveal to you the 'exceeding great and precious promises', and everything is transformed. It is He who reveals God to us as our Father, as 'the Father of our Lord and Saviour Jesus Christ', and our Father. You remember that Paul put it like this: 'Blessed be the God and Father of our Lord Jesus Christ, who hath blessed us with all spiritual blessings in the heavenlies in Christ' (Eph. 1: 3). The moment you realise that, your whole outlook is changed. You say to yourself, Well, though things are as they are, God is my Father, and I have the authority of the Lord Jesus Christ for saying that He has numbered the very hairs of my head, that He is not only interested in the fall of every sparrow, He is infinitely more concerned about me and everything that happens to me. He is the Father of Jesus Christ, and He is my Father; and as He cared for Him, He will care for me. He has said, 'I will never leave thee nor forsake thee.' Do you know anything about that? To feel, in the presence of God, though you may be almost overwhelmed by troubles and problems, a sense of joy and of happiness, because you are a child of God, that over-rules and overrides everything? That is what the Holy Spirit does.

Let me put it finally in this form. The apostle says in writing to the Romans, 'Ye have not received the spirit of bondage again to fear, but ye have received the Spirit of adoption, whereby we cry, Abba, Father' (8: 15). We know about bondage, do we not? We know about all the difficulties that I enumerated at the beginning—and that is sheer bondage. Trying to think of something to say, trying to work up a feeling—oh, what a bondage it is! There is no freedom there. How unlike the child speaking to his father, holding out his hands for the father to embrace him, mumbling his little nothings because he is glad to see his parent. That is how we should be praying, with a glorious freedom. 'Not the spirit of bondage again to fear!—but the Spirit of adoption, whereby we cry (with this elemental, childlike, filial cry), Abba, Father.' Do you know this *freedom in prayer*? Do you know this spiritual eloquence in prayer? Do you know what it is to be carried out of yourself in prayer? Do you know what it is almost to desire to go on praying for ever, and to find it difficult to stop? That is praying in the Spirit when it has reached its greatest heights. Here, then, is the way we have access to the Father, says Paul, through the Lord Jesus Christ, and by the one Spirit.

Let me put it all in one question. *Do you enjoy prayer?* Have you ever enjoyed prayer? Is it to you a most delightful occupation? If it is not, it is because you have forgotten that the operations of the Holy Spirit are absolutely essential to prayer. Therefore, when you next engage in prayer remember this. Pray to Him, ask Him to enliven you and to quicken you. He wi'l do so; He has already done it without your knowing it. The desire for prayer has been produced by Him, the very thought about it. He is the One who produces all these desires; He 'worketh in us both to will and to do'; so ask Him and He will increase it. Go to Him in your dryness, in your deadness, tell Him that you feel ashamed of yourself, tell Him that you want to know God, tell Him that you want to enjoy God, tell Him you want to know this freedom in the Spirit; and ask Him to make it possible, and go on until the answer comes. And it will come! Hear the word of the apostle again in Romans 8: 26 and 27, to this effect: 'We know not what to pray for as we ought; but the Spirit himself maketh intercession for us, with groanings which cannot be uttered'; 'He that knoweth the hearts knoweth what is the mind of the Spirit'. It is as wonderful as that, that even when we are utterly helpless and do not know what to pray for or what to do, and are desperate, as it were, even then—and have we not known it, thank God—we find ourselves groaning, not knowing what we are saying. It is the Spirit Himself making intercession for us, in us, through us, with groanings which cannot be uttered. If He does that apart from our request, without our asking Him to do so, how much more certain is it that if we truly ask Him and seek His aid, He will surely answer us! And beginning to pray in the Holy Spirit, we shall have a true access into the presence of God, and shall not only glorify God but begin to enjoy Him for ever.

25

CHRISTIAN UNITY

Now therefore . . .   Ephesians 2: 19

We turn our attention now to the apostle's two words, 'Now therefore'. In other words, we arrive at a point in our consideration of the second chapter of this great Epistle, at which the apostle, having completed his main statement, is summarising, or pausing for a moment to gather up the various things which he has been saying. And as he does so it is very important for us to do so. There is always a danger, when one deals with a great section of Scripture such as this, that in dealing with the various details, as we have been doing, and as we must of necessity do, one may very well lose the main trend or the main argument of the section. So it is very important that we should, from time to time, even as the apostle himself suggests to us, pause for a moment and consider what we have been discovering.

What a tremendous thing this is! It is important that we should look at it now for a moment as a whole. We have been taken through the steps; he has shown us exactly how God has done a great work through the Lord Jesus Christ, how the middle wall of partition—that law of commandments in ordinances—has been demolished. There is this entry, this access into the presence of God in the Lord Jesus Christ and through the Holy Spirit. The thing for us to bear in mind is this great matter of unity, the unity that exists between all who are truly Christian. That is the thing the apostle has uppermost in his mind—this 'one body', this 'one new man'; 'we both' have access by one Spirit, and so on. This is the thing he is so anxious we should all be clear about. And therefore it is good for us to notice in general what it is that constitutes this unity, what makes it, what brings it into being and keeps it going. Here we are face to face with one of these great and crucial statements of Scripture.

In looking at this, certain great principles will become manifest to us. For instance, you cannot consider a passage like this without being reminded again very clearly *what a Christian is, and what makes us Christian.* In showing how these Ephesians had been brought into the Church with the Jews, the apostle shows what had to happen to the Jew and the Gentile before either of them could ever have come into the Church, before either of them could ever go into the presence of God. So that here, incidentally, we are brought back again to this bedrock, this foundational position where we see clearly what it is that makes us Christian. In other words we are given a very wonderful definition of the Christian.

Another thing that we are shown is that *nothing else can ever bring men together truly but this gospel*. We discover that in this way. The apostle, in expounding and in showing how this wonderful unity has been brought about, has incidentally shown us what had to be done before this could be brought to pass. As we have an insight into the things that divide men and women, we are driven and forced to the conclusion that nothing but the power of God in Christ through the Holy Spirit in the gospel can ever really bring men and women together. This is surely a very important thing for us to bear in mind at the present time. When I say that, I am thinking not only of the Church but also of the whole general international situation. There is a great deal of false and glib and superficial talk about unity in the Church and amongst the nations. But as I understand the teaching of Scripture, and especially this particular section, there is nothing that is quite so dangerous, and in the end so fatuous and so completely futile, as all this vague and general talk of bringing people together and establishing what is called 'a unity'.

We have to recognise that there are times when there appears to be a unity: but it may prove only a superficial unity, only an appearance. Sometimes because of certain circumstances people get together, driven together, perhaps, by a common need or by a common danger, and they are to be seen talking to one another and co-operating and working together. But that is not of necessity a true unity, as history shows very plainly and clearly. There may be a coming together among men or nations, or between different sections of the Christian Church, for specific objects, and superficial people are tempted to say that at last the enmity has been abolished and all are one. But a community of interest for the time being is not a real unity. Read your secular history books and watch what the nations have done, notice how there have been strange combinations of nations at different times, and how it looked for the moment as if they really had formed a firm friendship which could never be dissolved. But then you turn over a few pages in your history book and you find these two nations, who seemed to have become one, fighting one another. The explanation is this. When they appeared to be in a firm friendship it was only because circumstances were such in the case of both nations that it paid them and it suited them to come together. You often get that during a war. A common enemy suddenly arises and the others (who really do not like one another and have always been opposed), because of this common danger, work together in order to keep that enemy down; but then the moment that has been accomplished, they begin quarrelling again with one another. What appeared to be unity was not unity, it was a façade, it was a mere appearance. That is not real unity.

Exactly the same thing applies in the realm of the Church. There are those who think and say that face to face with the great enemy, Materialism (call it Communism if you like), all must come together who call themselves Christian in any shape or form. We must not be bothered about definitions but must form a common front against this one great enemy. There are those, therefore, who would say that Roman Catholics and Protestants should work together and be one, forget all their differences, and all stand together to defend Western Civilisation, or whatever it may chance to be called, against this great common foe. And they think that that is unity. Now my contention is that the teaching of this paragraph of our Epistle, without going any further, shows us how superficial, and in the last analysis how futile all such talk is. If we have grasped the teaching of this section, which gives us an insight into man's nature in sin, and the things which really divide people fundamentally, then I think we must be driven to the conclusion that nothing but a fundamental solution, such as is offered by the gospel alone, and by nothing else, can ever really produce this true and real and durable unity. That becomes clear.

Then another thing that becomes clear is this. We are given an understanding of, and an insight into, *the nature of this true unity that exists amongst Christians*. The whole point is that it is only those who conform to the description given here who really are one. The apostle has been talking about it in terms of one body and has given us this marvellous analogy of the body which he so frequently uses. He has emphasised that it is a vital, an organic unity; it is not simply a matter of people being loosely attached to one another, it is not simply a matter of people for the time being forgetting differences and forming a kind of coalition. Not at all! It is a live unity, the unity that obtains in the body, where the fingers are joined to the rest of the body, not just stuck on, but in a living unity, a unity of blood and of nerves. It is something that is a whole, having various parts, not a number of parts put together to make a whole. You start at the centre and work outwards, instead of vice versa: Perhaps I can summarise it all by putting it like this, that the unity amongst Christians is a unity which is quite inevitable because of that which is true of each and every one. I sometimes think that

that is the most important principle of all. With all this talk about unity, it seems to me, we are forgetting the most important thing, which is that unity is not something that man has to produce or to arrange: true unity between Christians is inevitable and unavoidable. It is not man's creation; it is, as we have been shown so clearly, the creation of the Holy Spirit Himself. And my contention is that there is such a unity at this moment among true Christians. I do not care what labels they have on them, the unity is inevitable; they cannot avoid it, because of that which has become true of every single individual Christian.

Let me next show how these principles are stated here in detail. First there is this great postulate, that *men by nature, men because of their backgrounds, are hopelessly divided amongst themselves.* We have been shown it here in terms of the Jew and the Gentile, and the deep and violent prejudices that both had. That is man in sin. Man in sin is a mass of prejudices. And because all men are in sin and have these prejudices, disunity is inevitable. The Jew despised the Gentile, and the Gentile hated the Jew, and there was a middle wall of partition. The world is still full of that kind of racial prejudice— people do not hesitate to dismiss whole nations and to condemn them, to speak of them with sarcasm and scorn; and the condemned do exactly the same in their turn. It is true of classes, it is true of groups. The whole of humanity is divided up in this way. This is not something superficial, it is something deep down in the life of man, it is elemental. In a sense it is something which is beyond the control of man. He tries to control it, he puts on a veneer of gentlemanliness or politeness, he may smile at somebody whom he is at the same time cursing in his heart. We put on the show and appearances are kept up, but beneath it there is enmity and disunion; and the mere fact that people are smiling and shaking hands does not necessarily tell you anything about their hearts. They may issue their communiqués, and yet be planning and plotting to foil one another and to do various unfriendly things against one another at the same time. We are all familiar with this. The whole so-called art of politics, local or imperial or international, is based upon this very supposition, that you cannot trust anybody, and that you must keep your eye on your own best interests, making concessions when it suits you.

That then is the truth about mankind. And it is true on the individual level exactly as it is on the international level. It is, therefore, not only to be a tyro in these matters and to be naïve and uninstructed and illiterate in the knowledge of history, to assume that appearances are what they are: it is also profoundly dangerous. In other words, we come back to this: before there can be unity amongst men, there must be a radical change in them. There must be a change in their very constitutions. What need to be changed in every one of us by nature are our fundamental prejudices; not what we do on the surface for the sake of negotiation or for appearances, but what we really are, what we really believe in the depths. Until that is put right it is idle and a sheer waste of time to speak about unity.

What then is it that the gospel does in order to produce this true unity? How have these Jews and Gentiles come together? *Why are all who are truly Christian of necessity one?* Here are some of the answers.

We are all sinners, and nothing but the gospel brings people to see that. We are all sinners, every one of us. I will go further, *we are all equally sinners.* What determines whether you are a sinner or not is not the sum total of sins you have committed, it is your total attitude towards God. It is here we see how futile all superficial divisions and distinctions are. That was what had kept the Jew and the Gentile apart. The Jew said, We are the people of God and we have the Scriptures, the Oracles of God, and we have the law, and we have the ceremonial and the temple; these other people have none of these things. And they thought that that put them right, that it made a vital difference. But the whole purpose of the preaching of the gospel, says Paul, is to show the Jew that he is as much a sinner as is the Gentile. 'There is none righteous, no not one.' 'All have sinned and have come short of the glory of God.' The whole world has 'become guilty before God'. You see, at that point, how entirely superficial, and what a waste of time it is to indulge in our divisions between very bad people, bad people, good people, very good people, noble people. Those are our classifications, are they not? We call one man a sinner, an outsider; and judge another to be very respectable, very nice and very good. And we really attach significance to these divisions and distinctions. The moment you come to the gospel it is all demolished and becomes completely irrelevant. The test, after all, is not what we are among ourselves and according to our measures and standards. Every one of us has got to come before God. And face to face with God we are all sinful and we are all vile. We do not know Him. We have not served Him as we ought. We have broken His laws. Each one has gone his own way. 'All we like sheep have gone astray.'

We understand this perfectly well in the natural realm. But we somehow seem to fail to apply it in the realm of the spiritual. We have our standards for measuring light and the power of light, and so on. We talk about voltage and wattage, and things like that, and there are divisions and distinctions—shall I put on a 150 watt lamp or shall I put on a mere 15? What a difference! The difference seems to be most important. But bring the two, the 15 and the 150, and put them before the sun, and your differences do not matter at all. It does not matter whether you have a taper or a candle or a very powerful light, in the light of the sun they are all darkness, as it were, and the differences are irrelevant and do not count at all. It is like that in the spiritual realm. We are all face to face with God. And when I stand in the presence of God and His holiness and His law, it does not help me if I happen to think that I am perhaps a little less bad than somebody else; the question is, Am I good enough for Him? Am I good enough there? And what this gospel has done is to show men God, and themselves in the light of God; and they are all condemned, they are all under a common denominator. There is neither Jew nor Gentile, Barbarian, Scythian, bond nor free, wealthy nor poor, educated nor ignorant. All these things are irrelevant—black or white, this side or that side of a particular curtain. It does not matter, all have sinned. That is the first step to unity. Before there can be unity we must all be brought down to the dust. While any one of us is standing on his feet, as it were, and asserting himself, you will never get unity, because he is boasting of something, he is holding on to something that is peculiar to him. You will never get unity in that way; we must come to an end of self. But here, facing God in the gospel, we are brought to the dust, we are forced to see our utter sinfulness, and one by one we see exactly where we are in His presence.

This first answer leads inevitably to the second. Not only are we all equally sinful, but *we are all equally helpless*. Now that was the difficulty with the Jew; he did not realise his helplessness. He thought that his knowledge of the law somehow or other was going to save him. But he came to see that it could not. As the apostle puts it in the third chapter of Romans, 'By the law is the knowledge of sin'. Certainly! Very valuable in that respect! 'I had not know sin,' says Paul, 'except the law had said, Thou shalt not covet.' It pinpoints the thing. The law is of inestimable value in that respect. But the foolish Jew thought that his mere knowledge of the law somehow saved him. But it did not and could not. The law simply condemns: it does not help to save. This is vital to the whole argument of this apostle, and to the whole argument of the gospel everywhere. Listen to him saying it again in Romans 8: 3: 'For what the law *could not do*, in that it was weak through the flesh, God, sending his own Son in the likeness of sinful flesh and for sin, condemned sin in the flesh, that the righteousness of the law might be fulfilled in us, who walk not after the flesh but after the Spirit'. There it is, once and for ever. We are all not only sinners together, but we are all equally helpless in our sin. We may try with a great resolve or with tremendous will power to be better, but it avails us nothing. There are people who may lead a very select, abstemious and noble kind of life; they may give themselves to perfecting themselves and to raising themselves in the moral scale; but how futile it all is, for the task is to arrive at God! It is idle to boast about the respective horsepowers of your motor cars when you are confronted by a mountain that the most powerful car can never climb. And that is the position of man in sin. It does not matter how great a man's moral striving may be, in and of himself he can never bring himself to satisfy God and His demands. No man can stand in the judgment simply in his own righteousness and by his own efforts: when we realise this, we all must say,

> *Not the labours of my hands*
> *Can fulfil Thy law's demands;*
> *Could my zeal no respite know,*
> *Could my tears for ever flow,*
> *All for sin could not atone.* . . .

We are all one in our helplessness, in our weakness, in our hopelessness, in our ineffectiveness; we are all together in the dust. It is realisation of this that brings unity. Before, on his feet, one says, I am better than you are, I have gone further than you have gone. Lying helpless in the dust we realise that we have nothing to boast of, we have nothing to talk about. We are all silenced together. The competition is abolished. Negatively, we are all in the same position.

And that, of course, leads to the other thing that the apostle has been emphasising. *We have all come to the one and the same Saviour.* How he delights to repeat the name! 'But now in Christ Jesus, ye who sometimes were far off are made nigh by the blood of Christ'— you see how he repeats it at once! 'For *he* is our peace, who hath made both one'; '*He* has abolished in *his* flesh the enmity, even the law of commandments'; 'for to make in *himself* of twain one new man'; 'and that *he* might reconcile both unto God in one body by the cross'; 'and *he* came and preached peace'; 'for through *Him* we both have access'. It is always this blessed Person. Here we are beginning to look at it positively. We are all in the dust and in our ashes and rags together. Then we lift up our eyes and look together at the same blessed Person. I am not interested in a World Congress of Faiths. I cannot kneel down together with, and look up with people, one of whom is looking at Confucius and another at Mohammed and another at the Buddha, and another at some philosopher. I cannot! There is only One to look at, it is this blessed Son of God. And I have no sense of unity and no fellowship with any man who is not looking together with me at the same Saviour. 'There is one God and one mediator (and one mediator only) between God and men, the man Christ Jesus' (1 Timothy 2: 5). There is no unity apart from this. We are together in failure and hopelessness, and now we are looking together at the same blessed Person. And if we are not, what is the value of talking about unity? What is the value of talking about having things in common and claiming that we are all one, if there is any question about Him, as to whether He is Son of God or only man? If there is any doubt about it there is no unity, there is no fellowship. We must confess together that there is only one Saviour, one only Lord Jesus Christ, God and Man, two natures in one person, born of the Virgin Mary, crucified under Pontius Pilate, risen again. There must be no question about Him! There is no unity unless we are agreed about Him! The same Saviour, the same Person!

And then *we have the same salvation*! We must particularise, you see. It is not enough to say, Oh yes, I believe in Christ and I am one with all who believe in Christ. But what does believing in Christ mean? Well, you notice how the apostle puts it. He says that 'ye were at that time, without Christ, being aliens from the commonwealth of Israel, and strangers from the covenants of promise, having no hope, and without God in the world: but now in Christ Jesus ye who sometimes were far off are made nigh *by the blood of Christ*'. It is the only way. And I am not nigh to any man unless he has been brought nigh by the blood of Christ. I have no fellowship and no union with a man who does not like the theology of *blood*. He can tell me, if he likes, that he believes in Christ, but I know no Christ except the Christ who had to die for me and for my sins on the cross. I have no access to the Father except by 'the blood of Jesus'. A man who can bypass the cross is a man with whom I am not in fellowship, I care not what he calls himself. There is no unity except among those who belong to the blood-bought company, who share the same salvation in which the cross is inevitable, essential and central. 'There was no other good enough to pay the price of sin.' God, says Paul again in the third of Romans, must be just, when He acts as the justifier of the one who believes in Jesus. I cannot believe in a God who can wink at sin and pretend He has not seen it. God is 'holy and just and righteous' He has said that He will punish sin, and He must; and I believe He has done so in Christ there on that cross. It is that same Christ of the cross, who literally rose in the body from the grave and ascended to heaven for my justification. I am only one with those who are clothed with the same robe of righteousness, which is Christ's righteousness. There is no unity when people have these different clothings—one with his moral righteousness, another with the righteousness of some philosophy, and another with the righteousness of Christ. We are one with none but those who 'have washed their robes in the blood of the Lamb' and who are clothed immaculate with the righteousness of the Son of God. That is the argument; not only here, it is the argument everywhere. We share a 'common salvation'. That is the word that is used, you remember, in the Epistle of Jude.

All these things are common to all Christians. Furthermore, *we have the same Holy Spirit* dwelling within us and living within us, working within us, and doing exactly the same work in us. The apostle has already mentioned Him. It is by 'one Spirit' we have this access of ours unto the Father. 'Work out your own salvation with fear and trembling, for it is God that worketh in you'—the same God, the same Holy Spirit. How organic is unity! How different all this is from saying superficially, Let us all come together. There is a common enemy so let us all forget our differences! We need to be changed radically. It is our natures that cause the divisions, and anything that does not deal with our natures cannot possibly solve the problem. And all this is necessary to change our natures—the Holy Spirit must come. And He has come, the same Holy Spirit in us all, and producing in us—and this is perhaps in many ways the most wonderful thing of all—the same new nature. 'If any man be in Christ he is a new creature (a new creation), old things are passed away, behold all things are become new.' The Christian is not a man who has improved himself, or who has learned to control himself in a measure, and in the language of Scripture has 'cleaned the outside of the cup and the platter.' Not at all! He is a new man. He has been made a 'partaker of the divine nature'. And the divine nature is one of love.

How can you get unity unless there is love? But the Holy Spirit produces this new man, this new nature. This 'fruit of the Spirit' is found in all Christians, so you have inevitable unity. All Christians are born of the Spirit, born of the same Spirit. 'Ye must be born again', said Christ to Nicodemus. 'That which is born of the flesh is flesh, and that which is born of the Spirit is spirit.' This is absolutely essential. Men can never be one unless they all have this same common nature. In Christ we have it. He has made in Himself 'of twain one new man, so making peace.' This new humanity of His! And so, with this new nature, this new fundamental disposition within us, we who are Christian have the same interests, are concerned about the same things, and have the same desires. So that when we meet one another, at once we find that we have this community of interest and desire. It is not difficult to find something to talk about when you meet a Christian. You know him at once. You are talking about the same things, these spiritual matters; no longer talking about the world and its gaudy, superficial nothings; but about eternal interests, the soul, and God, and Christ, and salvation, and the rebirth, and all these things. Christians meet together and they talk together. That is how they are described in the Old Testament and in the New. These people know one another, they are drawn to one another, they understand one another; they do not need elaborate introductions, they at once get on to these common topics, and they are animated by the same desires and share the same hopes. How inevitable unity is amongst Christians!

Then that brings us to this, that *we have the same Father.* 'For through him (or by him), we both have access by one Spirit, unto the Father.' We belong to one another because we belong to God. We are children of the same Father. Now members of a family may disagree and quarrel at times, but there is a fundamental unity at the back of it all. That is the difference between true unity amongst Christians and this artificially produced unity which the world, and the Church, alas, talk so much about at the present time. You may look at members of a family and say, They seem to hate one another, look at them quarrelling. But if you try to get in between them you will soon find that they are one, for there is a blood unity. They belong to the same family, the same father. They have a right, as it were, a freedom to disagree, but there is always this basic unity. But in those other people, who seem to be so much at one on the surface, beneath, and in the heart, there is nothing solid, and the appearance of unity collapses in the hour of greatest need. As true Christians we have one Father. We are children of the same heavenly King. And, therefore, we have the same essential family interests.

Not only is the above true of us all as Christians, but *we even have the same trials.* We have the same temptations. We have the same problems. This sometimes makes one realise the unity more than anything else. When you think you are alone in your troubles and trials and tribulations, and you come to the house of God, as the man in the seventy-third Psalm did, you realise at once, 'Well, at any rate, I am not alone in this'. You meet somebody else and he begins to tell you of how he has been having an awful time. And when you ask him what has been happening to him he tells you the very thing that has been happening to you the same week. Because we are spiritual, because we have this new nature, we have the same enemies—the world, the flesh, and the devil—and they attack us all in the same way. So we understand, we bear one another's burdens, we sympathise with one another. 'There hath no temptation taken you but such as is common to man.' That is what Paul says to the Corinthians (1 Corinthians 10: 13). We are all sharing in the same battle, the same fight 'against the principalities and powers, against the rulers of the darkness of this world, against spiritual wickedness in high places'. But, thank God, in the fight we experience the same grace, the same deliverance, the same Saviour, the same Guide and Mentor and Friend.

And finally, *we are all marching and going together to the same eternal home.* As Christians we realise, as nobody else can realise, that this is but a passing world, this life is but a preparatory school. This is not our home; we are marching to heaven, to glory. We have the same hope set before us. There may be differences here—differences of nationality, differences of gifts. We may differ in appearance, and in a thousand and one ways—yes, but we are all going to the same place, to the same eternity and the same glory, the same God, the same heaven. We have our eye on the same 'recompense of the reward'.

Do you not now agree that my propositions at the beginning were justified? There is no such thing as unity except in people of whom these things are true. No other unity, so-cal'ed, is of any value. But at the same time we must add that anything which is allowed to divide people of whom these things are true, is sinful. So that for myself I care not what a man's label is; the people whom I really know, and in whom I am interested, are the people of whom these things are true. I am not interested in their country, in their colour, in their gifts, abilities, possessions, or any label that the world of men may attach to them. If a man tells me that he knows that he is a hopeless, vile, condemned, damned sinner, and that he relies only on the fact that the Lord Jesus Christ died for his sins, that His body was broken and His blood shed for his sins, that he trusts only to that atoning, reconciling work of Christ, that Christ was his Substitute, and that God in Christ by the Spirit has made a new man of him and given him a new nature, I am one with such a man. I belong to him and he belongs to me, and I will not allow anything finally to separate us. And it seems to me to be more and more sinful that we should allow anything to separate us. Is it right that such people should be dispersed amongst the various denominations as they are, and attached to people with whom they have nothing fundamentally in common but simply tradition? True unity is this unity of the Spirit, this unity of the new nature, this unity that is in Christ and Him crucified, the unity of His blood, the unity of the Lord Himself.

May God, in His infinite grace, give us ability to see these things. The unity of the Spirit is the only true bond of peace. Thank God, all who belong to Him, born of His Spirit, are His, and are one, in spite of their blindness and sinfulness and their failure to implement such a glorious truth!

26

NO MORE STRANGERS

*Now therefore ye are no more strangers and foreigners, but fellow citizens
with the saints, and of the household of God.*   Ephesians 2: 19

As we have been working our way through the various details of
the apostle's argument starting at verse 11, we have seen that the
apostle has been emphasising two things. The first is the greatness
of the change that must of necessity take place in us before we can
become Christian at all. There is no greater change known to man
in any realm or department than the change that we all undergo
when we become Christians. It is a new creation, nothing less. The
second thing that obviously emerges is the privilege of our position as
Christians and as members of the Christian Church, or as members
of the body of Christ. The two things are there, you notice, right
the way through. The Ephesians were *that*, they have become *this*;
and they are now one with Jews as they have also become Christians,
and together they are one body, the Church, and are worshipping
the one Father.

We come now to the privilege of that position. That is the subject
the apostle takes up in this nineteenth verse, and which he works out
in the remainder of this chapter. He has ceased to think in terms of
Jews or Gentiles, or of any differences; he is now describing to us the
privilege of anyone who is a Christian, whether he was a Jew or a
Gentile before. The difference no longer matters, all that is finished
with—one new man! Here, he is looking at this new man, this new
humanity, this new thing that has come into being, the Christian
Church. And his concern is to show us what a wonderful thing it is.
He does so by employing *three pictures*. The first is the picture of a
state—Christians are fellow citizens in a great kingdom, a great
state. The second is, they are members together of a family—of 'the
household of God'. And thirdly he thinks of Christians and of the
Christian Church as a temple in which God Himself dwells.

That is the big theme here—*the privilege of being a Christian*. He
wants these Ephesians to realise it. It is a return to the theme of the
nineteenth verse of the first chapter and its context. The apostle told
these people there that he was praying for them, asking that the
eyes of their understanding might be enlightened 'that ye may know

what is the hope of his calling, and what the riches of the glory of his inheritance in the saints; and what is the exceeding greatness of his power to us-ward who believe'. That is what he wants them to see—the privilege of being a Christian. And that is what you and I need to take hold of more than anything else. All the exhortations in this Epistle, and in every other Epistle, addressed to Christian people, really come out of this doctrine. If we but realised exactly what we are, and who we are as Christians, most of the problems in our daily life and living would automatically be solved. It is because we do not realise this, and the privilege of our position, that the problems arise. If we did we would never envy people who are not Christians, we would never try to live as near to them as possible and sometimes almost feel sorry because we are not still in their position. All that is due to a failure to realise what we are. So the apostle puts it in this wonderful manner. Did you notice how, before he comes to his three positive pictures, he starts with a negative? People do not like negatives today; but the apostle Paul does. 'Now therefore'; is he going to say something positive? No, he is going to start with a negative. 'Now therefore ye are *no more* strangers and foreigners, but . . . .' Then he comes to the positive.

The apostle obviously felt constrained to bring in the negative again. In other words he goes back to the eleventh and twelfth verses, where he had said, 'Wherefore remember, that ye being in time past Gentiles in the flesh, who are called Uncircumcision by that which is called the Circumcision in the flesh made by hands; that at that time ye were without Christ, being aliens from the commonwealth of Israel, and strangers from the covenants of promise, having no hope, and without God in the world'. He just glances back at that once more, and therefore starts with this negative, 'Now therefore, ye are *no more* strangers and foreigners'. Why do you think he does this? It seems obvious to me that his reason for doing so must be that *it is no use our going on to consider the privileges of our position unless we are perfectly certain that we are in that position.* It is no use being told exactly what applies to a certain position if you are not in that position. So it is essential that we should make quite plain and clear to ourselves that all this really does apply to us. Before I begin to look at my citizenship, or my membership of that family, or myself as a stone in that building, that temple, I must ask myself: Am I there? Is this all applicable to me?

In the case of the Ephesians there was no doubt or question whatsoever about this matter. The apostle says, Now therefore you are no more that, but you are this. It was clear, it was obvious, patent to everybody. These people, when pagans, had lived a certain type of life. The Jews on the other hand had lived a different type of life and followed a very different pattern of worship. Now no one could turn from paganism to Christianity and be in the Christian faith with converted Jews without having undergone a very great change. He had to leave certain practices and customs, he had to renounce certain gods whom he had worshipped before, and say that they were 'no-gods', and many other things. It was an obvious change. Paul said, 'You are no longer . . . , you are . . .' This is something which is always true in what one may call 'first generation Christians'. It was very true in the case of the early Church. It is still very true in connection with foreign mission work. Foreign missions go to places where the gospel has never been heard before. The gospel is preached to people who were in paganism and darkness. It is heard for the first time, and people believe it, and the change in them is obvious. First generation Christians! But it is not quite so simple when you come to the second generation Christians; and still more difficult when you come to the third, fourth, fifth—tenth—twentieth generation. So that whereas the thing was perfectly plain in the case of these Ephesians, it is not always quite so plain now. It is never as easy and as simple in a country which calls itself a Christian country, and where it is tacitly assumed by so many that everybody born in such a country must be a Christian. It is not so easy when people have been brought up in churches and in a Christian atmosphere, and have always gone to a place of worship and to Sunday School and joined in Christian activities. It is very important, therefore, that we should interpret this not only in the setting in which it was originally written but also in our own particular setting; for, as I shall try to show, the principle is exactly the same always; it is the application that differs. The apostle here was primarily concerned about the principle. He was not simply rejoicing in the fact that these Ephesians were members of a church as such, and that they had their names on a church roll. That is not what he is talking about. He is talking about the principle of life. He has been doing that all along in this highly spiritual paragraph. It comes to us, therefore, in this particular form of a question. It was obvious that these people had once been unbelievers but that they were now Christian. The question for us is, Is this as definite and as clear and as unmistakable in us as it was in the Ephesians?

The two words used by the apostle will help us to face this all-important subject. The first word, you notice, is the word 'stranger'. 'Now therefore, ye are no more strangers.' What is a stranger? *Strangers are those who find themselves among a people not their own.* When you are a stranger you are amongst people who are not your own people. They all belong to one another, but you are a stranger, you do not belong to them, they are not your people. The second word is the word translated in the Authorised Version as 'foreigners.' Sometimes you will find it translated 'sojourners.' Both terms are very good. What does this word mean? Originally it was a description of someone who dwelt near a community but not in it, for example, a man who lives just outside the city wall. He is near the city but he is not in it. He does not belong to the city; living nearby but not in. That was the original meaning, but now it comes to mean those who find themselves in a place which is not their own country. The first term 'stranger' conjures up more the idea of the family unit, of a kind of blood relationship, whereas this other word 'foreigner', or 'sojourner', compels us inevitably to think more in terms of a polity, a state, a country, or a kingdom. A foreigner is a man who find himself in a place which is not his own country. It means that though this man is living in the country he does not possess the citizenship of that country, he is not naturalised, he has not the right of permanent residence in that country. Or, to put it still more simply, he is a man who is living on a passport. Now these are the two words the apostle uses: strangers and foreigners, sojourners, people living there maybe for a long time, but still they are always sojourners, they are still foreigners. The other place is their home; they are living here on a passport and they have to renew it periodically. Now that is the picture the apostle sets before our minds. And you notice that when he comes to the positive he just reverses this; he starts with the citizenship and then he goes on to the family relationship. But we are concerned at the moment primarily with the negative.

Notice what a subtle matter this is. We have all often seen it in practice. There may be someone living in the family, someone who has lived in the family for years, and is almost one of the family, and yet not one of the family. Though this person may be sharing in the life of the family in almost every conceivable manner, still he or she actually does not belong to the family. And that is where the difficulty comes in. A stranger, a visitor might well think and say, This person is obviously one of the family. And yet, having known them for a while he would discover that that was not the case. It is exactly the same with a country. There may be people living in a country, resident for many years, and somebody coming on a visit to the country, looking at them would take it for granted that any one of them was actually one of that country, just a typical citizen— doing the same sort of thing as others, going to business in the morning, returning at night on the same train, following exactly the same routine. And yet actually that person does not belong to that country, is not a citizen, but is just living on a passport.

There we see in a picture the idea we have to get hold of in our minds. That sort of thing obtains in the Church of God; this very position, of living with a family but not belonging to it, being in a country and yet not being a citizen. It is possible to be in a company and yet not be of the company. You will remember that when the children of Israel went up from Egypt to Canaan, we are told, in a most extraordinary phrase, that 'a mixed multitude went up with them'. They went with them, they shared the same hazards, the same problems and difficulties as the children of Israel, but they did not belong to them. They were 'a mixed multitude'. But indeed the apostle Paul takes that further, in the Epistle to the Romans, when he says, 'They are not all Israel which are of Israel' (Romans 9: 6). What a phrase! You look at them as a mass and you say, They are all of Israel. But that does not follow of necessity. There is an Israel and an 'Israel'. There is an 'Israel' of the spirit, as well as the Israel of the flesh. There is a remnant in the mass. That is the apostolic teaching, and in these New Testament Epistles it is a most vital and important doctrine. You can be of a company and yet really not belong to it. The apostle John says the same thing about certain people who had gone out of the early Christian Church: 'They went out from us', says John, 'but they were not of us; for if they had been of us they would no doubt have continued with us' (1 John 2: 19). They had been among them, but they were not of them. They had been in the Church and they seemed to be Christians but they had never really belonged.

That is the kind of matter that is raised here for us. Let us consider it by putting it in the form of a number of principles. The first is that *the difference between the Christian and the non-Christian is clear and definite.* In spite of all I have been saying, the principle remains that there is a clear distinction between a Christian and a non-Christian. Paul puts it like this: 'You are—no more.' There is a change, a change over. Obviously there had been a change externally, but he is not concerned about the external, but about the internal. And therefore there need be no hesitation in asserting that every one of us at this moment is either a Christian or else not a Christian. We are either 'in Christ', or else we are 'outside Christ'. Aristotle once laid down as a proposition, and it is undoubtedly true, 'There is no mean between two opposites'. Opposites are opposites, and there is nothing in the middle, there is no mean between them. It is 'either—or'. In the seventh chapter of Matthew's Gospel, our blessed Lord and Saviour emphasises exactly this point. You cannot be on the narrow way and the broad way at the same time. You cannot be going through two gates at the same moment. You cannot be passing

through a turnstile and going through a wide gate at the same
moment. It is impossible. Now that is the thing that starts off the
difference between the Christian and the non-Christian. The
Christian goes in at a strait gate, he walks on a narrow way. The
other does the exact opposite. It has to be one thing or the other.
That is our Lord's statement. You notice how He goes on repeating
it—true prophet, false prophet; good tree, bad tree; good fruit, bad
fruit; and finally in that tremendous picture of the house on the rock
and the house on the sand. It is always one or the other; it is,
either—or. You are Christian or you are not Christian. And these
things are absolutes. You are no longer strangers and foreigners: you
are Christians, in the body.

The Christian position is not a vague one, it is not indefinite, it
is not uncertain. Of course, if you think of it mainly in terms of
superficial conduct and behaviour, then it may very well be vague.
I can easily draw a picture and show you two men. One is a man
who is highly moral, never does anybody any harm, his word is his
bond, he is honest and just and upright, a thoroughly good man in
every sense of the word. But look now at the other man. You cannot
say, looking at them generally, that the second man is as good as the
first man. He does things that he should not do at times, and he is not
such a lovable character perhaps. And yet it may be the case that
the second man is a Christian and the first man is not. For what
determines whether a man is a Christian or not is not his general
appearance and behaviour. That foreigner living in this land looks
exactly like an Englishman, he does the same things, and so on; but
the fact is that he is still a foreigner. The fact that he looks like the
other man does not mean that he is like him. The question is, is he
living on a passport or has he a citizenship? You see, the test is not
just the general, superficial appearance. This is the very thing the
New Testament is always emphasising. This is really a fundamental
point. Do we agree that either we are definitely Christian, or else
we are not? And that there is no such thing as an intermediate
position where one is hoping to be or trying to be a Christian? If you
are simply hoping or trying to be a Christian you are not one. To be
on the doorstep is not to be inside, and it does not help you to be
on the doorstep when the vital question is, Are you inside or not
inside? How often is this depicted in the Scriptures! Our Lord draws
His picture of people coming and hammering at the door and
saying 'Open unto us'; but the reply comes from the inside, No, you
are outside, you do not belong. We are either Christian, or we are
not Christian.

So the second point I would make, my second principle, would be this, to stress *the vital importance of knowing which we are*. Now here again Paul's illustration helps us. How does it become clear and obvious whether we are strangers and foreigners (sojourners), or whether we really belong? Eventually it always becomes clear. It does not matter how intimate a relationship may be, however friendly you may be with someone who is living with you in the family. We have a saying that puts it all in a nutshell—After all, blood is thicker than water. Certain points arise in life when actually the one thing that matters is the blood relationship. And it is at that point that the poor stranger begins to feel that he is only a stranger after all. He may have felt for years that the distinctions were irrelevant and may have said: I am one of them, I am a member of the family and have always been treated as a member of the family. But suddenly, in a crisis, he discovers that he is not. 'Blood is thicker than water.' You cannot explain these things; you may even say that there is a great deal that is wrong about such a situation. That may well be, but that is how it works out in practice. Something fundamental, elemental, suddenly comes to the surface; and you will find a whole family that may have been at sixes and sevens suddenly becoming one. And the poor stranger is conscious that he is an outsider.

Or take the other illustration which puts it perhaps still more clearly. Take a person who is a sojourner, a foreigner, in another land. He may have lived there twenty or thirty or forty years, and enjoyed living there, liked by all and happy. All distinctions seem irrelevant. What does it matter that he has a passport and that he had not a true citizenship and that he has to go and have it renewed and checked and so on? What does it matter, you say, he is quite one of us by now! But stay! Suddenly and unexpectedly the country to which that man belongs and this country in which he is living have a dispute; and the dispute cannot be settled, and war is declared. And this man who may have lived in the country for forty years suddenly realises that he is a foreigner, and that everybody looks at him with suspicion. He may be interned or sent back to his own country. He appeared to be a member of the company, a citizen of the country, and one with the true citizens; but when a crisis, a test, a trial comes, at once it is plain that he is a foreigner after all. We saw a great deal of that sort of thing in this country in 1914 and 1939. Sometimes it is almost tragic, but it happens.

We turn again, then, to the principle that you find running right through the Scriptures. Why is it important to know whether you are a Christian or not? I will tell you. It is at the time of testing that this thing becomes of vital importance to you. It is in the tests and the trials of life that this thing comes out. You go on for years while

you are well and hale and hearty. You are in the Church, you seem
to be of the Church, your interest is there and you are one with the
company. But suddenly you are taken ill and you find yourself for
months on a sick bed. It will not be long before you know whether
you are a Christian or not. It makes a vital difference then. Or when
there is an illness in a member of the family, when there is a bereave-
ment or a death, some terrible heart-rending sorrow. Oh, it is then
that it becomes all-important. If you are simply 'living on the
passport' it does not seem to help you. But if you really belong it
makes all the difference in the world. But let us take it on to the
ultimate. Our Lord Himself does this. Is not that the whole point
of the concluding section in the seventh chapter of Matthew? These
people who seem to be Christian and who say, 'Lord, Lord, have we
not prophesied in thy name . . . and in thy name done many
wonderful works?'—they were in the Church, they were active in the
Church, they were Church people. But He says, 'I will profess unto
them, I never knew you: depart from me, ye that work iniquity'.
A stranger after all, a foreigner in the last analysis; passport handed
back, shipped abroad, sent out of the country! Oh, the vital
importance of making absolutely certain whether we are still
'strangers and foreigners' or whether we really belong!

   To be practical let me put my third principle as a question. *How
may we know this? How can we settle this question? What are the tests?*
I am going to suggest some very simple answers, based upon the
illustration used by the apostle.
   I start with the most superficial thing of all. It is this: a general
feeling. I am not testing you, you are testing yourselves. You want
to know whether you are a stranger and a foreigner, or not? Well,
answer this question. Do you feel really at ease in the Church?
Are you quite at ease amongst Christian people? Do you feel quite at
home? Or have you got an uncomfortable feeling that you are
somehow an outsider? That is what happens when you go to stay
with a family, is it not? They are very nice and friendly, but you
feel that you do not belong, you are not quite at ease, you are
conscious of the fact that you are not in your own home, you cannot
relax. You are a stranger, after all, though it is all very kind and
affable and friendly. Are you at home in God's house? Are you at
home among God's people? Are you at ease? Or do you feel, in
spite of everything, that you are just an odd man out, a bit of an
outsider, that you do not really fit in? Or let me put it like this.
Are you as much at ease among God's people as you are in other
circles and in other types of company? With the other company—
the laughter and the joking, the fun, and perhaps the drinking and

the gambling, are you free with them, and have you much to say? Are you one of them? Is it like that? Are you conscious of being just a little bit out of your element in the church? This is tremendously important. When you put it in terms of a family you see how inevitable it is. It is one of these imponderables, as we call them, a thing you can scarcely put into writing or on paper, but you just know it. That is how I feel, you say; and your feeling is right.

Or take another approach. *Is there a real and a living interest?* When you belong to a company you are active in your interest, you are alive in your interest. More than that, you really delight in it, your heart is in it, it is what you love, it is where you like to be. You like to be at home, you like to be in your own country; you may admire others, but after all it is home. Now the same thing applies to this relationship. A man who truly belongs delights in it. It is not a matter of effort to him. It is not a mere matter of duty. It is something in which he enjoys himself and which he prizes above everything else. Let me summarise this whole section by putting it in the words of the First Epistle of John: 'We know that we have passed from death unto life, because we love the brethren'. We feel we belong to them. There are some of them we do not like, perhaps, but we love them, because they are brethren. We may like other people more than we like these, but it is not a question of liking, it is one of loving. Sometimes it happens that a member of a family likes a friend much more than a brother or a sister; that does not affect the relationship, this elemental, fundamental, organic thing that is deeper than everything else. 'We know that we have passed from death to life because we love the brethren'. General feeling!

Come to a second test. Understanding! When you are staying with a family this question of understanding becomes tremendously important; and it is the same when you are a foreigner in another land. I mean this. *Do you know and understand what is being talked about?* Is there anything which makes you feel more uncomfortable than to have the feeling that, though you are seated with the company, somehow or other you are outside the conversation and do not enter into what they are talking about? They all seem to understand one another, they use certain phrases, they look at one another in a significant way, they are all in it, it is a sort of free-masonry, as it were; but you, somehow, you are not in it. You are listening, you are part of the company, you are in the conversation, but you are not able to enter into it and to enjoy it. So I would put questions like this. Do you understand the language of God's people? The family has its own language. People say: I cannot stand this talk about justification, sanctification and all these terms—do you feel like that? God forbid that you should! They are precious terms to the children of God. *They* are not impatient with them. They are like a little child listening to grown-up people. It suddenly brings out a big word which it does not understand. What is the child doing? It is trying to prove that it is a member of the company. It is using a word that the father used. And the children of God are like that. They may not know what justification and sanctification mean, but because they are children they want to know, and they begin to read and study and ask questions. But if you are impatient with it all, you are just proclaiming that you are an outsider, and that you do not understand the language. Is the language of Zion sweet to you? Imagine the case of a man who has been away in another land and has had to speak a foreign language; he comes back on the boat, and even before he has got off the ship he hears his native tongue again, and oh, how he rejoices! So it is with the Christian!

But it is not only the question of language, there is something more. Do you know anything about the subjects they are discussing? Do you understand them, are you interested in the questions? Again let me use my illustration. We have all had this kind of experience. We are staying with a family perhaps. They are all so nice and kind and affable, and we are engaged in conversation. Then, suddenly, somebody comes in, and you can tell by looking at his face that something has happened which is of great concern to the family. And they all feel awkward, they want to talk about this together; but you are there and they cannot do so. So they talk in hints and suggestions and in an indirect round-about manner. You do not know what they are talking about. They behave like· that because you are a stranger—they like you, they are not insulting you, but you do not understand. There are these intimate problems and questions which they cannot share with you, though they like you very much, because you do not belong to the family. It is the same with a country. And it is like that in the Christian life. Are the questions and the subjects and the problems of the Christian life known to you? Are you interested in them? Or when you sit and listen to people talking about them, or perhaps as you listen to someone trying to preach, do you say to yourself: What is all this about? I do not understand it. Now if he were talking about the visit of some foreign statesman, or talking about some new measure introduced into parliament, of course, I would understand; but these other things—what is it all about, what is it? It is so boring. That is the sort of way in which you discover whether you are of the family or not.

Let me put it finally in a way which, I suppose, is one of the best ultimate tests. *Are you in on the secrets?* There are family secrets, there

are national secrets. Are you in on the secrets? It is possible for a
man to be interested in religion, to be interested in theology, to be
interested in philosophy; and as long as we are dealing with abstract
theoretical questions he appears to be right in, and one of the
family. But suddenly you begin to talk spiritually—I mean by that,
you begin to talk experimentally, you begin to talk about your own
soul and your own experience—and immediately the man who has
been so interested theoretically feels he is outside. Do you know
anything about that? I heard the other day of a man who was in
a certain theological seminary. He went there because he knew that
they taught the great doctrines of the faith and he was enjoying it
to his heart's content. But he was suddenly confronted by a problem,
and he wanted to talk to somebody about his soul, and to talk in
the depths about some secret. But he could not find any help. They
did not seem to understand, they did not want to talk about such
matters. As long as it was a question of arguing about philosophy—
marvellous! Interested in theology—yes, certainly! But when the
man had a soul need and wanted something experimental, he
suddenly began to feel he was living on an iceberg. Thoroughly
orthodox—but cold! It is possible to have a general interest, but
not this intimate, personal interest in the secrets of the life. That is
a vital test.

Other tests I would suggest would be these. *Are you conforming in
general to the laws and the customs of the country?* The apostle John says
that, to the Christian, God's commands 'are not grievous' (1 John
5: 3). They are grievous to everybody else, but not to the Christian.
The Christian says, 'How I love thy law!' David could say that in
the Psalm, and the Christian says it. We proclaim where we are
and what we are, by the way in which we live. You go from this
country, say, to France or to some other part of the Continent in
your car, and you start driving on the left side of the road, and in
two seconds you will know you are a foreigner. Exactly! And are
there not many people who are driving on the wrong side of the
road within the Church? They do not know it, perhaps, but they
are proclaiming that they are foreigners and strangers, they are
driving on the wrong side of the road. They do not know and honour
the laws and the commandments of the kingdom. They are not
behaving in a manner that is consonant and consistent with the
customs and the habits of this particular family and country.
Strangers and foreigners, though living in the company! Another
vital test is concern for the state and condition of the family or
country, and its well-being. This arises instinctively.

Finally, it comes to this. I have started on the superficial level and
have gone down deeper. There is a final proof. *Which have you got,*

a passport or a birth certificate? That is absolute proof, is it not? That is beyond feeling, interest, understanding and all these things. In the last analysis it is a legal question. Have you got a birth certificate or are you simply living on a passport? You ask, What is the Christian's birth certificate? I will tell you. It is above and beyond everything I have been saying. 'The Spirit himself beareth witness with our spirit that we are the children of God' (Romans 8: 16). It is 'the sealing of the Spirit' (Ephesians 1: 13). It is the assurance that can only be given by the Holy Spirit Himself, who has sealed us, and who is 'the earnest of our inheritance until the redemption of the purchased possession' (Ephesians 1: 14). Do not misunderstand me. You may be a Christian though you have no definite knowledge of the sealing of the Spirit. If you have passed my other tests, I would assure you that you are a Christian. But I exhort and urge you, do not be content with that. Insist upon having your certificate! Go to the heavenly Somerset House until you find it! Let nothing stop you. Seek it of the Lord. Apply to Him. I use Thomas Goodwin's term again, 'sue' Him for it until you have got it. And then you will know and you will be able to say: I am no more a stranger or a foreigner, I am a fellow citizen with the saints, I am of the household of God; I am a stone in the temple which God Himself inhabits.

27

HEAVENLY CITIZENSHIP

Now therefore ye are no more strangers and foreigners, but fellowcitizens
with the saints, and of the household of God.   Ephesians 2: 19

The apostle in these words puts before us the glories and privileges
and advantages of membership of the Christian Church. That has
been his theme, indeed, right through the chapter. He has been
concerned earlier to deal with the mechanism, or the way in which
it has been made possible for both Jews and Gentiles, and now he
contemplates the thing itself, and is anxious that these Ephesians
should enjoy it with him and should come to understand it and
realise what it means. He knows, and has told them in the first
chapter, that this is only possible as long as 'the eyes of their under-
understanding are enlightened'. It is quite impossible apart from
that. The Church is but an institution to people whose eyes are
not enlightened by the Holy Spirit. They may like it as an institution,
they may glory in it as an institution, but that is not what the
apostle would have these people see. He prays that the eyes of their
understanding may be enlightened that they may know 'what is the
hope of his calling, the riches of the glory of his inheritance in the
saints, the exceeding greatness of his power to us-ward that believe'
(1: 18). We have already begun our consideration of this verse by
showing how the apostle stresses the vital importance of our being
absolutely certain that we are in the position described in this verse.
We cannot hope to realise the privileges of the position unless we
know what the position is, and unless we are quite sure that we are
in it. We saw the importance of knowing for certain that we are
no more strangers and foreigners, of knowing, as I ventured to put
it, that we no longer live on a passport but that we really have our
birth certificates, that we really do belong. If we only realised what
it is to be a Christian and a member of the Christian Church, I
suggest that most of our problems, if not all of them, would be
immediately solved. If we could but rise to the height of our high
calling in Christ Jesus and realise what we possess in this position,
the little pinpricks and problems would become unthinkable; they
would fall off, they would be unworthy of consideration. Now that
in a sense is the argument of every New Testament Epistle. All the

Epistles are written to churches, to members of Christian churches, and what every one of them does is precisely what I have been saying. They all start by giving us a picture of our position as members of the Christian Church, and then, having done that, they say, Well now, in the light of that, this is obviously how you have to live. That is the analysis of every New Testament Epistle.

There is surely nothing more important today, therefore, from every standpoint, than for us to realise these things. It is important for us personally. Most of our trials and troubles, tribulations and problems would be viewed in an entirely different manner if we really saw ourselves as we are in Christ. And still more important, if the whole Church only realised what she is, we would already be on the high road to true revival and a mighty spiritual awakening. It is because we fail to realise these things that we do not pray for revival as we ought, and do not look for it and long for it. It is not surprising then that the apostle emphasises it so much. Here he puts it in the form of a number of pictures. We have three pictures presented together almost at once: the first, the Church as a great state or kingdom; yes, but it is also a family; yes, and it is also a temple. He has already given us one earlier picture where he compares the Church to a body, one body, one new man. And you will find that in the fifth chapter of this Epistle he uses yet another illustration, for there he says that the relationship between the Church and the Lord Jesus Christ is the relationship between a bride and a bridegroom. It is interesting to notice that the apostle thus uses a variety of pictures and illustrations; and it is important that we should be quite clear as to why he does so. Any one illustration is not enough. The truth is so great, so many-sided, so glorious, that he has to multiply his pictures and images. Each one of them conveys some particular aspect, and enables us to see some peculiar facet of truth which is not so well conveyed by the other illustrations and pictures.

We come now to *the first picture*. 'Ye are no more strangers and foreigners'! says the apostle. Well, what are we then? 'Fellow-citizens with the saints!' That is the first picture. What does this tell us? Very rich teaching! *He compares the Church here to a city, or a state, or a kingdom.* It is not surprising that the apostle should have done this. In those ancient times there were great state-cities, or city-states; certain cities were actual states in and of themselves. But over and above that, of course, there were great states, great kingdoms, great empires. The apostle at the time of writing this letter was probably a prisoner in Rome, the very metropolis and centre and nerve of the great Roman Empire. She was the capital city, and she had her peoples scattered abroad through the then civilised world, with governors and other important functionaries carrying out the behests and the orders of the central government and, ultimately, of the emperor. It is not surprising, therefore, that the apostle should have thought that the Christian Church is something like that. She is like a great state, a great empire, a great kingdom, and he uses the illustration to convey some very precious teaching to these Ephesians.

This is not a new idea that suddenly came to the apostle Paul. It is a most important conception that is found right through the Bible. There are great sections of the Scriptures which we simply cannot understand at all unless we grasp this particular idea. In the call of Abraham—which is one of the great turning points in history— God was taking the first steps in the formation of a nation for Himself. Until that point God dealt with the whole world, as it were. The first eleven chapters of the book of Genesis deal with the whole world and the history of the whole world and all its people. But at the beginning of chapter twelve in Genesis, in the call of Abraham, the record begins to deal especially and specifically with the history of one nation. There, at once, we are introduced to this whole idea that God's people are God's kingdom, God's nation— this whole conception of a state. In the nineteenth chapter of Exodus the same thing is repeated very clearly. God told Moses just before the giving of the Ten Commandments and the moral law, that the people were to realise that they were a 'holy nation', that they were 'God's citizens', that they belonged to Him, that He was their King, and they His people. That was to control the whole outlook of the children of Israel. Before God took them into the promised land He wanted them to realise this. The whole tragedy of Israel was that they failed to do so. They never realised just this very thing, that they were God's kingdom, a kingdom of priests, a holy nation unto God. And because of that failure all their tragedy descended upon them, and they cut the sorry figure that we see described in the Old Testament. But again, if you go to the Book of Daniel you will find this conception expounded in a most amazing manner. It is the great message of that book. Everywhere we read of kingdoms, fights between kingdoms and the relationship of this kingdom of God to those other kingdoms; the beasts that represent those other powers—Babylon, which already existed, Medo-Persia Greece, and Rome, which would later arise—and this kingdom. Indeed the message of all the prophets was an attempt to impress upon the children of Israel their peculiar relationship to God as citizens of His eternal kingdom. Then as you come to the New Testament you find this is a central theme in the teaching of our

Lord and Saviour Jesus Christ. Look at His parables of the kingdom. He always thought in terms of the kingdom. He said He had come to establish a kingdom. He said He was a King—He was crucified for saying that, in a sense, on the purely secular level. All His teaching is about the kingdom, and people entering into His kingdom. He starts by saying it to such a man as Nicodemus: 'Except a man be born again, he cannot see the kingdom of God'. It is integral to His whole message. The Sermon on the Mount has been well described as the manifesto of that kingdom. And it is found constantly in the writings of the apostle Paul. You find it likewise in the First Epistle of Peter. He quotes the very words of Exodus 19 and then adds, 'Which in time past were not a people, but are now the people of God' (1 Peter 2: 9-10). He applies that to all members of the Christian Church. And in the book of Revelation you find exactly the same thing. It is clear then that this is a vital doctrine in the Bible; and as Christian people it behoves us to study it and to grasp it, and to apply it to ourselves, that we may glory in it and rejoice in it as we are meant to do. What then is the teaching?

Let us look at it like this. What does this tell us about ourselves? What kind of definition of the Church does this give us? It is quite simple if you have a clear conception of a state or kingdom or city. The first thing it obviously emphasises is that *we are a people who are separated from, and made distinct from, all others*. Ancient cities all had a wall around them, the city wall. You can still see relics and remnants of these walls in various cities. There is still a part of this city of London called London Wall, and there are other cities such as Canterbury and Chester where you have the same thing. What was the purpose of the wall? Well, to separate the citizens. It shuts them in, it shuts others out. There were gates leading through the wall into the city; they were shut at a given hour and they were opened at another hour the next morning. The whole conception of the city, the polity, means separation, a drawing out of, a setting apart, a surrounding, and even an encasing.

Or if you do not think of it in terms of cities but prefer to think of it in terms of countries or of states, there is always a boundary to a state, a boundary to every country. It may be the sea, it may be a river or a range of mountains or it may be some artificially determined line which is drawn by authorities. It does not matter what it is, but there are always boundaries, and you cannot pass from one state to another without crossing the boundary. You have to pass through the customs and show your passport and have your goods examined because you are at the boundary! You cannot think of a state or a city or a kingdom without boundaries. And the business of boundaries is to say to certain people: So far but no further, and to say to those within the boundaries: This is your city, this is your country, this is the land to which you belong.

The importance of this doctrine should be self-evident. You cannot be a Christian without being a separated person. You cannot be in the kingdom of God and in the kingdom of 'the world' at the same time. There is this fundamental 'either—or,' whether we like it or not. This same apostle reminds the Galatians that God in the Lord Jesus Christ 'hath delivered us from this present evil world' (Galatians 1: 4). In writing to the Colossians he says, 'Who hath delivered us from the power of darkness and hath translated us into the kingdom of his dear Son.' (1: 13). What a tremendously important conception this is! If we are Christians we are separated people, we are no longer like everybody else. But someone may ask, But is not that being Pharisaical? Is not that being proud? Not at all! The Pharisee did separate himself, but it was the way in which he did it that was wrong; it was not the separation which was wrong, it was the spirit in which he did it. I am not advocating the better-than-thou attitude, but what I am saying is that as a citizen of the kingdom of heaven I am different from those who are not citizens of that kingdom. How ready we are to assert this on the national level—I am an Englishman, or whatever else it is. We are very careful to emphasise the distinction, that we are not something else. And yet when we come to the spiritual realm people object to it. That is narrow, they say, that is divisive. But let us be consistent, let us be logical, above all let us be scriptural. Whatever we may think about it, the fact is that as a Christian, as a member of the Church, you have been taken out of the world, you are separated. And unless you realise it and rejoice in it, surely there is very good reason for questioning whether you are Christian at all. It is basic, it is fundamental, it is one of the first things that should be obvious.

But let us go on to something else. The second thing that comes out of that, of necessity, is that the citizens are therefore *people who are bound together by a common allegiance to a ruler* and to authority and to law, and to a way of life. This is always true of a city, a state or a kingdom. Being thus separated, we are separated for certain specific objects and purposes. There was always a head of a city. He might be a king or he might be somebody appointed, but there was always a head. There is always a head to a state, there is always a king in a kingdom. There is no sense in talking about a kingdom unless you have a king. And the citizens of a kingdom are those who are bound together by a common allegiance to this state, to this king, to this supreme authority, president, or whatever he may be. As citizens we all acknowledge that together. There is this common bond, this common allegiance; we have these common interests together.

We see the importance of this when we apply the concept to the Church. We all acknowledge the same Head, the same King, eternal, everlasting. We have the same common interests. We recognise the same laws. And because of this, we have a common allegiance also to one another. As a direct consequence there are certain things that are peculiar to us which do not apply to other people. This is so elementary that I need not stress it. It is vital, of course, that we should realise that we are not simply speaking about the external, visible Church. The apostle in the whole context of this statement makes it plain and clear that he is thinking spiritually. Let us never lose sight of this fact. We are not simply talking about the Church as an organisation, a visible external organisation; the apostle's idea is spiritual, mystical and organic. It expresses itself externally, but the vital thing is this internal principle. For, alas, it is possible to be a member of the visible, external Church and yet to be ignorant of Christ, not to know Him, not to be truly, vitally related to Him. There have always been such people, there are still such people; they have been brought up in it, it is tradition, it is something that is part of the social and fashionable round but it is not living, it is not real. Their heart is in the world not in the Church. The greatest tragedy in a sense that has ever taken place in the history of the Church was when Christianity became the official religion of the Roman Empire, and that fatal association between Church and State began, which has befogged and confused the situation ever since. This idea of separation has been lost, and people have thought in terms of Christian countries, assuming that everybody in such a country must be a Christian. How utterly opposed to Paul's teaching! No, it is not merely the external. What Paul means is that as Christians we are citizens of Christ's kingdom. Where is Christ's kingdom? Christ's kingdom is wherever Christ reigns; therefore, Christ's kingdom can be in the heart of an individual. He reigns in the hearts of all who belong to Him and who have submitted themselves to Him. Christ's kingdom is on earth and in heaven, in His people. His kingdom is not of this world, it is invisible for the time being, but it is real. Christ's reign and rule and authority, wherever it is, is His kingdom. That is the thing about which the apostle is speaking. Christ is our Prophet, our Priest, our King, and all who recognise His rule, and who bow to Him in allegiance, are citizens of His eternal kingdom. The value and the importance of looking at it like this becomes evident when we realise that he tells us, that here and now we can be citizens of that kingdom which is to last for ever and ever. We enter it now, we shall continue in it through all eternity.

Let us look now at the third thing, which is: *the privileges of our citizenship of this glorious kingdom.* We are all interested in privileges, are we not! You know the sort of man who likes to boast that he has them and that he is 'well in' with the great. He can introduce you, he says. Privileges! How we want them, how we like to have them! The whole world is mad on privileges today. It is the result of sin. But if you are interested in privileges, listen to this. What are the privileges of this citizenship? The first and the greatest privilege is this—*our King*. People boast about their citizenship, about their countries, and about certain things in particular. They quote their history and talk about their great heroes; they put up monuments to them and write about them in books. They are proud of their association with them. But all that pales into insignificance when compared with our privileges as citizens of the kingdom of heaven. Above all else we glory in the fact that we have a King who is 'the King of kings, and the Lord of lords', the Son of God Himself—the King of heaven.

But let us go on to consider the sphere of this kingdom. And this is a most entrancing and wonderful theme. The sphere of all earthly kingdoms is on earth, and the centre, the capital, is always on earth. We belong to Great Britain, to a Commonwealth of nations, and we used to boast of the fact that her citizens were scattered throughout the earth, and that the sun never set on the British Empire. How extensive, how wonderful! And we have a capital city— London! And other nations have similar boasts. London—Paris— Washington! Capital cities! Extensive sway, a wide domain and dominion! The nations take great pride in that, and often their rivalries and jealousies have brought them into conflict. That shows their appreciation of the privilege, and their pride in the sphere and the extent of their kingdoms. But you remember how our blessed Lord defined and described His own kingdom in this respect. He said, 'My kingdom is not of this world'. He spoke of it as *the kingdom of heaven,* or 'the kingdom of the heavens'. And the apostle in writing to the Philippians says, 'Our conversation is in heaven'. (3: 20.) We are here on earth, but our citizenship is there. Somebody has translated it by the words, 'We are a colony of heaven'. Yes, we are on earth, but we are only a colony; our capital is not London, Paris or New York, but heaven itself.

What is the city to which you and I as Christians belong? According to the book of Revelation, it is the New Jerusalem that

is going to come down out of heaven and be established on earth—
the New Jerusalem! That is where the King lives, that is where He
is seated at the right hand of glory at this moment. Not an earthly
Jerusalem but a heavenly, an everlasting Jerusalem. What a privilege
to belong to such a great empire, such a wide domain! But it is not
only true to say that the headquarters, the capital, is in heaven. The
citizens of this kingdom are scattered throughout the whole earth.
It includes men and women out of 'all nations and kingdoms,
and people, and tongues'. As Isaac Watts puts it—

People and realms of every tongue
Dwell on His love with sweetest song.

What a kingdom, what a sphere! The Roman was proud of the
fact that he was a Roman citizen. Men belonging to great empires
have always displayed the same pride. Christian people, do you
realise that you are citizens of such a kingdom as this! Headquarters
in heaven; the King eternal, immortal, invisible, as your King!
And citizens in every kingdom and land and continent and clime!
Wherever we may live, and whatever our nationality may chance
to be, it makes no difference. We belong to Him, the headquarters
is the same—the heavenly Jerusalem. What a glorious kingdom!
What a privilege to be citizens in such a city!

But let me mention one other thing. You notice how the apostle
mentions our fellow-citizenship. 'Now therefore ye are no more
strangers and foreigners, but fellowcitizens with the saints.' Consider
your fellowcitizens! The saints, he says—you are fellow citizens with
them. Who are they? It is not the nation of Israel as such because
'they are not all Israel that are *of* Israel'. He is thinking of the
saints amongst the children of Israel. What Paul means here is
what the man who wrote the eighty-seventh psalm had in his mind
in verses five and six, 'And of Zion it shall be said, This and that
man was born in her, and the highest himself shall establish her.
The Lord shall count when he writeth up the people that this man
was born there.' You see what he means? On the natural level
men are proud to belong to a nation that can produce a Shakespeare
—the land of Shakespeare! The land of Marlborough! The land of
Wellington! The land of a Pitt; the land of a Cromwell; the land
of these great men that tower as statesmen, as poets, as artists, and
so on! We are proud to belong to such a nation—such and such a
man was born here, bred in our land, bone of our bone as it were,
and flesh of our flesh. But the Bible says, 'The Lord shall count
when he writeth up the people that this man was born there'. This
means the people to whom we belong. We are fellowcitizens with
Abraham, the greatest gentleman who has ever lived, the one who

was distinguished by being called 'the friend of God'. Is it not a marvellous thing to understand and to know that you belong to the same city, the same kingdom, as Abraham? And not only Abraham, but Moses, and David, and Isaiah, and Jeremiah, and all those mighty men of the Old Testament. We belong to them, we are in the same city, we have these common interests and this common allegiance. I must confess that it is to me perhaps the greatest thrill of all to realise that I am a fellowcitizen with the apostle Paul, that as Christians we are one with him, that we have his interests at heart, and that the same things that moved him move us. And we shall see him and spend our eternity with him, and all the other apostles.

But consider the story of the Church. I am glad that I belong to the same company, the same kingdom, as Augustine, and John Calvin, and Martin Luther, and John Knox and the Puritans, and Whitefield and Wesley and all the rest. We are all one, we belong to that company of people. No longer in the world, we belong to this separate kingdom, this kingdom of priests, this holy nation. Let me remind you of verses 22–24 in the twelfth chapter of the Epistle to the Hebrews, that put it so perfectly. 'But ye are come unto Mount Sion, and unto the city of the living God, the heavenly Jerusalem, and to an innumerable company of angels; to the general assembly and church of the firstborn, which are written in heaven, and to God the Judge of all, and to the spirits of just men made perfect; and to Jesus the mediator of the new covenant. . . .' That is where we have come. We belong there. We are no longer a little kingdom on earth at the foot of the Mount Sinai. We have come to the heavenly Jerusalem, and to this innumerable company of fellow-citizens.

But, finally, to make this picture complete, the ultimate privilege is to realise something of the future prospects and *the future glory of the kingdom*. At the present time it seems feeble. The masses are outside the Church, and many a foolish Christian is tempted to ask, Shall I go on with it, is there anything in it? Shall I go to church or shall I not? Anyone who says that, has not seen the real meaning of this kingdom. We are a despised, rejected few, today, perhaps, but there is a glory coming. 'In thee', said God to Abraham at the beginning, 'shall all the nations of the earth be blessed.' Count the stars in the heaven if you can, said God to Abraham; so great, and greater, will be your posterity. Count the grains of sand on the sea-shore; so innumerable will be the citizens of my kingdom which shall be formed of you and your seed. But consider also the message which was given to the prophet Daniel. You remember the vision that was given to the king of that great power that was going to dominate the world and to crush God's people—an image with a head of gold, the breast and arms of silver, the belly and thighs of brass, legs of iron, feet part iron and part clay? This power was towering over the earth as a colossus. But that was not the end. 'Thou sawest', says Daniel to Nebuchadnezzar, 'till that a stone was cut out without hands, which smote the image upon his feet that were of iron and clay, and brake them to pieces. Then was the iron, the clay, the brass, the silver, and the gold, broken to pieces together, and became like the chaff of the summer threshing-floors; and the wind carried them away, that no place was found for them; and the stone that smote the image became a great mountain, and filled the whole earth.' (Daniel 2: 34–35.) That is the kingdom of God that starts as a despised stone, and is as nothing face to face with a colossus; but it smites it and smashes it, and it disappears; and the stone becomes a great mountain that fills the whole earth. There is a day coming, says Paul to the Philippians, when 'at the name of Jesus every knee shall bow, of things in heaven, and things in earth, and things under the earth, and every tongue shall confess that Jesus Christ is Lord, to the glory of God the Father'. 2: 10–11.) Says John in the book of Revelation, 'The seventh angel sounded, and there were great voices in heaven saying, The kingdoms of this world are become the kingdoms of our Lord and of his Christ, and he shall reign for ever and ever' (11: 15). And you and I are citizens of that kingdom. It is going to conquer, it is going to prevail.

> *Jesus shall reign where'er the sun*
> *Doth his successive journeys run.*

And did you know this, that you and I are going to reign with Him? This is what Paul says in 1 Corinthians 6: 'Do ye not know that the saints shall judge the world? Know ye not that we shall judge angels?' It is a kingdom that cannot be shaken. It is a kingdom that shall have no end. It is the everlasting kingdom of God and of His Christ. And you and I, if we are Christians, are already in it, are already citizens of it. Thank God 'we are no more strangers and foreigners, but fellowcitizens with the saints'.

28

PRIVILEGES AND RESPONSIBILITIES

Now therefore ye are no more strangers and foreigners, but fellowcitizens with the saints, and of the household of God.   Ephesians 2: 19

The apostle, as we have already seen, is describing here in a positive manner the privileges of membership of the Christian Church. Having explained how the two parties, Jews and Gentiles, were brought together, he now shows them both together what their position is as members of the Church. In order to do this he employs a number of figures and pictures. The Church, he has already suggested, is like a body. But here he tells us that the Church is like a city, a kingdom—'fellow citizens'. He says that the Church is also like a family—'the household of God'. But the Church is also like a temple, in which God Himself dwells. We are looking for the moment at the first picture given in this nineteenth verse—the Church as a state, a kingdom, a city. Earlier we considered what this definition means in general. We considered also how one obtains this citizenship. And then we looked at some of the general privileges that belong to us as citizens of such a kingdom. We reminded ourselves of the character of our King, the extent of His kingdom, our fellowcitizens, and the future glory of this wondrous kingdom into which we have been brought.

But now we must look for a moment at some *further particular privileges that belong to us as members and citizens of this great kingdom.* The apostle was most anxious that the Ephesians should realise these things. They had been saved, they were in the Church, they had been sealed by the Holy Spirit. But he is not satisfied with that, he prays that the eyes of their understanding may be enlightened that they may know these further things, and among them this one in particular. And surely our main trouble as Christian people today is that we do not realise the privileges of our position as members of the Christian Church. The greatest need of all today is a true and an adequate conception of the nature of the Christian Church. It is because we who belong to her lack this that we fail to attract those who are outside. We make such a poor impression that they are not interested. Revival starts in the Church. True evangelism can never be carried on with a church that is not a living demonstration of the gospel. So from every standpoint the thing we need to concentrate on at the present time is the character, the nature, of the Church, and the privilege of our position in the Church.

Let us go on to consider some of these further privileges. There are certain things which we can add to the general privileges that we have already considered. They are all quite obvious as we work out this analogy of the Church as a kingdom.

Think, for instance, of *the benefits we enjoy* because we are citizens of such a kingdom. That is one of the first things one thinks of in connection with a kingdom. As a citizen of a country, you enjoy all the benefits of the reign and the rule and the laws of that particular community. It has often been the proud boast of the citizens of this country that she is the home of freedom—parliamentary democracy, and so on. Now those are things which we enjoy as the result of our citizenship in this country. There are people in other countries which have not got these privileges, they are still more or less in a state of serfdom. There are others under awful tyrannies. One of the best things about citizenship is that it does at once entitle you to enjoy all the benefits of the system and form of government, and the economy of a particular state.

We can transfer all this to the realm of the Church. The apostle has already reminded us of it in the very first chapter, where he says in the third verse, 'Blessed be the God and Father of our Lord Jesus Christ, who hath blessed us with all spiritual blessings in heavenly places in Christ'. That is a summary of all the blessings of this particular kingdom. They are endless, and it is quite impossible to attempt to describe them. But we must lay hold of the great principle that all spiritual blessings in the heavenly places in Christ are ours. The kingdom, the city, to which we belong is a kingdom, a city, in which all these blessings are given freely; it is the King's good pleasure that they should be given. He delights in doing it. He is interested in His citizens, He is interested in all His people; their welfare holds a special place in His mind and His heart. He is the Father of His people, and He is concerned about their welfare and their well-being in every single respect.

Other statements in the Scriptures to the same effect will help us to understand this. The apostle Paul, in his first letter to Timothy, uses the interesting expression, 'God, who is the Saviour of all men, specially of those that believe' (4: 10). The word 'Saviour' means the One who blesses, the One who looks after, the One who delivers out of trouble. And the Scriptures teach this everywhere concerning God. God 'maketh his sun to rise on the evil and on the good, and sendeth rain on the just and on the unjust'. There are men and women in the world today who never think of God and never mention Him except to blaspheme His name; nevertheless, they enjoy some of the common, general benefits and blessings of God's kingdom. All they have comes from God. He is 'the Saviour of all men', yes, but 'specially of them that believe'. He has a personal interest in believers, a special interest, a peculiar interest, and you and I as citizens of the kingdom are the recipients of these peculiar benefactions, these special blessings that He has for His own people. Everything is ordered for our good. 'We know', says Paul—there is no need to argue about this, there is no question or query about this—'We know that all things work together for good to them that love God'. (Romans 8: 28.) There is nothing beyond that. It is the simple truth that God, who controls the whole universe and cosmos, manipulates everything for the good of His own people. Everything is worked to this end. God has the control of everything, and as our King He manipulates all His resources for our good.

Take another statement by the same apostle: 'He that spared not his own Son but delivered him up for us all, how shall he not with him also freely give us all things?' (Romans 8: 32). Our Lord Himself also says that 'the very hairs of your head are all numbered', and that nothing can happen to us apart from our Father. Much of the teaching of the Sermon on the Mount is designed to inculcate this idea of God's special interest in and concern for His people. It is something that is integral to any conception of a kingdom with a king and citizens. And so we should remind ourselves of this most wonderful fact. In this kingdom of God and of His Christ to which we belong, all the resources of the Godhead are for us. That is the teaching everywhere in the Bible. The Old Testament has much to say about God's concern for His people. It is still plainer in the New Testament. We are the recipients of all these amazing, untold, unsearchable, riches and blessings of God's kingdom.

Another privilege is that we have *the right of access to the King*. That is true of the humblest citizen in the land. Ultimately he has a right of appeal to the king. The whole process of the law is there, in a sense, to enable him to exercise that right. He can take his appeal from one authority to a higher, and ultimately he can appeal to the king. Now that is true of every one of us as a Christian. We have a King, who though He is the King of kings and the Lord of lords, and the Ruler of the ends of the earth, knows and .is interested in His citizens individually. Are you burdened, are you heavy laden, are you struggling and striving? I would remind you that you have a right of access to the King. You can take your case to Him. Whatever great matter may be engaging His attention I assure you that if you hold up your hand as He is passing, and hold out your petition, He has time to listen to you, to look at you, and to deal with your case. Let us never feel lost in the Church or in the great world in which we live. Let us never think that we are so small and insignificant that this great and high King is not interested in us. The whole teaching of the Bible emphasises the reverse and the contrary. He is ready to listen to your humble cry.

How many instances of that there are in the life and ministry of our blessed Lord when He was here on earth! Do you remember how, when He was on His last journey up to Jerusalem, He was followed by a great crowd? But there was a poor blind man who cried out, 'Have mercy on me, thou Son of David'. The people tried to silence him. Keep quiet, they said, He is going to Jerusalem, He has not got time to deal with you. But He heard him. And He had time to stop and to speak to him and to heal him and to deliver him. He likewise had time for Zacchaeus. He also had time to deal with another blind man at the gate of the temple. It did not matter where He was, or how great the throng, the crowd. Do you remember the woman who touched the hem of His garment? There you have illustrations of His care and solicitude for people. In your need and in your desperation, therefore, remember that as a citizen of this kingdom, you are known to your King, and that He is ever ready to listen to your petition, and to hearken to your cry.

But let us consider another aspect of the matter. *The resources of the kingdom are shared amongst us.* We referred to this matter when we looked at our fellow-citizenship with the saints; but we only looked at it from the standpoint of its greatness. But it is very precious to us from the practical standpoint also. The fellowship that we enjoy with our fellowcitizens! Again it is an essential part of any conception of the state. We talk a great deal today about the Welfare State, the basis of which is meant to be, that the strong are to bear the burdens of the weak, the wealthy the burdens of the poor. It is a sharing so that none have a superabundance and others nothing. That is the idea. It is still more true of the kingdom of God. There is a specific injunction to the effect: 'We then that are strong ought to bear the infirmities of the weak' (Romans 15: 1). 'Bear ye one another's burdens, and so fulfil the law of Christ' (Galatians 6: 2).

Surely there is nothing that should be more precious to us than the way in which, as fellow citizens together, as members of the Christian Church together, we know and experience this in practice. Is there anything more encouraging to a Christian than to know that he is being prayed for by others?—that other people have got you and your burden and your problem on their hearts and are making intercession for you? They not only think of themselves;

you are a fellowcitizen, and you belong together. We pray for one another, we can sympathise with one another, we understand one another. I could elaborate this at length; but let me put it simply in this form. How often have we known the following experience! We have been feeling that we can scarcely pray, we have been discouraged, and perhaps the devil has been particularly busy, and we are entirely forgetful of the fact that we have this right of access immediately to the King Himself. While we are commiserating with ourselves, suddenly we meet another Christian and, beginning to talk, we find that he or she has the same problem or difficulty. Immediately we are eased and helped. And so we go forward together. We bear one another's burdens. 'The sympathising tear,' the understanding! We are marching to Zion together through a strange land. It is a very wonderful thing to realise that the resources of others, the strength and the ability of others, become available to us in our difficulties. And when they in turn are depressed and we are joyful, we can help them. There is an amazing fellowship amongst fellowcitizens.

But let us consider another great source of comfort, namely: *the protection that the kingdom affords us.* This is a very remarkable thing. It is true, on the secular level. All the power and all the might and all the resources of a kingdom are behind the humblest citizen and are available for his defence. Let me give you an illustration of this which always seems to me to put it very plainly and clearly. Do you remember from your study of history what happened in 1739? There began in 1739 what is called 'The War of Jenkins' Ear'. There was a certain Captain Jenkins sailing the high seas, and a Spanish coast-guard attacked him without any justification at all, and for a brief time occupied his ship. And, to add to the infamy of their action, they cut off one of the ears of Captain Jenkins. Captain Jenkins eventually got back to this country. He had kept his ear in a bottle of spirits, and when he returned he presented it to parliament. And because of that, this country, Great Britain, declared war on Spain in 1739—the War of Jenkins' Ear. Who was Captain Jenkins? It does not matter, he was a citizen of Great Britain, and he was not to be insulted by Spain or by any other country; and because they had insulted him, all the might and the power of this country was turned upon Spain in defence of that individual citizen. And when you and I travel abroad and perchance suffer some indignity or some insult, we should be mindful of the fact that the same power, and all the resources of our country, are behind us and concerned about our defence.

When we apply it to the realm of the Church all this is still more true. Take certain Old Testament examples. Here is a man of God hard pressed, his enemies surrounding him and attacking him. What action can he take? He says, 'The name of the Lord is a strong tower; the righteous runneth into it and is safe'. 'The name of the Lord!' There is a wonderful exposition of this in Psalms three and four, where the Psalmist tells us of how he was surrounded by all kinds of dangers and of desperate enemies. And yet this is how he writes, 'Thou, O Lord, art a shield for me; my glory and the lifter up of mine head. I cried unto the Lord with my voice and he heard me out of his holy hill. I laid me down and slept; I awaked, for the Lord sustained me. I will not be afraid of ten thousands of people that have set themselves against me round about. Arise, O Lord, save me, O my God, for thou hast smitten all mine enemies upon the cheekbone, thou hast broken the teeth of the ungodly. Salvation belongeth unto the Lord.' Zechariah puts it like this: 'For thus saith the Lord of hosts: After the glory hath he sent me unto the nations that spoiled you, for he that toucheth you toucheth the apple of his eye.' (2: 8). Do you want anything beyond that? 'He that toucheth you', says God to you as a Christian, 'toucheth the apple of my eye'—the most sensitive spot in the whole of My being. That is the protection. 'I', says the Lord Jesus Christ, 'give unto them eternal life, and they shall never perish, neither shall any man pluck them out of my hand.' (John 10: 28). Is there a safer place than that? 'If God be for us', says Paul, 'who can be against us?' (Romans 8: 31.) 'The Lord is my helper', says the writer of the Epistle to the Hebrews, 'and I will not fear what man shall do unto me.' (13: 6.) Says John in his first Epistle, 'greater is he that is in you than he that is in the world'. (4: 6.) The enemy may be attacking you and hurting you; do not hit back, says Paul, do not retaliate, for 'Vengeance is mine, I will repay, saith the Lord.' (Romans 12: 19.) 'They overcame him', says the book of Revelation, 'by the blood of the Lamb, and by the word of their testimony.' (12: 11.) That mighty dragon that arises against the Church of God, and casts out of his mouth a flood of water in an attempt to drown her, is ever trying to destroy God's people. What can they do? 'They overcome him by the blood of the Lamb and by the word of their testimony.' That is the way to defeat the devil as he comes with all his malice and all his terrible power. Says the apostle Paul finally, 'For the which cause I also suffer these things'—his persecutions and trials and tribulations—'Nevertheless I am not ashamed, for I know whom I have believed, and am persuaded that he is able to keep that which I have committed unto him against that day.' (2 Timothy 1: 12.) All is well, says Paul: you, Timothy, are having a hard time; I know what it is to have a hard time; I am not ashamed, I am not alarmed, I am not frightened, I am not shaken—for I know Him whom I have believed, I have committed it all to Him, and He will keep me and it and everything I regard as precious until that day. Oh, that we realised our privileges as Christians! Whatever your problem, whatever your position, whatever your trial, I plead with you, remember the resources, remember all that is true of you as a citizen of this great and glorious kingdom.

I hurry to emphasise another aspect which is equally important for us, namely *the calls, the demands, the responsibilities of our citizenship.* 'We are no more strangers and foreigners, but fellowcitizens with the saints.' We have been rejoicing in the privileges, but let us remember the responsibilities. They are emphasised everywhere in the Scriptures. The whole of the second half of this Ephesian Epistle is given to that almost exclusively. But let us remind ourselves briefly of some of the things that follow because of our privileged and exalted position. These again, as I mention them, will provide us with very subtle and delicate tests as to whether we belong to the kingdom or not.

The first is obviously this—*our pride in the kingdom.* The human analogy is obvious. Our pride of country, our pride of citizenship! Sir Walter Scott asks very rightly, 'Breathes there a man with soul so dead who never to himself hath said, "This is my own, my native land"?' Is such a character conceivable? 'This is my own, my native land!' It is natural, it is instinctive. People are not only ready to speak for their country, and shout for it, they will also die for it. People do this for anything in which they are interested. Is a man interested in music?—he is always talking about it. Is he interested in football? Will he not shout in support of his team? Have you not heard them doing so by the thousand? Interest in their side! Not content with that, they wear mascots, they wear special colours, they will pay much money to go and see their side playing. The enthusiasm and the excitement! That is the realm of their interest.

But what of us? We are citizens of a kingdom that does not belong to this world—the heavenly kingdom we have been describing. What of it? Are we proud of it? Are we showing to which side we belong? are we showing our colours? Or do we, when we are in the company of certain people, rather try to conceal the fact that we are Christians? When we are with people who do not observe Sunday, and who rather despise people who still go to church or chapel, do we try to give the impression that that is also our position? It is not surprising that the masses are outside the Church when we so often give the impression that we are a little bit ashamed of the fact that we are inside. But it is not only a matter of not being ashamed. If we realised the truth about our position we should be moved by it, we should be thrilled by it. Like the man who says, 'This is my own, my native land', we should glory in our kingdom and boast of it, we should be ready to shout for it and if necessary to die for it. We should extol it and its virtues and all its high and great and glorious privileges, and we should be anxious that all should know that we belong to it—as a man does in a foreign country. Men from this country, when abroad, do not hide the fact that they are Britishers, they want everybody to know it. And people coming here from other countries do the same, and rightly so! And in the same way we should all, as citizens of this glorious kingdom, be ever showing our allegiance and glorying in the fact that we belong to such a kingdom.

The next thing, of course, is: *country before self.* That is the test of a man's true appreciation of citizenship. When the country is in trouble, the cry is, 'For king and country!'—not for your own particular interests and concerns! Listen to the apostle Paul saying this: 'No man that warreth entangleth himself with the affairs of this life; that he may please him who hath chosen him to be a soldier.' (2 Timothy 2: 4.) He means that when a man is a soldier in the army, he is not at the same time in a profession or a business outside the army. He is entirely at the disposal of his commanding officer, of his king and country. He does not entangle himself with the affairs of this life when he wars, because the consequence would be chaotic. If a number of men in an army when the country is at war suddenly began to say: I am sorry I cannot fight today, I have got to go home and transact some business, the army would soon be defeated. Soldiers have had to sign themselves away, they have handed themselves over, they are at the disposal of the king and country. When you are in the army you do not decide when you are going to have a holiday. Apply that thought to the higher realm. 'For King and country!' 'No man that warreth entangleth himself with the affairs of this life; that he may please him who hath chosen him to be a soldier!' The kingdom and the King come first. And the test of whether we realise our citizenship in this kingdom is just that. Are we surrendered to the King and to the country? Have we handed ourselves over? Have we realised it is true of us that 'Ye are not your own, ye are bought with a price'? (1 Corinthians 6: 19 and 20.) We belong to Him, we are no longer our own.

The next thought in this logical sequence is: Because of my relationship to this kingdom it follows that *I am now a stranger in every other kingdom.* Paul says to these Ephesians, 'You are no longer strangers and foreigners, but fellowcitizens with the saints'; you were once upon a time outside this kingdom, strangers and foreigners, but now you are citizens of the kingdom. But that means this, remember, that you are now a stranger and a foreigner in the other country out of which you have come. What an important principle this is! Let me remind you of the way in which the apostle Peter uses this argument in his First Epistle: who 'were not a people, but are now the people of God.' 'Dearly beloved,' he says, 'I beseech you as strangers and pilgrims, abstain from fleshly lusts which war against the soul; having your conversation honest among the Gentiles, that whereas they speak against you as evildoers, they may by your good works, which they shall behold, glorify God in the day of visitation.' (2: 10–12,) You see the change? They were not a people: they are now a people. They were without the kingdom, strangers and foreigners outside the kingdom of God: they are now inside the kingdom of God. But because of that, he says, you are strangers and pilgrims in this world, you no longer belong to it. It is another way of saying what Paul says in Philippians 2: 20: 'Our citizenship is in heaven'; and because our citizenship is in heaven, we are strangers here. We are in the world but we do not belong to the world.

This is something that happens automatically. When you are visiting another country you do not become a part of that country; you are still a stranger, you are conscious of it and so is everybody else. And you and I as Christians have become strangers in this world. We do not belong to this world any longer, if we are truly Christian. We are like people away from home. We are here for a while, we are sojourners, we are journeymen, we are travellers; that is always the picture that is given of us in the Bible. Read the eleventh chapter of the Epistle to the Hebrews. The people mentioned there had counted themselves to be 'strangers and pilgrims in the earth'. They were 'looking for a city which hath foundations, whose builder and maker is God.' They dwelt in tents. They each one said, 'I am but a stranger here, heaven is my home'. It follows automatically, does it not? We are but strangers and pilgrims amongst the ungodly. They do not understand us, they are different. They may be antagonistic, they may persecute us. All is well, says Peter, just remember who you are, and remember that you do not belong to them any longer. There is no need to argue about this. You are either in God's kingdom or else you are outside; you cannot be in both at the same time. And it should be evident and obvious to all that you belong to this heavenly kingdom and not to that other.

I would put that in this form as my fourth principle. As strangers and pilgrims and foreigners in this world, let us always remember that the first call upon us is that *we represent our King and our country.* 'England expects that every man this day will do his duty', said Nelson on the morning of Trafalgar. The citizen of the Roman Empire in ancient days, wherever he went carried his peculiar cloak, the sign of the fact that he was a Roman citizen; and he was careful of it and of its honour. Very rightly so! Yes, says the apostle Paul again to the Philippians, 'Only let your conversation be as it becometh the gospel of Christ' (1 : 27). You are a stranger away from home, you know what you claim and you have told people what you are. Remember, they will be watching you. Never forget it. They will judge your King and your country by what they see in you. Look again, in Peter: 'Dearly beloved, I beseech you as strangers and pilgrims, abstain from fleshly lusts which war against the soul; having your conversation honest among the Gentiles.' They persecute you as evildoers, but prove to them by your good works that you are children of God.

This is how the New Testament always preaches sanctification and holiness. Something has gone tragically wrong with the preaching of sanctification and holiness when it is always offered to us as something for us, 'Life with a capital L,' or something that is going to be marvellous for us. The scriptural appeal for holiness is this: 'Be ye holy for I am holy, saith the Lord'. If you are not living a sanctified and a holy life you are a traitor to your country and to your King. You have no right to live as you like. You cannot dissociate yourself from your citizenship. You cannot say, It does not matter to anybody else what I do, I will live my life in my own way. Not so if you are a Christian. If you fall, we all fall with you; and the world laughs at us all. Above all, Christ is ridiculed. For a member of the Christian Church to live a worldly life is nothing but to be a cad and a traitor. In the secular realm people are shot for doing things like that. Insulting the flag! Letting down the country! Letting down the monarch! There is nothing worse. And you and I are citizens of this heavenly King and His glorious, holy kingdom. 'Dearly beloved, I beseech you as strangers and pilgrims, abstain from (keep clear from) fleshly lusts that war against the soul'—not for your own sakes only, but for the sake of those Gentiles looking on and for the honour of your King. 'Only let your conversation be as becometh the gospel of Christ.'

That is a good way of looking at Christian practice. In our daily life, when we are doubtful whether we should do something or not, or wear this or that, this is the test: Is it suitable? does it match? If I put on that coat, will it match my hat and my shoes? Is it becoming? Does it fit in with . . .? That is the very picture, the illustration used by the apostle. If it does not suit, and does not fit, and is not becoming and consonant with the rest, I must shed it. Let your whole conduct be governed by the gospel of Christ. All my actions should be controlled by that. There must be a wholeness. Each act must be seemly, must be fitting, must be suitable. So you must think of the great doctrines of the faith and ask, Is this sort of conduct consonant with that faith? Does it become the gospel of Christ?

Finally, it should be obvious that as citizens of this kingdom *we should always be concerned about the defence of the kingdom*, the defence of her laws and the defence of everything for which she stands. The flag! We must be ready to die for 'the flag'; that represents the country and all that belongs to her. And it is equally true in a spiritual sense of us. We are no longer strangers and foreigners, but fellowcitizens with the saints. In a day like this we are called upon to defend this 'flag,' the Bible. It is being attacked and ridiculed. Are you defending it? It is not enough just to give your testimony as a defence of the Bible. You have to study in order to defend the Bible. To start with, you have got to know the Bible. And you have to know something about books that will help you to defend the Bible. Goodwill and good intentions do not defend the country. A man defending the country has to go into the army and be trained and drilled and disciplined; whether he likes it or not, he is put through it, as we say. And you and I need to be 'put through it' to defend the flag, the country, the kingdom. Our Book is being attacked; our faith is being attacked; our Lord and Master and King is being attacked. 'We must be ready at all times,' says Peter, 'to give a reason for the hope that is in us'. (1 Peter 3: 15.) Can we do so? The kingdom is being attacked by a mighty foe, and you and I are called upon as soldiers to play our individual little parts. There is no greater honour, there is no higher privilege. Victory is certain and assured. But it would be a tragic thing, when the great and glorious day of celebration comes, if any one of us should feel that we have done nothing at all, that we merely sat by while somebody else did the work, the defending, the fighting, the labouring.

We need not all be great experts in the art of war. Let me use a human analogy. We are not all meant to be regulars; you need not, of necessity, be a whole-time worker, you can join the Civil Defence of the kingdom of God. Become a special constable. Find time for it. Have a concern. Give yourself to it. The kingdom is being attacked and ridiculed. Let us then jump to her defence in whatever little service we can render.

In other words, as citizens of this kingdom, our greatest desire, our chief ambition, should ever be to see her confines extended, and to see her becoming yet mightier and mightier and yet more and more glorious, until that day when 'the kingdoms of this world shall have become the kingdoms of our Lord, and of his Christ'.

'Ye are no more strangers and foreigners, but fellowcitizens with the saints' in this glorious kingdom. And for that reason we are but strangers and pilgrims in this world, with all its artificiality and loudness, and all its mad self-confidence which will come to nought. Thank God, we do not belong to that. We are but strangers in it: 'Our citizenship', thank God, 'is in heaven'.

29

OF THE HOUSEHOLD OF GOD

Now therefore ye are no more strangers and foreigners, but fellowcitizens with the saints, and of the household of God.   Ephesians 2: 19

Having considered the first picture which the apostle employs to show us the privilege of being members of the Christian Church, namely, that of citizens in a state, we now come to *his second picture*. True Christians are not only fellowcitizens with the saints, but they are also '*of the household of God*'. Here is obviously something different, here is an advance. But, again, let us remember that the two things Paul wants to bring out are this principle of unity and also the greatness of the privilege. But we may ask, Why does he thus use a second figure? And why indeed is he going on to use a third figure, which we shall consider later. The answer, I think, is obvious: it is that he felt that the first figure alone was not sufficient. It conveys an idea, it introduces us to a vital part of the doctrine, but it does not include it all. It is not sufficiently comprehensive. It has laid down one tremendous aspect, the one we have already considered, but there is much more to be said. Therefore, it behoves us to consider and to discover why it is that he employs this second illustration.

You will recall that in the first chapter the apostle has already introduced us to this idea of the family, where he says, 'Having predestinated us unto the adoption of children by Jesus Christ to himself, according to the good pleasure of his will'. Now, here, he takes up that idea again by telling us that as believers we belong to the family of God. 'Household' means family. In other words, we are children of God. Paul makes this point about Jews and Gentiles who have become Christians. All other distinctions, you remember, have gone, they have all been put aside, they have all been abolished. In this new thing that God has brought into being amongst Jews and Gentiles, the further great fact is that we are in the position of children.

What we have to do, therefore, is to *compare and contrast the idea of a state and the idea of a family*. And it is only as we do this that we shall realise why it is that the apostle brings in the second picture, and how this second picture is a very definite advance upon the first, and takes us more deeply into the truth about the unity of all Christians and the greatness of the privilege which we enjoy. We must consider, therefore, the points of contrast between a state and a family.

The first is that the relationship that exists and subsists between the members of a state is, after all, *a general relationship*, whereas the thing that characterises the relationship between members of a family is that it is *a more particular relationship*. All of us in this country are citizens of Great Britain, but we do not all belong to the same family. There are a number of families, we are all one in the State. That is what I mean by saying that the State relationship is something which is more general. On the other hand when you come to the family you have greatly narrowed down the relationship; it is a much smaller unit. And because it is narrower and more particular, it is therefore a much more intense relationship. So that we can use certain other terms. We can say that the connection between us in the State is a very loose connection. There is a connection, and it is enough to divide us from people who belong to other countries and to other kingdoms. We are bound together, but it is a loose connection. In a family, however, it is no longer a loose connection. Because it is particular, because it is narrower, it is more intense, and also closer. The apostle, therefore, is making a real advance in his doctrine about this unity. The unity that exists in the Christian Church between the members is not a loose attachment, it is an intense, close, intimate attachment.

But we can go further by putting it like this. In the second place, the unity that exists in the State is, ultimately, *an external unity*—whereas the whole point about family unity is that it is something which is *internal*. That needs no elaboration or demonstration. You cannot think of a family without immediately thinking of that something within, inside, that is making them one. That is not true in the realm of the State where we are held together by certain types of culture, by certain laws, and by certain common interests, all of which are, in a final sense, on the surface of our lives and outside us. Here it is essentially something inward, internal. In other words, the relationship between members of a state is a more remote relationship, whereas that between the members of a family is a more intimate one. I mean by that that we know most people in a vague and somewhat remote manner. We recognise people who live in the same street, or who work in the same office; we are acquainted with them, but we do not really know them, we are not intimate with them. It may be a kind of nodding acquaintanceship, a general friendship, but it is always remote. Whereas in the family, the central idea at once is that of intimacy and understanding, and of an inner bond.

Or let us think of it in yet a different way. Ultimately, our relationship to one another in the State is an *impersonal* one, whereas the whole point about the family is that the relationship is intensely *personal*. This is a very important principle, quite apart from its application to the Church. There is a tendency in the world today to emphasise and to develop impersonal relationships at the expense of personal relationships. You can think of many examples of this. The State itself does it. As the State becomes more and more powerful, and as it interferes more and more in our lives, it is tending to de-personalise us. We become units, we become numbers. The personal element has gone out. There is much evidence of that in this country at the present time. I am not making this point politically, I am making it as a most important point philosophically, and ultimately from the standpoint of personality and of individuality. The State always tends to de-personalise us. It is, of course, a part of the whole question of mass and mob psychology. You always tend to lose your identity somewhat in a crowd. That is why crowds can be so dangerous; and it may be that a day will arrive when there will even be need of legislation to prohibit people meeting together in numbers beyond certain limits. Whether we like it or not, a crowd has an effect upon us, and people tend to act automatically in a crowd. Hitler knew that very well and so exploited the whole idea. You can make people do things in a crowd that they would never dream of doing singly or individually. Somehow or another the personal element goes out. Indeed we need to observe and to watch this even in our educational systems. The more you impress loyalty to a side or to a school, the more you are tending to de-personalise children and to produce this impersonal relationship. I would even suggest that perhaps this is one of the main reasons for the appalling increase in divorce at the present time. People have thought less and less of themselves in this personal manner, and the loyalties have all been general—the country, the Crown, the school, the side, something like that, something outside oneself. Those things must not be neglected, I agree, for it is a terrible thing to be selfish and self-centred; but the tragedy is that we always tend to pass from one extreme to the other. In trying to teach children and others not to be selfish, surely we have gone to the other extreme if we have made them so impersonal that they are afraid to express their feelings, and so try to de-personalise themselves as to become lost in a mass, in a mob. You see, thus, that the apostle has definitely advanced the thought here. The attachment, the relationship in the State, is impersonal. But in the family—and this is the glory of the family—we are all persons, and the relationships are all personal and direct and immediate.

Then, finally, we can put it like this. The difference between the two relations is the difference between *a legal relationship* and *a vital, living, blood relationship*. What binds us together ultimately in the State is the law. There may be certain interests and outlooks in common; but the thing, after all, that makes us one and keeps the cohesion is the process of the law—it is legal. But that is not the case in the family. What binds in the family is blood. It is a vital relationship. The difference can be shown very easily in this way. You will find, particularly on the Continent of Europe, in various countries which are divided off from one another as states, that there is, nevertheless, the same blood in the people who belong to these different states. Think of the Slav people, for instance. They are of one blood and they possess certain characteristics; and though some may belong to one country and some to another, you can always recognise the Slav. And so it is with other types of nationality and of blood. A blood relationship is a more intimate, direct, vital, living thing than any relationship which is delimited and determined by the processes of the law and by the enactments of men.

The apostle, then, was not merely multiplying words when he says: 'Now therefore ye are no more strangers and foreigners, but fellowcitizens with the saints'—yes, and members of the 'household of God'. He has advanced, he has taken us to a higher realm, he is narrowing it down; and as you narrow relationship it always becomes more intense. We are always more intense in our relationships when we are smaller in number. That is psychology, that is human nature, is it not? So the term 'family' conveys all these great ideas which it is important for us to grasp.

Having shown the difference in that way in general, let us now come to *the particular application of all this to the Christian,* to members of the Christian Church. Why is it important that we should realise this family relationship? Why was the apostle so anxious that these Ephesians should realise it? It is because so many of us do not realise these truths that we are as we are, and that the Church is as she is. Do we realise that we are indeed of the household of God— that we belong to God's family? It is a vital part of the whole doctrine of salvation. That is why we must consider it.

I start with the greatest and the most important thing of all. *It is important that we realise this in order that we should understand, as we ought, the marvellous and wondrous grace of God.* I mean this: it would have been a very wonderful thing if God had just decided not to punish us, not to send us to hell. It was hell we deserved. In our

natural state and condition which the apostle has already described
—'living to the lusts of the flesh, fulfilling the desires of the flesh
and of the mind', and being 'the children of wrath even as others'—
we deserved nothing but hell. I say that it would have been a
wonderful thing if God had merely decided not to leave us in that
state and not to punish us. But God's way of salvation does not
stop at that. He elevates us to this dignity of children, He adopts us
into His own family.

It is all to be seen in the parable of the Prodigal Son. The son
went home and said to his father, 'Father, I have sinned against
heaven and in thy sight and am no more worthy to be called thy
son'. And he was about to add, 'Make me as one of thy hired
servants'. But the father cannot regard his boy, though he is a
prodigal, as a servant. It just cannot happen. He says, No, no, you
come back as my son; and he embraces him and he brings out the
robe and the ring and kills the fatted calf. My son! That is God's
way of salvation. It is important therefore that we should grasp this
principle in order that we should be able to magnify the grace of
God. What a plan of salvation! What a scheme of redemption!
Content with nothing but that we should stand in His presence as
His children! If we do not realise this we do not realise the greatness
and the riches of God's grace.

There, then, is the first and the most important thing, the thing
which in a sense includes all the others. It emphasises what I have
just been saying, that we must never think of our salvation negatively. We only start with the negative. The first thing we all need
is the forgiveness of sins and deliverance from the wrath of God. But
He does not stop at that. And we must never stop at that in our
thinking. Our thinking must be positive, we must see all this to
which it leads. The Christian is not merely a man who is forgiven
and saved from hell. Much more than that, he has been adopted
into the family of the eternal God!

Another most important point is this. You notice that this is true
of us only in and through the Lord Jesus Christ. *It is only true of
those who are 'in Christ'.* This is absolutely vital and pivotal, because
there is a loose teaching current today concerning the so-called
universal fatherhood of God, and the universal brotherhood of man.
The apostle here in this chapter teaches the exact opposite. All
blessing—and we must bear in mind that this nineteenth verse is a
summing up of what has gone before—everything, he has been
telling us, is 'in Christ Jesus'. None of these things are true apart
from Christ Jesus. 'Wherefore remember, that ye being in times past
Gentiles in the flesh . . . that at that time ye were *without Christ,*
being aliens from the commonwealth of Israel, and strangers from

the covenants of promise, having no hope, and without God in the world; but now *in Christ Jesus* ye who sometimes were far off are made nigh by the *blood of Christ*'; '*He* is our peace'. Then in verse 18, 'For *in him* (Christ), we both have access by one Spirit unto the Father'. There is no such thing as belonging to the family of God apart from the Lord Jesus Christ. Mankind is divided into two compartments—those who are outside Christ or without Christ and those who are members of the household of God. The Lord Jesus Christ said about the former: 'Ye are of your father the devil, and the works of your father ye will do'. How important it is to observe these things! God, as the Creator, is the Creator of all, and there is a kind of fatherhood in that sense. That is not the thing the apostle is speaking about here; that is not the truth the Lord Jesus Christ speaks of when He says, 'Your heavenly Father knoweth that ye have need of all these things'. No, this is the new relationship which has come into being only through the Lord Jesus Christ and His perfect work.

God, then, is not the Father of those who do not believe in Christ. And no man can go to God and ask for certain things and say, 'My Father', unless he goes 'by the blood of Christ', relying utterly upon His perfect work. This, as you know, is often denied today. People talk glibly and loosely and easily about going to God without even mentioning the name of the Lord Jesus Christ. They will awake one day to the realisation that He never knew them, that they are outside, that they do not belong to the family. Without Christ there is no such relationship. On the other hand let me emphasise that this is something which is true of all Christians. There are no divisions like this amongst Christians. All Christians are 'fellow-citizens with the saints and of the household of God'. So we must reject all teachings which say that there are some Christians who are not sons of God, and which draw a distinction between sons and children. Children and sons are one and the same thing, and you cannot be a Christian without being a child of God and a son of God. The terms apply equally to all Christians.

It is important that we should realise this, and for this reason. If you and I are the children of God, then we have no right to live as if we were but servants. We have no right to live in the kitchen of the house. We are children!—and all Christians who do not realise this, and who are living simply a servant kind of life are dishonouring God and detracting from the eternal glory of His grace. That is why it is important that we should grasp this further advance in the doctrine. If we fail to do so we fall into those various errors, and thereby we are detracting from the glory of the Lord Jesus Christ. We are taking Him from the centre, He is no longer crucial, His

blood is being put on one side and at a discount. He is not everything, and we do not glorify His Father as we ought.

That, then, is the first reason why we must grasp this. It is
essential to a true understanding of the doctrine of salvation.

But let me put it in a more intimate way. *It is only as we understand
this that we ever come to enjoy the privileges of this position.* Do you realise
what it means? We were considering the privileges of being a
citizen of a kingdom, and they were wonderful and glorious. But in
the light of the distinctions we have drawn you see how much higher
the privilege is when you look at yourself as a child of God, and not
merely as a citizen of His kingdom.

What are these privileges? Here is the first one. *God is our Father.*
The everlasting and eternal God! We can go to Him as our Father.
You remember how the Lord Jesus Christ Himself said, 'I ascend
unto my Father and your Father and to my God and your God'.
There is surely no greater honour and no greater dignity that can
ever come into our ken or comprehension than just this, that we
have upon us the name of God. It is not surprising that John, in the
prologue of his Gospel, puts it like this: that to 'as many as received
him gave he the power (the right, the authority) to become the
children of God' (1: 12). There is nothing beyond that, nothing
conceivable beyond that, that we are actually members of God's
own family. This is literally the truth about us as Christians. John
again says, 'Beloved, now are we the children of God' (1 John 3: 2).
We do not know what we shall be in all its fulness, he goes on to
say, but we do know this that we are already, *now*, the children of
God. The apostle Peter is equally concerned about it and says that
we are 'partakers of the divine nature' (2 Peter 1: 4). More and
more it seems to me that it is our failure at this point that really
explains why the Christian Church is as she is. And it does not
matter what we do or try to do; until we come back to this and really
understand this and feel it and experience its power, I see no hope
for the Church. We are the children of God, partakers of the divine
nature itself.

Then, because of that, the second thing that is true about us in
our relationship to God as our Father is that we have the right of
approach to Him which a child always has to a father. Paul has
already said that in a previous verse: 'For through him we both
have access by one Spirit'—not unto God, you remember, but—
'unto the Father'. This is so overwhelming that we can scarcely
receive it: but it is true. May I use a simple and an obvious illustration. Think of a man, the head of a great business, with hundreds,
perhaps thousands, of people in his employment and under his

control, an exceptionally busy man. Obviously such a man cannot be handling all the little details of the business or the works or whatever it is. He only deals with great principles; he has his managers and under-managers, foremen, and so on, and they deal with the details of things in their departments. If you take a little detail from some department to this great man, the head of all, the chairman of the company, he will just dismiss you, for he has not got time for such things. And yet I see him there one day seated in his office at his desk with all these great matters in his mind, and perhaps millions of pounds to handle, and for which he is responsible. He cannot even see the managers this day, he can only see some special directors. But suddenly he hears a little tap at his door. At once he puts everything aside. He recognises it; it is his own little child, a little toddler; and he goes himself and opens the door for him and spends time talking to him, perhaps playing with him for a while. Everything is put on one side. Why? It is his child. That is the doctrine we are considering. The God who made everything out of nothing, and to whom all the stars and the constellations are but as marbles to a child, the God who controls all things that are, and who is from eternity to eternity, to whom the very nations are but 'as the small dust of the balance'—He is your Father and my Father, and there is nothing howsoever small and trivial in your life and in mine but He is interested in it, and, as it were, is prepared to allow the whole universe to go on by its own momentum for the moment while He is listening to you and giving you His undivided attention. That is what this doctrine means.

How foolish we are! How we rob ourselves of some of the most precious things of the Christian life, simply because we do not lay hold of doctrine! We use the terms glibly, but we fail to analyse their content. This is what the apostle is saying: we are not only citizens—I reminded you that a citizen has the right of appeal to the king, but this takes us much further—I go as a child right into the presence of my Father, and He is always ready to receive me. Or, to put it the other way round, if only we realised God's interest in us and God's loving concern about us! How is it that we can read our Scriptures and peruse these glorious statements and never seem to grasp them at all? It is the Son of God who Himself has told us that as children of God 'the very hairs of our head are all numbered'. God knows about us in that sort of way and in that kind of detail. Our Lord was ever repeating this point. He says, 'Your heavenly Father knoweth that ye have need of all these things' (Matthew 6: 32). What are you worrying about and fretting your-selves about? If only you realised that He is your Father, who knows all about you, and knows all your needs and all your worries much better than you do yourself, as a parent knows more than the child knows about these things! Why do you not confide in that, why do you not trust in that, why do you go hesitantly and doubtfully to Him? 'Your heavenly Father knoweth that you have need of all these things.' We are members of the household of God. There is no danger of abusing this doctrine as long as we remember what our Lord said in the Lord's Prayer, 'Our Father, which art in heaven, hallowed be thy name'. As long as you start like that when you go to God as your Father, there will be no glib, unworthy familiarity, but the full Father-son relationship will remain, and you can go with confidence, with assurance, with certainty, knowing that because He is your Father, and because of His exceeding great and precious promises, He is always ready to receive you. What is most marvellous is not His power but the relationship. That is the guarantee.

That is the first aspect of the privilege. The second is: that because of our relationship to the Father, there is *a relationship to the Son*. The Lord Jesus Christ is referred to in the Scriptures as the 'first-born among many brethren'. And it is true. He says, 'My Father—your Father'. There is a relationship between us and Him. The author of the Epistle to the Hebrews says, 'He has not stretched out a helping hand to angels, but to the seed of Abraham' (2: 16). He did not take on Him the nature of angels, He took on Him man's nature; He has 'been made a little lower than the angels', He has come down to our level, He took on Him human nature from the Virgin Mary. He is our Brother, He is the First-born among many brethren; and He says, 'Behold I and the children which God hath given me'. Thus He is one with us, sharer of our nature. But as the Epistle to the Hebrews shows, it does not stop at that. Because that is true He understands us, He sympathises with us, He is in heaven to represent us. He is ever there with the Father interceding on our behalf. And the thought of that again is quite overwhelming. It is in Him and through Him and by Him we go to the Father.

But let us never forget that because of our relationship to the Father and the Lord Jesus Christ, we are entitled to say, according to this apostle: 'And if children, then heirs; heirs of God and joint-heirs with Christ' (Romans 8: 17). At this very moment, whatever your position may be, this is the simple truth about you, you are *an heir of God*. There is a glory awaiting us which is so marvellous that we are told very little about it even in the Scriptures. People sometimes ask, Why are we told so little about heaven, why are we told so little in detail about the eternal state? The answer is quite simple. Because we are sinful, because we are fallen, our language is fallen also, and any attempt to describe the glory of heaven would be a misrepresentation of it. So we are not given detailed descriptions. All we are told is this, that we shall be with Christ—and that ought to be enough for us. We shall be with Him. We shall be like Him. There are images used in the book of Revelation, but remember that they are only pictures and images; the thing itself is infinitely greater than that, the glory is indescribable. And you and I are heirs of that. 'Blessed are the pure in heart, for they shall see God.' 'Blessed are the meek for they shall inherit the earth'—and it will be a new earth, a glorified, renovated earth, 'new heavens and a new earth wherein dwelleth righteousness'. And it is ours; we are heirs of that and joint-heirs with Christ. 'If we suffer with him we know that we shall also reign with him,' says Paul to Timothy. What are you fretting at, Timothy, why are you whimpering and crying? Why are you so sorry for yourself? Do you not know that if you suffer with Him you shall also reign with Him and be glorified with Him? If we remembered this always we would talk much less, we would not grumble at all, and we would not be overwhelmed and upset by problems and difficulties. Our failures are really all due to our failure to realise and to grasp the fact that God is our Father, that every detail of our life is of concern to Him. Take everything to Him; 'take it to the Lord in prayer', whatever it is. He has used the term Father Himself. Do not think of Me, He seems to say, as some distant God away in glory and in eternity; I am there, but in Christ I have come to you, I am your Father, come to Me. As the Lord Himself gave the gracious invitation and invited all who are weary and heavy laden to come to Him, so God invites His children. 'Come unto me all ye that labour and are heavy laden, and I will give you rest' (Matthew 11: 28). That fretful child is breaking his heart because he wants something he cannot have—his father just takes him up and embraces him, and the child is satisfied without knowing why, because he knows that that embrace means that all the father has is his also. So God is ready to take us up and to enfold us in His love. Go to Him, Christians, He is your Father, you are 'members of the household of God'.

And, again, for the same reason, *we share the same Spirit*. The same Spirit that was in Christ is the Spirit that is in us. 'Because ye are children', says Paul, 'God hath sent forth the Spirit of his Son into your hearts crying, Abba, Father' (Galatians 4: 6). The Spirit of adoption! This is again a result of our being children of God, that He has given us His Spirit.

As I close, need I remind you of *the responsibilities of all this*? It is inevitable. Enjoying such a position, such a dignity, such glory;

participating in such privileges, oh, how great is our responsibility! Let me quote a few words spoken by our Lord Himself. Because of all this, 'Let your light so shine before men, that they may see your good works, and glorify your Father which is in heaven' (Matthew 5: 16). The child tells us a great deal about his parents, does he not? The child not merely tells us things about himself, he tells us much more about his parents. As you watch the behaviour of a child you are really learning a great deal about the discipline, or lack of it, at home. The child proclaims the parent. 'They shall see your good works, and glorify your Father which is in heaven.' Christ Himself again said, 'I am glorified in them (us)' (John 17: 10). And you remember how, in the Sermon on the Mount, our Lord again puts it like this, in talking about loving your enemies, 'Ye have heard that it hath been said, Thou shalt love thy neighbour and hate thine enemy; but I say unto you, Love your enemies, bless them that curse you, do good to them that hate you, and pray for them which despitefully use you and persecute you.' Why should we do all this? Here it is—'That ye may be the children of your Father which is in heaven' (Matthew 5: 43-5). That is why we have to do it, that we may be like our Father, that we may proclaim the family to which we belong. 'For if ye love them which love you, what reward have ye? Do not even the publicans the same? And if ye salute your brethren only, what do ye more than others? Do not even the publicans so? Be ye therefore perfect, even as your Father which is in heaven is perfect.' So the next time you are in doubt about some course of action, whether you should do a certain thing or not, do not spend your time arguing with someone as to whether it is right or wrong, simply ask 'Is that sort of thing worthy of my Father's son? Is it consistent with the family to which I belong, the Father who has put His own name on me and whom I represent among men?'

'Ye are no more strangers and foreigners, but fellowcitizens with the saints, and of the household of God.'

30

AN HABITATION OF GOD

And are built upon the foundation of the apostles and prophets, Jesus Christ himself being the chief corner stone; In whom all the building fitly framed together groweth unto an holy temple in the Lord: In whom ye also are builded together for an habitation of God through the Spirit.

Ephesians 2: 20–22

These verses carry on the thought of the previous verse where the apostle says, 'Now therefore ye are no more strangers and foreigners, but fellowcitizens with the saints, and of the household of God'.

We have dealt with the first two pictures which the apostle uses to enable us to see the privileges of being members of the Christian Church, and so come on now to *this third and last picture*. It is a picture of the Church as 'the temple of God', 'the house of God', *the building in which He dwells*.

It is always interesting to observe the working of the apostle's mind. Have you ever wondered, when reading this statement, why the apostle added this last, this third picture? It seems to me that there is only one explanation. The thought of a household suggested to him at once the thought of a house. It is a natural transition— from the household, the family, to the house in which they dwell. I say that it is interesting to observe the working of the apostle's mind, and I say so deliberately. It is important as we think of the doctrine of the inspiration of the writers of the Scriptures that we should always bear in mind that the doctrine of inspiration does not do away with the individual characteristics of the writers; otherwise there would be no variation in style at all, they would all write in exactly the same way. But though all these different writers are filled with, and controlled by, and governed and led by the Holy Spirit, their own individual characteristics are given full play. One should never, therefore, have any difficulty, when listening to, or reading a portion of Scripture, in knowing whether it has been written by Paul or by Peter or by John. They have their own individual characteristics, and here we have something which is very characteristic of the apostle Paul, namely, the way in which his mind moves always along lines of reason or logical links and connections. Household!—house!

335

We must now look at this picture. In dealing with the idea of the Church as the family of God, I was at pains to point out that this represented an advance in the apostle's thought from the first picture. I tried to show by a series of comparisons and contrasts why this was so, and how he was taking us up to a higher conception. As we come now to this third picture the question at once arises, therefore, Is he still advancing? Is this third picture a climax or is it an anticlimax? Some may well feel on first reading it that, whatever may have been true of the second, this third picture must be an anticlimax, because to go from a family to a house is surely to go down. It seems to be a going from the personal to the impersonal, from the human to the material. What is the position therefore? Is the thought of the apostle advancing? Is he taking us still higher? Or is he suddenly changing the trend and line of thought and bringing us to some kind of mechanical picture?

This is a very important question, not only from the standpoint of exactness and exegesis and exposition, but still more perhaps from the standpoint of spiritual truth. I propose, therefore, to show that *the apostle's thought is still advancing and that in this third picture he brings us up to a great climax, beyond which nothing is possible.* How can this be established? In this way—in its definition and description of the relationship that exists between the members of the Church. We have already emphasised that the apostle's leading principle all along is that of unity, and what he is trying to do in these three pictures is to bring out this great fact of unity. My contention is that in this third picture he is showing us the essence of that unity in an even greater way than he did in his first two illustrations. In order to justify this contention, all I need to do is to show the superiority of this third picture in that respect to the second picture, that of the family; because we have already shown that that was superior to the picture of the State.

I suggest that the members of a family, while they are more closely bound together than are the fellowcitizens in a state, are still in some respects in a free and loose association. The family, after all, is a collection of individuals, whereas when you come to a building that is no longer the case and there is *a truer merging of the parts.* Now the phrase which the apostle uses in the twentieth verse, 'in whom all the building', 'the whole building' provides the key to a true understanding. I know that there are those who would translate that expression as 'every building', but still the point he makes is the same. If you prefer to take it as 'every building' and think of each such building as a different section of the temple, still the different sections are parts of a whole, so you have still got the idea of a whole building. I suggest, therefore, that when you think of a building, as distinct from a family, there is a unity between the different bricks or stones in a building which is even closer than that which exists between the members of a family. The members of a family are separate and distinct individuals. All the members of a family are not identical; they do not have to submerge their characteristics in order to be members of a family. Individuality still remains and sometimes it is very striking, so much so at times that certain members of a family may bear a less close resemblance to one another than to other people to whom they are not related at all. They are members of a family, and yet this individuality is still maintained and remains, and the connection and the attachment is to that extent a loose one. The most essential point about a structure, a building, on the other hand, is the cohesion, what the apostle describes as being 'fitly framed together'.

I can perhaps put it best of all in this way: the members of a family, after all, can separate from one another. That does not mean they cease to be members of a family, but they can part company from one another. They may even quarrel, they may not even see one another, they may not speak to one another. I know that the fundamental union is still there and nothing can dissolve it; but as regards fellowship and communion and companionship and being together, they can, because they are distinct and separate entities, separate from one another and almost give the impression that there is no relationship or connection at all between them. But if you begin to do that sort of thing with a building, the end will be that you have no building. If you take a large number of stones out of a building your wall will collapse, your building will be non-existent. So that here, I think, the principle of unity is shown to be still closer and nearer. Separate the bricks or the stones in a wall, and the building is gone: but you can separate the members of a family and still the family remains as a unit. It is a looser connection than is the case in a building. I suggest, therefore, that the apostle is really advancing in his thinking, and that he shows us here that the relationship of Christian people as members of a church is indeed as close and as intimate as is that which obtains in the different parts and portions of a building.

But when we look at it *from the standpoint of privilege* the advance in the thought is yet more evident. We saw that the child is in a more advantageous position than the citizen. The humble citizen can appeal to the king, the head of the state, but not in the same way that a child can approach his father. That shows a more intimate relationship and a higher and a greater privilege. But here the apostle goes even beyond that. His conception of the Church here is that the Church is the holy temple of the Lord, 'builded together for an habitation of God through the Spirit'. Now the child has access to the father, but the child is still outside the father. But here the idea presented is of God dwelling within us, taking up His abode within us. Now that is as tremendous an advance in the thought, as the second was upon the first. Not only are we in that near relationship to God and have this freedom of access to Him; beyond and above all that, the final mystery and glory of the Church is that God dwells within her. She is the temple, the holy temple of the Lord. As His presence dwelt in that innermost sanctuary in the old temple amongst the children of Israel, so now He dwells in the Church amongst His people. There is nothing in the realm of thought that can advance beyond that.

It is, of course, similar to the teaching which our Lord gave just before the end of His earthly life when He said, 'It is expedient for you that I go away, for if I go not away the Comforter will not come unto you; but if I depart, I will send him unto you'. It was a great privilege to be there standing in the presence of the Son of God, looking at Him, listening to Him, being able to question Him and being helped by Him. That was marvellous, it was wonderful; but there is something better, and that is, that He should come and dwell in us and live in us and take up His abode in us. And He said, That is what I am going to do. I will come to you, I will manifest myself unto you, the Father and I will dwell in you, and take up our abode in you (John 14: 21-23). That is beyond speaking to Him externally. He now comes and dwells within—'I live, yet not I, but Christ liveth in me'. Now that is the idea, the kind of conception which the apostle holds before us in this third and last picture that he uses. What he says is that the Ephesians are parts of this great building, this temple of God—these Ephesians who were once so far away have been built into this temple and are being built into it.

This teaching, concerning the Church as a great building, *is given much prominence in the New Testament.* And as there is nothing more vital today than that Christian people should again grasp this New Testament teaching about the Church, there is nothing more urgent for us than to take hold of this wonderful teaching. You remember that it was first propounded by our Lord Himself in the great incident at Caesarea Philippi, when Peter made his confession, 'Thou art the Christ, the Son of the living God', and our Lord said to him, 'I say unto thee that thou art Peter, and upon this rock I will build my church'. There is the first use of the analogy; there is the basis on which all the others have built. I shall hope to refer to this particular statement later in order that we may have some understanding of what our Lord means by it; but it is dealt with indirectly and by implication by the apostle here.

Then there is the statement at the beginning of the third chapter of the First Epistle to the Corinthians, running from verse 9 to verse 17. There the apostle says that he is a 'master builder', and he has clearly got this whole conception of the Church as a building in his mind—'other foundation can no man lay than that is laid, which is Jesus Christ'. There are all sorts of people who are building upon this foundation, says the apostle, but they are not all building in the true way, and there is going to be a judgment, and every man's work will be tried. But it is the idea of the Church as a building that he is emphasising: 'Know ye not,' he says, 'that ye are the temple of God?' The whole trouble in the church at Corinth was that they had forgotten this, and as a result they were dividing themselves up— 'I am of Paul; I am of Apollos; I am of Cephas'; and so on. He says, Do you not realise that you are the temple of the living God?— you must not destroy God's temple in that way, you are violating the principle of unity. In this way, we are reminded of the all-importance of this doctrine. All the troubles in the Church finally come from our failure to realise the nature of the Church. That is why all these New Testament Epistles ultimately deal with the doctrine of the Church. These people had been saved, they were Christians without a doubt; but they were in trouble in many directions because they kept on forgetting what they were as members of the Church. They were segregating themselves, as it were, becoming individualists in a wrong sense, and so troubles and trials arose. The answer to all that is: come back and realise that the Church is like a great building.

Again he is really saying the same thing when he reminds these Corinthians, in the sixth chapter in the nineteenth verse, that the Holy Spirit dwells within them. He is thinking of individuals rather than the Church, but it is a part of the same concept. 'Ye are not your own, ye are bought with a price.' He tells them not to commit certain sins of the body. Why? Because 'your body is the temple of the Holy Ghost which is in you'. Again there is a very notable statement of it in the Second Epistle to the Corinthians, in the sixth chapter and the sixteenth verse, where he says, 'What agreement hath the temple of God with idols? For ye are the temple of the living God; as God hath said, I will dwell in them and walk in them. . . .' There it is once more, the Church as the temple of the living God. Again you have it in the First Epistle to Timothy, the third chapter and the fifteenth verse. I am quoting all this to show how vitally important it is in the New Testament teaching. 'But if I tarry long', says Paul to Timothy, 'that thou mayest know how thou oughtest to behave thyself in the house of God, which is the church of the living God, the pillar and ground of the truth.' It is the same idea still. And the apostle Peter uses exactly the same illustration. He says, 'Ye also, as lively stones, are built up a spiritual house . . .' (1 Peter 2: 5). There are other examples also that could be quoted, but these are the leading ones.

With all these passages in our minds, let us see what the apostle is really teaching us at this point in our chapter. It seems to me that we can divide his statement into two main sections. *First,* there is a general statement about this idea of the Church, especially in terms of unity and privilege. *Secondly,* there are the actual details of the construction. Whenever you look at a building it is important that you should bear those two things in mind. You can take a general view of the building; there are certain marked features which you can at once note. But then there is that other aspect to the study of a building—the examination of the foundation in detail, the way in which the walls have been built and what it is that holds it all together. There is that aspect, the more mechanical side. In a fascinating manner the apostle deals with both aspects here.

For the present I want to deal in particular with the first principle only; namely, *this general conception of the Church as a building.* As we look at it may the Spirit enable us to see ourselves as a part of this amazing process that is going on.

The first thing the apostle tells us is that the Church is a building *which is in process of being built.* I do not know of a better way of thinking of this present era, this present dispensation, than just to look at it like that. What is it that God is doing at this present time? What is it indeed that God has been doing ever since our Lord completed His work and returned to heaven? What indeed has God been doing in this world since the very fall of man? The answer is that God is erecting a building, and that building is the Church. It is a process that is going on. The apostle suggests it here in this word, 'and are built upon the foundation', which is, more accurately, 'are being built upon'. There is the idea of a process. It is here in another word, 'in whom all the building fitly framed together, groweth unto an holy temple in the Lord'. You can see the process going on, a building growing upwards and extending. I like to think of that as a picture of what is taking place in the world. You can read the secular history books, you can look at the history of the world and of the human race as the secular-minded man does, and you will find it very difficult to make anything of it at all; but when you look at it from the standpoint of the Bible you see very clearly what is happening. God has a great plan. He is the eternal Architect who has drawn up His plans and specifications, and He is building. And in every generation He is taking out certain stones, quarrying them, pulling them out, in the manner I hope to describe later, and adding them to the building. In some generations there have been mighty revivals and there has been a great addition, and you can see the building springing up, as it were; but then there are periods when nothing at all seems to be happening and a casual observer might say that there is no increase, no extension, that the walls are no higher and that nothing is happening at all. And yet the building is going on, one stone here and one there perhaps. It is all a part of this great process.

But we must remind ourselves that it is not only a part of God's purpose, but that it is also a certain purpose. This process of building has been going on for a long time. 'You have been built into it', says Paul to these Ephesians, but how many thousands, millions, have been built in since then! You and I have been added to it, built into it; we are a part of it; and the process is still going on. And it will go on until it is complete and finished. This apostle Paul in the eleventh chapter of the Epistle to the Romans talks about 'the fulness of the Gentiles', and of 'all Israel being saved'. Believe me, 'known unto God are all His people', and 'the foundation of God standeth sure'. Let the world do what it will, let hell be let loose, yet everyone whom God has chosen for this building will be in the building. We are placed in it, added to it, and it is the highest and the greatest privilege that can ever fall to the lot of any human being. Think of yourself then in this way, as a part of this glorious edifice, this tremendous temple, that God is building. He is quarrying these stones out of the world, and setting up this new building, this marvellous structure, this glorious temple. That is the first thought.

But I must emphasise at once the second thing which is suggested here, which is that *this is a vital process*. Again I must observe how fascinating it is to watch the working of the apostle's mind. He must have realised at once, the moment he started with this conception, that people might begin to think of the Church, and the building of the Church, in a mechanical manner. You just put a brick on top of a brick, you add a stone to a stone, put in a bit of mortar, and so on—what is more mechanical than building! The apostle, I think, was so afraid that people might misunderstand it in that way, that he brings in a term like this word 'groweth': 'in whom all the building fitly framed together groweth . . .' Can a building grow? Can something that is material and mechanical grow? It can, according to the apostle; and in order to make this clear he is almost guilty, if not actually guilty, of mixing his metaphors. He is mixing the metaphor of the growth of flowers, or of grass, and that of a building developing and advancing and extending and going up. It is interesting to observe that in the third chapter of the First Epistle to the Corinthians he again puts these two ideas side by side. He says in the ninth verse, 'For we are labourers together with God; ye are God's husbandry, ye are God's building'. At one and the same time the apostle says that he is a farmer and a master builder. You, he says, are like a field of wheat and you are also a building. He puts the two ideas together, he seems to blend them into one. The building growing—a vital process!

The apostle Peter does the same thing. Whether he got the idea from the apostle Paul or not, I do not know. (We know that he did read Paul's epistles, because he has told us that some of them are a little difficult to understand (2 Peter 3: 15, 16).) Did you notice the words I quoted just now from 1 Peter 2: 5: 'Ye also as lively stones . . .'? Can a stone be lively? Can a stone be living? Is there vitality in a stone? Peter says there is, for this is his metaphor, 'Ye also as lively stones (living stones) are built up a spiritual house.'

Indeed the apostle Paul here in the twenty-second verse again brings out this same idea: 'in whom all the building fitly framed together'—fitly framed together! He uses that very same idea in the fourth chapter when, in speaking about the body, he says 'from whom (Christ) the whole body fitly joined together and compacted, by that which every joint supplieth'. Now all that is quite simple in the case of the body, but is it as evident in the case of a wall, a building? The only way to understand it, according to the apostle, is to grasp the idea that it is a vital building, a living building.

This is one of the things that needs to be emphasised urgently today. There is all the difference in the world between just adding to the numbers on the roll of a church and the growth of the holy temple of the Lord. We are living in an age which is statistically minded, and you can read reports of countries and places where almost everybody seems to be a church member. But, alas, it does not follow that they are all being built into this holy temple of the Lord. It does not follow of necessity that they are 'lively' stones, that they are a part of this growth. The increase of the Church is vital, not mechanical. Men can add to the membership of a church, but God alone, can build, through the Holy Spirit, into the building of the Church. This growing unto an holy temple is a vital process. As you listen to, and read of, all this talk today about Church unity and a great world church, and the coalescing of different denominations, bear in mind this word 'groweth'. It is one thing merely to amalgamate together a number of organisations. That is not Paul's conception of the unity of the Church, nor of the increase of the Church. But that seems to be the controlling thought today. It is mechanical, it is statistical. You just add on here; you sit down and have a conference, and you decide to do that. What a contrast to this vital, living, dynamic process! 'Groweth unto an holy temple!' Living stones! Lively stones! I am emphasising it because I have no hesitation in asserting that it is very largely because this principle has been forgotten that the Church is as she is today. The Church has been pleading with men to join her. What a confession of failure to understand the nature of the Church! I never ask anybody to join the Church. I never will. I have never done so. To me it is grievously wrong to plead with people, almost to implore them, to join the Church. Indeed people have often been bribed to join a church. But all that is the very antithesis of this vital process in which the apostle is interested, this growing, the result of this tremendous operation. Let us always remember that it is a vital process.

That brings me to my third comment. You notice that the apostle says that *this is a 'holy temple'*. As you walk around this building and look at it, what is your main impression? Well, says the apostle, the main impression that this building gives is an impression of 'holiness'. He does not say a word about the size, he does not say anything about its ornate character. He does not say that there is anything showy about it. But he does say that it is holy. That is its great characteristic. '. . . groweth unto an holy temple, in the Lord'. 'In whom ye also are builded together for an habitation of God, through the Spirit.' Oh, how we have forgotten this characteristic! How sadly is it being forgotten today! Surely this was the fatal thing that happened when Constantine linked the Roman State with the Christian Church. It was forgotten that she is a holy temple, that the main characteristic of the Church is always that it should be holy— not that it should be large or influential. You remember the state-ment that was once made by a man, perhaps partly jocularly but, also, how truly! In discussing the question of miracles in the Church this man pointed out that it was when the Church could say, 'Silver and gold have I none' that she could go on to say, 'In the name of Jesus Christ of Nazareth rise up and walk'. The Church today can make neither of the statements. She has got the silver and gold, she has become great and powerful; but she has forgotten holiness. But this is *the* characteristic of the temple, a 'holy people', a 'place meet for God to dwell in'.

Would that in all our talking and thinking and arguing concerning unity today this principle were put at the centre. But it is not. What are being discussed today are various points of view about ordina-tion; whether bishops are of the *esse* of the Church or only the *bene esse*, and so on; mere mechanical matters! As if these were the things that count! As the apostle goes on to say in chapter 4, the one guarantee of true unity in the Church is the unity of the Holy Spirit, the unity of holiness, the unity of holy people. When holiness is the main characteristic, the unity looks after itself. When holiness is put at the centre, much has to go, before much can come in. Every revival, every great increase in the Church in her long history has always followed this pattern. It was when Wesley and Whitefield and others had had their 'Holy Club' that the revival came 200 years ago. You start with holiness, and then the numbers increase. But if you try to add to the number without the holiness, you will not have a 'temple in the Lord'. You will have a great organisation, you will have a flourishing business concern, you will have a marvellous institution; but it will not be the place where God dwells. It may be a place of entertainment and of much bustling activity, but it will not be the Church of the living God. Holiness is her main characteristic.

That brings me to the last thought for the moment, which is, that the Church in all these respects must always be thought of in *terms of the blessed holy Trinity*. How constantly does the apostle come back to this! We saw it in the eighteenth verse, 'For through him (referring to the Son) we both have access by one Spirit unto the Father'. The three Persons! Do you notice his emphasis? 'Jesus Christ Himself (here is the first mention of Christ in these particular verses) being the chief corner-stone'—Jesus Christ! What else? 'In whom'—Jesus Christ!—'all the building, fitly framed together, groweth unto an holy temple in the Lord'—the Lord Jesus Christ again; 'in whom'—still the Lord Jesus Christ. Paul cannot leave Him alone, he cannot forget Him. He goes on emphasising it and repeating it. As we read through these first two chapters of this Epistle to the Ephesians, how often do we find this repetition of the name, Jesus Christ, the Lord, Christ Jesus, in whom, in Him, even in Him; on and on he goes, always referring to Him! There is no Church apart from Jesus Christ. There is no unity apart from Jesus Christ. That is why a so-called world congress of faiths is a denial of Christ and of the Church. And that is why any movement or organisation that claims to put men right with God which does not put Christ everywhere—central, beginning, foundation, end, everywhere—is not Christian. It may do a lot of social good, it may help people, it may perhaps even produce a change in their lives; but if Christ is not essential it is not Christian. Notice the repetition of it here again—'Christ Jesus Himself'—in whom, in whom, in whom! There is nothing apart from our relationship to Him. And then, 'an habitation of God'—the Father!—coming to dwell within. He manifested His presence in the Shekinah glory in the temple in the 'holiest of all'; and He comes to dwell in the Church. And He does so through the Spirit. The Son! The Father! The Holy Spirit! It is always the order—the Son takes us to the Father, and the Father and the Son send the Spirit. And so we have this 'holy temple in the Lord'.

Do you not see the importance of this doctrine? People went into the ancient temple to meet with God. It was the place where His presence and His honour dwelt. The practical, vital importance of this doctrine for us is, that God dwells now in the temple which is the Church. And it is in us and through us that people look for Him and, in that first sense, come to Him. Are we giving the impression to those who are outside, that the Church is the temple of the living God? Do they see something of this holiness, this awe, that belongs to God Himself in us—that He dwells and walks in us?

There, then, are some general principles deduced from the general language of the apostle. We shall go on to consider in detail what he tells us about the construction. It is absolutely vital. In all this modern interest in union and in the Church, nothing is more fundamentally important than that all our thinking should be controlled by the Scriptures. We must beware lest human ideas intrude, and we must make sure that in our desire to 'do' something, we may not be wasting our energy, and so find when the day comes when every man's work is tried by fire, that our work will prove to be nothing but wood and hay and stubble that will all be burned, and we shall suffer loss—though, by the grace of God, we ourselves may still be saved—yet, so as by fire (1 Corinthians 3: 13 and 15).

31

THE ONLY FOUNDATION

And are built upon the foundation of the apostles and prophets, Jesus Christ himself being the chief corner stone; In whom all the building fitly framed together groweth unto an holy temple in the Lord: In whom ye also are builded together for an habitation of God through the Spirit.

Ephesians 2: 20–22

We have seen that the apostle uses three pictures here in order to convey to these Ephesian Christians a true conception of their position in the Christian Church, and therefore a true conception of the nature of the Christian Church herself. We have already dealt with two of them. The first was the picture of a state, a kingdom, a country. We are all members, citizens, of the kingdom of God. But secondly he compares the Church to a family. And we are all the children of God and members of the household of God. But even that was not enough. He goes on to this third picture which we have already begun to consider, this picture of the Church of God as a great building in which God dwells.

Now it is obvious that the picture suggested itself to the apostle partly because of what he had just been saying in an earlier verse about the temple under the old dispensation. His great point is that the middle wall of partition between the Jews and the Gentiles had been broken down. The middle wall of partition, of course, was to be found in the temple. The Gentiles were in the Court of the Gentiles, and there was a wall that prevented their going in to the Court of the People. And the people in turn were not allowed to go into the 'holy place,' and none save the high priest into the 'holiest of all'. He was thinking therefore in terms of a temple which had separated people. But now all that has gone, and there is a new temple; and God dwells in this new temple, the temple consisting of His own people. It is no longer a Jewish temple. That has gone for ever; 'There is neither Greek nor Jew . . . Barbarian, Scythian, bond nor free; but Christ is all, and in all'. There is this new thing. The temple in which God now dwells is the Church, His own people.

I have already reminded you, and now remind you again, that there are two great principles which we must hold very firmly in

346

the forefront of our minds if we are to follow this teaching. The apostle is concerned to show two things: one, the unity, the essential unity that must ever be true of the Christian Church and of all who are truly Christian. This is not a debatable matter, it is something that God has made and that God Himself has produced in Christ. He has 'made of twain one new man', this new thing, the Church. And the unity is quite inevitable. The second thing, and it follows from that unity, is the privilege of our position. The apostle in this picture of the Church as this temple, this holy building in which God takes up His residence, brings out those two truths very clearly. We have looked at it in general, but we must go on to a more detailed consideration.

The apostle teaches that the building is a thing that is constantly developing by a lively, a living, an active process. 'Groweth'—it is something that grows; and we are all 'fitly framed together'. It is not mechanical—we must never think of unity in terms of mechanics or cold statistics. No, it is something vital—'groweth'. It is a living process. We also saw that it is holy. The apostle is not interested in size, he is interested in quality. Holiness! 'Holy temple in the Lord!' We saw, likewise, that the three Persons of the blessed Trinity are always of necessity involved. But the apostle does not stop at mere general description. He looks at the temple and he first of all gives a general account of it. But this matter is so important in his estimation that he must come to details. He gives us the plans and the specifications of this building, this temple. And, because the apostle takes the trouble to do this, we must deduce that he regarded it as a matter of the greatest importance.

This whole question of *the nature of the Church, the unity of the Church, is indeed a fundamental matter*. The apostle dealt with it in his own day and generation because it was obviously very essential that he should do so. It is equally essential that we should do so today. The great word of today is the word 'unity'. There is possibly more talk and more preaching and more writing of books and articles about unity in the Church today than concerning any other single subject. Indeed, it is the main topic under discussion in all sections of the Church in all countries. Therefore, whatever our views may be, it behoves us to be clear in our thinking. It is very wrong for any Christian to say that he is concerned only about his own personal experience, and in no way concerned about these larger matters. You must be. You cannot live in isolation. We all live together, we have fellowship with one another. 'No man liveth unto himself. No man dieth unto himself.' And indeed if we do not think about these matters we shall find ourselves being influenced by others, and involved in their decisions. Let me use an illustration. We read constantly in the newspapers these days that the real problem in the industrial world as regards strikes and disputes is very largely due to the fact that the vast majority of the members of the trades unions simply do not take the trouble to go to the meetings and to vote. The result is that a few keen persons, who may be Communists, always go, and because they go and the others do not, but allow it to pass by default, the policy of a union may well be governed by a mere handful of people while all the others who may not really be in agreement have to abide by the decisions. The sheer slackness and indolence, the refusal to take an active interest, allows the position to go by default. Exactly the same thing will happen in the Christian Church. It has often happened that Christians in a state of indolence, and refusing to be bothered and to apply their minds to these things, have allowed decisions to be made for them by a bare handful of officials. It is our duty, I say, as Christians to understand something of what the apostle teaches here concerning this question of unity.

Let me give you some further reasons for doing so. *There are many ways in which you can get a kind of unity, but what matters is the unity which corresponds to what the apostle teaches here.* The Roman Catholic Church believes in the unity of the Church more than any other body. They are always saying so. The very word 'catholic' tells us that. It is the universal Church, and the Roman Catholics are amazed that Protestants ever left them or that there have ever been any divisions at all. They say that we should be one, that the Church should be united. No church preaches unity more than the Roman Catholic Church. But we know what they mean by that. They mean uniformity; they mean that we all become absorbed again; they mean that we all return to Rome. My point is that they are very much interested in unity. So if we simply talk about unity and say that nothing matters but unity, then logically we ought all to go back into the Roman Catholic Church. They call themselves Christians as we do. Very well then, we might reason, if we are all Christians together, why separate, why be different? Let us all be one, let us all become Roman Catholics.

Now when it is put like that we do not like it; but when precisely the same argument is used within Protestantism we think it is a wonderful argument. But the principle is still precisely the same. You do not, and must not start with unity. Unity is something that results from something else. You cannot create unity. Take for instance this picture that the apostle has used about a family. The unity between the members of a family is not something created artificially. Unity is inevitable because of their relationship. And every form of unity is the same. Unity is a result. You do not start

with unity; unity is something that exists because certain fundamental principles are in operation.

Consider another illustration. We read in the newspapers a few
years ago of the way in which the tenth anniversary of the founding
of the United Nations Organisation was celebrated. In connection
with that they had a meeting which they called a 'Festival of Faith.'
And the festival of faith consisted of this, that there was a great service
in which Jews and Mohammedans and Buddhists and Confucianists
and Christians all took part together and recited the same prayers
together. The argument was this—oh, how often is the argument
used today! People say, We all believe in the same God. The
Mohammedan, the Hindu, the Buddhist, the Christian, all believe
in the same God. Truth is like a great mountain; there is the one
summit, but there are many ways of going up to it. Why should you
say that you alone are right? What right have Christians to say
that they alone are right and that all the others are wrong? It does
not matter which way you climb up the mountain as long as you
get to the top. So let us all come together in a great festival of the
faiths, a great congress, a world congress of religions. We believe
in the same God, therefore why haggle about these things? That is
the kind of argument that is being used. I wonder sometimes what
such people would think of the apostle Paul if he were alive today.
I wonder what many in the Christian Church would say about him.
Notice what he says to the Galatians: 'Though we or an angel from
heaven preach unto you any other gospel than that which we have
preached unto you, let him be accursed' (Galatians 1: 8). Ha! they
would say, impossible man, individualist, isolationist! He alone is
right, everyone else is wrong. He won't come in with the rest of us,
he is always standing out on certain points. Is it not clear that
through allowing ourselves to be influenced by vague general talk
we become utterly unscriptural at times without realising what we
are doing? No, we must be careful to observe the God-given plans
and specifications. It is not enough to be shouting the word 'unity'
and saying that the great thing is that we should all get together.
There is something infinitely more important—truth! For a unity
which is not based upon truth is false. It is man-made; it is not
God's plan, and is therefore unreal and spurious.

The apostle here gives us clear teaching concerning all this.
Build, he says, upon the foundation. He brings us to the vital
principle at once: *there can be no true building without a right foundation.*
You have got to start with foundations, says Paul. You cannot talk
of a building without knowing something about its foundation.
That is absolutely vital and central. Therefore, in the light of the

modern tragic confusion, we must take the trouble to go into detailed descriptions and expositions and definitions to show exactly what the apostle says.

Here is the only basis for true unity: *the foundation of the apostles and prophets*. What does Paul mean? We must start by asking the question, *What is an apostle*? This whole matter of unity cannot be understood unless I know what an apostle is and what a prophet is, because the Church is 'built on the foundation of the apostles and prophets'. The following are the essential points about an apostle. An apostle was one who had seen the risen Lord. By definition an apostle is one who is a witness to the resurrection, because he has seen the risen Lord. That was one of the qualifications of Paul himself. He saw the risen Lord on the way to Damascus. If he had not done so, he could never have been an apostle. He might have been a preacher, he might have been a prophet, he might have been a great teacher; but he could never have been an apostle if he had not seen the Lord on the road to Damascus. So that is why, in writing to the Corinthians, he says that he himself is 'as one born out of due time' (1 Corinthians 15: 8). He did not see the risen Lord at the same time as the other apostles, he had this special manifestation to himself in order that he might be made an apostle. He puts the same point in a phrase at the beginning of the ninth chapter of the First Epistle to the Corinthians: 'Am I not an apostle? Am I not free? Have I not seen Jesus Christ our Lord?' That is the proof of the fact that he is an apostle. But not only that! An apostle was one who was specially called and designated and sent as a preacher of the gospel by the risen Lord Himself. That again is a vital part of the calling of an apostle. Read the twenty-sixth chapter of the book of Acts, and there you will find the account of how the Lord Himself commissioned the apostle Paul on the road to Damascus. So an apostle is one who, having seen Him risen from the dead, was specially commissioned by Christ to go out to preach the message. And further, the apostles were given a very special authority. They were given power to work miracles and to found churches, and it was these that attested their authority as apostles. Those then are the three main characteristics of an apostle. We shall see in a moment how vital it is that we should bear all of them in mind. Without those three things no man was an apostle and this makes 'apostolic succession' an impossibility.

We move on to the prophets. *What is a prophet?* There has been a great deal of discussion about this. The older commentators all agree in saying that this word 'prophet' refers to the Old Testament prophets, those who prophesied of the coming of Christ, those who prophesied the coming of the kingdom, and in that sense laid a foundation. But there is also a great body of opinion on the other side which says that this is not a reference to the Old Testament prophets, but rather a reference to the New Testament prophets, the prophets who functioned in the New Testament Church. They argue that this must be the case for the reason that if the apostle had been thinking of Old Testament prophets he would have said 'on the foundation of the prophets and apostles'; but he says 'on the foundation of the apostles and prophets'. Therefore he is clearly thinking in New Testament terms. They go further and say that he does the same thing in the fifth verse of the third chapter, where we read, 'which in other ages was not made known unto the sons of men as it is now revealed unto his holy apostles and prophets by the Spirit'. And again in the eleventh verse of the fourth chapter he says: 'He gave some, apostles; and some, prophets; and some evangelists; and some, pastors and teachers'. So on these grounds they argue that this is patently a reference to the New Testament prophets, the prophets in the Christian Church.

That then raises the question, What is a prophet?—whether in the old dispensation or the new. The answer is that a prophet is one who receives a direct message from God. He is one to whom the truth is revealed directly by the Spirit—not as a result of reading the Scripture or anything else, but by a direct message given, which he in turn is to impart to others. The apostle Paul defines it for us: 'he that prophesieth', he says, 'speaketh unto men to edification and exhortation and comfort' (1 Corinthians 14: 3). In the Christian Church in the early days there were these people called prophets. They had no New Testament Scriptures then; neither the Gospels nor the Epistles were available to them: but there were these people who were given spiritual truth and understanding by direct revelation and were enabled to speak it. The prophet in the Old Testament did exactly the same. God revealed truth to him and enabled him to speak it. That is the characteristic of a prophet.

To what exactly is the apostle referring here, when he says, 'on the foundation of the apostles and prophets'? He puts the apostles first because of their utter absolute uniqueness. You get the same in Revelation 21: 14, where we read of the holy city, new Jerusalem, coming down from heaven, that its wall had twelve foundations and in these were written the 'names of the twelve apostles of the Lamb'. As regards prophets we may agree that he is referring to the Old Testament prophets *and* to the New Testament prophets, but especially the latter.

In what sense, then, is it true to say that the Church is built and established and founded upon the foundation of the apostles and prophets? It means partly upon the men themselves as believers, the men as exercising faith. They were the first believers—the apostles and prophets—and in that sense the whole superstructure rests upon them. There is no doubt at all but that that is partly the meaning, that they were the first to be laid there in this great building as foundation stones. So it is right to say that this partly refers to them as believers, as those exercising faith in the Lord Jesus Christ.

But that in turn leads to the second thing, and probably this was even more in the mind of the apostle than the first; *the teaching of the apostles and prophets*. This after all is the real foundation. None of us can come into the Church without believing. It is as the result of believing that we derive all our benefits, and are made what we are. The difference between Christians and non-Christians is that between believers and non-believers. Un-believers are not in the Church: believers are in the Church. What did they believe? They believed the teaching. So that the foundation, in the last analysis, is the teaching of the apostles and prophets, their doctrine. They taught what they believed themselves; they gave expression to the faith by which they lived; so the two things really become one.

This, therefore, is the vital thing for us to understand and to grasp at a time like this. What makes us members of the Church, what makes us part of this great temple, this wonderful edifice that is being built, is our faith, is our acceptance of the teaching, the doctrine. This is basic and fundamental. It was the thing about which the apostle wrote in the first chapter of the Epistle to the Galatians. 'I marvel', he says, 'that you are so soon removed'—you notice how abruptly he says it. Immediately after his very brief preliminary salutation he says, 'I marvel that ye are so soon removed from him that called you into the grace of Christ unto another gospel: which is not another'—because there is not another, and there cannot be another. How strongly and dogmatically he speaks! Whether we like it or not, Christianity is a most intolerant faith. It says that this and this alone is right and true. The apostle even says 'But though we, or an angel from heaven preach any other gospel unto you than that which we have preached unto you, let him be accursed'! (Galatians 1: 8). There is no other gospel. 'Other foundation can no man lay than that is laid' (1 Corinthians 3: 11). In other words, the only basis of unity today, as it was the only basis of unity in the early Church, is the apostolic message. And whatever men may think or say we must assert this. Let them call us intolerant, isolationists, or what they will, we must take our stand with this man of God! It is not my opinion or anybody else's opinion that matters—what does the Word teach? What did the apostles teach? I know nothing apart from that. It is not modern knowledge or research or understanding or a modern idea of God that matters. What these men taught is the only gospel.

Now this is clearly something that can be defined. If it cannot be defined how could the apostle reprimand the Galatians? They knew what he taught and he reminds them of its content. The idea that Christianity is so marvellous that you cannot define it, that it is just a wonderful spirit which cannot be reduced to propositions, is a denial of the New Testament teaching. The Epistles were written in order that we might know what we are to believe and what exactly we stand for. None of us can plead ignorance of this teaching; it is all in this second chapter of the Epistle to the Ephesians. And this is the foundation—that man by nature is dead in trespasses and sins; that he is under the wrath of God. It is the apostle who says so. And, therefore, unless you believe that man, by nature, is dead in trespasses and sins, and that there is such a thing as the wrath of God upon sin, whatever else may be true of you, you are not in this holy temple in the Lord, in which God dwells. This is an essential part of the foundation. But thank God it does not stop at that, it goes on to tell us about the grace of God. It goes on to tell us about the Lord Jesus Christ, His Person and His work. It tells us that He is the only begotten Son of God. Though a man calls himself a Christian, if he does not believe in the deity of Christ I say he is not a Christian! I must be intolerant! I cannot afford to compromise at this point. If Christ is not the Son of God I am yet in my sins and I shall go to hell. And His work! Have we not noticed as we have worked our way through this second chapter —and I have taken time deliberately because we cannot afford to skim over these things—the emphasis on the blood of Christ? It is by His death, by His sacrificial death, by His substituting Himself for us to bear the punishment of our sins, that we are saved. It is by the blood of Christ! 'Wherefore remember, that ye being in time past Gentiles in the flesh, who are called Uncircumcision . . . that at that time ye were without Christ, being aliens from the commonwealth of Israel and strangers from the covenants of promise, having no hope and without God in the world. But now in Christ Jesus ye who sometimes were far off are made nigh, by the blood of Christ'! And yet people scoff at the blood of Christ! There are people who call themselves Christians who scoff at it. There are leaders in the big denominations who say that it is scandalous to talk about a substitutionary atonement. And I am asked to be one in fellowship with them. How can I be? It is impossible. I have no choice; this is fundamental. The blood of Christ! 'He bore my sins in his own body on the tree.' It is by that alone that I am delivered, and by the power of God in regeneration, and the gift of the Spirit.

Union with Christ! That is the doctrine—all that the apostle has been teaching us in this wonderful chapter.

That then is the foundation of the apostles and prophets. Not vague talk about Christianity! Not a wonderful spirit in which we all, loving one another, get together and are not concerned about definitions! If you want that spurious kind of unity you can have it, but when 'the day' comes and the judgment arrives, you will find that what the apostles said in writing to the Corinthians, 'Other foundation can no man lay than that is laid' is the only truth. He preached 'Jesus Christ and him crucified' to the exclusion of everything else. He was intolerant. Do not listen to that other teaching, he says to the Galatians, it is spurious, it is a lie, it is not a gospel, it is a denial of the gospel. The foundation of the apostles and prophets! We either accept their teaching and their message or else we do not.

Let us now draw some very up-to-date deductions from this doctrine. The first is that *the Church is founded, not on the apostle Peter only, but on the apostles and prophets*—all the apostles, and the prophets. That is our answer to Roman Catholicism, and it is indeed as simple as that. But says someone, what about Matthew 16, at Caesarea Philippi, when our Lord says 'Thou art Peter, and on this rock I will build my church'?—it must have been Peter only. The answer is what I was saying just now, that it was Peter's confession. Peter had just made his great confession! Our Lord had turned to His disciples with the question, 'Who do men say that I, the Son of man, am?' 'Some say that thou art Elias; and some, John the Baptist; and others, one of the prophets.' 'But who do ye say . . . ?' said our Lord. And Peter put himself forward as the spokesman, as was his habit, and said, 'Thou art the Christ, the Son of the living God'. And the Lord replied saying, 'Blessed art thou, Simon son of Jona, for flesh and blood hath not revealed this unto thee, but my Father which is in heaven'. What does that mean? Peter having seen the truth confesses it, and on that rock, Christ says He will build His Church. The confession, the belief, the faith! And that is not only true of Peter. The apostle Paul is not contradicting the teaching of our Lord here. According to Roman Catholic teaching he would be doing so. Many contrast the teaching of Christ with the teaching of Paul, but there is no contradiction. The foundation is the apostles and prophets, all of them, not only Peter. It is this confession that was first made by the apostles and prophets. That is the only foundation of the Christian Church. And therefore we cannot be one with those who say that all is founded on Peter alone and that everything depends upon Peter. That is a false basis.

But it is equally important for us to make this second deduction, that in the light of what we have seen to be the truth about the apostles and prophets *there can be no repetition of apostles and prophets.* They are the foundation. You do not repeat a foundation. A foundation is laid once and for ever. And therefore all talk about apostolic succession is a denial of our text. There are no special successors to the apostles. Indeed there are no successors to the apostles. An apostle was a man who had seen the risen Lord and could therefore be a witness to the resurrection. Are there such people today? An apostle was one who was specially commissioned by the Lord Himself in a visible manner. Are there such today? He was given special powers, miracles and others, and infallibility, in order that he might preach and teach infallibly. Are there such today? And yet in all this talk and argument about reunion, this seems to be the big thing—apostolic succession! And because of that, nonconformists, free church ministers, must all be ordained again by a man who is a 'direct successor' of the apostles! Without this you cannot have unity, and you cannot have communion together! How important it is to study the Scriptures! There is no such thing as apostolic succession; by definition it is something which is a sheer impossibility. You can have a sacerdotal succession, you can have a succession of men who appoint one another in perpetuity but there is no such thing as apostolic succession. And therefore all this talk that you cannot have unity without a re-ordination, or some special relationship to a bishop, is a denial of this postulate. It is faith alone and subscription to the truth that makes one a part of the building.

That brings me to the third deduction, which I put in this form. *Obviously there can be no addition to this foundation.* In the matter of teaching, I mean. If the foundation is the teaching of the apostles you cannot add to it. So I do not believe in the 'Immaculate Conception'; I do not believe in the 'Assumption' of the Virgin Mary; I do not believe in all these other things that the Roman church has added, and other churches have added. You cannot add to a foundation, you cannot take from a foundation. Here is a *corpus* of truth, here is a body of doctrine. You cannot add, you cannot subtract, you cannot touch a foundation. You may think that you can, but you would be wrong. What you are doing is just to put yourself outside the building. The foundation has been laid once and for ever, and it can never be repeated. God is the Builder and He builds upon 'the foundation of the apostles and prophets'.

So that the next very practical deduction is, that it is not enough for us just to say that we are Christian or that we want to be Christian, and that nothing further is needed. The vital question is, What do you believe? You cannot be a Christian without knowing what you believe. It is impossible. It is the truth that brings us to God, it is by the truth we are sanctified. It is only as we know the truth concerning our blessed Lord and Saviour, and ourselves and our need, and what God has done in His grace, that we can be parts and portions of this great edifice.

Therefore my last deduction must be that to talk in terms of numbers or of size or of organisation or anything else is extremely dangerous in these matters. The unity of the Church is the result of two things: purity of doctrine and purity of life. It is 'a holy temple in the Lord'. It is 'a habitation of God'.

It is built on the foundation of the apostles and prophets. And observe how the apostle hastens to add this: '*Jesus Christ himself being the chief corner stone*'. What is a chief corner stone? Let me quote a definition: 'A corner stone is a primary foundation stone at the angle of the structure by which the architect fixes a standard for the bearings of the walls and cross-walls throughout.' The corner stone not only holds together all these other subsidiary foundation stones, it also binds them together and it binds all the walls together. It is at the corner, and everything is supported by it and everything is welded together by it. And the chief corner stone is Jesus Christ Himself. Isaiah had prophesied this when he said 'Behold, I lay in Zion for a foundation, a stone, a tried stone, a precious corner stone, a sure foundation' (28: 16). And the apostle Peter, you remember, quotes that in his First Epistle in the second chapter and the sixth verse. But you remember that our Lord Himself said this: 'The stone which the builders rejected, the same is become the head of the corner'—referring to Himself and to His glorious and triumphant resurrection. They are rejecting Him, He says, but they will find that He will become the Headstone of the corner, that He is the basis of the whole building, binding all together, sustaining the weight of the entire superstructure. There is no unity apart from Jesus Christ. It is our relationship to Him, it is our dependence upon Him that matters. He is central, He is vital, He is all-important. I repeat again this striking phrase: 'in whom all the building fitly framed together groweth unto an holy temple in the Lord; in whom ye also are builded together for an habitation of God through the Spirit'.

The practical question therefore which we ask ourselves is this: Do I know what I believe about the Lord Jesus Christ? Do I know Him? Am I in Him, in this vital relationship? We shall have to answer that question, because the apostle deals with it in detail. 'In whom the whole building', he says, 'fitly framed together. . . .'

If that is not true of us we are not in it. But at the moment I confine my question to the foundation. Are you based solidly upon the foundation of the apostles and prophets? Or are you just interested in a vague, nebulous Christianity that says that you must not be concerned about doctrine because doctrine separates? Is that your position? It was certainly not the position of the man who said, 'But though we or an angel from heaven preach any other gospel . . . let him be accursed'. We must know in whom we have believed. We must know what we believe. This apostle speaks of 'my gospel'; and there is no other gospel. Is it yours? Do you know and confess that, as you were by nature, you were a child of wrath, dead in trespasses and sins? And that were it not for the grace of God in Jesus Christ, were it not for His atoning, sacrificial, substitutionary death you would still be in that position? Do you know that He died for you, gave Himself for you and for your sins, and that by the power of His Holy Spirit He has regenerated you, has quickened you, has raised you from the death of sin; and that you are seated even now in the heavenly places with Christ, because you are in Him and joined to Him, by the grace of God?

32

FITLY FRAMED TOGETHER

And are built upon the foundation of the apostles and prophets, Jesus Christ himself being the chief corner stone; In whom all the building fitly framed together groweth unto an holy temple in the Lord: In whom ye also are builded together for an habitation of God through the Spirit.

Ephesians 2: 20–22

We now come to a further study of this third picture. We have taken a general view of it, but we have also noticed that the apostle is not content with this alone, though it is important. In addition to giving us a general description of the building, and therefore of the nature and the character of the unity belonging to the Church, the apostle also deals with the details of the plans and specifications.

We have already given some consideration to the all-important foundation. The first thing Paul tells us is that the Church is 'built upon the foundation of the apostles and prophets, Jesus Christ himself being the chief corner stone'. I do not go back over that again, but surely we must all realise that a foundation is of absolutely central importance. We must never take any risks with a foundation. Our Lord has established that point in His parable of the two houses, one upon a rock and one upon the sand. A foundation is absolutely vital and we have already seen what that foundation is, and how the Lord Jesus Christ Himself is the chief corner stone, binding all the subsidiary stones together, binding all the walls together, thus supporting and uniting the entire structure.

Now having done that, the next thing the apostle deals with, the next thing we are obviously interested in, is this—Where do we come in, in all this? We are built upon the foundation, we are parts of the walls that are going up in the erection of this great temple which God is building for Himself and for His own habitation, this holy temple in the Lord. In other words we come to a consideration of our part and our place and position in this amazing building of God. The apostle rejoices in the fact that the Ephesians are being built into it. The work had started before they came in, but they are added to it, they are put in, and so the building goes on. Others, many others, have come in since. You and I as Christians are in. We must be careful to observe what the apostle tells us about who are built into it, and how they are built into it. Those are the two things that matter. Who is it that has a place and a position and a part in this great structure? How did they ever come there? How are they put there? The apostle deals with both questions very clearly.

There are three things that we must bear in mind. Obviously every part of this structure must bear a particular relationship to the foundation. That goes almost without saying, and yet it is such an important point that I must emphasise it again. In a temple such as this which is being built, in any great and magnificent building, there must always be a correspondence between the various parts. You cannot put shoddy material here and there into a perfect building. If you are going to erect some unusual building, some great holy temple, every part must correspond with every other part. And so it is vital for us to remember that *we as individual parts in this great temple of God must correspond to the foundation, must be truly and rightly related to that foundation.* This is something which is of crucial importance. Let me remind you of how the apostle Paul has put this truth in the third chapter of the First Epistle to the Corinthians. This is a word particularly for those of us who are privileged to preach and to be pastors. We are the builders under God, labourers together with Him. And this is what the apostle says, 'Other foundation can no man lay than that is laid', 'But let every man take heed how he buildeth thereon'. You can build on it, he says, gold or silver or precious metals. That is valuable; but there are people who also want to build with wood and hay and stubble; and that is not at all good. Wood and hay and stubble are not consistent with the foundation that has been laid. The foundation is so precious, and the chief corner stone also, that nothing but gold or silver or precious metals are adequate. To put in wood and hay and stubble is unworthy. Not only that, he says; they will not last, they will not stand. This work is going to be tested—'the day will declare it.' And it will be a testing by fire. And when the fire comes, the wood and the hay and the stubble and the shavings will all vanish in a moment and there will be nothing left. Jerry-building never passes the test. There are people who are so anxious to run up a building quickly that they are not careful about what they put into the walls—anything to run up a building and just cover it over with a little paint. It looks marvellous, and the ignorant and the uninitiated are impressed. They say, How wonderful! Others seem to be building so slowly that undiscerning people say, He is doing nothing at all. But 'the day' will declare it. We are building not for time but for eternity, and the master architect is

God Himself who sees everything that is being done and will test it at the end. There are men, says the apostle, who seem to have done wonders, but when 'the day' comes they will find that all their work has been destroyed, there will be nothing of it left. They themselves, if they are truly Christian, will still be saved though all their work is lost, but they will be saved only 'so as by fire'.

Let every man, therefore, says the apostle, take heed how he builds on this foundation. In other words it comes to this, that the business of this under-builder is not simply to rush up a wall, but to make certain that everything that goes into the wall is in correspondence with the foundation. He must build into the Church not merely numbers on paper or on a roll, but those who are really established on the foundation of the faith. The kind of person who wants to be a Christian just in order to get certain benefits cannot go into this wall. It is only those who realise that they are dead in trespasses and sins, and utterly hopeless and helpless, and who depend solely upon the grace of God in Christ for their salvation; who realise that, had He not shed His blood for them and for their sins, they would still be lost, and who are resting only upon the finished, perfect, sacrificial, substitutionary atonement of Christ and the power of the Spirit—it is they alone who go into these walls. Not those who have merely been brought up to go to a place of worship or who are passably moral. There must be this definite relationship to the one and only foundation.

Let us go on to the second matter. I mention this separately because the apostle so emphasises it. We must not only be related to the foundation in that way, *we must be specifically related to the chief corner stone*. Everyone who is truly a member of the Christian Church is not only related to the faith of the apostles, he is also in a very definite relationship to the Lord Jesus Christ Himself. You remember that we started with the faith, the apostolic faith, the apostolic confession, with that irreducible minimum of Christianity which we have here in this second chapter of this Epistle to the Ephesians. But I do not stop at that, because to give an intellectual assent to that is not enough. If you do not give an intellectual assent to it you are quite certainly not in the building at all. But merely to subscribe to these tenets is not enough. We must be 'in Christ'. We must be joined to Christ. We must know this vital union and relationship to Him. The chief corner stone holds everything together— that is why the apostle keeps on repeating it: ' . . . in whom all the building, fitly framed together groweth unto an holy temple in the Lord: in whom ye also are builded . . .' The whole chapter has been emphasising it. We have been quickened together with Christ, we have been raised together with Christ, we are seated together in the heavenly places in Christ Jesus. This is something that can neither be evaded nor avoided. We not only believe and accept the truth as it is in Christ Jesus, we must be incorporated into Him, we must be in vital union with Him. 'I am the vine, ye are the branches,' He has said Himself, and it is the same idea. So that as members, as parts, in this great edifice, we are all related to the foundation, and we are all in this vital mystical manner related to Him.

Some of the other illustrations the apostle uses bring that out still more clearly. The illustration of the body at which we have already glanced does it still more perfectly. A body is not a collection of parts stuck together. The whole essence of the unity of a body is that it is vital and organic. A body is not formed by sticking fingers on to hands, and hands on to forearms, and forearms on to arms. On the contrary they are all vitally and intimately and organically related. So are we all related to Christ, in Christ, parts of Him, belonging to Him, all held together by Him. That then is also obviously something of fundamental importance.

That brings us to the third thing, the one we must now consider in detail, that is, *our relationship to one another*. Think of a building and of the stones in a building. They are all related to the foundation, they are all related to the chief corner stone, but they also bear a relationship to one another. You cannot have a wall without an inter-relationship of the parts. This is the principle the apostle illustrates in this most important and picturesque statement which is translated in the twenty-first verse by the words '*fitly framed together*'—'in whom all the building', or as you have it in the Revised Version 'in whom every building fitly framed together', or 'all the building fitly framed together'. The important phrase is the 'fitly framed together'.

This is a most interesting expression. We have it here in three words, but the apostle actually used only one word in the Greek. There is another very interesting thing about this word. It is a word that is only found here and in the sixteenth verse of the fourth chapter of this Epistle in the entire Bible. It is not found anywhere else. But there is something else that is still more interesting about it. It is a word that was obviously made and invented and formed by the apostle Paul himself. He did not borrow it; he had not seen it anywhere else. This is the first use of the word that is known. I emphasise that for this reason, that obviously the apostle regarded this particular point as being an exceptionally important one, so much so that he coins a word in order to bring out his idea. And yet, though the apostle took all that trouble, it is pathetic to notice the way in which some of the translations which are so popular at the present time have missed the precise meaning altogether. Take for instance, the Revised Standard Version. It translates it as just 'joined together', missing the whole point of the word that the apostle coined. The apostle could have used many words to bring out the idea of joined together. Moffatt in his translation gets a little nearer. He talks about 'welded together'. But even that is wrong, for you do not weld stones together, and the apostle's whole conception and picture is in terms of building with stones.

Actually, the word used by the apostle means 'harmoniously fitted together'. It is a double compound, three words put together and made into one. The fundamental word means 'binding' or 'joint,' and that in and of itself suggests coming together. But then on to that he put a prefix *sum* which means simply 'together', the same idea as you have in 'symphony' or in any one of such compounds. Joint, together—together-joint. Now 'joint' itself suggests the idea of 'together,' but he says 'together-joint' to make quite certain that we grasp it. And then he added a third word to these two, a word which really means 'to collect' or 'to gather' or 'to pick out.' This third word is often used for fitting words together or joining words together to form a sentence. When a man is speaking or writing certain words suggest themselves to him. He picks one and rejects the other. Then he does the same with the next word, he rejects one and picks another. Then he puts all the chosen words to form a sentence. The word the apostle used suggests that process. So we have got 'together—joint—choose,' (pick out). And he put these three words together to make one word which is translated in the Authorised Version as 'fitly framed together.'

Obviously there is some profound doctrine here. The apostle would never have taken the trouble to make a word like this, to invent a word, unless he had wanted us to be very clear about the ideas he was conveying. I trust that we shall all be able to follow his picture. Alas, we are living in days when buildings are made of bricks and not of stones, and therefore perhaps some are too young to understand the apostle's picture as they should. Rid your mind of the idea of a brick building. Think rather of a great, massive building of stone. Look at that man, or rather those men, who are erecting this building. Have you ever seen a real craftsman, the old type of mason at work? Have you ever watched him building a wall? Have you ever seen him pulling a stone out of a heap of stones and looking at it and then looking at his wall and finding that it is not suitable, throwing it away, and picking out another which he trims and then places in position? That is the picture the apostle is using; 'fitly framed together'—individual stones being added to and placed in position in a wall. What are the ideas he conveys by this language, this pictorial expression?

The first thing is the whole idea of choice. I repeat, anybody who has ever watched a real builder knows exactly what this means. Let us remember that we are considering our place and position as members of the Church of Christ. We are looking at ourselves as parts of this great wall, this great edifice that is being erected to make a temple, a habitation for God to dwell in. As God dwelt in the old temple, in the Shekinah glory in the 'holiest of all,' He dwells and will dwell for all eternity in the Church, in His people. And you and I are in this Church. How did we get there? Here is the first thing, the question of choice. It is a very individual matter, this. Look at that mason, that builder. He has built his wall up to a certain level; but he wants to go on, and at the moment he needs a rather big stone to fill a certain position. He has a heap of stones which have been carted to him. He runs his eye over them. Ah, he says, this will do. He pulls out a stone and looks at it, but he finally decides that it will not do. He has to throw it back. He takes another, he may take several, and reject them; and then eventually he finds and puts in the one he wants. All that is involved. There is a personal and a particular selection. Every stone is picked out and placed in position individually. There was no such thing as mass production when they built in that way in the old days. When building with bricks, one is as good as another. But not with the kind of edifice of which the apostle was thinking. That is not how the old temple in Jerusalem was built, and that is the picture that he has in his mind. No, there is this deliberate, personal, particular, individual selection. And, thank God, that is true of everyone who becomes a Christian. There is no mass production in the Christian Church. Some people seem to think there is, but there is not and cannot be. Thank God, in a world in which the individual is increasingly becoming lost, he remains at the very centre in these matters.

Let us look at the matter from another angle by means of a change of illustration. There is only one way of entering the kingdom of God and that is through a turnstile. It is not a wide open gate, it is a turnstile—'strait is the gate'; 'narrow is the way'; one by one. You cannot go in crowds into the kingdom of heaven, it is an individual transaction between God and the soul. Regeneration is individualistic. And that is the basis of the Christian faith; it is the essential principle in connection with the walls of this building, this temple of God. You cannot be saved in families, still less in groups or classes, or nations. One by one, one taken and another rejected!

It is all brought out again by the apostle in his picture of the wood, hay and stubble in 1 Corinthians 3. Our Lord Himself made it equally plain in His parable of the drag-net which is thrown into the sea and gathers up a great mass, a great crowd of fishes; but then there is an examination, and the good ones are kept, but the bad ones are thrown back. They are in the net for a moment, but they are not kept, they are thrown back. The builder takes hold of a stone. Is it going to be put in? It looks as if it might be used. But it is not. Back it goes, thrown out, rejected. All that appears right to you and me, is not right in the eyes of God. It is a terrible thought, this, but the Bible teaches it everywhere. There will be many people at the Day of Judgment who thought that they were in the building, but Christ will say to them, 'I never knew you, depart from me ye that work iniquity'. It is an individual selection, it involves a choice, and a rejection. That is the first thing.

The second point is that all the stones in this building are not identical. Have a look at some magnificent stone building and watch for this point. The stones are not equal in size, nor in shape, nor in anything else. They are all different, and yet they are all harmoniously fitted together and form a part of the magnificent wall. Some are very big, some are small, some are of medium size. They differ in size and in shape and in many other respects. Again, I say, thank God for this. This again is a very important point which seems to me to be ignored and forgotten today. I had the privilege of being present at a discussion of ministers and clergy not long ago at which a very pertinent question was put by one of the company. He asked, Why is it that Christianity today only seems to be appealing to a particular type? He added, Patently we are not touching the working classes, so-called. We are only touching a certain class, a certain stratum of society. Why is it? I think it was a very profound question. My answer to the question was that there is something radically wrong with our fundamental conception of the Church. Class appeal is the sort of thing that attaches to psychology, but it is contrary to the whole genius of Christianity. The glory of Christianity is that it touches all types and kinds and conditions of men. This element of variety and variation, and the lack of sameness, is most interesting. The essential characteristic of a stone wall in contradistinction to a brick wall is that the stones vary in size, but are fitted together to form the pattern. There is not a dull, drab, uniformity in the Church. It is a characteristic of the cults that all their devotees tend to be the same always. In the Christian Church there is diversity in unity. Therefore we should always regard with suspicion any kind of teaching that leads to a kind of sameness in the results. There are certain people who, by the very way they speak and the phrases they use, almost tell you where they were converted. They are mass-produced, they are all the same. They say the same things and they say them in the same way, and they all do the same things. They are like a series of postage stamps. That is not the principle the apostle is enunciating here. We were never meant to be like that, we were meant to be different. All in the same wall, yes, but very different from one another—some big, some medium, some small; some this shape, some another shape, yet all equally in the wall. That is the true unity, not the dull, drab uniformity we see today in so many aspects of life, and, alas, in the Church. Let me put it plainly and simply by saying this: as Christians we are not all meant to be the same. Our individual characteristics are still to be here. Some of us are born vehement: well we are meant to be vehement. Others are quiet and phlegmatic; let them continue as such. There is nothing more ridiculous than to see a phlegmatic person trying to be like a vehement or mercurial person. And yet it often happens; all trying to be the same. We are not meant to be the same. Ah, but, you say, I always like a Christian who is bright and cheery. Well, I do not! There are times and conditions when such a Christian depresses me terribly. The forced laughter, the affected joviality! There are times when I thank God for a serious, sober-looking individual, who assures me that he is taking a profound and deep view of life, and that he knows something of what the apostle meant when he said, 'In this tabernacle we do groan, being burdened'.

We are not all meant to preach. But there is a teaching today which almost seems to say that we are. The moment a man is converted he has to give his testimony, then preach. But we are not all meant to preach. We are not all meant to go to the foreign mission field. We are not all meant to be whole-time workers in the cause of God. There are people who give the impression that we are. In their conferences they bring pressure to bear upon the young people, and make them feel that they are almost sinners if they do not volunteer for the foreign field. But that is a very false teaching. We are not all meant to be the same. We have all got our part to play, our function to perform; it is not the same in each case. There is the big stone that carries a tremendous weight. There is the smaller one—it is equally important, it fits in at that point where nothing else would fit.

Let us then get rid of this idea that we must all be the same, and let us discover what God would do with us and have us be. The history of the Church bears eloquent testimony to the fact that sometimes, some unknown, obscure Christian whom the Church had not heard very much about, spending his or her time in prayer and in intercession, had done very much more than the great and the popular preacher who built a good deal of wood and hay and stubble which will not stand at the Day of Judgment. Let us learn to look at these things spiritually. Some of us, perhaps, as Christians, are called simply to be kind to people, to be friendly and sympathetic, to do little more than to sit and listen to them. You can help people tremendously by just listening to them and allowing them to unburden their hearts. But there are some of us who are so active and so busy, and doing so much talking, that we never give them a chance to speak; we never have time to listen, and therefore we do not help them. Let us grasp this vital principle, that there is this great variety and variation in the stones that are to be found in the same building, the same holy temple in the Lord, this building of God. You may not be big and great; well, do not glory in the fact that you are not, but remember that the fact that you are not does not mean that you are not in the building. He knows. He sees us all. Go back to 1 Corinthians 12, and see how there the apostle has worked out this principle in great detail, in terms of the body. The whole body, he says, is not an eye, it is not an ear, it is not a hand, it is not a foot. All these different parts are in the same body though some are more comely than others. But he emphasises that our less comely parts are as essential as our more comely parts. Therefore let us not be foolish and desire to be all the same and identical. Let us not think in terms of mass production or of bricks. Let us think of a stone wall, and let us thank God that, whatever we may be, He has taken hold of us and has placed us in the wall, that He knows us as much as He knows the great stone, the shapely stone, the massive stone. It is marvellous to me, and wonderful, that we are put there one by one, and that the humblest Christian is as much known to God as the greatest and the mightiest saint, that He sees the exact place for us in the wall, and puts us there, and puts us there in exactly the same way as He puts in all the others.

Let us then not try to cut across or to violate God's plan and God's method and way of building. Let us beware of this terrible psychological danger that confronts the Church today—the mass production idea, leading always to the same result and producing the same particular type. It is a serious thing when the Church is only producing a certain type of Christian, and only appealing to a certain type or a certain class of person. When this gospel is being truly preached it touches every section of society. The history of the Church proves this. The danger today is that we should all merely be nice and quiet and respectable people, still holding on to our morals, and that the Church should consist only of such people—the middle classes only. It was never meant to be like that.

Let us reconsider our preaching, our teaching, and especially our methods, lest unconsciously we slip into the psychological method and thereby persuade ourselves that we are constructing a wonderful building, only to discover at the end that we have not been adding to the temple of God, and find ourselves at 'the great day' with very little to show for all our effort and all our excitement. That is the second thing.

Let me add just a word on *the third principle: it is the question of the preparation and the shaping.* I can only introduce it here because it is such a great subject. We shall have to go into it in detail later. I have told you that the builder, the stonemason, sees that at this point he requires a certain shape and size of stone, and that looking at his mass of stones he casts his eye over them and picks one out. Ah, he says, this will do. Having rejected some he says, Now this is going to be just right. But it is not quite right as it is, because this stone· has got to be fitted into and on to what is already there. There are stones beneath it and there are stones each side of it. This is the right type of stone in general but it has to be fitted into those each side and to those that are beneath, and then still later something has to be put on top of it. Have you ever watched a mason doing his work? Many times as a boy I did this, and it always fascinated me. He took the stone and then with his various types of hammer he knocked bits off. He trimmed it, he shaped it, he fashioned it, he chipped bits off it. He tried it. Then he took it back again because it was not quite right. He would knock off another piece, perhaps with the chisel and the hammer. And so he went on dealing with it until it was just right. Then he put it in, and stood back. Satisfied he put the mortar on, then he took his next stone and did the same to that. Now that is what the apostle means by 'fitly framed together.' Something has to happen to us before we can be *fitly* framed together. The builder does not throw the stones together anyhow. No, there is a marvellous symmetry about it all. Look at buildings and you will see that. And, of course, it is obvious that in some cases more of this trimming, chipping and chiselling is necessary than in the case of others. But we all need it. And we all get it. And we can never be parts of the wall until that has happened to us.

There is nothing more fascinating, it seems to me, in the long history of the Church and her people, than to see this principle in operation and in practice. There have been some men who have needed a lot of chiselling and shaping, and they have had it. They became mighty stones afterwards. There were others who seemed to be almost right as they were. There was very little that needed to be done to them. You must have found this in your own experience as you have looked at different Christian people. It is not the amount that matters, the principle is that there is always the necessity for this procedure and process in greater or lesser measure.

How is it done? It is done by preaching and teaching. That is the whole business of preaching and teaching; it is to fashion us, to prepare us. We have all got these odd angles and corners, and as we are by nature, we do not fit in. They have got to be chiselled off. Angularities, awkwardnesses, awkward people in the Church! We are all awkward people in a sense, some less so, some more so. We are rough-hewn stones as we come out of the quarry, blasted out of it as it were. We are more or less the right shape but there is much need of chiselling before we fit properly into our particular places in the wall. And until we are so shaped we are not put in. How we all tend to forget this! If we read the New Testament, if we listen to the preaching and the teaching, we shall see the absolute need and necessity of this preparation. There are people who say, I am this sort of person. I am that sort of person. I must always say what is on my mind. If everybody was like that what sort of a church would you have? What kind of a building would you have if all the stones were angular and difficult like that? It would be impossible, you could not build; such corners have to be chipped off. Now that is where personal discipline comes in. We have got to be less difficult as persons. We have got to fit in—fitly framed together.

We must forget ourselves and think of the wall, the building, and realise together that it is the Lord who decides where we are to be and what we are to be, and what particular function we are to perform. And, believe me, if you are in this building, or are going to be in this building, you will be formed and fashioned. It is God's building, let us remember, and if you and I do not apply the teaching and the instruction and the message of the Scriptures as we ought, God has another way of doing it. Read the twelfth chapter of the Epistle to the Hebrews and you will see what I mean. 'Whom the Lord loveth he chasteneth.' If the appeals and arguments of the gospel do not make you discipline yourself, and if these corners and irregularities are not got rid of, He has got a mighty chisel and a mighty hammer, and He will knock them off you. We all know something about this in our personal experiences. He humbles us, He brings us down, and He has many ways of doing it. He can do it through illness or sickness, or death, or sorrow, failure, misunderstanding; a thousand and one things. And He does it. Thank God He does. For if He did not do it to us, none of us would finally be fit to be in that wall. It is whom the Lord loveth, He chasteneth. If He does not love you, He does not bother about you, He throws you back, and there you can be with all your angularities and oddities for the rest of your life saying, I am this sort of person! Very well! be that sort of person!—but you are not in the holy temple of the Lord, and never will be while you are like that. This is a very solemn and serious matter, a matter of eternal importance to us. We must be made conformable, and fit in with others, if we are to be in this holy temple. So if we do not realise this principle and see the importance of this vital preparation, and submit to it, we shall be rejected, and though we may not realise it in time, we shall certainly realise it in eternity.

33

THE GROWTH OF THE CHURCH

And are built upon the foundation of the apostles and prophets, Jesus Christ himself being the chief corner stone; In whom all the building fitly framed together groweth unto an holy temple in the Lord: In whom ye also are builded together for an habitation of God through the Spirit.

Ephesians 2: 20-22

We are still studying this third picture which the apostle gives us of Christian people in the Christian Church, in which he says that the Church is a kind of building, a great temple, in which God dwells and is yet going to dwell in a still larger and fuller manner. We have looked at this picture in general. But the apostle does not merely give us a general description of this building, he tells us in detail something about the plans and the specifications which were observed, and must always be observed, in the erection and building of such an edifice.

We started, therefore, of necessity, with the foundation. We are 'built upon the foundation of the apostles and prophets, Jesus Christ himself being the chief corner stone'. Following that we came more directly to a consideration of ourselves and that which is true of us—that as stones in this building we are all related to the foundation, we are all related to the Lord Jesus Christ, we are all related to truth; but, and this is the thing that he seems here to emphasise most of all, we are all also related to one another. In other words the important phrase here is this word which has been translated by the three words 'fitly framed together'. That is the word that we must take up again. There are all these individual stones in this wall, in these walls that are going up, and they are all 'fitly framed together'.

All these things are pictures, and it is obvious therefore that any one picture cannot convey the whole truth. That is why the apostle uses three different pictures here; no one of them is sufficient in and of itself. So that previously, in dealing with this question of the preparation of the stones, I indicated that a certain amount of preparation was necessary beforehand, and also that in a sense the preparation continues throughout life. That is the kind of paradox you find in the New Testament concerning the Church. On the one hand we are given the impression that God already dwells in the

Church—and He does. And yet there is this other idea that the Church is still being built—'for an habitation' into which He is going to come to dwell when it has been completed. In the same way we, in a sense, are already prepared, but we also still need this process. But other illustrations are used to bring that out.

Now let us come back to this great question of how exactly these stones are put into the building. 'In whom ye also are builded together', says Paul, 'for an habitation of God'. You Ephesians, he says, have been brought into this building, you are parts of this fabric now, you are parts of this great temple that is being built in the Lord for an habitation of God through the Spirit.

A most important question for our consideration is this: *When does the preparation take place*? Primarily and most essentially this preparation takes place before we are ever in the Church at all. We can never be parts of this edifice, we can never be stones in these walls, without our being already prepared. Let us go back, therefore, to a verse in the Old Testament—1 Kings 6: 7, 'And the house, when it was in building, was built of stone made ready before it was brought thither: so that there was neither hammer nor axe nor any tool of iron heard in the house, while it was in building.' That is a part of the account of the building of Solomon's temple. It is a very important bit of history. Indeed, as we are studying this particular section, it is of great importance that we should go back to the Old Testament and read there about the building of the tabernacle in the wilderness, and also the building of Solomon's temple in Jerusalem. There is no doubt at all that the apostle Paul had those very pictures in his mind, and it is equally clear that what is taught with regard to the building of the tabernacle and the temple has relevance to what we are considering at this moment.

When God instructed Moses to build the tabernacle, He took him up into a mountain and gave him detailed instruction. God did not simply say to Moses, Now I want you to build a tabernacle for Me in which My presence can dwell, in which My Shekinah glory can appear. He gave him detailed instructions, entering into questions of measurements, colours, and so on. Everything was given in detail. And then having given him the plans and specifications, God said to Moses, 'See that thou make all things according to the pattern shown thee in the mount'. It appears that instructions were also given to Solomon (2 Chronicles 3: 3) in a similar way. It is important, therefore, for us to bear all this in mind; it has a deep significance. Listen to it again: 'And the house, when it was in building, was built of stone made ready before it was brought thither: so that there was neither hammer nor axe nor any tool of iron heard in the house,

GOD'S WAY OF RECONCILIATION

while it was in building'. That statement contains very important doctrine which throws great light upon the exposition given by the apostle here with regard to the nature of the Christian Church.

The first principle to observe, it seems to me, is this: *the preparation is done in secret*. Undoubtedly there were people there in Jerusalem watching the building and the erection of the temple. But they did not see the preparation of the stones. That work had been done before the stones were ever brought to the site of the temple and put into their positions in the wall. Here is a great New Testament principle. Before any of us can be truly members of the Christian Church—(and you see the importance of distinguishing between the mere having of our names upon a church roll and really being members of Christ and of His Church)—before any of us can be truly in the Church, a mighty work of preparation is essential. It is a work that is done by the Holy Spirit, and it is done in the depths of the soul. It is a mysterious work and a secret work. The world knows nothing about it. As the people in Jerusalem knew nothing about the preparation of those stones, so the world knows nothing at all about this. It is possible for us to be working in an office with other people, or even living in the same home with people, and for this mighty work of preparation to be going on in us, without their knowing anything about it. It is not something which is done externally, outwardly, superficially; it is a work that is done in the vitals of the soul.

The apostle in writing to the Corinthians puts it like this: 'Ye are . . . the epistle of Christ . . . written not with ink, but with the Spirit of the living God: not in tables of stone, but in fleshy tables of the heart' (2 Corinthians 3: 3). It is an internal work, a mysterious work, which goes on in that part of man which is called the soul. You may remember a famous anatomist scoffing, a few years ago, about the soul. He said that he had dissected many bodies in the dissecting room but he had never come across an organ called the soul. Of course he had not! That is one of the secret things that a materialistic anatomist cannot understand. Still less could such a man understand the work of the Spirit in the soul. The work is as secret as this, that the man himself on whom the work is being done sometimes does not know what is happening. The Spirit of God often deals with us for some time before we come to a realisation of what is happening. All we know is that we are being caused to ask certain questions which we have never asked before. All we know is that we suddenly become dissatisfied with ourselves and with our lives, and we do not know why. Somebody else may say that we are not well, perhaps, and that we should go to see a doctor; and we may agree. We may think that we are tired, or may seek some other explanation. It is a mysterious work. New interests seem to arise, new longings and desires and aspirations, and we say, 'What is this? I do not understand myself. Something seems to be happening to me. I am not as I was. What is it?' And we do not understand. We are ignorant of this secret work of the Spirit. But it is there, and it is a part of the preparation. The work was done before the stones were brought to Jerusalem.

I must not stay with this, but you remember how our Lord put it in speaking to Nicodemus, who completely failed at that point to understand His doctrine. 'How can a man be born when he is old?' says Nicodemus. 'Can he enter the second time into his mother's womb and be born?'—I do not understand! Quite right, said our Lord, in effect, 'The wind bloweth where it listeth; and thou hearest the sound thereof but canst not tell whence it cometh and whither it goeth; so is everyone that is born of the Spirit'. You see the result, you do not see how it happens, you do not understand. 'Thou canst not tell whence it cometh and whither it goeth'. It is unseen, it is invisible, but you see the effects, the outcome, the finished product. 'So is everyone that is born of the Spirit.'

In other words I lay it down as a fundamental proposition—and it is most important to emphasise it today because there is such grievous misunderstanding about the matter—that *to become a Christian means that we are subjected to a power and to a force that is beyond our understanding.* Do not misunderstand me. That does not mean that Christianity is irrational; what it means is that it is super-rational, supra-rational we might well say. There is nothing—and I delight in this, and therefore often repeat it—there is nothing, once you are inside it, that is so rational, so logical (as we have an illustration here in this Epistle to the Ephesians) as the Christian faith. But if you are outside it, you do not understand it; there seems to be something mysterious and almost strange about it. Why? Because it is God's work, because it is the direct action of the Eternal. He is no longer acting through the laws of nature, He is acting directly, He is acting immediately. Let me again call the great apostle to expound himself. He puts it like this in the First Epistle to the Corinthians and in the second chapter. He says that when the Lord Jesus Christ was in this world the princes of this world did not recognise him, 'for had they known him they would not have crucified the Lord of glory'. They saw but a man, the carpenter of Nazareth. They said, Who is this fellow? They were amazed at His knowledge and learning; but they did not understand, they did not know He was the Son of God. But the apostle says, 'the Spirit hath revealed them unto us'; even the Spirit who 'searcheth all things, yea, the deep things of God'. He goes on, 'for we have received, not the spirit that is of the world, but the Spirit that is of God, that we may know the things that are freely given to us of God'. And again he goes on to say, 'The natural man receiveth not the things of the Spirit of God, for they are foolishness unto him; neither can he know them because they are spiritually discerned'. He then adds this, 'He that is spiritual (that is, the spiritual man) judgeth all things, yet he himself is judged of no man'. In other words, by definition a Christian should be a problem and an enigma to every person who is not a Christian. How important all this is as a test for each one of us. If a man who is not a Christian can understand you, and all you do and say then, to that extent at least, you are not giving evidence of the fact that you are a Christian.

The Son of God when He was in this world was a great problem to people. They asked, Who is this? He is an ordinary man, He has never been trained as a Pharisee, He is not one of the scribes, He is not a priest, He has never had the learning and the teaching; yet look at Him, listen to what He is saying. He seems to know; look at His miracles—Who is this? He was a problem and a puzzle to them. And you remember how in the early chapters of the book of Acts we are told that the same was true of His followers? Peter and John healed a man at the Beautiful Gate of the temple, and the rulers could not understand it. They put them on trial, and all they could say about them was that 'these men had been with Jesus'. That is all they knew. Ignorant men, unlearned men, yet filled with power!—What is this?

That is the secret aspect of this work, this preparation. The Christian, because he has been formed and fashioned by the Holy Spirit is a man whom no one except another Christian can understand. The Spirit's work is not irrational, but beyond reason, confirming that profound dictum of Blaise Pascal, 'The supreme achievement of reason is to bring us to see that there is a limit to reason'. Here we are in a realm where God acts immediately and directly. So a Christian is not merely a man who decides to adopt a number of propositions and a point of view, or to espouse a philosophy. A Christian by definition is one who has been formed and fashioned and brought into shape, and made fit and meet to be a stone in this wall, in this edifice, which is going up as 'a holy temple in the Lord', as an habitation of God. A Christian is a man who has been born again, changed, renewed, regenerated. These are the New Testament terms. He is ' a new creation'.

But that brings us to a second principle: *that all this must happen to us before we can become a part of the Church*. Our fundamental text there in 1 Kings 6: 7, brings that out above everything else. 'The house while it was in building was built of stone, made ready *before* it was brought thither.' We are not in membership of the Church in order to become Christians. We are in the Church because we are Christians. The reason for becoming a member of a church is not that you may eventually become a Christian; it is because you are already one. The membership of the Church was never meant to be a mixed multitude—consisting of those who are Christians, of those who hope they are Christians, of those who hope they may become Christians, and of those who are there, well, just because they have not even thought enough to stop coming and who are mere traditionalists. This again, I must remind you, is a tremendously important point, and especially at this present time when the question of the nature of the Church is raised acutely by all the talk about union and reunion and unity. It is our duty to acquaint ourselves with what has been taught in the past concerning these matters. Now at the time of the Protestant Reformation this became an urgent and a crucial matter. Martin Luther taught that the Church is the community of believers. John Calvin emphasized that the Church consists of the total number of the elect. You notice the emphasis?—community of believers, total number of the elect, the chosen, the called out. And you remember that the Puritans, who in a sense were the originators and the founders of what are called the 'free churches' (the first Independents, the first Baptists, and others), put their emphasis upon what they called 'the gathered Church'. They meant that the Church really consists of the gathering together, or the meeting together of saints, of believers. They became increasingly unhappy with the idea of a 'state church', because, according to the 'state church' idea, everybody who lives in a parish is a member of the Church and a Christian. Now Nonconformity rejected that completely. They said, Because a man happens to live in a parish he is not of necessity a Christian. Merely because people happen to live in this country they are not Christian. They asserted that the Church consists only of those who have been prepared, the born again, the regenerated, the renewed, the saints, the believers, God's people; and the Church is the gathering together of these. That is the Church, the 'gathered Saints'.

You see the importance and the relevance of all this at this present time, when there is a tendency to become looser and looser, and vaguer and vaguer, in definitions; to say that all who call themselves Christians must be regarded as Christians, and that we are all one, and so forth. Indeed, it is even suggested sometimes that we should not over-stress even the term 'Christian'. We have a so-called 'Congress of World Faiths', including anybody who believes anyhow in God. All such are said to be one, over against those who do not believe in God.

It is vital that we should consider all this, not only in the light of history but still more in the light of Scripture—this Scripture in Ephesians and that statement in 1 Kings 6: 7. In other words, surely the teaching of the Scriptures is plain and clear. It is that the Church consists only of those who believe the true doctrine and who live a Christian life. 'The foundation of God standeth sure, having this seal, The Lord knoweth them that are his. And, Let every one that nameth the name of Christ depart from iniquity.' (2 Timothy 2: 19). There are some who are denying the faith, says Paul to Timothy: they are denying the resurrection, they say it is already past. Do not be troubled; they seem to men to be Christian, but God has always known where they stand. He knows all things, His foundation stands sure. He cannot deny Himself though we may deny Him. He knows what He is doing. He ultimately is the Architect of the Church.

We can go on then to say, that surely there is nothing that is quite so foolish and calamitous when we are thinking about the Church as to think in terms of size and numbers. But that is the controlling thought today. World Church!, they say, The only way to fight Communism and these other things that are opposed to Christianity is to become one; we must gather our great battalions, and then stand up to the enemy. But how utterly unscriptural it is! We sing in our hymns about 'the faithful few', and the Bible is full of the doctrine of the remnant. God does not work through big battalions, He is not interested in numbers; He is interested in purity, in holiness, in vessels fit and meet for the Master's use. We must concentrate, not on numbers, but upon doctrine, upon regeneration, upon holiness, upon the realisation that this is a holy temple in the Lord, a habitation of God.

This is taught very clearly by the Lord Himself. You sometimes get the impression as you read the Gospels, that the Lord Jesus Christ spent a great deal of His time in refusing people. Today we press people to decisions, we do all we can to draw them in willy-nilly. But that was not our Lord's way. A man came running after Him and said, 'Master, I will follow thee whithersoever thou goest'. What a wonderful addition to the Church! we say. But our Lord turned to that man and said, 'Foxes have holes and the birds of the air have nests, but the Son of man hath not where to lay his head.' Go and think about what you are doing, says our Lord, I do not want mere excitement, I want you to realise what it may cost you. And, you remember, He goes on to speak to a man who asks that he may first of all go home and bury his father, and He says,

'Let the dead bury their dead'. Again, 'No man having put his hand to the plough and looking back is fit for the kingdom of God'. He tests, He seems to be rejecting, He examines. Count the cost, He says. What a foolish man, He says, is he who starts building a castle but has not first computed how much it will cost, and whether he has the ability and the wealth to go on with it! He speaks in a similar way about a man who sets out to make war against another country and does not know the number of his troops and reserves. Oh, the folly of that, He says. Stop! Consider! He seems to be rejecting men. He was concerned about the purity of the Church, not the size, not the number. And when He left the world He left but a handful of ordinary, ignorant, untutored, illiterate men to continue His work. That is His method.

And it has always been like that in every period of revival and reawakening. It was an extremely difficult thing to become a member of a Puritan church. Read the trust deeds of the first Independent and Baptist churches and you will find that it was an excessively difficult thing to obtain admission to membership. Have you ever read the rules that John Wesley drew up for admission into his societies? Men and women were examined and tested in doctrine and in life! It is when that kind of procedure is adopted that you get revival. God can only dwell in a pure church—not necessarily a large church, but a pure church, pure in doctrine, pure in life. It may sound a surprising thing, but I have no hesitation in asserting even today that the greatest trouble with the Church now is that she is too big. She is too much like a mixed multitude. It is only when men are vessels fit and meet for the Master's use that He uses them. It is only when it is a holy temple that the eternal Resident comes in. The whole teaching of the Scriptures is to this effect. And it is substantiated and supported and proved by the subsequent history of the Christian Church. It is still true to say that no one knows, the world does not know, what God can do when one man is completely committed to Him. All great revivals and reformations have come from the most insignificant beginnings. One man—Martin Luther! Odd individuals in the seventeenth century! The little Holy Club in Oxford in the eighteenth century! It has always been like that. Let us cease to think in terms of big business when we are talking about the Church. Let us come back to the New Testament. It is a holy temple in the *Lord*! When He comes in, with one feeble man He can convict thousands. Through the preaching of the apostle Peter on the day of Pentecost, three thousand were truly added to the Church.

Before we close let us look at one further principle. *There is to be no noise during this building process.* Go back again to 1 Kings 6: 7, and this is what you find written: 'And the house when it was in building was built of stone made ready before it was brought thither.' Then—'So that there was neither hammer nor axe nor any tool of iron heard in the house, while it was in building'. What a vital principle this is! Being interpreted and put into its modern dress it is this. There should be no discussion and no debate and no disagreement in the Church about vital truths. There is to be none of this noise of chiselling and hammering and forming and preparation *in* the Church. That happens before you come into the Church. There should be no discussion in the Christian Church about the Person of the Lord Jesus Christ. There should be no discussion in the Church about the position and condition of man in sin. There should be no discussion in the Church about the substitutionary atonement, and regeneration, and the Person of the Spirit, and all the doctrines of grace. There must be no noise of discussion about these things. All that should have happened beforehand.

Now let us be clear about this, because this again can be misunderstood. When I say that there should be no discussion and noise of debate in the Church I do not mean that the Church should not be interested in doctrine: I mean that the doctrine should be agreed upon from the very outset, so that there is no longer any need of discussion. But that is being misunderstood today, and is being put in this form. Ah, men say, we must not have any discussions about doctrines because they always divide; therefore let us not have them, but let us all agree to call one another Christians whatever we may believe. One man may say that Jesus of Nazareth was only a man, others say that He was also the Son of God. What does it matter really? After all we can all agree about His teaching, that it was very noble and elevating, and that if we all only practised it, there would not be all this trouble in the world today. So they say, Let us stop arguing about His Person. And then what about the death on the cross? One man says it is just the greatest crime in history, the supreme tragedy of all time. Another says, No, that is not enough: God sent Him to die; He died 'according to the predeterminate counsel and foreknowledge of God'; He died in order that He might bear the guilt of our sins, and if He had not died we would be yet in our sins. But the tendency today is to say it does not matter what you believe. Many say: The death of Christ after all is very wonderful and very moving, therefore we can all look at it, we can interpret it in different ways. It does not matter, we all believe in Him, and we are all trying to be like Him and to follow Him. We are all Christians, therefore let us carry on!

But that is the absence of doctrine, and what we are taught here is the exact opposite. There should be no noise of this debate and discussion in the Church—not because there is no doctrine, but because we should all be agreed about the doctrine, because we all subscribe to it. That is how it happened in the early Church. When was it that the Holy Spirit descended upon them? It was when they were all of one accord in the upper room. One accord! Again we read about His coming upon them and that they were all of one heart and of one mind. The early Church, we are told, continued steadfastly in the apostles' doctrine (teaching) and fellowship and breaking of bread and prayers. There was no noise of discussion and debate. Why? Because they all agreed! They knew He was the Son of God; the resurrection had proved it to them. He had expounded the Scriptures, He had explained His death, they had all sat at His feet and they had believed the doctrine. They were all of one accord. No noise! Why?—because they were agreed on doctrine; not because they avoided doctrine. Do you not see why the Church is as she is today? What has been happening in the Christian Church for the last hundred years? We have already given the answer. The Church has been arguing about fundamental doctrines. Why are an alarming number of churches almost empty today? Why are the figures going down from year to year? It is the Church herself that is responsible. Fifty years ago in London the whole Church was debating about what was called 'the new theology'. The debate was mainly about the Person of Christ!—was He really the eternal Son of God? Or was He only a man? Those were the questions. They were arguing about foundations, about the foundation of the apostles and prophets! Many did not believe it. There was noise in the Church because they were arguing about fundamentals. Is it surprising that the Church has become ineffective, and that she does not count, and that men are not saved, and that the Spirit is not operating?

There is to be no noise of hammer or of axe or of any tool of iron in the Church. Men and women are to be clear about these things before they come into the Church. Indeed, you cannot be in the Church truly except you are already right about these matters. The Christian Church was never meant to be a cockpit in which men argue and fight and debate and wrangle about the vital matters of Christ and His work. The Church is the gathering of those for whom these matters have been settled once and for ever, who know whom they have believed, who know what they believe, who are on the foundation of God, and who all come together—not to argue and debate about these matters, but to wait upon Him, to worship Him, that He may come among them, that He may fill them with His own presence and with joy unspeakable and full of glory, that

He may fill them with power to speak to others and to spread the good news, and to win men from the shackles and bondage of sin.

Note what I am saying. I am not saying that Christian people should agree about every detail. I am emphasising fundamentals. There are certain matters about which all Christians are not agreed, certain details about prophecy, certain matters like the mode of baptism, and many others. Those are not foundation principles. Christian people are never to wrangle and to quarrel and to fight about them. They should discuss them as brethren. But there must be no discussion about fundamentals, because they are fundamentals. The preparation is to take place before the stones are brought to the Church. There is no noise here, we *know* Him as Son of God and Saviour. The greatest need in the Church at this hour is to understand these principles. Now great world-wide conferences are being held one after another. But how do they spend their time? Not in prayer to God, not in waiting for the Spirit, not in being filled with the Spirit. They spend their time in trying to find a basis of agreement. They try to find an irreducible minimum about which they are not going to disagree. They spend their time on that, and meanwhile the world goes from bad to worse. They have this fatal notion that doctrine is a cause of division; whereas the truth is, that nothing unites except doctrine. For the only unity worth talking about at all is the unity of the Spirit which produces the same belief in the same Lord, in the same faith, and in the same baptism. It is the unity of those who are like-minded and of one accord, who have no confidence in themselves, and who rely only upon the Son of God and His perfect work on their behalf. The word to the modern Church, therefore, as it was the word of God to Moses of old, is simply this, 'See that thou make all things according to the pattern shown thee in the mount'. The mount of the Sermon on the Mount! The mount of transfiguration! The mount of Calvary! Mount Olivet, the mount of the ascension! There are the great peaks. Let us in our day and generation, whatever may happen to us, and whatever the Church, the visible Church, may say of us, whatever the world may say of us, let us build according to the pattern shown us in the mount. Let there be no uncertainty or hesitancy or discussion or noise of debate about the contents of this second chapter of Paul's Epistle to the Ephesians, for the foundation is—man dead in trespasses and sins, helpless and hopeless; raised by the grace of God; saved by the blood of Christ; regenerated and renewed and joined to Christ by the Holy Spirit and made a stone in the holy temple in the Lord.

Prayer
ch 24

citizens — Birth cert   26,27